Each volume of this series of companions to major philosophers contains specially commissioned essays by an international team of scholars, together with a substantial bibliography, and will serve as a reference work for students and nonspecialists. One aim of the series is to dispel the intimidation such readers often feel when faced with the work of a difficult and challenging thinker.

Plotinus is the greatest philosopher in the 700-year period between Aristotle and Augustine. He thought of himself as a disciple of Plato, but in his efforts to defend Platonism against Aristotelians, Stoics, and others, he actually produced a reinvigorated version of Platonism that later came to be known as "Neoplatonism." In this volume, sixteen leading scholars introduce and explain the many facets of Plotinus's complex system. They place Plotinus in the history of ancient philosophy while showing how he was a founder of medieval philosophy.

New readers and nonspecialists will find this the most convenient and accessible guide to Plotinus currently available. Advanced students and specialists will find a conspectus of recent developments in the interpretation of Plotinus.

THE CAMBRIDGE COMPANION TO

PLOTINUS

The Cambridge Companion to
PLOTINUS

Edited by Lloyd P. Gerson

CAMBRIDGE
UNIVERSITY PRESS

PUBLISHED BY THE PRESS SYNDICATE OF THE UNIVERSITY OF CAMBRIDGE
The Pitt Building, Trumpington Street, Cambridge, United Kingdom

CAMBRIDGE UNIVERSITY PRESS
The Edinburgh Building, Cambridge CB2 2RU, UK   http: //www.cup.cam.ac.uk
40 West 20th Street, New York, NY 10011-4211, USA   http: //www.cup.org
10 Stamford Road, Oakleigh, Melbourne 3166, Australia

First published 1996
Reprinted with corrections 1999

Printed in the United States of America

Typeset in Trump Mediaeval

A catalogue record for this book is available from the British Library

Library of Congress Cataloguing-in-Publication Data is available

ISBN 0-521-47093-5 hardback
ISBN 0-521-47676-3 paperback

CONTENTS

v

CONTRIBUTORS

HENRY J. BLUMENTHAL is Reader in Greek at Liverpool University. He is the author of *Plotinus' Psychology* and has edited several books on Neoplatonism, including *Neoplatonism and Early Christian Thought*. Some of his articles are collected in *Soul and Intellect: Studies in Plotinus and Later Neoplatonism*.

JOHN BUSSANICH is Associate Professor of Philosophy at the University of New Mexico. He is the author of *The One and its Relation to Intellect in Plotinus* and *Ancient Philosophy After Aristotle* (forthcoming).

STEPHEN R. L. CLARK is Professor of Philosophy at Liverpool University. His most recent books include *God's World and the Great Awakening*, *How to Think About the Earth*, and *How to Live Forever*. He is the editor of the *Journal of Applied Philosophy*.

KEVIN CORRIGAN is Professor of Philosophy and Classics at St. Thomas More College, University of Saskatchewan. He is the author of *Plotinus' Theory of Matter-Evil* and *The Question of Substance: Plato, Aristotle, and Alexander of Aphrodisias* (forthcoming), and many articles on ancient and medieval philosophy.

CRISTINA D'ANCONA COSTA is Research Assistant at the Università di Padova, Instituto di Storia della Filosofia. She is the author of *Recherches sur le Liber de Causis*, a translation of Thomas Aquinas's commentary on the *Liber de Causis*, and articles on Plotinus and Proclus.

JOHN M. DILLON is Regius Professor of Greek, Trinity College, Dublin. He is the author of *The Middle Platonists; The Golden*

vii

Chain: Studies in the Development of Platonism and Christianity; Alcinous. The Handbook of Platonism; and scholarly editions of works of Iamblichus, Philo of Alexandria, Proclus, and Dexippus.

EYJÓLFUR KJALAR EMILSSON is Professor of Philosophy at the University of Oslo, Norway. He is the author of *Plotinus on Sense Perception* and many articles on Plotinus.

MARIA LUISA GATTI is Professor of Philosophy at the Università Cattolica del Sacro Cuore, Milan. She is the author of *Plotino e le metafisica della contemplazione* and many articles on the Platonic tradition.

LLOYD P. GERSON is Professor of Philosophy at the University of Toronto. He is the author of *Plotinus* in the Arguments of the Philosophers series; *God and Greek Philosophy: Studies in the Early History of Natural Theology;* translations of Aristotle and Hellenistic philosophy, and many articles in ancient philosophy.

GEORGES LEROUX is Professor of Ancient Philosophy at the Université du Québec, Montreal. He is the author of *Plotin. La liberté et la volonté de l'Un (Ennead VI.8)* and many articles on Plato and Neoplatonism.

DENIS O'BRIEN formerly Fellow of Gonville and Caius College, Cambridge, has since 1971 been Directeur de Recherche at the Centre National de la Recherche Scientifique, Paris. His books include *Empedocles's Cosmic Cycle. A Reconstruction from the Fragments and Secondary Sources; Études sur Parmenides; Theories of Weight in the Ancient World* in four volumes, two of which are forthcoming; *Plotinus on the Origin of Matter,* and many articles on ancient philosophy.

DOMINIC J. O'MEARA is Professor at the University of Fribourg, Switzerland. He is the author of *Plotinus. An Introduction to the Enneads; Pythagoras Revisited. Mathematics and Philosophy in Late Antiquity;* and many works on various aspects of ancient and medieval Platonism.

SARA RAPPE is Assistant Professor of Classical Studies at the University of Michigan. She is the author of articles on Plato, Plotinus, and the Platonic tradition.

JOHN RIST is Professor of Classics and Philosophy at the University of Toronto. His many books include *Plotinus. The Road to Reality; The Mind of Aristotle; Stoic Philosophy; Epicurus. An Introduction; Augustine. Ancient Thought Baptized;* and many articles on ancient philosophy.

FREDERIC M. SCHROEDER is Professor of Classics at Queen's University, Kingston, Ontario. He is the author of *Form and Transformation. A Study in the Philosophy of Plotinus* and many other works on Plotinus and late Aristotelianism.

ANDREW SMITH is Professor of Classics at University College, Dublin. He is the author of *Porphyry's Place in the Neoplatonic Tradition* and the Teubner edition of Porphyry's *Fragments*.

MICHAEL F. WAGNER is Professor of Philosophy at the University of San Diego and the author of articles on Plotinus and early medieval philosophy.

THE *ENNEADS*

The following is a list of the treatises comprising the *Enneads* with the titles that appear in Porphyry's edition. The chronological ordering is indicated in brackets.

Introduction

I A COMPANION TO PLOTINUS

This volume, like the others in the series, is intended to serve as an aid to the reading of a major Western philosopher. One service that the editor and contributors would be glad to perform is to change the mind of those who cavil at the use of the term "major" or even "philosopher" in reference to Plotinus. Read them and him for yourself and decide. Do not be put off by ignorant detractors or uncritical enthusiasts or by the essentially empty label "Neoplatonist," which in some circles has become nothing more than a term of abuse.

How best to assist someone who wants to read Plotinus, whose works, regardless of their quality, are intensely difficult, is not easy to determine. First of all, his thought is not simply divisible into the traditional categories of metaphysics, epistemology, ethics, and so on. And so it would be positively unhelpful to suggest otherwise by offering a tidy package of essays each of which "does" a given subject. Second, Plotinus's writings can hardly be characterized as systematic, although there *is* a Plotinian system in the sense that there are basic entities, principles of operation, and an effort at a unified explanation of the world. The system, however, does not for the most part cut up nicely into the written works, such that an introductory exposition of a work would provide one of that system's building blocks. Third, Plotinus is a philosopher deeply and self-consciously rooted in a long and complex tradition. To try to represent his views without some appreciation of this context could only result in grotesque distortions and it would make this book at best a treacherous "companion."

The expedient employed here is something of a compromise,

attempting to combine elements of different possible approaches. The first essay should give one an overview of the philosophical context of Plotinus's writings. The next three together provide an outline of the three "hypostases" or basic entities of Plotinus's system and their operations. Essays five through nine discuss specific philosophical problems that Plotinus deals with on the basis of his fundamental principles. Essays ten through thirteen concern Plotinus's treatment of issues that cut across what today would be said to belong to philosophy of mind, ethics, and philosophy of religion. Essay fourteen concerns Plotinus's remarkable use of the Greek language in his sometimes tortured efforts to convey his philosophical vision. Essays fifteen and sixteen provide the reader with some signposts leading from Plotinus to the increasingly complex history of later Neoplatonism and its encounter with Christianity. Some important topics are only touched on – aesthetics and mysticism, for instance. The airing of controversies regarding interpretation of texts has been largely suppressed, not by editorial fiat, but by the far more effective expedient of space limitations. I am reasonably confident that in generally having ignored deeply contentious issues of interpretation we have not done a disservice to the neophyte. More experienced readers of Plotinian scholarship will after all have some idea of what the issues are and what is the range of scholarly opinion, and they can evaluate what is said here accordingly.

II THE LIFE AND WRITINGS OF PLOTINUS

We know rather more about the life of Plotinus that we do about most ancient philosophers. His disciple Porphyry, a distinguished philosopher in his own right, not only undertook an edition of his master's works – the edition that is the basis for all modern editions – but added to it a biography, *The Life of Plotinus*. Unfortunately, Plotinus was exceedingly reticent regarding his personal history and so, though we know that he was born in Lycopolis, Egypt in A.D. 205, we cannot be certain that he was a Greek rather than a member of a Hellenized Egyptian family. Porphyry tells us that in his twenty-eighth year Plotinus recognized his vocation as a philosopher. What occupied him until that time is unrecorded. Searching for a teacher of philosophy he came to Alexandria where he encountered Ammonius. Little is known about this man, who was perhaps a Christian. In any case, he satisfied Plotinus's thirst for learning for a decade. In 243 Plotinus decided to study Persian and Indian philosophy and to that end attached himself to an expedition of the Emperor Gordian III to Persia. That expedition was aborted with the assassination of Gordian by his troops. Evidently abandoning his plans to travel east, Plotinus established himself in Rome in 245, where he lived until his death in 270 or 271.

Porphyry tells us that during the first ten years in Rome Plotinus lectured on the philosophy of Ammonius, writing nothing himself. Thereafter, he began to set down his own thoughts in a succession of "treatises" of various lengths and complexity. They are frequently occasional pieces, written in response to questions raised in "class" by Plotinus's students. For that reason, they are intensely dialectical, that is, they consider the strengths and weaknesses of opposing arguments before coming (usually) to some resolution. These treatises were arranged by Porphyry into six groups of nine each (hence the title *Enneads* from the Greek work for "nine"). This arrangement ignores the actual chronological order in which the works were produced, an order that Porphyry scrupulously records in his *Life*. Although the division into fifty-four treatises is somewhat artificial (some larger works are split up in order to make the groupings even in number), the thematic arrangement is fairly perspicuous. The treatises move from the earthly to the heavenly, from the more concrete to the more abstract. More plainly, they begin with human goods (I), proceed to discussions of various topics in the physical world (II–III), then on to the soul (IV), knowledge and intelligible reality (V), and, finally, the One, the first principle of all (VI).

Plotinus thought of himself simply as a disciple of Plato. He probably would have been deeply disturbed to be characterized as the founder of something called "Neoplatonism." But perhaps our hindsight regarding Plotinus's achievement and influence are superior to his own modest assessment of himself. For it is undeniable that Plotinus's Platonism is not a simple meditation on the master's work. First of all, between Plato and Plotinus a great deal of philosophical activity occurred, including the work of Aristotle, the Stoics, Epicureans, Skeptics, and various lesser figures usually referred to with the somewhat pejorative sobriquet "Middle Platonists." Much of this work is critical of Plato. Some of it, like that of the Skeptics belonging

to Plato's Academy, makes contentious claims to be authentic trans-
mitters of Plato's true meaning. All of this material, and more (for
example, the commentators on Aristotle), Plotinus knew intimately.
Consequently, it is not surprising that his understanding and expression of the wisdom of Plato should be filtered through his responses to
the challenges of Plato's critics. Above all, in responding to Aristotle's criticisms of Plato, Plotinus was moved to say many things
that are arguably Platonic in spirit, though not explicitly found in the
dialogues. One additional complication in this regard should be mentioned. For Plotinus, Plato was not just the author of the dialogues,
but also the author of all the letters we possess in the *corpus* and the
"unwritten doctrines" testified to by Aristotle, among others. For
this reason, Plotinus had a somewhat more capacious conception of
what Plato taught than that of many contemporary scholars.

The treatises in the *Enneads* make many demands on the reader.
They are packed with allusions to various ancient and contemporary
philosophical positions and quotations from the works of major authors. Their style modulates from the literary to the dialectical to
the intensely analytical. One not infrequently has the impression of
passing from the clear light of expository prose into a dense fog of
allegory and abstraction and then out again. These features can all be
very discouraging. It is hoped that the essays in this book will provide some support and inspiration for those who have not yet taken
up the challenge of actually reading Plotinus. Perhaps they will also
serve those who have read some of his works before, but without
much profit. In any case, they are intended to provide a fairly complete introduction to the thought of Plotinus, who is probably the
dominant philosopher in the 700-year period between Aristotle and
Augustine of Hippo. If it is true that Plato is not responsible for what
later disciples made of him, neither is Plotinus. Precipitous judgments regarding Plotinus's philosophy should be avoided.

III FROM PLATO TO PLOTINUS

When Plato died in 347 B.C., the headship of his Academy passed on
to his nephew Speusippus and then, upon his death in 339, to
Xenocrates. These two philosophers were in a sense the first Platonists. They developed Plato's thought in ways which are both
understandable and highly contentious. In particular, they empha-

sized what we would call the "reduction" of Forms to first principles, a One and a Dyad or principle of multiplicity. The more one believes that Plato had an unwritten teaching and that Aristotle basically describes this accurately in his works, the more sympathetic one will be to the claim that the views of Speusippus and Xenocrates are authentic expressions of Platonism. But the doctrine of first principles is not completely absent from the dialogues, at least, we must add, on some interpretations. Obviously, in the first generation after Plato there were already efforts under way to systematize his thought.

Since the tradition of a Platonic Academy was to continue to exist in some form up until A.D. 529, there was ample opportunity for friends and enemies alike to define and redefine Platonism. Among those who found it desirable to be identified with Plato in some way were the Skeptics in the Academy in the third and second centuries B.C.; the syncretic philosopher Antiochus of Ascalon (c.130–c.65 B.C.), who, against the Skeptics, argued for the underlying agreement of Platonic, and certain Aristotelian and Stoic doctrines; and Philo of Alexandria (c.20–15 B.C.–c.45 A.D.), the Jewish philosopher who claimed to find in Plato and the Stoics the appropriate understanding of the revelation of the Old Testament. This list could be expanded considerably. If Plato was not all things to all men, he was at least the beginning of wisdom for many with markedly different agendas.

IV PLOTINUS'S PLATONISM

Perhaps the only thing many people know about Plotinus, if they know that name at all, is that he was a Neoplatonist. Usually thinkers are referred to as "neo" with a bit of a sneer. This seems to me rather odd, since for a long time "new" has been practically a synonym for "good" in our culture. In any case, many are surprised to learn that the terms "Neoplatonism" and "Neoplatonist" are actually of eighteenth-century vintage, terms of the historian's art intended to indicate a perceived development within the history of Platonism. By that token, one might suggest that Speusippus and Xenocrates are Neoplatonists, but for the fact that it is thought necessary to discover some anti-Platonic agent in the interim for the "neos" to react to. There have even been eminent scholars who have spoken only half in jest of Plato's Neoplatonism.

If "Neoplatonist" does not stand for anything Plotinus would recognize, what then is the difference, if any, between Plotinus's Platonism and Plato's? The answer to this question of course depends on our deciding what exactly Plato taught, if anything. Even if we limit ourselves to what F. M. Cornford called "the twin pillars of Platonism," the theory of Forms and the immortality of the soul, a myriad of delicate exegetical issues come readily to mind. I believe the best way to distinguish Plotinus's Platonism both from Plato's and from the versions of Neoplatonism that came after Plotinus is to focus on Plotinus's responses to the most serious objections raised against Platonism. These objections – principally Aristotelian and Stoic – naturally presume specific interpretations of Plato's claims. Plotinus's Platonism is, roughly, the reformulation of these claims in response to these objections. These reformulations rarely correspond with exactness to anything to be found in the dialogues. The crux of the issue is whether they represent unexpressed meanings of Plato's own words or plausible inferences from them or genuinely new claims that share with Plato's own some more general commitment – or perhaps an amalgamation of all these.

For example, it is now widely recognized that to speak of *the* theory of Forms is both inaccurate and unhelpful. So, rather than asking whether Plotinus adheres to the theory of Forms it is better to ask whether he adheres to the principles underlying any theory of Forms. The answer to this question is emphatically and unequivocally yes. Among these principles are: that eternal truth exists; that eternal truths are truths about eternal entities; and that eternal truth is complex. In addition, Plotinus shares with Plato the principle that eternal truths and the reality which grounds then have a paradigmatic status for the sensible world, such that the latter represents or imitates or shares in the former. Finally, and this is only slightly more controversial, he shares with Plato the principle that eternal complexity or multiplicity cannot be ultimate. That is, there must be some first principle of all that is absolutely simple and stands in some sort of causal relation to the complex that accounts for eternal truth. Now it will be granted that philosophers who share these principles can nevertheless concoct theories or hypotheses on the basis of these that differ in subtle and not so subtle ways, all the while recognizing the common ground they share. So it is with Plotinus and Plato.

A similar point can be made about the immortality of the soul. No one would bother about the soul's immortality unless that meant the immortality of the person or self. Unquestionably, both Plato and Plotinus share the view that persons are not bodies; that they have a destiny which is nonbodily; and that this destiny is superior to any bodily state. This sets them apart from Aristotelians, Stoics, Epicureans, Christians, and others. But exactly what Plato taught about the incarnated self and that self's discarnate status is controversial and obscure. Plotinus evidently thought so as well, sometimes ruefully admitting that Plato's meaning was anything but obvious. So, we can ask, is Plotinian soul–body dualism identical to the Platonic version or a new creation? Plotinus probably thought he was defending claims that Plato meant to be accepted as true or perhaps would have expressed if he had been faced with the sorts of criticisms Plotinus himself squarely addressed. Was he right in thinking this? It is hoped that this volume will provide some help in formulating an answer to this question and ones like it.

We can approach the matter from the other direction and ask what is original in Plotinus. Actually, this does not amount to asking what is non-Platonic in Plotinus, for not only was he a direct inheritor of a tradition of Middle Platonism, but even despite his fundamental opposition to Aristotle and the Stoics, he was prepared to learn from them as well. So, Plotinus was not original in calling the first principle of all "the One" nor in making Forms internal to intellect nor even in distinguishing an empirical from an ideal self. Yet, when one begins to probe beneath the surface similarities between what is said in the *Enneads* and what can be found in earlier philosophers, it is at once evident that Plotinus is rethinking the grounds for the claims he has inherited. He is not content, for instance, simply to insist on the existence of "the One" or to cite Plato as an authority for its existence or to rely on some traditional slogan like "unity is prior to multiplicity." Rather, he sets himself the analytical task of displaying the weaknesses of opposing views and seeking out his own unassailable arguments for the One's existence. It must be admitted that on occasion he produces such a veritable avalanche of arguments (usually against Stoic views) that one might be forgiven for suspecting that quantity is being substituted for the knockdown argument that eludes him. But this is not the norm. More typically, his writing glows with the bold and imaginative use of reason. This is not the place to try to say to what extent his efforts to reach familiar destinations by new paths actually led him to redescribe the destinations themselves. In any case, like Plotinus himself, we should focus on finding the truth and let originality take care of itself.

V TRANSLATING PLOTINUS

Since this book is aimed in part at the Greekless reader, all the texts of Plotinus quoted are in translation, occasionally by the contributor, but more usually by A. H. Armstrong. The translation by Armstrong in seven volumes (*Ennead* VI takes up two) in the Loeb series with facing Greek text is certainly the best available in English. A translation by Stephen MacKenna, completed more than sixty-five years ago, has achieved a sort of legendary status in some circles, but despite its unquestionable passion and rough beauty, it is not a very reliable guide to Plotinus's actual words. Armstrong's version gives witness to some of the almost insurmountable challenges facing the translator. Plotinus's thought is constantly straining at the discipline of expository prose composition. Porphyry tells us that, owing to his poor eyesight, Plotinus never revised anything he wrote. To my knowledge no one who has read Plotinus's Greek has ever questioned this astonishing statement. In addition, he was basically conservative in his use of philosophical terminology. This means that generally he prefers to use a familiar word in unfamiliar ways rather than coin a new one. So, the translator has constantly to face a desperate choice between being true to the letter or the spirit of the text. No doubt, a case can always be made for the latter over the former, as MacKenna's admirers will be quick to point out. But the truly Greekless reader is then entirely at the mercy of the translator's understanding of the text, and it is no insult to MacKenna to say that when the text is Plotinus's, this is indeed a perilous prospect. Probably one cannot find ten sentences in a row anywhere in the *Enneads* where there is not at least one fundamentally disputable philological issue, that is, words and phrases the basic meanings of which are in doubt. I say this without intending to strike dread into the heart of anyone thinking about reading Plotinus's works. It is simply a fact one has to face, whether in Greek or with the guide of a distinguished scholar like Armstrong.

One final note on the method of referring to the *Enneads* used in this book. For example, V.3.5.1–4 refers to *Ennead* V, the third treatise, fifth chapter, lines 1–4, as found in the critical edition of Plotinus's works by Paul Henry and H.-R. Schwyzer. This is the standard method of citation. The titles of the individual treatises in the *Enneads* are not Plotinus's, as Porphyry informs us, but those which over time prevailed among the first readers.

1 Plotinus: The Platonic tradition and the foundation of Neoplatonism

I PLOTINUS AND HIS PHILOSOPHICAL SOURCES

The problem of the relation between Plotinus and Platonism belongs within the wider context of the connection between Plotinus and his philosophical predecessors.

Plotinus has gathered the legacy of nearly eight centuries of Greek philosophy into a magnificently unified synthesis. The philosophers mentioned explicitly in the *Enneads* are few enough and include no one outside the Hellenic period. They are Pherecydes, Pythagoras and the Pythagoreans, Heraclitus, Anaxagoras, Empedocles, Socrates, Plato, Aristotle, and Epicurus. Nevertheless, citations and allusions are far more numerous than direct references, and these, along with biographical material, permit us both to deepen and to broaden significantly our knowledge of Plotinus's sources by tracing the trajectory of speculation through Plotinus's predecessors. (For a proper evaluation of the relation between the citations and allusions it is crucial to recall with Szlezák[1] that if Plato is explicitly mentioned more than fifty times and Aristotle a mere four times by Plotinus, the number of allusions to each, as listed in the *Index fontium* of Henry and Schwyzer,[2] is far greater, around nine hundred for Plato and five hundred for Aristotle).

Within such an exceptionally rich tradition, we should mention Pythagoreanism in particular among the influences on the philosopher of Lycopolis, for the conception of principles and numbers, for anthropological doctrines, both ascetic and religious; Parmenides, for the identity of being with thinking, on which Plotinus's second hypostasis rests; Plato, above all in the mystical, theological, and

Translated by Lloyd P. Gerson

metaphysical dimensions of his thought.[3] On the doctrinal plane, the aspects of Plato that interested Plotinus, as we shall see below, were not the aporias of the Socratic dialogues, with their ironic and maieutic cast, and even less those relating to the connection between philosophy and education in the ideal state, but rather those that were metaphysical and mystical or ascetic. The dialogues cited explicitly in the *Enneads* are: *Phaedrus, Philebus, Republic, Symposium*, and *Theaetetus*. The *Index fontium* of the *editio minor* of Henry and Schwyzer[4] indicates references to: *Alcibiades, Apology, Cratylus, Epinomis, Phaedo, Philebus, Gorgias, Ion, Hippias Major, Laws, Minos, Parmenides, Statesman, Protagoras, Republic, Symposium, Sophist, Theaetetus, Timaeus* and, among the *Epistles*, the second, sixth, and seventh.

Porphyry, in his *Life of Plotinus* (14.4–7), observes that imperceptibly mixed into the writings of Plotinus are Stoic and Peripatetic teachings, and that in particular the *Metaphysics* of Aristotle is extensively employed.

Plotinus does not have the same esteem for Aristotle that he cherishes for Plato and the Pythagoreans. Although Aristotle is criticized, in particular for his identification of the primary principle of all with thinking of thinking, his doctrines are crucial for the Plotinian conception of the second hypostasis, identified with the Aristotelian *nous*; the question of the soul; categories; and for many aspects of physics. Regarding Aristotle, the *Index fontium* of Henry and Schwyzer[5] refers to many writings that suggest the enormous importance of Aristotelian elements in Plotinus: *Prior Analytics, Posterior Analytics, Categories, On the Soul, History of Animals, On the Heavens, On the Generation of Animals, On Generation and Corruption, On Interpretation, On Memory, On the Motion of Animals, On the World, On the Parts of Animals, On the Senses, On Sleeping and Waking, Eudemian Ethics, Nicomachean Ethics, Metaphysics, Meteorology, Physics, Politics, Topics*, and numerous fragments.

In addition, Stoicism, towards which Plotinus is even more critical, owing to its fundamental materialism, nevertheless had a decisive role in Plotinus's thinking. The Stoic accounts of God, the soul, nature, and matter have all influenced Plotinus's conception of *logos*, necessity, his account of the passions and other questions in the philosophy of human nature, and several logical notions. In this regard, after Theiler,[6] who has firmly located Plotinus midway between Plato and the Stoics, examining the question principally from the terminological and historical point of view, it is appropriate to mention the important work of Andreas Graeser.[7] In the first part of his book, the texts regarding Plotinus's relations to the Old Stoa on the one hand and to Posidonius and Epictetus, on the other, are presented; the second part of the book contains studies of Plotinus and the Stoic categories of being, causality, free will, and *sunaisthêsis*.

Above all, Plotinus's thought cannot be understood without taking into account the revival of interest in metaphysical, theological, and ascetic or spiritual matters in Alexandria between the first and third centuries A.D. In this period, in the Alexandrian environment, flourished Philo Judaeus and the Middle Platonism that influenced Plotinus especially in metaphysics and philosophy of human nature, as we shall see, and the Neopythagoreanism that involves a recovery of the doctrine of principles and numbers in a metaphysical dimension. Finally, Alexandria saw the establishment of the school of Ammonius Saccas, attended by Plotinus for about eleven years.

It seems undeniable that Philo, living between the first century B.C. and the first century A.D., and producing for the first time in history a fusion of elements of traditional Greek thought with elements of Hebrew culture, was also an influence on Plotinus, particularly in the matters of *logos*, of spiritual powers, of the intelligible world, and in the accounts of theology and mystical asceticism.[8]

Between the end of the ancient period and the first two centuries of the imperial period there occurred a genuine and unique rebirth of the Pythagorean tradition in Neopythagoreanism,[9] which had its own significant characteristics, among which was, most significantly, the reaffirmation of the existence of the immaterial or incorporeal, something that was absent in the systems of Hellenistic philosophy. This incorporeality came to be conceived on the basis of the doctrine of the Monad, the Dyad, and Numbers, inserted into a hierarchical system of derivation. In the philosophy of human nature, the Neopythagoreans held the immortality of the soul and gave a mystical coloring to their insistence that the end of man consisted in separation from the sensible world and union with the divine. One notes that in the preface to his book *On Ends*, Longinus presents Plotinus as the philosopher who in his writings has given a clearer exposition than his predecessors of the principal theory of Pythagoras and Plato.[10]

Describing the meetings of the school of Plotinus, Porphyry[11] tells us that first, Plotinus would have the texts read that were to constitute the point of departure for the day's lessons. The principal texts cited were those of Severus, Gaius, Atticus (Middle Platonists of the second century A.D.), Cronius (Neopythagorean Middle Platonist of the second–third century A.D.), and of Numenius of Apamea of the second century A.D., whose works were a fusion of Middle Platonism and Neopythagoreanism. Numenius, affirming the absolute incorporeality of being, articulated its structure into a hierarchical triad of three gods (that he believed to have found in the *Second Epistle* of Plato), in which was contained the Neopythagorean doctrine of the One and the Indefinite Dyad. With Numenius, above all in his conception of three gods, of contemplation as creation, of the presence of everything in everything, and of the personal mystical union with the Good, one arrives truly at the threshold of Neoplatonism. There are such striking affinities between the Numenian and Plotinian doctrines that Plotinus was actually accused of plagiarizing Numenius, and a disciple of Plotinus, Amelius, in response, wrote a book in defense of his master, titled *The Doctrinal Differences Between Plotinus and Numenius.*[12]

According to the testimony of Porphyry, Plotinus had read out from among the Peripatetics the commentaries of Adrastus of Aphrodisias (second century A.D., author of historical and lexicographical studies of the Aristotelian *corpus*; author also of commentaries on the *Categories* of Aristotle and the *Timaeus* of Plato); those of Aspasius (second century A.D.; his commentaries on the *Categories, On Interpretation, Metaphysics,* and *On the Heavens* are lost; there remains only a part of his commentary on the *Nicomachean Ethics*); and those of Alexander of Aphrodisias (second century A.D.), the most eminent Aristotelian commentator in antiquity.

Notwithstanding these debts, the philosophy of Plotinus cannot in fact be considered eclectic or syncretic, for in the *Enneads* are to be found basic themes that provide an entirely new inspiration and unity for the ancient doctrines.

It is sufficient to mention here the observation of Porphyry[13], to which we shall return, that stresses that Plotinus never simply read the texts of prior commentators, but showed extraordinary originality in his speculations and infused the spirit of Ammonius Saccas into his studies. Porphyry testifies that Plotinus quickly grasped the passage read and intervened to explain in brief a profound theory. Indeed, he criticized those who were simply philologists and not philosophers like his fellow student, Longinus.

Certainly, as Dodds has noted[14], one can find for every passage in Plotinus sources and precedents, but the essence of his system is contained in its comprehensive meaning, and cannot be reduced to a mosaic; his true originality stands in its overarching design, not in the parts out of which it is made.

II PLOTINUS AND THE HISTORY OF ANTIQUE PAGAN PLATONISM

The history of Platonism does not coincide simply with that of the Academy, which ended in the first century B.C. with Antiochus of Ascalon. Platonism is not a closed system with a simple character; rather it has a variegated and complex history.

Arnou[15] has justly described a "Platonism in process" that diversifies itself as it progresses: it is a question of a current of thought that is developed in various forms, based on a permanent foundation of a few metaphysical and ethical-ascetic features. Among these should be stressed, in particular, following the common polarities, the admission of two levels of reality, one sensible and the other intelligible, of which the second is the true cause of the first, which is not capable of explaining itself; the distinction in man of two parts, corresponding to the two levels of reality, that is, body and soul (related to the intelligible and incorruptible); the association of ethics with eschatology in a religious vision of the world; the conviction of the necessity of separating the soul from the body.

Regarding the troubled history of the Academy, the ancients themselves[16] had already distinguished five phases: (1) the first Academy of Plato and his successors, the astronomer Eudoxus of Cnidus, Heraclides of Ponticus, Speusippus, Xenocrates, Polemon, Crates, and Crantor; (2) the second Academy of Arcesilaus, the sceptical philosopher who lived at the end of the fourth and the beginning of the third centuries B.C.; (3) the third Academy of Carneades, skeptic of the third to second centuries B.C., Clitomachus of Carthage, skeptic, who lived in the second century B.C., disciple and popularizer of the thought of Carneades; (4) the fourth Academy of Philo of Larissa, eclectic and refined skeptic of the second century B.C., and Carmides, who practiced Carnedean rhetoric; (5) the fifth Academy of Antiochus of Ascalon, eclectic thinker of the first century B.C., teacher of Cicero, who came to the view that Stoicism was substantially identical with Platonism and Aristotelianism, differing only in form and certain dogmas of logic, physics, and ethics.

In the speculative sphere, beginning with the first disciples of Plato, there was a decline within Platonism, especially in its mathematical and "immanentist" tendencies and then, finally, antimetaphysical, culminating in the skepticism of the second and third Academies and the eclecticism of the fourth and fifth.[17]

In 86 B.C. Sulla conquered Athens and along with it the Academy and Aristotle's Lyceum. In this way, the Academy, which had undergone a progressive doctrinal development even from its beginning and culminating in skepticism and eclecticism, experienced the devastation of its foundation and library.

While at Athens in the first century B.C., the Academy was dying, outside of Athens, particularly in Alexandria in Egypt, it was rising again, with Eudorus and others, in the first and second centuries A.D., as a metaphysical and ethical-ascetic system. The resurgence was gradual but continuous, mutating and reconfiguring itself constantly in metaphysical matters, breaking the ties with the materialism and skepticism of the philosophy of the preceding centuries.

The Platonism that developed in the first and second centuries A.D., while it no longer had the characteristics of ancient Platonism, also did not have the characteristics of Plotinianism, and showed fragmentations, oscillations, and contradictions. For this reason, standing astride the old and the new, it was dubbed by scholars "Middle Platonism":[18] an essential link in the chain of development of Western thought, whether that be in relation to the history of pagan Platonism or the early Church Fathers, who derived from it numerous doctrines.

The most important characteristic of Middle Platonism is the recovery of the Platonic dimension of incorporeality. The fundamental feature of the metaphysics of Middle Platonism for the history of later philosophy is the fusion of the Platonic conception of Ideas and the Aristotelian conception of *nous*. The Middle Platonists considered the Ideas, in their transcendent aspect, as thoughts in the mind of God, that is, the intelligible world came to be identified with the contents of a supreme Intellect; in their immanent aspect they understood the Ideas as forms of beings. The basic text utilized by Middle Platonists for their rethinking of Plato was the *Timaeus.* Apart from the rediscovery of transcendence, the Middle Platonists posited as the supreme end of man the imitation of God, or assimilation to the divine and to the incorporeal.

In order to comprehend the origins of the Plotinian system within the tradition of Platonism, it is necessary briefly to recall, apart from the internal phases of the development of the Academy in relation to the rise of Middle Platonism, the mysterious figure of Ammonius Saccas, the teacher of Plotinus, who lived at Alexandria between the second and third centuries A.D. The relationship between Plotinus and Ammonius recapitulates in certain respects that between Plato and Socrates.

Given that he did not wish to write anything, the thought of Ammonius is difficult to reconstruct, though he must have been a philosopher of exceptional profundity. We can recover a few elements of his thought from Porphyry's *Life of Plotinus* (3.14). He relates that Plotinus, having become disillusioned by all the famous intellectuals of Alexandria, was, at twenty-eight years old, led to the school of Ammonius by a friend. When he met Ammonius he exclaimed, "this is the man I have been seeking" and he stayed with him until he was thirty-nine. The same source tells us that Plotinus owed Ammonius a considerable debt, both in his method of study and in his doctrine, and he recalls that when, many years later, Plotinus noticed entering his own school a fellow student of Ammonius, he ceased at once his lesson, claiming that when a speaker knows that his hearer can anticipate what he is going to say, his enthusiasm ceases.

As for the cultural origins of Ammonius, Porphyry always maintained that he was born and educated in a Christian family, but, dedicating himself to philosophy, had reverted to paganism. The Neoplatonist Ierocles and Nemesius relate that Ammonius wanted to harmonize Plato and Aristotle and that he held that all reality derived from God, distinguishing three levels intimately connected, within the real: (a) the supreme reality, that is, God the creator, the celestial realities, and the gods; (b) intermediate reality, constituted by ethereal nature and good demons; (c) lowest reality, that is, human souls, men, and terrestrial animals.[19]

Ammonius had founded a school in Alexandria around 200 A.D. that marks the decisive link between the Middle Platonic tradition and the beginnings of Neoplatonism. Its disciples were, in particular, Erennius, Olympius, the Neoplatonist Origen, Plotinus, and Longinus. Plotinus remained with Ammonius from 232 to 243 A.D., the year in which, desiring to acquire direct knowledge of the wisdom of the Persians and the Indians, he followed Gordian III on his Oriental expedition. That expedition was aborted owing to Gordian's assassination in Mesopotamia. Returning to Antioch, Plotinus, now forty, and having attained full maturity as a philosopher, decided to remove himself to Rome, where he arrived in 244 A.D. There he founded a school which became almost at once extremely famous. Many among those most prominent at the time were attracted to his person and his teachings: philosophers, rhetoricians, philologists, physicians, political figures, senators; even the emperor Gallienus and his wife Salonina attended his school.

III PLOTINUS: EXEGETE OF PLATO OR INNOVATOR?

As many scholars have stressed, Plotinus himself insisted that he was a simple "exegete" and continuator of Plato. This affirmation can only be properly understood in context. In fact, in the celebrated and much quoted passage in which it appears, he claimed that his own theories of the three hypostases were not new, but were advanced long before, even if they were not stated in a clear and explicit fashion.[20] However, according to him, they expressed nothing other than an interpretation of Platonic writings. It goes without saying that his speculation tended to harmonize with Plato. For example, after his treatment of the genera of being, Plotinus took care to emphasize that his doctrine of essence was in accord with that of the founder of the Academy.[21]

Regarding the question of the exegesis of Plato, Brisson,[22] after having duly recorded the important observation of P. Hadot, who has shown that for almost two thousand years philosophy was conceived of as exegesis, concluded that this was the precise notion of philosophy shared by Plotinus and by his followers.

According to Dörrie,[23] Plotinus the "traditionalist" cannot be separated from Plotinus the "innovator." Every innovation was introduced by him only on the condition that it be in accord with the tradition, to which he wished, without any doubt, to be faithful. The originality of Plotinus does not manifest itself directly, but in the interpretations and in the judicious corrections that he introduces, based on the texts of the commentators that he used. The criteria according to which he accepted or rejected the doctrines of his predecessors are at the same time the criteria of his originality: a theology and a metaphysics centered on the triad of transcendent hypostases and on the doctrine of procession.

Dörrie concluded, however, that in Plotinus one can see a kind of coincidence of opposites; in him are found both aspects. One cannot be found without the other. His innovations were rooted in a tradition that he knew harmonized with his metaphysical system, centered on the procession of plurality from the One. Plotinus was both "traditionalist" and "innovator," that is, he was an acute searcher for and servant of the truth.

Szlezák[24] has claimed that the assertions of Plotinus concerning his relation to the philosophical tradition are puzzling in the extreme. In the *Enneads* one moves from derisory remarks regarding those who adhered to the opinions of the great predecessors,[25] to peremptory assertions by the philosopher of Lycopolis that he is nothing other than an exegete of Plato.[26]

At the same time, Szlezák has argued that on one side Plotinus pointed to union with the first principle of all as a goal of philosophy, in a progressive overcoming of all forms of thinking, ending in the unification of "the alone with the alone,"[27] while on the other side it seems evident that the Plotinian way to the One did not pass through ascetic practices of the anchorites, but through the speculative attainment of the intelligible.

For this reason, the judgments of interpreters on such a question differ. For some scholars, the debt of Plotinus to Plato was absolute. Plato is beyond all criticism or polemic according to Plotinus, who considered himself nothing more than Plato's disciple (Zeller, Theiler, Schwyzer, Armstrong, Krämer).[28] According to others, Plotinus is completely autonomous with respect to the tradition, including Plato, availing himself of Platonic doctrines in an independent manner (Rist, Eon).[29]

For Dodds, the references by Plotinus to his predecessors were simply superficial. In particular, he tended to cite Plato only instrumentally in a discussion, as authority for his own conclusions. For

others, the unresolved problems in the texts of his predecessors provided the decisive inspiration for the Plotinian reconfiguration of
these problems (Merlan, Armstrong).[30] Finally, for still others, a re-
working by Plotinus of doctrine occurred in a limited way indicating
that he is simply the representative of a long and well-established
tradition, that of classical metaphysics (Krämer).[31]

If at one time we were astonished at Plotinus's ahistorical and arbitrary use of the Greek tradition (Zeller),[32] some recent interpreters
have attributed to him a clear awareness of the historical conditioning of his thought (Matter, Gräser),[33] or even a systematic justification reflecting his utilization of philosophical texts (Eon).[34]

As Faggin has rightly insisted,[35] even if Plotinus does not claim
originality, wishing thereby to testify to the vitality and continuity
of the Platonic tradition, all the same there is in him an undeniable
creativity centered on the remarkable doctrinal novelty in his proces-
sions of the hypostases. Consequently, the greatest continuator of
Plato among the Neoplatonists was not Iamblichus, who struggled
with obscure esotericisms, nor Proclus, who ontologized and div-
inized numbers and relations, but Plotinus, who, in the *Enneads*,
has presented a powerful synthesis in which Platonic thought is
represented and developed with the appropriate religious, mystical,
and metaphysical sensitivities.

Charrue, studying Plotinus as a reader of Plato, especially of the
Parmenides, Timaeus, Phaedrus, Phaedo, Sophist, and book six of the
Republic, has argued that for Plotinus the only reading that truly
counted was that of Plato, a reading which revealed precisely the
meaning and implications that Plotinus intended for his works.[36]
Plotinus's work had the characteristics of a synthetic representation,
a conscious and careful elaboration of texts; his reading of Plato was
actually more of a rereading, the fruit of thought that had profoundly
matured. Plotinus has beyond question extracted many elements
from his sources, but in doing this he has transformed fundamental
parts, that is, the content and the essence of their doctrines, alert to
the search for truth (he held that it was necessary to believe that some
ancient philosophers had discovered the truth, but that one must
examine who has correctly assembled it and in what manner it was
understood).[37]

Carefully examining the texts, Charrue has observed particularly
that Plato, though never being cited alone by Plotinus, but always

together with other philosophers, was, however, always regarded in the first rank, owing to his precision (*akribeia*).[38]

Of major importance is the programmatic implication of Plotinus's statement that he did not wish to be other than an interpreter of Plato,[39] which highlights the fact that Plotinus wanted to return to the ancients as sources of truth that was difficult to recover, and the anti-Gnostic polemics of II.9.5 and 6, in which the Gnostics were accused of censuring and contradicting the ancients and of introducing, in opposition to them, novelties that distanced themselves seriously from the truth. By contrast, the doctrines of the ancients on the intelligible realm were thought to be truly wise and superior to those of the Gnostics. From the historical point of view, the truth, for Plotinus, was known only by the ancients; from the theoretical point of view, it is a property of the intelligible world. The Platonists, as we read in an important text,[40] are the third race of men (Plotinus distinguishes in a descending hierarchy Platonists, Stoics, and Epicureans), divine owing to the acuteness of their vision, with whom one is elevated above the terrestrial mist. The region of the truth belongs to them.

Plotinus was not concerned with the personage of Plato in his treatises, that is, with his life, his psychology, or his nature; this would have been in conflict with the Plotinian spirit, characterized by a total absence of biographical preoccupation. He was, it is said, ashamed to be in a body and almost never talked about himself. It was rather the Platonic doctrines that interested him, in which there were obscure and incomplete sides, calling for an accurate interpretation. In particular, he considered Plato to be a philosopher who posed problems or aporias that often did not have definitive solutions.

For example, according to Plotinus, Plato did not always affirm the same things regarding the soul[41] such that one can clearly grasp his intention, although he always disvalued the sensible realm and censured the soul for its continued connection to the bodily. On the one hand, in the *Phaedrus* the loss of wings was considered to be the cause of the fall of the soul and of its sojourn on earth, while on the other, in the *Timaeus*, Plato comes to say that the soul was a gift of the goodness of the Demiurge. Plotinus, though recognizing for every dialogue an autonomous and distinct existence, nevertheless formed a global interpretation of them. Beyond the differing intentions of different writings, there was a single purpose that guided a unifying exegesis, according to a common and permanent vision.[42]

According to Charrue, the Plotinian reading of Plato was heuristic. For example, regarding the knowledge of the intelligible world, Plotinus affirmed that Plato has left "to us" the task of seeking and discovering such things, so long as we wish to be worthy of the name "Platonists."[43]

In order to be truly Platonists and exegetes of Plato it was necessary to realize a philosophy similar to his own; Plato had to be reconstructed. Thus, one understands all the better the affirmations of St. Augustine, for whom Plato continued to live in Plotinus. In this manner, the exegesis of Plotinus differed from that of others in this period; he never wrote commentaries as did his predecessors (or as Proclus would later do), nor did he write introductions, like the *Eisagoge* of Albinus (Alcinous). For Plotinus, exegesis was not simply commentary, but embodied a nobler task. He thought above all of meaning: in writing he did not occupy himself with style, nor with the formalities of composition, but rather he concerned himself solely with meaning (*nous*).[44] Plotinus never relied uncritically on the commentaries that he had read out in class, being independently minded in speculation and bearing the "spirit of Ammonius" in his studies.[45] What was this "spirit of Ammonius," asks Charrue? A phrase of Ierocles helps us understand. Ammonius "understood well" the doctrine of Plato and of Aristotle and "he united them in one and the same spirit (*nous*)."[46] It is significant that the terms used by Porphyry to describe the method of Plotinus coincide with that which Ierocles uses to qualify the exegesis of Ammonius.

Basing his interpretation on the accusation by Plotinus that Longinus was a philologist and not a philosopher, Charrue concluded that the interpretation of Plotinus was "philosophical exegesis." For the philologist, the text is in itself untouchable, and everything has to be subordinated to it, while the philosopher studies the texts, but only for the thought. They are the point of departure for philosophical reflection. Plotinian interpretation of Plato consisted of a "metaphysical reading." Plotinus vivified or revivified the thought of Plato. His Platonism is a "Platonism in action"; he had discovered how to apply the method and the ideas of the founder of the Academy.[47]

Regarding these problems, Szlezák, convinced that in order to comprehend the distinctiveness of Plotinus one has to get at the truth of the attitude and the means by which Plotinus appropriates the philosophical tradition, has analyzed with great acuity the Plotinian "self-testimonies" and the judgments of critics of his argument,[48] concluding that the Plotinian interpretation of Plato was decidedly unhistorical.[49] The position of Plotinus was this: a leap of faith in Plato that cared nothing for the problem of originality, nor for historical accuracy. Rather, it focused on that which was of permanent value in philosophical doctrine.

IV PLATONISM AND PLOTINIAN NEOPLATONISM: CONTINUITY OR RADICAL INNOVATION?

In the history of the interpretation of Platonism it is possible to distinguish some steps between Plato and the Neoplatonists.

Late antiquity and the Middle Ages have known Platonism in the guise of Neoplatonism, making no distinction between the two systems. Plotinus and the later Neoplatonists considered themselves legitimate inheritors, interpreters, and continuators of Plato; this did not prevent them from integrating into basically Platonic doctrines the speculative patrimony of antiquity in its various currents. As Meinhardt has rightly stated,[50] this holds in particular for Aristotle who was understood by the commentators of late antiquity above all as a disciple of Plato. In the Middle Ages, Platonism was transmitted in various Neoplatonic forms. St. Augustine, who considered himself a Platonist, learned the philosophy of Porphyry and of the Neoplatonists of his time; again, in the sixth century Boethius considered the doctrine of the three hypostases as Platonic; in the entire medieval period that which was read of Plato (only a few dialogues), in particular the *Timaeus*, came to be interpreted through the Neoplatonic commentaries.

In addition, after the Middle Ages, Plato continued to be understood in this manner. Thus, Renaissance Platonism, which knew directly the Platonic writings, is in fact Neoplatonism. Marsilio Ficino, who asserted that through Plotinus Plato himself spoke, and who produced translations of both the dialogues of Plato and the *Enneads* as well as of other Neoplatonists, contributed in large measure to the continuation of Neoplatonic interpretations, blending the legacy of Platonic and Neoplatonic thought with his own peculiar vision of the world, in polemical confrontation with Aristotelianism and Scholasticism. The same goes for the Cambridge Platonists of the seventeenth and eighteenth centuries. We might note that they did not even possess a distinct concept of Neoplatonism.[51]

By contrast, in our century, starting from the discoveries of the preceding century, we find stressed with increasing clarity a neat historical separation between the two systems: the thought of Plotinus and of his successors was presented with full documentation as a philosophy with original characteristics in comparison to Platonism.

In particular, Meinhardt has emphasized that the rise and development of the concept of Neoplatonism in the arena of the history of German Philosophy has gone through various stages beginning with the devaluation and refutation of Neoplatonic thinkers. In the modern age they came to be thought of as falsifiers of Plato; there was here the prohibition of compromise among the Platonists; their sect was declared "eclectic" and, in addition, by J. Brucker, the lowliest denizen of the Alexandrian underworld. The term "Neoplatonism" is used in 1744 by A. F. Büshing, who spoke not only of an eclectic sect but also of "new Platonists"; in 1786 C. Meiners produced a "History of New=Platonic Philosophy," continuing, however, to consider it in a negative light. Finally, in 1793 G. G. Fülleborn chose to express with the title "Neoplatonic Philosophy" the common name for the "famous Neoplatonists," though he still regarded them in basically a negative manner. In any case, the gradual formation of the term "Neoplatonism" reveals a change in the view of the philosophy of Plotinus and of his successors, no longer described as an eclectic excrescence, but as an authentic form of Platonism.

Meinhardt[52] has urged that it took a philosophy of the speculative power and systematic form of German idealism in addition to a more precise grasp of the historical features of the philosophers of the Imperial Age before there could be a true change in the valuation of the Neoplatonists. That which was already prepared by Fichte and Schelling came to fruition with Hegel, for whom Neoplatonism was "a recovery of the spirit of man, indeed, of the spirit of the world." In the 150 years following, even if the judgment of Hegel was not endorsed, in any event the term "Neoplatonism" was ever after understood as a current of thought that should be definitively reinserted in the history of Platonism.

One must remember that in the last years of the twentieth century, owing to the evolution of specialized research on the currents and thinkers of late antiquity antecedent to Plotinus, and to the interpretation of Plato in the light of the theory of principles handed down through the indirect tradition, the close connection between Plato and Neoplatonism beginning with Plotinus was put in relief, but at the same time the theoretical differences between the two systems were also stressed.[53]

Krämer[54] has adduced evidence to the effect that the Aristotelian testimony on the "unwritten doctrines" of Plato plays a not inconsiderable role in the *Enneads*. Two elements, above all, connect the emerging Platonic thought of the indirect tradition with Plotinus: the doctrine of the One above being and the plurality of the levels of being. To these can be added other themes, such as the central positions of the ideal numbers and the relations between bodies and figures and geometrical dimensions which had, however, lost their theoretical force. The major differences between Plotinus and Plato are the elimination of politics from philosophy, the transformation of the dualism of principles into an extreme radical monism connected with the question of the derivation of a multiplicity from unity, and, finally, the spiritualization of the system. Nevertheless, Krämer concludes that there is a peculiar historical influence of the unwritten writings of Plato on Neoplatonism that, interpreted in the most Platonically conservative manner, has transmitted basic concepts of the metaphysics of Plato to the medieval and modern traditions.

Merlan[55] has stressed the closeness between Platonism and Plotinian Neoplatonism. While in many periods they were considered identical, the nineteenth century arrived at an opposing point of view that insisted on a complete differentiation between the two systems. By contrast, the present tendency is once again to narrow the gap between Platonism and Neoplatonism rather than to amplify it.

The fundamental characteristics of Neoplatonism according to Merlan[56] are the following seven: (1) there exists a plurality of spheres subordinated hierarchically one to the other, that go from the highest to the sensible world, which exists in space and in time; (2) the derivation of every lower sphere from a higher, in virtue of a relation of the implicit to the explicit rather than that of a concrete efficient cause and effect; (3) the derivation of the highest sphere of being from a principle that, insofar as it is cause of being, is beyond being, that is, superior to every kind of determination of being; (4) this supreme principle is designated "One"; it is removed from every sort of determination and is therefore absolutely simple; (5) every inferior sphere of being implies either an augmentation of the number of beings that it contains or an incremental determination up to the spatial-temporal, which possesses the minimum of unity; (6) the knowledge of the first principle is radically different from that of any object; it is not a matter of predicative knowledge, as in the case of beings that imply some determination; (7) the principal difficulty of Neoplatonism consists in the explanation and justification of why and how there occurs a passage from the One to a plurality and, in particular, of the role of a material principle in this passage.

Reale,[57] commenting on Merlan's work, argues that even if it is true that these characteristics are present in Neoplatonism, the problem must nevertheless be considered from a different perspective. From the interpretation of Plato in light of the "unwritten doctrines" one discovers that these elements were already visible in Plato himself; that is why what Merlan calls "Neoplatonism" really began with Plato and would seem to be more correctly called "Platonism." All the same, there are important differences between Platonism and Neoplatonism, by means of which it is necessary to distinguish them precisely, without separating them radically.

Reviewing Merlan's book,[58] Dörrie observes that Neoplatonism is born of a fusion of Pythagorean, Aristotelian, and Academic elements, according to a form that is different from the tradition, with the addition of a new element, that of the mystical-religious, by means of which contemplation comes to be conceived of as ecstasy and the assimilation to God as a unification with the One itself.

Reale, in order to demonstrate satisfactorily the identity and difference between Platonism and Neoplatonism, has taken a different approach and has emphasized the principal theoretical novelty of Neoplatonism, consisting in the systematization of Platonic thought.

While in Plato and in the Academy the structure of the real came to be explained by means of the bipolarity of the two opposing principles, the One and the Indefinite Dyad, in Neoplatonism, beginning with Plotinus, the One was placed at the pinnacle of all, according to a kind of monopolarity, from which all reality is derived. Besides the concept of the monopolarity of the One, another element that definitively characterizes Neoplatonism is the doctrine of the productivity of the One, that in Plotinus became self-productivity, *causa sui*. The Neoplatonic One-Good was an infinite superabundant force that produces by means of successive instruments, making everything to be. In the third place, while the Platonic principle of the One-Good was perfectly definable and expressible and was not communicated by means of writings owing to a conception of the relation between orality and writing tied to an archaic mentality, for Neoplatonism the first infinite principle was structurally indefinable as well as ineffable. Furthermore, in Neoplatonism the connections between the diverse spheres of reality came to be explicated in a more clear and precise manner, in Plotinus with the doctrine of creative contemplation, that constitutes the heart of this processional metaphysics, and in Proclus with the development of the dialectical triads, according to the circular triadic laws of perdurance, procession, and return.

A great scholar of the thought of Plotinus and of its historical sequelae in Western philosophy, Werner Beierwaltes,[59] has observed that in the "systematic" appropriation of parts of Plato by Plotinus, above all in reference to the *Second Epistle* and to the *Parmenides*, one cannot sustain the contention that Plotinus was original according to the modern meaning of that word. Nevertheless, this does not mean his doctrine was a mere reproduction of the tradition, without an autonomous interposition of his own thought.

It is a question rather of a transformation of the philosophical and theological legacy, that understands the thought of predecessors as being elaborated within a rich matrix and analyzes them thoroughly in an "ambivalent game" of philosophical identification with the tradition and of innovation. Plotinus did not interpret nor cite nor take passages in their context, but proceeded in a rigorously selective manner. (Schwyzer[60] in examining the Plotinian interpretation of the *Philebus* has already noted that Plotinus did not concern himself with the main questions of the dialogue, but read in it above all affirmations regarding the first principle, using isolated assertions, and paying no attention to context, considering the *Philebus* simply as one expression of the true philosophy. This indeed goes for his use of all the Platonic writings, in which every element was subordinated to the treatment of the central themes.) The early dialogues, owing to their aporetic structure, were of no interest to him; he sought in Plato not aporias but solutions; not a method, but a doctrine. For this reason, he concentrated on phrases and on the key words, recovering from them their true value, apparently heedless of their context.

Plotinus, "interpreter" of the philosophy of Plato, *in* this interpretation, and *by means of it*, in spite of a conceptual form that would be unthinkable without Plato, has succeeded in producing and developing a new form of thinking that did not concern itself so much with following the letter of the Platonic text as with tracing a supposed intention of Platonic philosophy, which was to be verified by a strictly historical point of view.

In particular, the mode in which Plotinus has interpreted the *Parmenides* of Plato in its basic intentions, encompassing it in his own doctrine of the three hypostases in their differentiation, but reciprocally related by means of a kind of circular relation, became the point of departure of a schema of thought that, as a map of the unities of reciprocal relations, has remained authoritative throughout the successive developments in the history of Neoplatonic philosophy. Beierwaltes has conclusively shown, borrowing a definition of Klibansky,[61] that the Plotinian philosophy remained, despite its uniqueness, within the ambit of the "continuity of the Platonic tradition."

V THE INNOVATIVE LINES DERIVED FROM THE PLOTINIAN INTERPRETATION OF THE PLATONIC TRADITION

Recapitulating the observations made in the preceding paragraphs, one must insist that the fundamental differences between the thought of Plato, ancient Platonism, and the Neoplatonism of the philosopher of Lycopolis were of a theoretical nature, and are centered on two main axes in the whole Plotinian system: the doctrine of the "procession" of the hypostases from the One that is developed according to a circular triad, and that of "creative contemplation."

These constitute the key to the systematic reading of the entire Plotinian philosophy.[62]

Starting from these points, Plotinus has realized an authentic and unique reconstruction of classical metaphysics, arriving at positions quite new in relation to Plato and to all preceding philosophy.

Let us look, first of all, at the fundamental problem of the "procession." One must above all remember that for Plotinus the ultimate questions of metaphysics were two and not one, as was the case in the entire philosophical tradition that preceded him. The principal problem of Greek metaphysics in its classical form was: why and how do a many derive from One? Plato in the *Philebus* had observed that it was marvelous to think that the many could be one and that the one could be many: the question of the relation between the One and the many was, for philosophers, from beginning to end the cause of the greatest wonder. Plotinus, who knew of this theme, "already notorious among the ancients,"[63] has, without question, posed and solved this problem in a unique manner.

In any case, beyond this, Plotinus has formulated another exceedingly difficult question that no one of the Greek philosophers had ever posed before: why does the One exist and why is it what it is? One notes that posing this question means to put in question the Absolute itself, asking, so to speak, for the why of the first principle of all. In particular, this problem would be an absurd outcome within the context of the metaphysics of Plato and Aristotle, in which the first principle was something unconditioned, the ultimate explanation, of which it was constitutionally impossible to ask for its reason. (Aristotle had said that this sort of question was structurally deceptive, in virtue of its leading to an infinite regress: in the ambit of his doctrine of substance, the question of why in relation to a principle would have implied a following question regarding the why of the why, and so on to infinity.)[64]

Plotinus, who was probably occupied by such a question owing to the influence of the problem raised by Christians and Gnostics, has given to it a highly revolutionary response in the context of Greek thought, holding that the cause or the reason for the being of the One was freedom: the One exists because it is free self-productive activity. In the heart of one of the most portentous treatises of the *Enneads*, VI.8, dedicated to the problem of the freedom of the One,[65] Plotinus has presented, in an extraordinary passage that penetrates and then transcends the theoretical horizons of Platonism and Aristotelianism and touches the highest peak of Western thought, a true and strict demonstration of the existence of the One, beginning with the desire for the Good inherent in all things. Plotinus has observed that every entity aspires to the Good and believes itself to have achieved the highest state of being when it participates in it; so long as one does not possess it, one wishes for something else, but when one possesses it, one wishes oneself: thus, being and willing coincide. For this reason, being belongs to the Good itself, coinciding with it, in fact, in a certain sense creating itself, all the more because the Good in itself and through itself wants to be what it is. (Indeed, adds Plotinus, if, *per absurdum*, the Good were all to change itself into something else, it would not be able to want to be other than itself, because it is perfect and has nothing that it wants more than to be itself.) In the Good, choice, will, and being coincide: it is the creator of itself. To summarize: while other being are satisfied with themselves only because they participate in the Good, in the Good is contained the choice and the will for its own being. The first principle posits itself and creates itself as well, and is self-productive activity. In it activity and being coincide.[66]

After having examined the Plotinian solution of the problem of the why of the One, with the revolutionary affirmation that it is self-creating and self-possessed, we see the solution to the other problem, that of the explanation of the existence of the many. The Plotinian response to this question as well, as we shall indicate, represents one of the vertices of the metaphysics of antiquity and constitutes a unique element at the heart of it.

Given that in describing the derivation of entities from the first principle, Plotinus employs numerous imagistic features of sensible experience, the most famous of which was that of light (the genesis of things from the One was compared to the radiation of a light from a luminous source in diminishing degrees, that is, in successive hypostases), a few interpreters, taking these images literally, have understood the derivation of the many from the One as a form of emanation, as a physical, mechanical, necessary flowing.[67] Contrary to what so many scholars have held, it is important to stress that the images must not be understood as intended to deceive, making it seem as if for Plotinus the One would be subject to necessity in generation, as occurs in the case of falling water, or heat or light or an overflowing force. Indeed, by means of these images of a physical character, he seeks to explain the action of the infinite One, self-caused, making use of that which is infinitely different from it, insofar as everything else is caused by something other than itself, that is, everything that is not the One. The doctrine of Plotinus was much richer in images utilized by him for purely didactic purposes, aimed at showing that the first principle produces everything else while remaining absolutely stable.

In truth, one must observe above all that by an attentive analysis of the context of the images presented one is able to discover that for Plotinus the first principle remains (*menei*) in its transcendent state while it generates, without its substance being impoverished; the generated is inferior to the generator, and does not impoverish it nor does the generator have need of the generated in any way.[68]

More fundamentally, in order to comprehend the derivation of things from the One in its true meaning, concealed behind the images, it is necessary to focus on an important passage in the *Enneads*, V.4.2, that the interpreters have habitually ignored, in which Plotinus has explained how the production from the first principle occurs.

In this text are distinguished two activities of being: (a) the activity *of* being and (b) the activity *from* being; (a) the activity of a being coincides with that which the thing is and (b) the activity that is from the being follows necessarily from it and is distinct from it. For example, in a source of heat that is (a) the activity of heat which coincides with its nature (this is the activity of the flame) and (b) an activity that derives from the flame and arrives outside of it. Applying this distinction to the One: (a) there is an activity that is unique to the One, that is that owing to which the One is permanently that which it is, that is, self-creative freedom, absolute power; and (b) there is an activity coming from the first; it is a question of power, an exceedingly great *energeia*, because it comes from the greatest power: this activity produces all things. The activity *of* the One is self-creative freedom, while the activity *from* the One follows necessarily from the first, but is a necessity *sui generis*, that is, a necessity that follows from an act of freedom.

In truth, what we have said in order to explain the production of the many from the first principle is still not complete. This is one of the aspects in which the thought of Plotinus emerges in its radical originality. In fact, the generation of the intelligible hypostases and, in part, of the physical cosmos, as Plotinus implies, beyond the two activities mentioned, includes a further activity that is equally essential, namely, the *epistrophê*, that is, the return to the contemplation of the generating principle. If one were to pay sufficient attention to this activity, it would perhaps be understandable how inadequate is the emanationist interpretation that does not allow one to grasp this contemplative return.

In many passages of the *Enneads* Plotinus has highlighted the metaphysical return of the generated to the generator, owing to which the first acquires its own determination. We see, for example, this return in the passage from the first to the second hypostasis. The power that comes from the One does not directly generate *nous*, but rather an indeterminate and shapeless intelligible matter, that determines itself and becomes the world of forms only as a result of contemplating the first principle. In particular, in an important passage,[69] in this contemplative turning Plotinus distinguished again two moments: the turning towards the One of matter, that came to be shaped and limited, fecundating itself (thus was born being, a synthesis of matter and form); then the moment of self-reflection on this fecundated power, with the birth of thought.[70]

The triadic rhythm in the procession is evident from all these passages. For this reason, it emerges ever more clearly from an accurate analysis of the texts that the term "emanation" does not apply to the metaphysics of Plotinus. In this derivative procession the determining element is the return or conversion rather than the flowing. In addition, studying the terms with which the three moments are expressed, one may note that Plotinus has in large part anticipated Proclus, presenting a circular triadic law that unfolds according to an articulation of stability, that is, immanent activity in each hypostasis; progression, that is, activity that derives from each hypostasis; finally, turning and return, that is, conversion to the preceding hypostasis. In the process of the derivation from the One, indeed, there was no question of a flowing of the substance of the first principle, but of its potency, much less a kind of physical necessity, but a necessity that follows from the supreme act of freedom, the self-willing of the first hypostasis.[71]

Further, if the noun most appropriate for indicating the Plotinian doctrine of derivation from the One is "procession," the adjective that better qualifies it is "contemplative": the moment in which the hypostasis being is generated coincides with contemplation.[72] Indeed, the cardinal point, the key to the structure of the procession of Plotinian metaphysics, was contemplation or *theôria*. To be more precise, one must emphasize that not only was it one of the three moments of the procession, but that the three moments of the procession were actually three moments of contemplation. Consequently, one can say that in the *Enneads* everything for Plotinus was contemplation and derived from contemplation.[73]

In the first place, the philosopher of Lycopolis held that "everything is contemplation." According to his metaphysical conception, everything was endowed with this supreme activity, beginning with the One, which turns to itself in the simplest regard, implying no complexity or need. So too the second hypostasis contemplates, defined by Plotinus as "living contemplation," self-reflective and contemplative activity par excellence, where subject contemplating and object contemplated coincide. In addition, the third hypostatic level, the soul, was, for Plotinus endowed with *theôria;* the diverse grades in the soul, the diverse souls, have their greater or lesser unity and multiplicity dependent on it. Consequently, all beings, insofar as they participate in soul, in reason and *logos*, in a certain sense contemplate. This applies in a special manner to man who, exiled from the Absolute, has to return to it, following the correct "way of return" which has the character of contemplation, articulated in the ascetic-religious steps of ethics, of erotics, of dialectic and of mysticism, in which Platonic philosophy is adapted and transformed.[74]

In the second place, in the doctrine of Plotinus "everything comes from contemplation." The spiritual activity of seeing and of contemplating is transformed in the *Enneads* into a creative metaphysics; in all reality and, in particular, in man, the more profound is the *theôria*, the more fecund is the resultant action. Plotinus held that to create means to introduce forms into matter and that this happens owing to contemplation, the supreme activity by means of which, in the diminishing hierarchy of Plotinian ontology, a being comes to participate in form, in perfection, in the creative power of the productive principle, to the extent that it is possible for it.[75]

On this point, above all at the vertices of the hypostases, the activity of the One, its simple intuition of itself, produces the activity from the One, from which is born the intelligible matter that, next, turning to contemplate the One and filling itself with the One, determines itself as being and thought. In a second grade, the self-contemplation of *nous*, that is, the activity of *nous*, produces the activity from *nous*, from which is derived a matter that in its turn contemplates the second hypostasis, and is born as soul. Finally, from the extreme limit of the soul of the universe, that for Plotinus is *physis* or nature, sensible matter is derived. As the product of the contemplation of a metaphysical level greatly debilitated, it is incapable of turning back to nature itself in order to contemplate it. In contrast to the preceding hierarchical levels, in this case *physis*, turning to matter with a second act of contemplation, gives it form, thereby producing physical reality.[76]

It is a question, therefore, of a true and unique "contemplationist metaphysics," in which contemplation, as "creative," constitutes the reason for the being of everything.

The theme of *theôria* was one of the authentic signs of ancient speculation: from Thales who in Plato's *Theaetetus* was pointed to as a symbol of the theoretical life, to Pythagoras, and Anaxagoras, presented in the *Protrepticus* of Aristotle in an analogous fashion, to the celebrated affirmations of Plato in the *Republic*,[77] in which it is held that true philosophers are those who love to contemplate the truth, to the "marvelling" spoken of by Aristotle, the aim of philosophy was fixed as disinterested knowing, as pure contemplation of the truth. In the Greek world, *theôria* had, in addition to this dimension, also an essentially ethical value, a consequence and realization of the preceding. To the new vision of the whole generated by the contemplation of the truth corresponded a diverse and hierarchical perspective, having both an ethical and a political character. In an emblematic manner the Platonic myth of the *Phaedrus* had emphasized that souls, on the plane of truth, were contemplating the truth and they were nourished by it; therefore, the differences among men depended on the diverse grades of their contemplative activity. Consequently, also in the ascetic-mystical conception of Plotinus, contemplation of the truth and the richness and fecundity of life came to be inseparably bound together.

Finally, for Plotinus the doctrine of contemplation is also asserted within the widest possible perspective, coming to be the linchpin and the synthesis of his entire system, as "creative contemplation," a characteristic that accommodates all the hypostases and all beings, and a key to the reading of the procession and of the return to the

One, according to three exceedingly rich and strictly correlated values that we have presented. The hypostases and the beings are born from infinite contemplation and, in particular, through contemplation, man is able to turn toward the infinite, toward the Absolute.

Consequently, one can conclude that, whether it be the notion of freedom as the reason for the being of the One, which opens a profound perspective on the root of the necessity of the productive procession, or whether it be the doctrine of "creative contemplation" as cognitive concept, ethical-ascetic, ontogonic and ontopoietic, they permit us to grasp the fundamental point, the essential nucleus of the metaphysics of Plotinus in its radical originality in the entire history of Greek thought and, in particular, of the rich current that constitutes a true and unique part of the tradition of Platonism.

NOTES

1 Cf. Szlezák 1979, 19, n39.
2 Note that Szlezák refers to the *editio maior* of Henry and Schwyzer (1973, 436–62), but the data produced correspond in the main to the *editio minor*. In this study we follow the *editio minor* both for the *Life of Plotinus* and for the *Enneads* themselves.
3 One must not forget that, according to Porphyry (*Life of Plotinus*, 2.40–3), the traditional birthdays of Plato and Socrates were celebrated in Plotinus' school. Regarding Socrates, it is important to stress that his name appears in the *Enneads* only eight times, but always as an example of an individual man, while his doctrines are never considered. Cf. Szlezák 1979, 44.
4 Cf. Henry-Schwyzer 1982, 348–65.
5 Cf. Henry-Schwyzer 1982, 329–38.
6 Cf. Theiler 1960, 63–103.
7 Cf. Graeser 1972, passim, which contains many significant comparisons, in addition to a rich bibliography and critical apparatuses.
8 Cf. Radice 1992, 97, 241; for Philonic influence on Plotinus see above all H. A. Wolfson 1952, on the divine attributes and C. Elsas 1975 who examines three threads of influence: Philo-Middle Platonism-Plotinus; Philo-Numenius-Plotinus; and Philo-Gnosticism-Plotinus.
9 On Neopythagoreanism cf. Reale, IV, 1991[8], 366–409 (English translation, 237–62).
10 Cf. Porphyry, *Life of Plotinus*, 20.71–6. Longinus explained that the writings of Numenius Cronius, Moderatus, and Thrasyllus regarding

these arguments were far inferior in exactness in comparison with those of Plotinus.

11 Cf. Porphyry, *Life of Plotinus*, 14.10–14.

12 Cf. Porphyry, *Life of Plotinus*, 17.1–6. See Reale, IV, 1991[8], 410–26 (English translation, 263–72).

13 Cf. Porphyry, *Life of Plotinus*, 14.14–16. See the observations of Charrue, *infra*, on this problem.

14 Cf. Dodds 1973, 129.

15 Cf. Arnou 1935, col. 2260; see also Blum 1989, coll. 977–85.

16 Cf. Sextus Empiricus, *Outlines of Pyrrhonism* 1.220.

17 Cf. Reale, III, 1991[8], 83–122; 499–542 (English translation, 57–83; 329–56).

18 Cf. Reale, IV, 1991[8], 307–64 (English translation, 205–34); Zintzen 1981, passim.

19 Cf. Reale, IV, 1991[8], 461–70 (English translation, 297–302); Schroeder 1987b, 493–526.

20 Cf. V.1.8.10–14.

21 Cf. VI.3.1.1–2.

22 Cf. Brisson et al. 1982, 57.

23 Cf. Dörrie 1974, 195–201.

24 Cf. Szlezák 1979, 9–51; the *status quaestionis* is addressed at 10–11.

25 Cf. III.7.1.8–13.

26 Cf. V.1.8.12.

27 Cf. VI.9.11.

28 Cf. Szlezák 1979, 10 and n9.

29 Cf. Szlezák 1979, 10 and n10.

30 Cf. Szlezák 1979, 10–11 and n12.

31 Cf. Szlezák 1979, 11 and n13.

32 Cf. Szlezák 1979, 11 and n14.

33 Cf. Szlezák 1979, 11 and n15.

34 Cf. Szlezák 1979, 11 and n16.

35 Cf. Faggin 1992, xix–xx.

36 Cf. Charrue 1978, 17.

37 Cf. III.7.1.13–16.

38 Cf. V.1.8.24.

39 Cf. V.1.8.10–14.

40 V.9.1.

41 Cf. IV.8.1.23–50.

42 One notes that expressions like "often Plato" or "always" frequently punctuate Plotinian interpretations of the passages of Plato's dialogues, and stress their global unity. Cf. Charrue 1978, 31.

43 Cf. V.8.4.52–6. See Charrue 1978, 29.

44 Cf. Porphyry, *Life of Plotinus*, 8.4–6.
45 Cf. Porphyry, *Life of Plotinus*, 14.15–16.
46 Cf. Photius, *Library*, 461a 35–6 (ed. Henry).
47 Cf. Charrue 1978, 266.
48 Cf. Szlezák 1979, 14–51.
49 Cf. Szlezák 1979, 51.
50 Cf. Meinhardt 1984, coll. 754–6.
51 Cf. De Vogel 1953, 43–64; Meinhardt, 1984, coll. 754–5.
52 Cf. Meinhardt 1984, col. 755.
53 De Vogel 1953, passim; Krämer 1964, passim; Szlezák 1979, passim; Merlan 1975, passim.
54 Cf. Krämer 1982, 235–7.
55 Cf. Merlan 1990, passim.
56 Cf. Merlan 1990, 47–53 (English original, 1–5).
57 Cf. Reale's introduction to the translation of Merlan 1990, 25–7.
58 Cf. Reale's introduction to the translation of Merlan 1990, 22, 25.
59 Cf. Beierwaltes 1991b, 26–38; 1991c, 23–141; Dodds 1928, 129–42.
60 Cf. Schwyzer 1970, 81–93.
61 Cf. Klibansky 1939, passim.
62 Cf. Gatti 1982, 31–42, 171–7 (see notes 4 and 5 on page 32 for references to the works of J. M. Rist, H. F. Müller, A. Covotti, J. Trouillard, and V. Cilento). Also, Reale 1983, 153–75; Reale, IV, 1991[8], 606–16 (English translation 293–8).
63 Cf. V.1.6.1–8. See Plato, *Philebus* 14c.
64 Cf. Reale, IV, 1991[8], 610 (English translation, 394–5).
65 Cf. Leroux 1990, in particular, the introduction, 23–123, and the bibliography, 429–47.
66 Cf. VI.8.13.
67 Cf. Gatti 1982, 34–6; Reale 1983, 154–63; Reale, IV, 1991[8], 519–26 (English translation, 334–9). See III.8.10; IV.3.17.12–31; IV.4.16.20–31; V.1.6; V.4.a. and 2; VI.8.18. Also, Rist 1967, 66–83.
68 Cf. V.4.2.19; V.5.5.1–7; VI. 9.3.45–9; VI.9.9.1–7. Cf. Arnou 1967[2], 162.
69 Cf. V.2.1.1–18.
70 It is necessary to recall that the various phases of the generation of the hypostases were distinguished by Plotinus only according to a logical point of view and for didactic purposes, in order to present a metaphysical structure of the relations between the conditioned and the conditioning, and not according to a chronological scale, given that the hypostases are eternal. Cf. II.4.5.24–8; V.1.6.19–22; VI.6.6.4–5; VI.7.35.29. See Gatti 1982, 41.
71 Cf. Gatti 1982, 34–6; Reale, IV, 1991[8], 606–12 (English translation, 393–6).

72 Cf. Gatti 1982, 33–4, 63–5, 84–5, 174–6; Reale 1983, 163–72; IV, 1991[8], 612–16 (English translation, 396–8).
73 Cf. III.8.7.1–2.
74 Cf. Gatti 1982, 44, 47, 54–9, 64–78, 91–2, 173–4.
75 Cf. Gatti 1982, 84–5, 175–6. See III.8.7.21–2.
76 Cf. Gatti 1982, 78–92. See IV.3.9.20–9.
77 Cf. Plato, *Republic* 475e.

2 Plotinus's metaphysics of the One

Of the three first principles (*archai*) or hypostases, One, Intellect, and Soul, the One or Good is the most difficult to conceive and the most central to understanding Plotinian philosophy. It is everything and nothing, everywhere and nowhere. The One is the source (*archê*) of all beings and, as the Good, the goal (*telos*) of all aspirations, human and non-human. As the indemonstrable first principle of everything, as transcendent infinite being, and as the supreme object of love, the One is the center of a vibrant conception of reality many of whose facets resist philosophical analysis. Efforts to understand or to define the nature of the One, Plotinus believes, are doomed to be inadequate. We speak *about* it, but in reality these efforts only amount to "making signs to ourselves about it"; it is not possible for anyone to say what it is (V.3.13.7, 14.1–7).[1] Despite this insistence on the ineffability of the first principle Plotinus talks about it constantly, making radical claims about its universal role in the structure of reality. Only by reflecting on the internal logic of his metaphysics can we recognize the multi-faceted nature of this unitary principle.

I TALKING ABOUT THE ONE

Three interrelated factors motivate Plotinus's philosophy of the One: tradition, reason, and experience.[2] Since the influence of his predecessors, especially Plato and Aristotle, on Plotinus is discussed in Chapter 1, here we will examine the contributions made by rational argument and personal experience toward articulating the metaphysics of the One.

His ways of speaking about the One warrant attention because thought and speech achieve greater or lesser degrees of clarity and accuracy in proportion to their proximity to the One itself. The One's existence is certainly not in doubt: otherwise, thought and speech would be impossible (VI.6.13.44–9). But being the first principle of reason requires that the One transcend determinate being and even the highest type of thought (cf. VI.9.4.1–16). Discussions about the first principle, therefore, usually stress the limits of reasoning and insist on transcending analysis and conceptualization. By contrast, on many other topics Plotinus readily offers explanations of the doctrines he holds and argues for the truth of his philosophical and religious views, for example, against the Gnostic view that the physical universe is evil in II.9. Nevertheless, the transcendence and ineffability of the One should not, I think, be taken as evidence of deep-seated hostility to reason, for Plotinus's skepticism about the capacity of language and thought to grasp the One is itself inspired by intense reflection. He is convinced that discursive thinking is a weakened form of thought, which is inferior to and relies on intellection (noêsis), the immediate, intuitive, and comprehensive understanding that, when we have access to it, provides the most accurate view of the One available to us: for "if there is anything before it, Intellect knows clearly that this is what it derives from" (V.5.2.15–16). Since so much of what Plotinus says about the One is an expression of the noetic vision of intelligible reality, we should note what he says about it. Intellect, intellection, or intelligible being are: (1) incapable of error (V.5.1.1–2); (2) eternally knowing (V.5.1.4); (3) not based on demonstrative proof (apodeixis) (V.5.1.7, 2.13–14); (4) self-evidently true (V.5.2.16, VI.9.5.12–13); (5) unnecessary to search for (V.8.4.36–7); (6) not acquired by reasoning (logismoi) (V.8.4.35); (7) changeless (III.7.3, IV.4.1); (8) nondiscursive, nonpropositional (V.3.17.21–4, V.5.1.38–40, V.8.5.20–2); (9) a kind of unknowing (V.8.11.33–4); (10) radiant and transparent (V.8.4.5–9, 10.5–8; VI.7.12.22–30).[3]

Since even pure visionary thinking cannot grasp the One, far more limited is the derivative faculty of discursive rationality (dianoia), which utilizes reified conceptual objects for analysis and reasons successively, that is, inferentially (V.3.2–3, 7–9). Now Plotinus does mention demonstrations that the One is the ultimate goal of philosophizing – but these "proofs" are clear to individuals who already accept its existence (I.3.1.2–6). It is perhaps more accurate to say that for the true philosopher, who has direct access to the intelligible world (VI.5.7.1–9), the existence and truth of both Intellect and the One are self-evident, indemonstrable starting-points for further reflection on the nature of the One and its effects. Discursive reasoning must retreat before intuitive thought and visionary experience, which for Plotinus justify the claim that " 'whoever has seen, knows what I am saying,' that the soul then has another life and draws near . . . and has a part in him, and so is in a state to know that the giver of true life is present and we need nothing more" (VI.9.9.46–50). To achieve this transcendent level of existence requires both philosophical reasoning and affective training:[4]

[starting from the soul's experience of the Good] we must speak of it . . . proceeding by rational discourse. The knowledge or touching of the Good is the greatest thing, and Plato says it is the "greatest study" [Rep. 505a2], not calling the looking at it a "study," but learning about it beforehand. We are taught about it by comparisons [analogiai] and negations [aphaireseis] and knowledge of the things which come from it and certain methods of ascent by degrees, but we are put on the way to it by purifications and virtues. (VI.7.36.2–9)

Both cognitive and emotional training seem to be necessary conditions for achieving the highest stage of human development – mystical union with the One – though Plotinus is not always clear about whether they are sufficient. It must be recognized, however, that for Plotinus rational inquiry or 'learning' lacks to a considerable degree the critical, tentative, and revisionary attitude considered essential to the practice of philosophy today. Simply put, for him philosophy ultimately attains the truth. Yet Plotinus's deep skepticism about the capacity of language and thought to reach the One's ineffable reality may, unexpectedly, be the most vital and appealing feature of his thought.[5]

Learning about the One has positive and negative aspects. The affirmative way, as we have seen, includes: (1) the recognition of properties that may pertain to the One by way of reasoning, for example, from effect to cause, as well as the use of analogy, metaphor, and symbol; and (2) the emotional discipline that produces psychic excellence – the engine to climb the hierarchy of being. However, doubts persist whether affirmations can tell us very much at all about the One in itself: "For to say that it is the cause is not to predicate something incidental of it but of us" (VI.9.3.49–50). Not surprisingly, then, the negative way to the One is often thought to be superior.[6]

Language cannot specify what the One is, only what it is not (V.3.14.6–7). Even the designations One and Good are deficient signs of the One's reality (II.9.1.1–8, V.5.6.26–30, VI.7.38.4–9, VI.9.5.29– 34). Paradoxically, these reflections on the limits of reference are emblems of Plotinian optimism, just as intense emotional purification (*katharsis*) is the tonic of the spirit. Working together, these disciplines actually produce philosophical and spiritual progress by deconstructing language, thought, and the empirical self. The goal of this universal way, then, is not emptiness but the unveiling of the noetic self and the One beyond it.

Both reasoning to the first principle and meditations on symbolic theophanies of the One (e.g., the rising of the sun of the Good in V.5.7–8) point beyond themselves, beyond understanding, to unmediated visionary experience of the first principle:

The perplexity (*aporia*) arises especially because our awareness (*sunesis*) of that One is not by way of reasoned knowledge (*epistêmê*) or of intellectual perception (*noêsis*), as with other intelligible things, but by way of a presence (*parousia*) superior to knowledge. (VI.9.4.1–3)

Therefore, Plato says [*Letter* VII. 341c5], 'it cannot be spoken or written', but we speak and write impelling towards it and wakening from reasonings to the vision of it, as if showing the way to someone who wants to have a view of something. For teaching goes as far as the road and travelling, but the vision is the task of someone who has already resolved to see. (VI.9.4.11–16)

Communication between those who have had "the good fortune to see" (VI.9.11.1–4) apparently counts as meaningful discourse about the One, a sort of mystical dialectic; "but we are not prevented from having it [sc. the One], even if we do not speak it. But just as those who have a god within them and are in the grip of divine possession may know this much, that they have something greater within them, even if they do not know what" (V.3.14.8–11).

Clearly, philosophizing about the One in a Plotinian way eventually requires lofty existential qualifications: thus, the One "is always present to anyone who is able to touch it, but is not present to one who is unable" (VI.9.7.4–5). We should think of Plotinus as a "mystical empiricist," that is, a thinker who is committed to the view that ultimate reality can be grasped in itself, in mystical experience that transcends the duality of subject and object and all familiar cognitive and affective states. This transformative type of philosophy works toward an experiential goal. Thus, philosophizing about the One has the concrete aim of nullifying itself, an attitude that is neither nihilist nor antiphilosophical, but which points toward a "soteriontology."

I propose charting a course for the One that will traverse three distinct but interrelated perspectives: (1) The One in itself: its transcendent or formal properties. (2) The One and others: (A) The One as efficient cause and immanent presence; (B) The One as final cause and transcendent goal. (3) The One as everything and nothing – a dialectical perspective on the One as source and goal that transcends distinction and nondistinction and provides a comprehensive view of the One in itself.

Perspectives (1) and (2) are closely linked in that the nature of the One in itself grounds the Plotinian metaphysics of causation according to which what is perfect produces, as in the comparison of the One's perfect nature to a fire and its productive power to the heat radiating from it (see Section III, The One as efficient cause). The first perspective on the One we will consider concerns the "substance" or inner "actuality" of the One without any reference to its effects, while the second perspective explores the "external" causal activity of the One.

II THE ONE IN ITSELF

(1) Since we cannot say what the One is but only what it is not, negative predications appear least susceptible to ignoring its complete dissimilarity to its effects and hence to violating the One's absolute transcendence. Strictly speaking, the term "One" does not reify the One as a distinct object or entity (II.9.1.1–8, VI.7.38.4–9, VI.9.5.29–34), but removes all plurality and compositeness, thus laying the cornerstone of a distinctive philosophical theology:

There must be something simple before all things, and this must be other than all the things which come after it, existing by itself, not mixed with the things which derive from it, and all the same able to be present in a different way to these other things, being really one, and not a different being and then one; it is false even to say of it that it is one, and there is "no concept or knowledge" of it; it is indeed also said to be "beyond being." For if it is not to be simple, outside all coincidence and composition, it could not be a first principle; and it is the most self-sufficient, because it is simple and the first of all. . . . A reality of this kind must be one alone. (V.4.1.5–16)

Even if "One" and "Good" do not convey the reality of the first principle, the negative properties unity, uniqueness, and simplicity must be accepted as true if there is to be any understanding of the One at all. Simplicity grounds ontological priority and uniqueness (cf. VI.8.10.10–14). The distinctness of the One from everything else supports the further claim that the One has no relations to other things, whereas the relations of others to the One are real (cf. VI.8.8.12–15, VI.9.6.40). Unity specifies, negatively, that the One is nothing other than itself. Besides indicating what the One is not, the properties of priority, unity, and uniqueness also identify the One affirmatively as a hyperontic entity distinct from sensible and intelligible beings. (This is not to say, however, that the One is one member of the genus being.) Unity also signifies the One's indistinctness from other things, implied in the words "to be present in a different way to these other things." Evidently, two distinct senses of unity are relevant: (i) exclusive or pure unity; (ii) inclusive unity, the unity of indistinction. Consideration of ways in which these two senses of unity might be combined is taken up in Part IV.

(2) The simplicity, self-sufficiency, and uniqueness of the first principle anticipate the medieval concept of necessary being, but the necessity/contingency distinction is not the centerpiece of Plotinius's metaphysics of the One. The One necessarily is what it is (VI.8.10.15–20), but this necessity is identified with the One's absolute freedom, thereby insuring that the One is not constrained to be what it is by anything external to it or independent of it.[7]

The simplicity of the One is based on the claim that it is non-composite, that is, without parts or internal relations, and in fact without external relations either. Thus, the One is beyond being and form because form involves complexity, determinateness, and definability. Noncompositeness is the basis for the radical assertion that the One is formless (amorphon) and infinite (apeiron), without limitation or determination (amorphon: VI.7.17.17, 40, 33.4; VI.9.3.39; apeiron: V.5.10.18–22). Let us focus on these properties in succession: simplicity, infinity, and being without relations.

(3) The One must be simple because it is perfect, and being perfect it must be independent from all things, with all things dependent on it. Plotinus is thus committed to divine aseity. But how can the doctrine of simplicity and aseity be consistent with the attribution of many properties to the One? Granted that the properties of good-

ness and formlessness, say, are predicated of the One without introducing complexity into its nature, should we conclude that as a property simplicity is identical with goodness, or with infinity, or, generally, that the One's attributes are all the same or are mutually entailing? Perhaps simplicity operates as a generic property whose species are goodness, etc. If Plotinus means that each property is identical with every other one, he shows no concern for the logical objections to identifying distinct properties that are not coextensive. He rejects the objection that the One as property is an abstract object because its reality transcends all possible descriptions, but this point does not justify the conclusion that the One is a concrete particular. Working out the relations among the One's properties deserves further study.

(4) Most references to the One's infinity concern its infinite power (*dunamis*) to generate the intelligible world (V.4.1.23–6, V.5.10.18–22, VI.9.6.10–12, II.4.15.17–20, VI.9.6.7–8; cf. V.5.11.1–2), the topic of Part III.A. "Unlimitedness" is clearly a negative attribute that does not define the One's nature at all, but indicates only that the One's infinite nature (*apleton phusis:* V.5.6.14–15) is not subject to internal or external limitations. Formlessness (V.5.6.5) attests that the first principle is not limited in the way that being or essence is limited (V.5.5.6, 11.2–3); and formlessness entails self-sufficiency (VI.7.32.9–10), as does simplicity (I.8.2.4–5, II.9.1.9; V.4.1.12–13).

(5) The notion of perfection is closely associated by Platonists with being and by Aristotle with actuality, but Plotinus attributes perfection to the One beyond being, perhaps on the grounds that its perfection derives from its own reality (*ousia*) (V.1.6.38, V.6.2.13). It is perfect because it is completely itself, fully actual, and a perfect actuality (*energeia:* cf. VI.8.20.9–16) "containing everything and lacking nothing" (cf. *Physics* III.6.207a9: "that which has nothing outside itself" is perfect [*teleios*]). Perfection, as we shall see, is a property essential to the One's productivity.

Now Intellect too is perfect (III.6.6.10–17, V.1.4.14–15; perfect life: V.3.16.29; cf. V.1.10.12); actual (II.5.3.31, VI.2.20); self-sufficient (V.3.13.18–21; the One as beyond self-sufficiency: V.3.17.14); and it is even infinite in power and extent (V.7.1, VI.5.12, VI.6.18). Of course, in the case of Intellect these "perfections" coexist with the deficiences of thought, duality, and plurality. Nevertheless, the use of the same properties with regard to both One and Intellect raises questions (to be taken up below) whether these properties are predicable by degree and what it means for the One to contain everything.

(6) That the One is without external relations is a corollary of divine aseity and simplicity. Here Plotinus agrees with classical theists that the relations of created things to the first principle are real, whereas its (apparent) relations to other things are not, and hence are Cambridge properties. Being without relations follows from the One's independence and ontological priority (VI.8.8.12–15, 11.32). However, Plotinus makes the remarkable claim that the One is internally related to itself: "He himself is by himself what he is, related and directed to himself, that he may not in this way either be related to the outside or to something else, but altogether self-related" (VI.8.14.25–7). It is preferable, I think, to interpret this statement as driving home the point that the One is what it is rather than a literal reading that its internally differentiated parts are interrelated. Equally troublesome, if taken literally, is the claim that the One is cause of itself (VI.8.13.55, 14.41, 16.14–15), which is better construed to mean that the One has no cause, that is, that it is a necessary being whose being is completely self-derived.[8] Plotinus himself seems to deliteralize the notion of self-causation in the assertion that "he [the Good] is not to be classed as made, but as maker; we must posit that his making is absolute" (VI.8.20.4–6).

III THE ONE AND OTHERS

The starting point for reflection about the One is the things that come from it (III.8.10.34–5, 11.33–9; V.3.14.1–8). Statements about the One that employ properties of composite things are inadequate but not false, since the analogical or equivocal use of terms is justified (VI.8.8.1–7; cf. VI.9.3.49–51). The One, therefore, is and is not the first principle of all things (arché: VI.8.8.8–9). The One is a cause in two respects: as the causal origin of reality and as the universal object of desire, that is, as efficient cause and as final cause: "the source therefore of being and the why of being, giving both at once" (VI.8.14.31–2). Efficient causality occurs in the procession (proodos) of lower realities, the second explains their reversion (*epistrophê*) back to the One.

The One as efficient cause

(1) Efficient causality – from the side of the effect – is passage from (i) nonexistence to existence and (ii) potentiality to actuality. To the One's efficient causality can be applied the counterfactual conditional: without the cause the effect would not have occurred (III.8.10.1–2, IV.8.6.1–3, V.5.9.1–4). Most importantly, the simple and noncomposite One is conceived as the cause of the existence of all complex and composite things (III.8.11.40; V.2.1.7–8, 13–14; V.3.15.28–30, 17.12; V.5.5.5–7; VI.6.13.50; VI.7.32.2; VI.8.19.12–20). It is the cause both of things' coming into existence and of their being sustained in existence by continuous participation in the One (V.3.15.12, 17.8–9; VI.7.23.20–4, 42.11).

That the One is cause of being means that it imparts oneness to things as well (V.3.15.11–15; V.5.3.23–4; VI.9.1.3–4; 2.15–29; VI.6.13.52); so when things cease to be one they cease to exist.[9] Here Plotinus uses the Aristotelian point (*Met.* 1054a13ff.) that unity and being have different intensions but the same extension. Plotinus promotes, therefore, an even purer version of degrees of being and degrees of unity metaphysics: the greater the unity, the closer the proximity to the One and the greater the value of the entity (III.8.10.20–6, VI.2.11.9–18, VI.9.1.14).

In bringing things into existence and sustaining them the One's efficient causality differs from Aristotelian efficient causality among sensible substances, with its more limited focus on (i) initiating motion or (ii) explaining how an object or event gives rise to another that is numerically distinct from it, but which is like it in kind. The One, in sharp contrast, is the ultimate ground of being of all things.

(2) Plotinus analyzes the generation of Intellect as the primary case of the One's causality: the doctrine of emanation and return, or, more precisely, "procession" (*proodos*) and "reversion" (*epistrophê*). These logically distinct, successive, but nontemporal events of procession and reversion will be discussed separately under the rubrics of efficient and final causality, respectively. Three notions are in play in the following accounts of procession: (i) the prior actuality

principle; (ii) the principle of undiminished giving; and (iii) the principle of immanence.

All things when they come to perfection produce; the One is always perfect and therefore produces everlastingly; and its product is less than itself. (V.1.6.37–9)

Now when anything else comes to perfection we see that it produces, and does not endure to remain by itself, but makes something else. This is true not only of things which have choice, but of things which grow and produce without choosing to do so, and even lifeless things, which impart themselves to others as far as they can: as fire warms, snow cools, and drugs act on something else in a way corresponding to their nature. . . . How then could the most perfect, the first Good, remain in itself as if it grudged to give of itself or was impotent, when it is the productive power (*dunamis*) of all things. (V.4.1.27–36)

In each and every thing there is an activity (*energeia*) of the substance and there is an activity from the substance; and that which is of the substance is each thing itself, while the activity from the substance derives from the first one, and must in everything be a consequence of it, different from the thing itself: as in fire there is a heat which is the content of its substance, and another which comes into being from that primary heat when fire exercises the activity which is native to its substance in abiding unchanged as fire. So it is also in the higher world; and much more so there, while it [the One] abides in its own proper way of life, the activity generated from the perfection in it and its coexistent activity (*energeia*) acquires existence (*hupostasis*), since it comes from a great power, the greatest indeed of all, and arrives at being and substance, for that is beyond being. That is the productive power (*dunamis*) of all, and its product is already all things. (V.4.2.28–39)

(i) Plotinus employs Aristotle's prior actuality principle, which holds: (a) everything complete or perfect tends to reproduce itself; (b) the cause is in actuality what the effect is potentially but will be actually (*Phys.* 201a27–34, *Met.* 1049b23–6, GA 734a30–2; cf. VI.7.17.6–8); (c) the identity (in natural things) of efficient and formal cause; (d) the effect resembles the cause and is *in* its cause (*Met.* 1032a22–5; cf. IV.3.10.32–42, V.5.9.1–10) or participates, Platonically, in its cause. Each point is modified by Plotinus in some respect when applied to the One's productivity, in conjunction with the non-Aristotelian principle (e) that the cause is greater than the effect.

In his use of (a) and (b) Plotinus describes the One's "essence" or "substance" as activity (*energeia*) and what proceeds from this activity as both "activity from the substance" and as power or active potentiality (*dunamis*).[10] In itself the One's existence (*hupostasis*) is one with its activity (VI.8.7.47), with its will (VI.8.13.56–7), and with its "essence" (VI.8.12.14–17).[11] Insofar as it is efficient cause the One's operational attributes are activity and power. Do *energeia* and *dunamis*, which figure in Aristotelian causal connections between sensible substances, substantialize the One? Plotinus answers this objection by insisting that "the first activity (*energeia*) is without substance (*ousia*)" and that this fact is "his, so to speak, existence (*hupostasis*). But if one posited an existence without activity, the principle would be defective and the most perfect of all imperfect" (VI.8.20.9–13; cf. V.6.6.8–11). To rule out any duality VI.8.7.46–54 *identifies* activity, existence, and being, often invoking the qualifier "as if" (*hoion*); (cf. also VI.8.16.15–18, 25). Typically, Plotinus asserts that the One is beyond actuality (I.7.1.17–20, V.3.12.16–28, VI.7.17.9–11), especially when he wants to distinguish it from Aristotle's first principle, the divine Intellect.

The Aristotelian background can be summed up in this way. In his analysis of efficient causality, especially in *Physics* III. 1–3 (cf. *Met.* IX.7), Aristotle locates causal agency in the form/actuality of sensible substance: that is what transmits properties to or causes the existence of the product. Plotinus employs the physical model of property-transmission to explain the first stage of the One's generation of Intellect: the procession of potential Intellect.[12] Aristotle's first principle, the Prime Mover, can not be the universal efficient cause because its actuality cannot be directed outside itself.[13] But its final causality determines the structure of the second stage, the change from potential to actual Intellect: on the cognitive model the mind actually thinks when actualized by the object of thought and desire (cf. Section III, The One as Final Cause).

(ii) The principle of undiminished giving is exemplified by the external activity of the One, its overflowing productive power (*dunamis*), which is metaphorically likened to water flowing from a source or spring, and to the life-force springing from the root of a plant, and to light radiating from the sun (cf. Plato, *Rep.* 509b9–10). Because it contains nothing "The One . . . overflows, as it were, and its superabundance makes something other than itself" (V.2.1.7–9).

What is above life is cause of life; for the activity of life, which is all things, is not first, but itself flows out, so to speak, as if from a spring. For think of a spring that has no other origin, but gives the whole of itself to rivers, and is not used up by the rivers but remains itself at rest, . . . or of the life of a huge plant, which goes through the whole of it while its origin remains and is not dispersed over the whole, since it is, as it were, firmly settled in the root. (III.8.10.2–12)

The activity, which, so to speak, flows from it like a light from the sun, is Intellect and the whole intelligible nature, but that he himself, staying still at the summit of the intelligible, rules over it; he does not thrust the out-shining away from himself . . . but he irradiates for ever, abiding unchanged over the intelligible. For what comes from him has not been cut off from him, nor is it the same as him. (V.3.12.39–45)

According to the principle of undiminished giving the One (a) pro-duces eternally, (b) from an inexhaustible reality (VI.9.9.3–4), (c) with-out undergoing any change or alteration (III.8.8.46–8), and (d) without deliberation or inclination to produce (V.1.6.25–7, V.3.12.28–33; cf. V.5.12.43–9) and without knowledge of its products (VI.7.39.19–33). The natural phenomena of water flowing and radiating light that symbolize the generation of plurality from the One are well suited to illustrate each of these points. Natural entities or processes can more easily than voluntary agents be assumed to act in a continuous man-ner, without intentionality, and to exercise their causal agency from abundant stores of energy. Light has the appealing feature of being not just a quality of a certain medium, but an activity springing from a certain substance (cf. IV.5.9). The productive power on display in this imagery and examined discursively elsewhere (V.3.12.39, 16.1–3; VI.8.1.10–11) illustrates the One's omnipotence.[14] It follows that the first principle's causal power has generated everything that is meta-physically possible: "it is not possible for anything else to come into being; all things have come into being and there is nothing left" (V.5.12.46–7).

These natural metaphors of procession create problems for Plotinus. Although they signify the nondeliberativeness he ascribes to the first principle, they also imply that the One's giving cannot not have occurred and cannot cease.[15] Plotinus's solution to this problem is simple if not completely convincing: what proceeds from the One does so necessarily (II.9.3.8, III.2.3.1–5, IV.8.6.1–3, V.1.6.31) – instanced, again, in the necessary connection between fire and heat – but the One itself is not compelled to generate reality. It simply causes the existence of everything by the principle that what is perfect produces. In VI.8 Plotinus adds the important and un-Aristotelian point that this perfection is the Good's freedom to be itself beyond necessity, to which all its products are subject (VI.8.9.10–15). He adds that the One generates as it wills and wills what ought to be, what comes from it (VI.8.18.41, 49; 21.16–19), maintaining also that such willing introduces no deliberation or duality into the One.

(iii) The immanence of the One, that is to say its omnipresence (cf. VI.8.16.1, V.5.8.24), is necessary in order that it be the universal cause of all things. For the One to "fill all things" requires that it be "everywhere," as well as "nowhere" (cf. III.9.4). Being everywhere and nowhere are mutually entailing for Plotinus since the One must be "alone by itself" and simple "if it is to be seen in other things": compositeness requires prior simplicity (V.6.3.10–15). In the fire/heat model the immanence of the One is represented in the external activity that surrounds and is attached to its source, an image of its archetype (V.1.6.32–4). Plotinus notes the dynamic continuity between the One and its product Intellect at V.1.6.50–4: there is nothing between them, they are separated only by otherness; "neither cut off nor identical" (V.3.12.44). Continuity is perhaps best expressed by the notion of life:

All these things are the One and not the One: they are he because they come from him; they are not he, because it is in abiding by himself that he gives them. It is then like a long life stretched out at length; each part is different from that which comes next in order, but the whole is continuous with itself, but with one part differentiated from another, and the earlier does not perish in the later. (V.2.2.24–9)

An alternative model for representing ontological continuity and dependence is the geometric image of radii (intelligible beings) drawn from the center (the One) of a circle (cf. 1.7.1.23, VI.8.18.7–30).

Each of the three principles of prior actuality, undiminished giving, and immanence has specific applications to the initial stage of the generation of Intellect. The first establishes that what began as the external activity of the One produces an indefinite, potential entity (VI.7.21.5), something that is potentially what its cause is actually, but in the end will be inferior to it.[16] The second stipulates that (i) the procession of Intellect is eternal (II.9.3) and without temporal limits: the stages of the generation are logically but not temporally distinct; and (ii) that the One's infinite power produces an indefinite potentiality, that is, an entity that can "become all things." The third ensures the presence of the One throughout the procession and actualization of Intellect: what is distinct from the One eternally desires and participates in it (III.8.11.24–5).

Plotinus refers to this potential, inchoate, or pre-Intellect in various terms, which we can classify in two groups: (i) the indefinite dyad (V.1.5.6, V.4.2.7–8), motion (*kinêsis:* V.6.5.8, VI.7.16.16–18), otherness (II.4.5.28–30); (ii) potentiality (*dunamis:* III.8.11.2), desire (*ephêsis:* V.3.11.2, V.6.5.10), indefinite life (*zôe:* VI.7.16.14–15, 17.13), indefinite seeing (V.3.11.12, V.4.2.6, V.6.5.10, VI.7.17.14–15), and intelligible matter (II.4.5.24–37). The sources of these terms are, roughly: (i) the Platonic "greatest kinds," namely, Otherness and Motion as well as the late Academic indefinite dyad and (ii) "Aristotelian" matter and potentiality (in the cognitive model of actualization, desire and vision are potentialities). The actualization of this first, potential stage in the life of Intellect occurs by means of the One's final causality, to which we now turn.

The One as final cause

The One's final causality operates in two distinct domains: (1) the actualization or perfection of Intellect; (2) the mystical return of the soul to its source.

(1) The actualization of Intellect is the primary instance of the One's final causality. The One gives being and the why of being (VI.8.14.32). The genesis of Intellect is for the sake of the One, its first principle. And the end (*telos*) for potential Intellect is its actuality (*energeia*), its perfection (cf. *Met.* 1050a7–10). The actualization of Intellect is modeled, first, on the simile of perception and knowledge and the comparison of the Good to the sun in *Republic* 507–9 and, second, on Aristotle's account of perception and thought. In the latter the faculty of sight is a passive potentiality that gets actualized as seeing through contact with the sensible form, as wax is imprinted by a signet ring (*DA* 424a18–28). Likewise, in the case of thought the noetic faculty is "potentially identical in character with its object without being the object" (*DA* 429a16–7); and it is

"before it thinks, not actually any real thing" (*DA* 429a24). So thinking is caused by the object of thought; and it may be because for Aristotle the mind is moved by the object of thought and desires it (*Met.* 1072a30, *DA* 433a9–b18) that Plotinus describes potential Intellect as indefinite motion and desire for its end the Good, though Aristotle himself distinguishes motion from activities like perception and thought (*Met.* 1048b28–30). Plotinus often weaves together Platonic and Aristotelian elements: the Good "moved what had come into being to itself, and it was moved and saw. And this is what thinking is, a movement toward the Good in its desire of that Good; for the desire generates thought and establishes it in being along with itself" (V.6.5.7–10). For Plotinus the Aristotelian object of cognition and the Platonic Good in *Republic* 508e–9d offer complementary, if subordinated, accounts of final causality: the Aristotelian theory provides a precisely structured model that can be grafted onto the Platonic hierarchy of being with its transcendent Good.

Light also plays a significant role in the One's actualization of Intellect, as a rough equivalent of the cause's external actuality. The One is a "generative radiance" (VI.7.36.20), the source of light that serves as the medium of noetic thought (V.5.7.16–21, VI.7.21.13–17). Here too Plotinus combines the Platonic account of the Good as illuminating power (*Rep.* 508d4–6) with the Aristotelian theories of perception and thought. Light serves as the medium for transmitting the sensible object to the sense organ. The cause of thought is the productive intellect, which is compared to light (*DA* III.5).[17]

Where Plotinus departs from the Aristotelian cognitive model is on the crucial point of the latter's provision for the reception of form: the grasping of the sensible or intelligible object in itself is what defines the actualities of perception and thought. For Plotinus, however, Intellect cannot grasp the One in itself because it is beyond being and form. The potential Intellect is in fact actualized or perfected by contemplating or "looking at" the One (V.1.7.16, V.3.11.10–16, V.4.2.4–8, VI.7.16.16–22), but what it sees is not, so to speak, the One itself but the image of the One its inchoate vision has multiplied (V.3.11.7–9; VI.7.15.12–24, 16.10–13). The products of this fragmented vision are: (i) the actuality of pure thought (*noêsis*) and (ii) the multiplicity of forms or beings (V.3.11.14–15, V.4.2.43–8).

In the account of the generation of Intellect certain complications, which have a bearing on the One's final causality, result from (i) the One's radical transcendence and (ii) combining the Platonic and Aristotelian analyses of the first principle's causality. To recapitulate: the One is the efficient cause of the potential Intellect (procession), which the One perfects, as the goal of Intellect's desire for completion (reversion). On the other hand, "Intellect also has of itself a kind of intimate perception of its power, that it has power to produce substantial reality. Intellect, certainly, by its own means even defines its being for itself by the power which comes from the One, and because its substance is a kind of single part of what belongs to the One and comes from the One" (V.1.7.11–15). Similarly, "that Good is the principle, and it is from that that they are in this Intellect, and it is this which has made them from that Good. . . . Intellect therefore had the power from him to generate and to be filled full of its own offspring, since the Good gave what he did not himself have" (VI.7.15.14–16, 18–20). With good reason these passages have convinced some that Intellect, and not the One, is the primary cause of intelligible being or essence, whereas the One is the cause of Intellect's existence.[18]

The view that Intellect generates being or essence depends on three points. (i) The great difference between the One and Intellect: the One gives what it does not possess. (ii) The principle that the recipient alters what it receives requires that the external activity or active potentiality generated by the One is altered and diminished; it is then the internal activity of Intellect, whose desire for the Good generates intelligible beings. (iii) Though the Good continually operates as final cause, this causality comes second to Intellect's self-creative activity. One version of this interpretation is quasi–idealistic: "it is not the One which actualizes the sight (or capacity to think) of Pre-intellect, but *the One as seen (or thought)* by Pre-Intellect."[19] But precisely because Intellect's view is distorted one wonders whether Plotinus gives an account from the One's "point of view." Such an "objective" interpretation would call for the priority of the One's causality in the actualization of Intellect and in the generation of its essential attributes being, goodness, beauty, and the like. It would employ the language of image and participation to convey the likeness between the two principles. III.8.11, for example, states that "it is the Good which brings fulfilment to the sight of Intellect" (7–8); and when Intellect attains the Good it becomes conformed to the Good and is completed by the Good, since the form which comes upon it from the Good conforms it to the Good. A trace of the Good is seen in it, and it is in the likeness of this that one should conceive its true archetype, forming an idea of it in oneself from the trace of it which plays upon Intellect. The Good, therefore, has given the trace of itself on Intellect to Intellect to have by seeing. (16–23)

This important passage combines Aristotle's cognitive model of actualization with the Platonic model of illumination (the analogy of the sun and the Good), in company with the Platonic-Pythagorean notion of the One limiting the indefinite dyad (cf. V.1.7.26–7; V.4.2.7–9), to highlight the One as primary cause of Intellect's actualization. Similarly, the goodness of the life that comes to the potential Intellect is responsible for the goodness of actualized Intellect (VI.7.18.2–7, 41–3; 21.4–6). On the question of the generation of being and substance Plotinus observes that the Good is "the generator of substance" (VI.7.32.2); "each of the beings which come after the One has in itself a kind of form of it"; "being is a trace of the One"; "that which came to exist, substance and being has an image of the One since it flows from its power" (V.5.5.10–13, 22–3; cf. also V.1.7.1–4). These texts raise some difficulties for the view that Intellect is the sole or even primary cause of being and substance. Prima facie they seem to make the One the formal or essential cause of Intellect. But this judgment would contradict claims made elsewhere that One and Intellect are radically dissimilar and that the One gives what it does not have.

If Plotinus is not flatly contradicting himself, and I don't think he is, it might be the case that he makes some statements about the genesis of Intellect from the vantage point of the One – his version of the "god's eye view" – and some from Intellect's point of view; or that some statements have different meanings when considered from each point of view. Both images – the imposition of limit and definition by the One on the indefiniteness or passive potentiality of the inchoate Intellect, or the form of the Good that "comes upon" the potential Intellect – seem to require less ingenious exegesis when viewed from the side of the One than from Intellect's. If indeed the use of these two perspectives helps to clarify things, note that V.1.7.11–15 quoted above, the passage that refers to the fact that Intellect "defines its being for itself by the power which comes from the One," also says that "its substance is a kind of single part of what belongs to the One." Perhaps superimposing the two views only blurs our vision!

The primacy of the Good in the actualization of Intellect is also prominent where the Good is described as the maker of beauty: "the productive power of all is the flower of beauty, a beauty which makes beauty. For it generates beauty and makes it more beautiful by the excess of beauty which comes from it, so that it is the principle of beauty and the term of beauty" (VI.7.32.31–4). Since procession is an eternal process the One continually brings things into existence and thus also continues to actualize Intellect: "Now as well it is keeping those things in being and making the thinking things think and the living things live, inspiring thought, inspiring life" (VI.7.23.22–4). Both as passive potentiality (i.e., potential Intellect) and as actual thought, Intellect *eternally* depends on the One as external transcendent cause for activation and realization of its possibilities. The derivation of goodness, beauty, life, and so on from the One to Intellect, via efficient and final causality, does not make the One a formal cause of Intellect, in the sense of univocally predicating properties that are possessed to the same degree by both paradigm and instances. The reality of the One is certainly not predicated univocally of its effects.[20] Yet, as we have seen, difficulties stand in the way of imputing formal causality completely to Intellect, since everything it has and is derives from the One. Even if Intellect is the proximate cause (from within Intellect's perspective) of the generation of being and essence, the internal activity of Intellect, that is, its power to generate, is derived from the One's external activity; and it is only in its reversion to the One that it becomes actualized as Intellect, substance, and thought (cf. V.3.11.12–16). On a comprehensive and balanced view it is perhaps best to say that both these perspectives on the actualization of Intellect are essential and that neither is primary in every respect.

The One as mystical final cause

Plotinian mysticism is a large and complex subject that can only be considered here briefly insofar as it concerns the metaphysics of the One.[21] The fundamental principle grounding the actualization of Intellect as well as Plotinus's ethical and psychological teleology is that everything desires the Good. However, the Good's final causality is not limited to Intellect's actualization nor to an individual soul living virtuously or taking up the intelligible life. The higher aspect of the Good's final causality is to draw lower realities upward toward itself, to the supreme realization of union with the Good: "The soul's innate love (erôs emphutos) makes clear that the Good is there. . . . For since the soul is other than God but comes from him it is necessarily in love with him" (VI.9.9.24–7).

The soul's desire for full participation in the intelligible realm is an essential stage in its mystical ascent to the Good. When it attains the intelligible world the individual soul discovers that its true self is an eternal part of the intelligible (IV.7.20.14–20, IV.8.1.1–7). On one view the individual soul transcends itself, becoming "completely other," a fully actualized member of the intelligible world (IV.4.2.23–32, IV.7.10.28–37, V.1.5.1–4, V.3.4.10–14, VI.5.12.16–25, VI.7.35.4).[22] A short passage conveys the message: "whoever has become at once contemplator of himself and all the rest and object of his contemplation, and, since he has become substance and intellect and 'the complete living being,' no longer looks at it from outside – when he has become this he is near, and that Good is next above him" (VI.7.36.10–14).

The noetic life lived by the soul is both intellectual (I.3.4.10–17) and visionary (V.8.4.5–9, 12.3–7; VI.7.12.22–30). What Plotinus seems to have in mind is a mystical awareness of a distinctly philosophical character, which combines both cognitive and affective elements.[23] Yet this noetic mystical activity is not the ultimate reality: "there comes to be the intense kind of love for them not when they are what they are but when, being already what they are, they receive something else from there beyond" (VI.7.21.11–13). The intellectualized soul shifts its attention from an intellectual contemplation of forms to an awareness that intelligible beings reflect or even serve as a reflective medium for the light radiating from the Good: "then truly he is also moved to the Forms, and longs for the light which plays upon them and delights in it. . . . For each is what it is by itself; but it becomes desirable when the Good colours it" (VI.7.22.2–6). At this stage the soul realizes that in the beauty and goodness of the intelligible world it "has not yet quite grasped what it is seeking" (VI.7.22.22), that these sublime realities are not self-constituted but derive from a higher reality. The distinction between the "beings as they are" and the "beings as reflecting the One" corresponds to the two distinct capacities of Intellect: "one power for thinking (*dunamis*), by which it looks at what transcends it by a direct awareness and reception. . . . And that first one is the contemplation of Intellect in its right mind, and the other is Intellect in love, when it goes out of its mind 'drunk with the nectar' " (VI.7.35.20–5). The ascended soul, filled with love for the Good, participates in Intellect's erotic, supraintellectual aspiration for the Good and "sees by a kind of confusing and annulling the intellect which abides within it" (VI.7.35.33–4).[24] Transcending Intellect, being, and thought is the final stage of the mystical ascent: the soul "is carried out of it [i.e., the intelligible world] by the surge of the wave of Intellect itself" (VI.7.36.17–18) to vision of the Good as pure light. Elsewhere the soul is "lifted by the giver of its love" (VI.7.22.18–19), a particularly activist characterization of the Good's final causality. Far from ignoring the possibility that these positive descriptions of the Good compromise its radical transcendence, Plotinus insists that it is precisely because the first principle is formless and shapeless that it is "most longed for and most lovable, and love for it would be immeasurable" (VI.7.32.24–6). The infinite, indeterminate nature of the Good requires a capacity or activity on the part of the soul that is infinite and undefined in order to be united with it. The Good "is its beginning and end (*archê kai telos*); its beginning because it comes from there, and its end, because its good is there. And when it comes to be there it becomes itself and what it was" (VI.9.9.20–2). Becoming simple and unified, the soul is "one with" the Good (3.10–3, 10.9–11), all thought or awareness of duality having been left behind (10.14–7; 11.4–16, 31–2). Union with the Good is "the end of the journey" (11.45).[25]

IV THE ONE AS EVERYTHING AND NOTHING

If we are to understand comprehensively Plotinus's thinking about the One it is necessary to recognize not only his philosophical and experiential approaches to the first principle but also the dialectical perspective within which they operate. This perspective is not unfamiliar, since it involves, initially, simultaneous application of the positive and negative theologies in understanding the One both as cause and as end or goal. But more is involved than the methodical alternation between negation and affirmation. Since only a beginning can be made here I propose examining two clusters of texts, the first on the One as efficient cause, the second, on the One as mystical final cause.

(A) As we saw in Section III (The One and the Others), the One is the productive power of all things while being none of them. The famous opening passage of V.2.1 articulates puzzling implications of this claim:

> The One is all things and not a single one of them: it is the principle of all things, not all things, but all things have that other kind of transcendent existence; for in a way they do occur in the One; or rather they are not there yet, but they will be. How then do all things come from the One, which is simple and has in it no diverse variety, or any sort of doubleness? It is because there is nothing in it that all things come from it. (V.2.1.1–5)

The radical disjunction between the One and its products acquits Plotinus of the charge of pantheism and of propounding an emanationist scheme, at least in the literal sense that the One's being actually constitutes the many existent things. Our difficulties stem from the fact that Plotinus does not leave us with the unambiguous picture of a radically transcendent One that is absolutely incomparable. He also asserts in the strongest terms that the One contains everything (IV.5.7.16–17, V.5.9.33–5, VI.4.2.3–5, VI.5.1.25–6), the grounds for its omnipresence and indeed for efficient causality:

> How is that One the principle of all things? Is it because as principle it keeps them in being, making each one of them exist? Yes, and because it brought them into existence. But how did it do so? By possessing them beforehand. But it has been said that in this way it will be a multiplicity. But it had them in such a way as not to be distinct: they are distinguished on the second level. (V.3.15.27–31; cf. also V.4.2.16, VI.7.32.14, VI.8.21.24–5)

> For something like what is in Intellect, in many ways greater, is in that One; it is like a light dispersed far and wide from some one thing translucent in itself; what is dispersed is image, but that from which it comes is truth; though certainly the dispersed image, Intellect is not of alien form. . . . He is then in a greater degree something like the most causative and truest of causes, possessing all together the intellectual causes which are going to be from him and generative of what is not as it chanced but as he himself willed. (VI.8.18.32–41)

Earlier in the same chapter Plotinus compares the relation between the One and Intellect to that between archetype and image (26–7), "evidence of something like Intellect in the One which is not Intellect" (21–2; cf. also VI.8.16.16). On a minimalist view these texts refer only to the existential dependence of Intellect, and all else, on the One. But it is necessary also to explain why Intellect's power, light, and perhaps its thinking come to it from the first principle. The two principles are also alike in that both are actualizations, though Intellect is not self-sufficiently so as is the One (VI.8.16.15–17). The statement that there is "something like Intellect in the One which is not Intellect" alludes to something more than efficient causality of existence.

How should we construe this difficult doctrine? One approach has been to argue that the statements about the One in VI.8 do not violate the strictures of negative theology with its insistence on the radical transcendence and ineffability of the One since Plotinus explicitly states that his language should not be interpreted literally, that the properties ascribed to the One, especially the noetic ones, are, strictly speaking, inapplicable to it. In VI.8 Plotinus refers to the One as existence (7.47), actuality (16.15–8, 20.9), being (7.49–50, 20.9–16), substance (7.52), life (7.51), self-will (13.38), cause of itself (14.41–2; 16.14–15, 21, 29; 20.2–6), free will (13.1–8, 16.38–9, 21.12–15) and as being everywhere (16.1–2; cf. III.8.9.25, III.9.4.1–7). These positive descriptions of the One, he says, are "for the sake of persuasion" and the phrase "as if" must be added as a qualifier in each case (VI.8.13.1–5, 47–50). Plotinus consistently maintains that these properties and activities do not admit plurality into the One but comprise an absolute unity (e.g., 20.23–7). Since it is because the One is perfect that it generates reality, these properties help to identify recognizable features of its perfect existence and thus serve the purpose of persuasion by explaining the One's efficient causality and by diminishing the paradoxicality of the notion that the One gives what it does not have.

Construed in this way these expressions are not simply opaque symbols of the One's transcendent reality. Not enough is explained by claiming that negative theology trumps the positive. A more promising recent proposal holds that the the One's indistinct possession of intellectual content points to the virtual existence of beings in the One, not their eminent existence.[26] On this view the eminent existence of the forms of being in the One, along Thomistic lines for example, would violate its simplicity. Thus, the real meaning of the claim that the One contains everything (or that the One *is* all things: VI.5.1.26; *contra:* V.5.12.47–50) is that everything is causally dependent on the One and has its being in reference to the One (cf. V.5.9.36–8). However, it appears doubtful that the virtuality/eminence distinction is flexible enough to explain how the One's being, substance, life, consciousness, and so forth, are predicable of its effects at all. To the extent that Plotinus ascribes, for example, perfect life or pure consciousness to the One he seems committed to some version of an eminence view, on which things exist perfectly in the One – though, of course, it would be wrong to refer to discrete "things."[27] The omnipresence of the One and its similarity to things must be reckoned with: the One "is like the things which have come to be much more originally and more truly and more than as it is on their level in that it is better" (VI.8.14.33–4). This is not to say that the One's properties are univocally predicable of its products: the One's life is not life in the same sense or to the same degree as Intellect's. Nor, on the other hand, is it easy to make sense of these difficult texts if we construe the One's properties (or its perfect activities) as purely equivocal. Surely the One's actuality, that is, the One *as* actuality, surpasses intelligible actuality, but there must also be a sense in which they are similar in nature. This interpretive dilemma might be seen as a variation on the philosophical difficulties that afflict relations between Forms and particulars in Plato's *Parmenides*, though Plotinus's situation is complicated by the fact that unlike the Forms, the One is both ineffable and universal efficient cause.

It might be useful to speculate that in working on this problem Plotinus practices a form of Aristotelian focal analysis, introduced in *Metaphysics* IV.1–2. For Aristotle every instance of being has its being in reference to primary substance (*ousia*). Aristotle's focal meaning, of course, applies to primary substances that can be either sensible or supersensible, that possess discursive definitions, and perhaps even particularity, none of which conditions apply in the case of the One. Yet focal meaning, in combination with Platonic participation, provides some means for understanding the relations and the similarity of things to the One. Such a Plotinian "method" combines Platonic degrees of reality metaphysics, with its gradable univocity (different entities possess more or less of the same property), with a modified Aristotelian *pros hen* equivocity, where a property applies to the One in a primary sense and derivatively to other beings.[28] When he focuses on the transcendent One itself, however, Plotinus prefers pure equivocity: its nature is completely *sui generis*, incomparable.

(B) Bringing this dialectical perspective to bear on the relationship between the One in itself and the effects of its efficient causality suggests not only that the One's indistinct possession of things means causal dependence but it also means that everything is somehow unified in the One. As unification is an aspect of reversion *qua* One as final cause, the inclusive interpretation of the One and others must also consider its function as mystical goal, particularly with respect to these remarkable passages in VI.8:

And he, that same self, is lovable and love and love of himself, in that he is beautiful only from himself and in himself. For surely his keeping company with himself could not be in any other way than if what keeps company and what it keeps company with were the one and the same. But if what keeps company is one with what it keeps company with and what is, in a way, desiring is one with the object of desire, and the object of desire is on the side of existence and a kind of substrate, again it has become apparent to us that the desire and the substance are the same. (VI.8.15.1–8)

But he is, if we may say so, borne to his own interior, as it were in love with himself, the "pure radiance" [*Phaedrus* 250c4], being himself this which he loves: but this means that he gives himself existence, supposing him to be an abiding active actuality and the most loved of things in a way like Intellect. . . . If then he did not come into being, but his activity was always and a something like being awake, when the wakener was not someone else, a wakefulness and a thought transcending thought which exists always, then he is as he woke himself to be. (VI.8.16.12–16, 30–3)

Detailed analysis of these texts is not possible here[29] but note that in the first the One, or Good, is described not only as object of love but also as the lover and as love itself – all united into one reality. The inner life of the One provides the paradigmatic structure for the erotic trajectory of the soul's mystical life, which is dramatically presented elsewhere in distinct stages. The ascended soul is filled with eros for unification with the Good (VI.7.31.17–18, VI.9.9.33–4, 44–7) and even becomes eros (VI.7.22.7–10, 31.8–9), while both the One, as object of love, and the soul's love are infinite (VI.7.32.24–8). That other modality of desire in the One, free will (*boulêsis*), also has its correlate in the ascended soul: the One's free will can be seen as just another description of the soul's liberation in union (cf. VI.8.7.1 and 20.17–19).[30] The mystical union of the One and the soul occurs because the latter becomes like the former (VI.7.24.11–14, 44) and both these previously distinct entities are then characterized with the same properties. The persuasive purpose of VI.8.15–16 is not, therefore, primarily to portray the Good in an exceptionally dramatic but strictly inaccurate fashion; rather it is intended, I think, to open a glimpse into the One's inner life, which the soul can aspire to and participate in fully.

It is paradoxical, to say the least, to depict an absolute unity as lover and beloved since love arises only between distinct beings longing to overcome separation. Similarly, in the second passage, the reference to the One's self-vision immediately calls to mind the unity in diversity of the second principle, Intellect. However, when Plotinus attributes some sort of awareness to the One he emphasizes that it (cf. V.4.2.17–19) transcends the intellectual thought, which presupposes a distinction between subject and object: "a wakefulness and a thought transcending thought (*hupernoêsis*)" (VI.8.16.32); the One has "a simple concentration of attention (*epibolê*) on itself" (VI.7.39.1–2); and it is in a nondualistic way pure intellectual actuality (VI.7.37.15–16, VI.9.5.50–5). Note also that consciousness is ascribed to the One in conjunction with its containing everything:

the One is not, as it were, unconscious; rather all things belong to it and are in it and with it; it is completely self-discerning; life is in it and all things are in it, and its intellection (*katanoêsis*) of itself is itself and exists by a kind of self-consciousness (*sunaisthêsis*) in eternal rest and in an intellection different from the intellection of Intellect. (V.4.2.15–19; trans. Armstrong, adapted)

The nature of the One's awareness is a complex topic.[31] Here I suggest that instead of – perhaps in addition to – defining the One's awareness as the unity of subject and object we should think of it as absolute or infinite consciousness without an object, a nonrelational awareness that lacks intentionality and compositeness. Rather than the One *possessing* quasi-thinking, awakening, actuality, love, and so forth as properties, these might be understood as referring to its existence or goodness in different senses. One advantage of this interpretation is that an objectless, radiant, and luminous consciousness describes rather well the reality participated in by the ascended soul, which, enveloped in light (V.5.7–8), in mystical union is incapable of distinguishing itself from the One. The absolute consciousness adumbrated here can be seen either as (i) the unattainable goal of the ascended soul's unified awareness or, as I prefer to take it, (ii) as identical with the unified soul's awareness. On either view the soul's mystical cognition transcends being and thought (VI.9.11.11, 40–5) and all duality and difference (VI.7.34.11–14, VI.9.3.10–13, VI.9.10.14–17); it is "another kind of seeing" (VI.9.11.22–3).

If we follow Plotinus in meditating on the metaphysics of eros and consciousness (or of being) in this dialectical perspective the dispersed life of the soul appears to flow into the inner life of the One. The puzzling statement that the One is "borne to his own interior, as it were in love with himself" (VI.8.16.12–13, Armstrong adapted) thus amounts to an attempt to envision the motion of the relative universe *toward* the absolute as motion *within* the absolute itself. This is, then, a visualization of the doctrine that the One contains everything. From this viewpoint within the One dissimilarity and transcendence are set aside in favor of presence, immediacy, and luminous consciousness.

Straightforward discursive analysis may resist the implications of the dialectical perspective, but it offers another glimpse into the minds of those who have attained the One, their true selves (cf. VI.9.9.20–2). It seems to me, therefore, that Plotinus does not temporarily suspend the negative theology in order to converse with those incapable of thinking about the One without attributes or without images, that is to say by descending to speak the language of positive theology to weaker minds. Rather he practices this mystical dialectic, which includes both the so-called positive and negative theologies – but transcends them, going beyond distinguishing and not distinguishing the One from all things. Plotinus's own method of teaching about the One unfolds in three stages: (i) constantly alternating between the positive and negative ways; (ii) transcending the two ways' logic of distinction and indistinction through this comprehensive dialectic; (iii) transmitting direct experiential awareness of the One.[32]

NOTES

1 See the admirable discussion of this theme in Schroeder 1985.
2 See Armstrong's classic 1973 and 1974 articles on these subjects.

3 For Plotinian Intellect as nondiscursive thought see Lloyd 1970, 1986, and 1990, 164–8.
4 On this theme see Hadot 1986, 234–44, 1994, chs. 5–7; and Bussanich 1990.
5 Further speculation along these lines in Armstrong 1975.
6 This view is strongly expressed by Armstrong 1977b, Sells 1985 and 1994, and Trouillard 1955a.
7 Plotinus here employs one of the Aristotelian senses of necessity: "the necessary in the primary and strict sense is the simple" (Met. V. 1015b11–12).
8 Cf. Leroux 1990, 341–3.
9 Gerson 1994, 9 with nn.20–1 argues that the One is not the cause of unity in anything else, whereas essential oneness derives from the intelligible world (V.5.4.20–5, 5.6; VI.2.9.7–8, 33–4; VI.6.11.19–24). It is not clear, in my view, that Plotinus makes such a precise, albeit attractive, distinction.
10 The perfume illustration seems to be taken from Aristotle Met. 993b25–6. Plotinus also makes the essence/effect distinction using the Platonic language of being and trace, e.g., at VI.8.18.2–7, on which see Bussanich 1988, 164.
11 See Gerson 1994, ch. 1 for an incisive analysis of the identity of essence and existence in Plotinus's One.
12 Lloyd 1987, 167–70; 1990, 98–105.
13 Lloyd 1976, 147–8. Cf. Gerson 1994, 24.
14 Plotinus diverges from classical theism by endorsing omnipotence but denying omniscience: cf. VI.7.39.19–34, 40.38–43.
15 For an excellent analysis of freedom and necessity in Plotinus see Gerson 1993 and Rist 1967, ch. 6.
16 Lloyd 1987, 177 identifies the One's external activity with potential Intellect.
17 On the Plotinian metaphysics of light see Schroeder 1992, 24–39.
18 Lloyd 1987, 165–75. Gerson concludes that Intellect, as essential being, has no cause: 1993, 570.
19 Lloyd 1987, 175.
20 Cf. Gerson 1994, ch. 4 section 1.
21 For discussions of mystical themes in Plotinus see Rist 1967, ch. 16, 1989; Beierwaltes 1985, chs. 1, 5; Hadot 1994, ch. 4; O'Daly 1973, ch. 4; and my 1994.
22 A spirited debate continues on the question whether the ascended soul "becomes" or merely "participates" in the life of Intellect. See Schibli 1989, Hadot 1987a and my 1988, 128–9.
23 See the classic study by Wallis 1976 and also Beierwaltes 1986 and Lloyd 1990, 133, 166, 180–4.

24 Rist 1989, 190–7 offers profound remarks on the spiritual aspects of the Plotinian Intellect.

25 Armstrong 1977a 59: "Our self does not lose its identity even in this ultimate union, and all its lower powers and activities remain in being, ready for use when required." Similarly, Rist 1967, ch. 16 and Gerson 1994, ch. 10 argue strongly against a permanent identity of the soul and One in mystical union; *contra*, Bussanich 1988, 180–93; 1994, 5325–8.

26 Atkinson 1983, 172; Gerson 1994, 32–3.

27 See Leroux 1990, 96, 108.

28 I am indebted to Gerson 1991, 333–4 for a valuable discussion of *pros hen* equivocity and gradable univocity in Aristotle.

29 For detailed analysis see Leroux 1990, 354–65; Rist 1964, 78–83, 97–103; and my 1988, 208–20.

30 Hadot 1994, 50: "The Good is what all things desire; it is what is desirable in an absolute sense. . . . by willing itself and being what it wants to be, it freely creates the love that beings feel for it, as well as the grace they receive from it."

31 See Beierwaltes 1985, 42–50; Rist 1967, ch. 4; and Bussanich 1987. On the lexicography of consciousness terms see Schroeder 1987a.

32 On the dialectic of distinction and nondistinction applied to a transcendent absolute see McGinn 1990.

3   The hierarchical ordering of reality in Plotinus

Never use the words higher and lower.

Charles Darwin

If we have any preconceptions about Plotinus, before looking at him more closely, these preconceptions are likely to include the notion that his world is a "hierarchy," or "chain of being," stretching from some mysterious transcendent cause, the One, down through a succession of levels to the bottom level, matter. This notion, derived from the doxographic surveys to be read in our manuals of the history of philosophy, influenced also perhaps by our ideas of later ancient and medieval philosophical systems, is likely to strike us as strange and constitute a major obstacle to wishing or being able to understand Plotinus better. For such a hierarchical world-view will be felt to be anachronistic and unacceptable if we stay within the implicit metaphysical materialism of our time, if we adhere to vague social and political feelings about equality, if we find that talk of "degrees of being" is philosophical nonsense, if we insist that it is *we* who make our (different) world-views.

If nonetheless we try to come to terms with Plotinus's hierarchical world-view, we soon meet with difficulty of another kind. The term "hierarchy" was first coined in the early sixth century A.D. by a Christian author much influenced by the *later* Neoplatonism of Proclus, Pseudo-Dionysius. The term is not found in Plotinus, nor are other expressions (in particular 'chain of being') sometimes used today to refer to Plotinus's view of reality.[1] The danger in this anachronistic use of terms is that we will tend to project back on Plotinus ideas associated with such terms in Pseudo-Dionysius and in his

66

medieval successors. And it becomes very easy to read into Plotinus the meanings which we would give today to notions of hierarchy.[2]

A procedure for dealing with this difficulty in such a way as to have some chance of coming nearer to Plotinus's own views would appear to be this: to pick out terminology which Plotinus himself uses explicitly in order to formulate a structuring of things to which we would tend to refer as "hierarchical." In particular I suggest taking the terms "prior" (*proteros*) and "posterior" (*husteros*) as expressing a way of ordering things. Plotinus himself uses these terms in connection with the structure of reality and uses them reflectively, that is in connection with discussion of the kinds of order which these terms serve to express. In this he is following the example of Plato's Academy and of Aristotle, where the terminology had been used in the formulation of theories of the ordering of reality.

In the following Section (I) I would like to review rapidly this Platonic and Aristotelian background before sketching (Section II) some of the ways in which Plotinus distinguishes between kinds of ordering in terms of priority/posteriority and showing (Section III) his use of these distinctions in connection with the structure of reality. This approach should help limit the impact of anachronistic projections of later ideas back on Plotinus and bring us a little nearer to Plotinus's own views. If this can be done, then a first step has been taken toward a genuine confrontation between Plotinus and modern philosophical views hostile, or perhaps in some respects friendly, to "hierarchy."

I

In a recent book (1992), J. Moravcsik has distinguished between two approaches in ontology, (1) an approach which aims at developing an "inventory" of reality, sorting out the different kinds of things there are, and (2) an approach which is more concerned with establishing what is fundamental and primary in reality, that on which things depend. These two approaches are not mutually exclusive: "fundamental" ontology may involve making an "inventory," a classification of the kinds of things there are, but this inventory need not be, for the purpose of finding foundations, systematic and complete. Moravcsik suggests that inventory ontologies are more characteristic of modern philosophy, whereas an interest in what is fundamental marks Plato's philosophy. What is fundamental in Plato is of course the Forms. We could say the same of Aristotle and describe the great debate between him, his master and other members of Plato's school as concerned largely with what should count in reality as fundamental, as primary, as that on which things depend.

A characteristic attitude adopted by Aristotle in this debate was his insistence on the need to distinguish clearly between the different possible meanings of the often ambiguous words used in the debate. The multivocity of the word "being" is an obvious example. But Aristotle also pointed out that other words used in the debate about what is fundamental, notably the terms "primary," "prior," "posterior," are also ambiguous and can mean different things, meanings which he classified in a number of places in his works.[3] I would like to review first some aspects of his classification of kinds of priority and posteriority, before showing its relation to his disagreement with Plato as to what should be identified as fundamental in reality.[4]

Aristotle's most elaborate classification of kinds of priority/posteriority is found in *Metaphysics* V.11. Three main groupings may be distinguished in the text.[5]

1 "Prior" as what is "nearer" in a given class (*genos*) to the "first" or "principle" (*archê*) in the class. The cases given are those of priority in terms of place (1.1), time (1.2), movement (1.3) (what is nearer the first mover), power (1.4) (what is more powerful is prior), and order (1.5), as in the ordering of a chorus or of the strings of a musical instrument.

2 "Prior" taken in the sense of what is prior in knowledge (*gnosei*), either as regards definition (*logos*), where the universal is prior to the individual (2.1), or as regards sense-perception, where the individual is prior to the universal (2.2).

3 "Prior" as regards "nature and being" (*kata phusin kai ousian*), "that is, those which can be without other things, while the others cannot be without them, – a distinction which Plato used" (1019a1–4, trans. Ross). Aristotle then goes on to relate to this kind of priority his concepts of the subject, of substance and of actuality, and says that all senses of the prior/posterior are said in some way in relation to this last sense (1019a11–14).

These three groups occur in various other places in Aristotle's work, where, of the first group, priority in time (1.2) is usually mentioned,[6] as is, of the second group, priority in definition (2.1).[7] But it is the third sort, that used by Plato, which seems to be the most important according to Aristotle. We should consequently examine it more closely.

Priority by nature and being expresses a relation of what might be termed "nonreciprocal dependence": A depends on B (or cannot be without B) in such a way that B does not depend on A. The example given in the *Categories* is that of the number series 1, 2, . . . , in which for there to be 2, there must be 1, but not vice versa; the constitution of 2 presupposes 1; 1 is thus that on which the existence of 2 depends.[8] The relation of nonreciprocal dependence is described in more detail, again with mathematical examples, in Alexander of Aphrodisias's commentary on Aristotle's *Metaphysics*, in a passage which may be based on Aristotle's lost work *On the Good:*

Both Plato and the Pythagoreans assumed that numbers are the principles (*archas*) of the things that are, because it seemed to them that what is prior and incomposite is a principle, and that planes are prior to bodies (for things that are simpler [than another] and that are not destroyed along with it are by nature (*phusei*) prior [to it]), and that lines are prior to planes by the same reasoning, and that points . . . are prior to lines, being totally incomposite. . . . [9]

Alexander goes on to tell us, as does Aristotle, that according to Plato sensible objects depend on the Forms for their being, that the Forms are numbers and depend themselves on two causes that are prior (in the sense specified above), the "one" and the "indefinite dyad."

The Platonic notion of priority "by nature" thus concerns a relation between things (A, B, . . .) including these features: nonreciprocal dependence (for A to be, there must be B, but not vice versa; the destruction of B means the destruction of A, but not vice versa) and composition (A is a composite constituted from something more simple, B, whereas B is not constituted from A). The mathematical examples suggest that if things in reality are constituted from prior, more simple elements, the latter also exist in themselves, in independence of what is constituted from them.

Aristotle of course rejects the fundamental ontology in Plato that specifies what makes up the order of priority "by nature" that is constitutive of reality. Forms cannot exist independently of, or separate from, sensible objects, and numbers do not exist "prior" (in the Platonic sense) to such objects. Aristotle replaces Forms and numbers with his own structure of dependence: that of attributes on natural substances; that of the changes in the natural world on celestial motions; that of celestial motions on an unmoved mover, divine intellect, "... on such a principle then depend (êrtêtai) the heavens and the world of nature" (*Met.* 1072b13–14).

In a passage in the *Physics* (260b15–261a26), Aristotle distinguishes between priority in terms of nonreciprocal dependence and priority by being and nature. This is rather confusing if compared with chapter 11 of *Metaphysics* V (summarized above), where it is precisely the (Platonic) relation of nonreciprocal dependence that is called priority by nature and being. However in speaking of being and nature, in the *Physics* passage, Aristotle seems to have in mind degrees of perfection or completion in something. In this sense we can readily see how a series of terms related by nonreciprocal dependence need not coincide with a series of degrees of perfection: *A* can depend on *B* without being necessarily inferior to *B*.[10] However it does seem that Plato's order of dependence coincides with an order of perfection: the Forms clearly have a mode of existence in relation to which sensible objects are deficient and imperfect, and the Form of the Good of the *Republic*, source in some way of the Forms, surpasses them "in power and dignity" (509b9–10). The perfection in terms of which the Forms are superior to sensible objects is complex, involving not only independence, but also immutability, self-identity, and integrity, that makes them "more real," the privileged objects of knowledge, the primary locus of moral and aesthetic values.[11] Aristotle also seems to claim something similar for his version of reality as a structure of dependence: in natural substances, the form, actuality, or finality of the object is what is primarily constitutive of it, what is most intelligible in it, its perfection;[12] celestial substances constitute a higher level in terms of perfection of existence; and the unmoved mover, divine intellect, as pure (immaterial) form or actuality is of such perfection as to be the highest object of thought and the object of imitation by lower things. Thus the order of priority by nature and being, both in Plato and in Aristotle, implies much more than a relation of nonreciprocal dependence: this relation involves also an order of perfection of existence, of knowledge and of value. And, as Aristotle suggests in chapter 11 of *Metaphysics* V, other kinds of priority can be related back to the central order of priority by nature and being.[13]

II

In evoking the debate in fundamental ontology between Aristotle, Plato, and the Platonists of the Academy, as this debate turned on the issue as to what should be identified as prior according to nature and being, I have referred indiscriminately to Plato's dialogues and to the Plato represented by Aristotle and his commentator Alexander. This is Plotinus's point of view: he has no worries, as we might have, about the reliability of Aristotle's reports about Plato, about what it is that is being reported (Plato's unwritten doctrines?) and how it relates to the dialogues. Plotinus simply assumes that Aristotle informs us of Plato's central metaphysical ideas (see, for example, V.4.2.7–9). Plotinus is deeply read in Aristotle's work and is familiar also with Alexander's commentaries. It is not then surprising that he is well aware of the Platonic and Aristotelian classifications of kinds of priority/posteriority and of their philosophical importance. As in the preceding section, I propose looking first at Plotinus's formulation of different kinds of priority, moving then to his use of them in developing a fundamental ontology that is a Platonist response to the ontologies of Aristotle and of the Stoics.

Plotinus distinguishes between many kinds of priority throughout the *Enneads:* priority in time, in place, in knowledge, in nature, in truth, in order, in power.[14] Priority in place and time (= 1.1 and 1.2, in the classification of *Metaphysics* V. 11) are usually opposed to the other kinds of priority.[15] Priority in knowledge, knowledge taken as sense-perception (= 2.2), is opposed to priority by nature (= 3).[16] Priority in order (= 1.5) is distinguished from priority in power (= 1.4), which is related to priority in truth.[17] In the structure of things priority in power and in truth overlap with the kind of priority to which Plotinus attaches most importance, priority by nature (= 3), that which Aristotle had associated with Plato and which was also for him of central importance. It seems to be of this kind of priority that Plotinus is thinking when he says:

I do not mean "another kind" in the sense of a logical distinction, but in the sense in which we Platonists speak of one thing as prior and another as posterior. The term "life" is used in many different senses, distinguished according to the rank of the things to which it is applied, first, second and so on. . . . [18]

Armstrong's addition of the word "Platonists" here in his translation can be justified to the extent that the kind of priority involved in the passage is the priority by nature that Aristotle had identified as Platonic.

Plotinus's conception of Platonic priority by nature can be characterized as follows. It refers to a relation of nonreciprocal dependence in which, in a series of terms, the posterior depends on the prior and cannot exist without the prior, whereas the prior exists independently of the posterior and is not destroyed with the destruction of the posterior.[19] Thus the posterior has its existence in some way, and as long as it exists, from the prior without impinging on the independence of the prior. Plotinus refers in illustration to the number series (cf. V.5.4.20–5), but more often speaks more generally of a series of compounds constituted from a noncomposite prior, or of a multiplicity constituted from a prior "one."[20] What is prior is then more "simple," more "one," and the first is the most simple, absolute "one" (cf. V.4.1.4–5).

In formulating the concept of priority by nature, Plotinus tends to emphasize the following aspects. The series involved constitutes a succession (first, second, third, . . .) in which continuity and proper order of succession are important. These features are characteristic of the series of numbers, but Plotinus also seems to have in mind a passage in the second Platonic letter.[21] The continuity of the number series, as it was conceived in his time, is such that the posterior terms are thought of as contained potentially in the prior terms, the monad containing potentially all the numbers constituted in succession from it.[22] For Plotinus also the posterior terms in a series according to priority by nature are already present potentially "in" the prior terms.[23] Furthermore, as the posterior is contained potentially in the prior, so the prior is contained in the posterior as constitutive of it. Yet while being a constitutive presence in the posterior, the prior is independent of the posterior (nonreciprocal dependence): thus it is both part of ("in") the posterior, and apart from, different from ("beyond," *epekeina*) what is posterior to it (cf. III.8.9.1–10).

These features of an order of priority by nature are brought together and summarized at the beginning of V.4:

If there is anything after the First, it must necessarily come from the First; it must either come from it directly or have its ascent back to it through the beings between, and there must be an order of seconds and thirds, the second going back to the first and the third to the second. For there must be something simple before all things, and this must be other than all the things which come after it, existing by itself, not mixed with the things which derive from it, and all the same able to be present in a different way to these other things, being really one, and not a different being and then one; it is false even to say of it that it is one, and there is "no concept or knowledge" of it; it is indeed also said to be "beyond being." For if it is not to be simple, outside all coincidence and composition and really one, it could not be a first principle; and it is the most self-sufficient, because it is simple and the first of all: for that which is not the first needs that which is before it, and what is not simple is in need of its simple components so that it can come into existence from them.

III

Returning now to the debate in fundamental ontology between Plato and Aristotle, we can ask how Plotinus makes use of the distinctions between kinds of priority/posteriority that emerged in this debate and how in particular he applies his conception of priority by nature in reaching his version of a fundamental ontology. In the following pages I attempt no more than to trace some of the lines that a fuller treatment of this subject might follow.

(i) We might begin with the question of the priority of soul with regard to body. In speaking of the making of the soul of the universe, Plato's Timaeus tells us:

Now God did not make the soul after the body, although we are speaking of them in this order, for when he put them together he would never have allowed that the elder should be ruled by the younger. . . . Whereas he made the soul in origin and excellence prior to and older than the body, to be the ruler and mistress, of whom the body was to be the subject. (*Timaeus* 34b10–c5, trans. Jowett)

Thus Timaeus's order of exposition (the account of the making of the soul as coming *after* that of the four elements of the world body) is the reverse of the order of priority according to generation, worth, and power (i.e., priority by nature), in which body is posterior to soul. However the Stoics, as Plotinus understands them, reversed the natural order and saw soul at its various levels as evolving from states of body:

> But as for saying that the same breath was growth-principle before, but when it got into the cold and was tempered became soul, since it becomes rarefied in the cold – this is absurd to start with; for many animals come into existence in heat and have a soul which has not been cooled – but anyhow they assert that growth-principle is prior to soul which comes into existence because of external happenings. So they find themselves making the worse first, and before this another of less good quality, which they call "character," and intellect last, obviously originating from the soul. Now if Intellect is before all things, then they ought to have made soul come next to it, then growth-principle, and have made what comes after always worse, as is the natural state of affairs. (IV.7.8³.1–11)

Against the Stoic position, Plotinus uses the Aristotelian argument of the priority of actuality to potentiality (8³.3.11–17): if body is at first merely potentially soul and intellect and then evolves toward being them, how could it do so in the absence of some prior actuality, that of soul and intellect, which would bring it to *this* actuality or inspire it with the actuality to be achieved? As actuality is prior and superior to potentiality, so are intellect and soul prior and superior to body as potentially ensouled. On the basis of this and of other arguments Plotinus thus argues in IV.7 that soul is prior by nature to body, as independent of body, as that on which body depends, as constitutive of body while being separate from body, a different and superior nature.²⁴

(ii) Plotinus extends this relation of priority by nature between soul and body to cover the general relation between intelligible being and body:

> But the other nature, which has being of itself, is all that really exists, which does not come into being or perish: or everything else will pass away, and could not come into being afterwards if this real existence had perished which preserves all other things and especially this All, which is preserved and given its universal order and beauty by soul. (IV.7.9.1–5)

The theme of the relation of nonreciprocal dependence, the priority by nature obtaining between intelligible reality and body forms the focus of one of Plotinus's most developed and interesting metaphysical studies, VI.4–5.[25] In exploring the difference in nature separating the intelligible, as prior by nature, from body, Plotinus emphasizes the spatial character of body and hence the nonspatial character of intelligible being. Since intelligible being is multiple and ordered, as we will see, this order cannot be spatial, but manifests other sorts of order:

And how is there the first there, and the second as well, and after that others? . . . And certainly things are first and second and third in order and power and difference, not by spatial positions. For nothing prevents different things from being all together, like soul and intellect and all bodies of knowledge. . . . (VI.4.11.2–3 and 9–12; cf. IV.3.10.1–6)

Time characterizes body, being produced by soul in its generation of the universe, and so should also be distinguished in the kind of order it yields (temporal priority/posteriority) from the order of priority structuring intelligible reality.[26] We can therefore say that temporal and spatial succession apply to the last stages in the order of the constitution of things by nature. Thus temporal and spatial order are, as wholes, posterior by nature to the other sorts of order characterizing intelligible being. To examine intelligible order, we might consider the order in soul and the order linking soul and intellect.

(iii) There are different forms and levels of life (plants, animals) for which soul is responsible, and different souls (individual souls, world soul). Plotinus argues that all souls are one and that the multiplicity of souls and the various levels of living functions relate to this one soul. How this could be he explains in terms of his concept of priority by nature in which posterior terms are constituted by the prior. This can be seen in the case of the levels of life in the passage from I.4.3.16–20 quoted above and is proposed at the end of the treatise (IV.9) where the unity of soul is argued:

How, then, is there one substance in many souls? Either the one is present as a whole in them all, or the many come from the whole and one while it abides [unchanged]. That soul, then, is one, but the many [go back] to it as one which gives itself to multiplicity and does not give itself; for it is adequate to supply itself to all and to remain one; for it has power extending to all things, and is not at all cut off from each individual thing; it is the same, therefore, in all. (IV.9.5.1–7)

Indeed the continuity of the series of priority by nature that is life can be extended to express the structure of reality in general:

All these things are the One and not the One: they are he because they come from him; they are not he, because it is in abiding by himself that he gives them. It is then like a long life stretched out at length; each part is different from that which comes next in order, but the whole is continuous with itself, but with one part differentiated from another, and the prior does not perish in the posterior. (V.2.2.24–9)

(iv) If the world depends on soul, soul cannot be regarded as the absolute prior by nature, Plotinus argues, because soul presupposes and depends on intellect, which must consequently be independent of, and different from, soul. Here again, Plotinus has Stoic ontology in mind, since the Stoics claim, he believes, that intellect evolves from, and is posterior to, more primitive states of body and soul, whereas for both Plato and Aristotle intellect is prior by nature to body and soul. Plotinus's anti-Stoic argument again appeals to the Aristotelian principle of the priority of actuality to potentiality: how could intellect as actuality develop from a potentiality in soul if there were no prior actuality of intellect? (V.9.5.2–4 and 25–6; II.5.3.25–31). The actuality that is intellect is the knowledge which inspires soul (a knowledge that soul does not of itself possess) in constituting the world. Thus intellect is the paradigm of the sensible world:

Intellect is before it, not in the sense that it is prior in time but because the universe comes from intellect and intellect is prior by nature, and the cause of the universe as a kind of archetype and model, the universe being an image of it and existing by means of it and everlastingly coming into existence. . . . (III.2.1.22–6)

(v) Intellect is, like soul, a unity and multiplicity. We could therefore explore the series that it constitutes as well as other aspects of the structuring of intelligible reality in terms of priority by nature, order, power, and difference.[27] However it is perhaps more important in the present context to move to the ultimate stage in the series of priority by nature that constitutes reality, the stage at which intellect, as prior by nature to all else, is itself found not to be the absolute prior, that on which all depends, but to presuppose in its constitution something other than it, something absolutely noncomposite, or simple, something absolutely one, the "One."[28]

In arguing that intellect is not absolutely prior, Plotinus is rejecting Aristotle's fundamental ontology in which divine intellect, the unmoved mover, is what is first by nature. Plotinus claims that this cannot be the case, since intellect is not merely a multiplicity of objects of thought, but also a duality of thinking and of object thought. Intellect is therefore a composite and as such must be posterior by nature (see, for example, VI.9.2; III.8.9).

Plotinus's conception of the One thus relates to his application of the notion of priority by nature to the analysis of (Aristotelian) divine intellect as composite. The One is that on which all else depends, what constitutes all else, present as such in, and part of, all else, yet also different from, and independent of, all else, thus "beyond" all else and in particular beyond, in the order of succession, intellect as the second term. And as intellect is identical with intelligible being, so is the One "beyond being." In this way Plotinus arrives at a conclusion which he can relate to Plato's description of the Form of the Good as surpassing the Forms "in power and dignity" (*Rep.* 509b9–10): "dignity," since Plotinus's order of priority by nature corresponds, as it does in Plato and Aristotle, to levels of perfection of mode of existence (independence, completion, unity);[29] "power," since the One constitutes all else.

In V.5.12, Plotinus speaks of the One's priority in power in connection with the political structure of monarchical power, thus evoking Aristotle's sense of priority by power (*Met.* V.11 = 1.4). But the kind of power involved is clearly far different and far greater, since it is that required to constitute reality. In VI.8.20.28–33 Plotinus also speaks of the "rulership" of the One and distinguishes its absolute priority in power from priority in order: "... the first; but this means not in order (*taxei*), but in authentic mastery and purely self-determined power (*dunamei*)." The distinction between priority "in order" and priority "in power" seems to be related to the idea explored in V.5.13.21–3 that the One cannot be one of the members of a series or group sharing something in common and distinct from each other by some difference. Such an order characterizes intelligible being (see above p. 75) from which, as a whole, the One must be separate as that which constitutes it (see also V.5.4.12–16).

We can consequently say that as temporal and spatial succession (in the material world) are subordinate to other kinds of priority (by order, difference, dignity, power, and nature) as emerging at the lowest stages of the order of priority by nature, so the priority by order and difference characterizing intelligible being is subordinate as relating to a stage posterior to the absolute first in the succession of priority by nature which is also priority by dignity and power. In other words, priority by nature, we might say, constitutes the fundamental structure of things, whereas other kinds of priority develop as secondary manifestations and subordinate articulations of what is prior by nature. Thus what is absolutely prior by nature, the One, produces a posterior reality, intellect, in which the power of the One is expressed in structures of order and difference; intellect in turn produces, as posterior by nature to it, soul, in which the structure of intellect is expressed in a further articulation; and finally soul produces, as posterior by nature to it, the material world, in which intelligible structures find expression in the succession of time and space.

IV

Various areas of Plotinus's philosophy have been scarcely more than touched on in this sketch of the way in which concepts of priority/posteriority relate to Plotinus's main positions in the debate over fundamental ontology. However what has been noted suggests the following conclusions as regards Plotinus's notion of a "hierarchical" structure of reality.

(1) The expressions "hierarchy" and "chain of being" are both too vague and too open to anachronism to be useful in coming nearer to Plotinus's views. We can substitute for them the terminology and classifications of types of priority/posteriority formulated by Plato and Aristotle and used by Plotinus in articulating the structure of reality.

(2) Plotinus's distinctions between types of priority/posteriority correspond to those found in Plato and Aristotle and, like them, he attempts a coordination and subordination of these types as they relate to the structure of things. Thus temporal and spatial priority are subordinate as wholes to other kinds of priority as coming at a later stage in the series of priority by nature, whereas, further up in the series, priority by order and difference are subordinate as wholes to the absolute priority by nature, power, and dignity of the One. If subordinated, these kinds of priority remain distinct and their distinctions are useful in clarifying complex relationships such as that

between the unified structure of intelligible being and sensible being, or that of the unity and multiplicity of soul.

(3) In Plotinus, as in Plato and Aristotle, the central kind of priority is priority "by nature," which is also priority by power and dignity. It is this kind of priority that is the concern of fundamental ontology as an attempt to identify what is fundamental in reality, that on which things depend. Plotinus seeks to restate Plato's version of a fundamental ontology, but he does this partly in connection with criticism of Stoic ontology, partly in reaction to (and in the light of) Aristotle's views.

(4) Plotinus's conception of priority by nature is largely inspired by Plato's, as reported by Aristotle and as suggested in some passages in Plato's dialogues. Plotinus develops Plato's conception in such a way as to bring out the following relational patterns that span every area of the structure of reality as he sees it. Reality is a structure of dependence, the posterior depending on the prior, being constituted by the prior, incapable of existing "without" the prior which can exist without it. The prior is thus part of, or in, the posterior (as constitutive of it), just as the posterior is potentially in the prior (as coming from it): causes are "in" their effects and effects are "in" their causes. But while a part of the posterior, the prior is also apart from it as independent of it. Thus the prior is both immanent in the posterior and transcends it: the One is "everywhere" and "nowhere." As independent and as prior, the cause is different from the posterior, its effect, superior in perfection and more powerful: causes (in the special sense of cause implied by the notion of priority "by nature") are superior to their effects.

(5) What might sometimes appear to us as paradox, contradiction (the One is everywhere/nowhere, in all/separate from all; effects are in their causes, and vice versa) or ambiguity (is it the One, or intelligible being, that is "everywhere"?) can thus be understood as tightly packed expressions of Plotinus's very rich conception of priority by nature.

(6) If these suggestions bring us nearer to Plotinus's way of seeing the structure of things, it would seem that an appropriate point of departure for critical discussion would be the analysis of what it is that should count as criterion of the "fundamental" in reality (priority by nature, for Plotinus), in the context of the project of a fundamental ontology, should such a project be considered meaningful.

NOTES

1 Cf. O'Meara 1975, 1–3. However the image of a "chain" (*heirmos*) of causes does occur in Plotinus (III.1.2.31; 4.11; III.2.5.14), in contexts suggesting a Stoic conception of causal networks.

2 Cf. O'Meara 1987 for some examples.

3 Cf. Cleary 1988 for a study of these passages. Cleary makes the comparison between the multivocity of "being" and the multivocity of "prior," "posterior."

4 The various difficulties raised by the interpretation of the relevant passages in Aristotle cannot be discussed here (coherence of the lists of types of priority, variations and relations between them), for which cf. Cleary 1988. My review must assume a response to these difficulties.

5 Cf. Cleary 1988, 34–52.

6 Priority in time is described as the first and most proper sense of "prior" in *Categories* ch. 12.

7 *Cat.* ch. 12; *Phys.* 260b15–19; 265b22–3; *Met.* 1028a31–3; 1049b10–12; 1077b1–4.

8 *Cat.* ch. 12, 14a30–5, which I take with 14b11–24; cf. Cleary 1988, 25, who uses the expression "non-reciprocal dependence."

9 Alexander *In Met.* 55.20–56.1, trans. W. Dooley, 84. For the priority of the incomposite (simple), cf. Aristotle *Met.* 1076b18–20. On Platonic priority "by nature," cf. also Cleary 1988, 14–15.

10 An example might be the series of psychic functions in Aristotle's *De anima*, in which the higher functions presuppose (are not found "without") the lower.

11 Cf. Vlastos 1973, essays 2 ("A Metaphysical Paradox") and 3 ("Degrees of Reality in Plato").

12 Cf. Morrison 1987.

13 Cf. Aristotle *Met.* IX.8, where it is argued that actuality is prior to potentiality in being, definition (knowledge), and time; cf. also *Phys.* 265b22–7.

14 Cf. Sleeman and Pollet 1980, s. v. *proteros*.

15 III.2.1.23–5; III.7.9.61–5; IV.4.1.26–31; V.5.12.37–40; VI.4.11.9–10.

16 VI.3.9.36–9; cf. VI.1.28.3–6.

17 VI.8.20.31–3; cf. V.5.12.38–9. For priority in truth, cf. Cleary 1988, 86.

18 I.4.3.16–20; cf. IV.4.28.67–8. I use here and in what follows Armstrong's translation (sometimes slightly modified).

19 III.1.2.30–4; III.2.1.22–6; IV.8.6.10; V.2.2.26–9 (cf. I.4.3.16–20); VI.1.25.17–18; VI.4.8.1–4.

20 III.8.9.3; IV.9.4.7–8; V.4.1.5–15; VI.3.19–22; VI.9.2.31–2.

21 [Plato] *Ep.* II.312e: "It is in relation to the king of all and on his account

that everything exists. . . . In relation to a second, the second class of things exists, and in relation to a third, the third class." (trans. Post); cf. Plotinus VI.7.42.3–10. For a political image of proper order of succession cf. also V.5.12.26–30.

22 Cf. Nicomachus *Introductio arithmetica* 113.2–6; Anatolius *De decade* 29.13–18: "the monad is prior to all number, from which all come, being itself [generated] by nothing . . . were it to be destroyed, there would be no number . . . if not in actuality, in potentiality it is odd, even, even-odd, cube, square, and all the rest."

23 Cf. VI.2.13.7–9. In this sense the prior terms are "common" to the posterior terms and yet are not a genus separate from the series of terms; cf. VI.2.11.40–9; 17.15–19; VI.1.25,15–20; VI.3.9.35–7; 13,15–23. Lloyd has examined this feature of such series (which he calls "P-series") in (1962) and (1990).

24 Cf. also the argument against the conception of soul as harmony (IV.7.8⁴.11–12).

25 Cf. VI.4.8.2–5: ". . . but if there is something which is immaterial, and has no need whatever of body because it is prior by nature to body, itself set firm in itself, or rather not in any way needing a setting of this kind. . . ." For the connection between the relations soul/body and intelligible/sensible reality in VI.4–5 cf. Emilsson 1993.

26 Cf. III.5.9.24–9; IV.3.25.15–16 (on temporal priority); IV.4.1.25–31; IV.4.16.

27 See, for example, VI.6.4 on the priority/posteriority of numbers in the structure of intelligible being.

28 For a new and provocative discussion of the sense in which the One is noncomposite, cf. Gerson 1994, ch. 1.

29 As Plotinus succinctly puts it: "the better is by nature the first" (V.9.4.3).

4 On soul and intellect

Readers of the *Companion* who have arrived at this chapter should be well aware of the fact that Plotinus was a Platonist. One might add that in spite of the fact that he has always been regarded as the founder of Neoplatonism, he himself would not have known what the Greek equivalent of that word might have meant, since all the Platonists of late antiquity regarded themselves as Platonists *tout simple*, and their philosophy as the exposition of the underlying truths of Plato's philosophy which Plato himself sometimes omitted to make explicit. The degree of self-deception involved in this self-concept is perhaps nowhere clearer than in their discussions of soul and intellect. That is so because, while their conception of soul (*psuchê*) was fundamentally Platonic and dualist, their explanation of its operations owed much more to Aristotle and other post-Platonic philosophers than it did to Plato himself.[1]

For Plotinus the dualism was as clear, if not as clear-cut. Though he was aware of materialistic theories of the nature of the soul, such as those of the Stoics,[2] he was hostile to them and would have had little time for the great volume of modern discussion which goes under labels like materialism, physicalism, or functionalism. That is equally true for those theories which, under headings like epiphenomenalism and supervenience, allow for other than fully materialist explanations of what Plotinus would have seen as the most important functions of the soul and intellect – the thinking functions of mind.[3]

Though Plotinus's dualist concept of the soul may be historically derived from Plato's, within his own philosophy it can be argued for from the soul's status as part of the intelligible hierarchy that forms the backbone of Plotinus's system. For him the three hypostases of

82

that hierarchy may exist within each individual (V.1.10.5–6), though their higher levels may not be accessible to all. That is because only those who are intellectually and morally – for a Platonist there is little, if any, difference – most advanced can "raise" their souls to make contact with those levels. Even if the position of the individual soul in relation to other forms of soul is not immediately clear, it follows from its being soul as such that it is both immaterial and essentially separate from body. Hence, there is an immediate problem about how it functions in association with that body which it acquires, or which acquires it, on incarnation.[4]

Before we deal with that let us locate the soul in question in the intelligible world: to save space I shall assume that it is on a lower level than the hypostasis, but coordinate with world-soul, which differs from it only by virtue of the superior body, or bodies, for which it is responsible.[5] Both are seen as more diffuse extensions or, as Plotinus often puts it, images or reflections, of the level of soul which constitutes the hypostasis (cf. e.g., I.1.10.10–11). The soul we are discussing is in the first place soul in the strict sense, excluding the intellect which may, or may not, be part of it: generally, as we shall see, it is not, or at least not without qualification.

That is the situation at the higher end of the continuum which Plotinus tells us that soul forms. There is a similar obscurity at the lower end. Here Plotinus is clear on one point: the soul that with something material constitutes the individual does so not with matter, as is the case with Aristotle's informing hylomorphic soul, but with body (sôma), which is itself a compound of form and matter. In other words the individual is not soul + matter, but soul[1] + soul[2] + matter. This position leads to a problem about the provenance of soul[2]: either soul[2] is there already when soul[1] comes to join body, and in that case it is provided by the world-soul insofar as that informs all matter in the world or directly makes its contents (cf. II.1.5.6–8), or it is a lower part of the individual soul, soul[1], which must somehow send it ahead in order to have a body in which to be incarnated. To describe the latter situation, or at least to give an indication of how he conceived it, Plotinus talks about the soul producing a preliminary sketch of itself before it comes "down" (VI.7.7.8–12), "down" because Plotinus uses the standard imagery by which soul is above body and descends to it, while maintaining, more clearly and successfully than did Plato, that, qua immaterial, it is actually everywhere and nowhere.[6] This, for an immaterialist doctrine of the soul, correct view applies to the soul "within" the body as much as to soul "elsewhere," thus contrasting with Plato's notion of a tripartite soul with each of the three parts having a specific location in the body, a notion which inevitably causes problems about how the soul works in the several activities for which it is responsible. In contrast to Plato's location of each of his three parts in separate parts of the body, Plotinus guardedly says that the activity of a faculty takes place in some part of the body, thus maintaining something of Plato's concept but removing its materialist implications. Plotinus will describe sense-perception as having its starting point (archê) in the brain (IV.3.23.9–21), explaining this by saying that the nerves start there.[7]

One of the characteristics of Plotinus's philosophy is that he will look at the same problem from different points of view, emphasizing different aspects of his thought accordingly. This characteristic shows itself in his approach to the question of which parts of soul come from where. Thus we may say that when he is considering the arrival of soul in body, he may see that body as part of the material world as a whole: in such contexts the body has its basic element of soul, what we have called "soul²," from the lowest level of the world-soul, sometimes referred to as nature (phusis), which eternally transforms matter into body (VI.4.15.8–17). When, however, he is more concerned with the unity of the individual as a single vertical section of the cosmos, he will see even this lowest level of soul as part of that individual. These two viewpoints are less inconsistent than they might at first sight appear to be because in the end – perhaps one should say the beginning, though neither is strictly appropriate – the world-soul and the individual souls are, qua soul, one and the same, a position most fully explored in IV.9 and the early chapters of IV.3.[8] For the identity of individual souls we may quote, by way of example, IV.9.4.15–18: "But this means that there is one and the same soul in many bodies, and, before this one in the many bodies, another again exists which is not in many bodies, from which derives the one in the many . . . " (cf. IV.8.3.11–12).[9]

This identity of individual souls raises the question of how, if soul is in control, individual human beings are not identical. That is a question to which Plotinus does not give a fully satisfactory answer. He usually takes the position that individuation is due to the body, a position that might have satisfied Aristotelians when it was generally accepted that that was Aristotle's explanation too,[10] but which is fundamentally incompatible with the position that body depends for its nature on a soul that is superior to it. In the same way he will allow geographical and other environmental differences as well as heredity to play their part in the formation and disposition of an individual (cf., e.g., III.1.5.27–8). A possible compromise may be seen in V.7.1.18–21, where he appears to attribute individuation to both matter and form: "there cannot be the same forming principle for different individuals, and one man will not serve as a model for several men differing from each other *not only by reason of their matter but with a vast number of special differences of form*" (my italics). Unfortunately we cannot be certain which points in this treatise are Plotinus's own and which are points he raises for discussion or demolition, a difficulty which also aggravates that of deciding whether or not Plotinus believed the ultimate basis of the individual's discrete existence is a Form.[11] At other times Plotinus will allow that the experience of past lives will contribute to the character of an individual (IV.3.8.5–9), but it might be argued that this too does not explain why the individual to whom such experiences are attached is different from any other in the first place.

Just as materialists have problems with apparently immaterial phenomena and functions of the mind, so dualists like Plotinus find difficulties in giving an account of the nature of the soul's symbiosis with, and control over, the body. Plato regarded this relation as almost axiomatic and frequently wrote as if no explanation was needed; for Aristotle the explanation consisted in his doctrine that the soul is the form of the body. One of Plotinus's great merits as a philosopher is that he was not content to leave unexplained matters which others had dealt with by assertion: this remains true even if he does not succeed in offering explanations which we can accept – or even ones with which he himself could rest content. Recognizing the difficulties, he made several attempts to explain how, as he carefully puts it, "soul is with the body."[12] In chapters 20 to 22 of IV.3, the first of Porphyry's divisions of the huge treatise on *On Difficulties About the Soul* (IV.3–5), he considers various ways in which a thing might be in another, or more specifically a soul relate to a body.[13] At this stage the only notion that fits his criterion of a symbiosis where the soul remains unaffected by body, an important criterion, and one which represents Plotinus's professed formal position even if he does not always succeed in maintaining it in practice, is that soul is present to the body as light is to air (IV.3.22.1–4). The notion of "presence to" is crucial: Plotinus repeats it several times in the course of these few lines. Nevertheless Plotinus does not rest content with this analogy, and corrects it later in the treatise, exploring some of the implications of the symbiosis and substituting heat for light (IV.4.29), the point being that heat will affect the air in a way that light does not.[14] This analogy does not, of course, explain how the soul can take cognizance of what happens in the body, let alone be influenced by it, an influence which Plotinus is prepared to allow when he discusses the operations of the several divisions of the lower soul, or, to put it another way, of the several powers or faculties of that soul.

Here we need to consider just how Plotinus envisaged the structure of the soul. Given that his psychology drew in different ways on Plato and Aristotle, he had two possible models, Platonic tripartition and the Aristotelian division into faculties: a third could have been the so-called moral psychology of the *Ethics* and *Politics* which divided the soul simply into a rational and an irrational part, sufficient for Aristotle's purposes in those works where he did not require the degree of accuracy appropriate to more scientific work.[15] In fact we find both the first two, and in practice often the third. Can we decide what Plotinus really thought on this question? If we examine the occurrence of the two types of division it soon becomes clear that they are found in different contexts, tripartition when Plotinus is doing ethics but his own version of the faculty division when he is doing psychology. An example of the first is his use of tripartition when he is describing justice on Platonic lines as the correct functioning of three parts of the soul in the right relation of dependence on the highest, each doing what is appropriate to it (*oikeiopragia*). In his treatise "On Virtues," I.2, Plotinus assigns what Neoplatonists called the civic virtues, those appropriate to life in a *polis*, and so *inter alia* in Plato's *Republic* state, to three parts of the soul: ". . . practical wisdom which has to do with discursive reason,[16] courage which has to do with the emotions,[17] balanced control which consists in a sort of agreement and harmony of passion and reason, justice which makes each of these parts agree in 'minding their own business where ruling and being ruled are concerned' " (I.2.1.17–21).

Readers of Plato will find this familiar enough, though the wording suggests a middle Platonic intermediary.[18] Other less clearly Platonic occurrences of tripartition are likewise found to be in ethical contexts, so for example at III.6.2.22–9. In his big psychological treatise, however, Plotinus himself argues at some length that the two lower parts of the tripartition are inadequate for a serious consideration of the operation of anger[19] and the higher emotions on the one hand, and what Greek philosophers called the desires, but we might classify as physiological drives, on the other (IV.4.28.1–70). As did Aristotle, Plotinus believes that we have a power of appetition (orexis) which crosses the boundaries of the Platonic tripartition, and that the correct way to deal with both anger and the desires is to see them as different kinds of appetition rather than activities of separate parts of the soul (69–70). Both come from the vegetative and reproductive area of the soul (IV.4.28.49–50), another Aristotelian division, and the irrational part of the soul – our third type of possible division, parallel to Aristotle's informal psychology – should not be divided into desiring and spirited parts (63–8). Thereafter the term for Plato's reasoning part appears, with one exception, only as a synonym for Plotinus's Aristotle-type faculty of reason: the one exception is in a list of possible ways of classifying qualities given in VI.1.12.5–6.

So it is clear that once he had examined tripartition in the context of explaining how the soul works Plotinus had no further use for it. We may therefore be sure that it was the division into faculties which he took as the only possible basis for the explanation of activities involving the soul. His list of faculties, however, is not the same as Aristotle's. Where it differs it does so mainly because of the difficulties arising from the superimposition of an Aristotelian psychology on the Platonic concept of the body–soul relation. Thus, there are three points where disagreement is likely: at the bottom, where to Plotinus's way of thinking, soul is most closely associated with body but still distinct from it; in the middle where Plotinus makes a sharper distinction between those faculties which require the body for their operation and those which do not; and, arguably, at the top: here the degree of difference depends, of course, on one's understanding of the crucial chapter (III.5) about the active intellect in the De anima.

At the bottom Plotinus finds a way of using Aristotle's notion that the soul is the form of the body without actually accepting it by taking the soul, when he does so, as being added to an already ensouled body (cf. IV.3.23.1–3, IV.7.8⁵.2–3). This, in the strict analysis to be found in IV.3–4, is what makes the body, as Plotinus puts it, so-qualified (toionde sôma: IV.4.18–21 passim),²⁰ this being what would be body as opposed to soul for Plato, and whose soul Plotinus distinguishes from what he variously calls the vegetative soul, following Aristotle, or simply nature, the two terms being cognate in Greek (phutikon and phusis respectively). It is the states of this body-so-qualified which are the basis for the activities of the vegetative soul. Those are conveyed to higher levels by a power of representation, traditionally translated imagination (phantasia): this power operates both downwards from its position at the centre of the soul's faculties, and upwards, enabling it to become aware not only of feelings in the body but also of reason and intellection, whose products can be referred to lower faculties of the soul for action (VI.8.2–3). This double operation of the imagination causes special problems for Plotinus, to which we must return.

It is at the next level, that of sense-perception, that we can observe one of the ways in which Plotinus adapted the Aristotelian account of the soul's role. Let us remember the crucially important point that for Aristotle it was not the soul, but the person by means of the soul, who performed the various functions discussed in the De anima (408b13–15). Plotinus's change consisted in making the soul more active in perception, insisting that sense-perception is an energeia in the sense of active function rather than that of actualization in which it plays so large a part in Aristotle's explanation of cognition. This applies from the level of somewhat undefined feelings, such as discomfort or changes of temperature, in the body (cf. III.6.1.1–24) through all the senses to vision, and ultimately to the intellectual cognition which had traditionally been modeled on it, but might also be taken as its model, a view that might be expected to be held by a Neoplatonist with his top-down view of the world, but in practice appears less often than would naturally follow from such a viewpoint. What is clear is that sense-perception, and vision in particular, differs from intellection primarily, if not exclusively, by having material objects and therefore requiring material organs as intermediaries between the soul and the sensible world with which this area of it is concerned (IV.3.23.3–7).

That sense-perception is an activity of the soul, but one requiring a corporeal environment for it to function means that we are now in the area of soul where Plotinus is particularly concerned to distinguish those activities which do and do not require the body as instrumental. Here it is necessary to bear in mind that, while Plotinus clearly has some scientific interest in perception as well as other operations of the soul in the material world, and while he is prepared to devote some of his treatises exclusively to problems pertaining to that world, all this interest is subsumed in the overriding concern to find the best possible life and the means of attaining it. Since that life for Plotinus consists in living as far as possible at the level of intellect he must be as clear as possible about the ways in which other aspects of life relate to that one, and in what respects they must be adjusted to attain it. So there are two reasons why he should be particularly concerned with sense-perception in general and vision in particular.

One part of the concern with the best life is the quest to maintain the integrity of the soul, or as Plotinus puts it, to make it free from affections (apathes).[21] At the level of sense-perception that is done by maintaining that the soul is not affected by sense-objects, but merely takes cognizance of the stimuli from them which impact on the body, that is the sense-organs. The faculty of sensation, in its various manifestations in the several senses, makes identifications and discriminations (kriseis, traditionally, but not always helpfully, translated as "judgements") (III.6.1–6, passim. Cf. IV.4.23.20–33).

That means that it is in no way passive, and the risk of being unable to maintain the soul's integrity which is present when the soul is exercising lower functions (cf., e.g. I.8.8.30–7) is no longer present – except, of course, insofar as attention to the physical world is a distraction from concentration on higher reality at which we should aim as far as is possible for each one of us (I.4.10.6–21; cf. IV.3.30.13–16).

This concept of sense-perception as active is most clearly set out in the treatise on On Difficulties About the Soul, so, for example, in IV.4.23–5. We should note the definition of sense-perception with which Plotinus begins chapter 23, together with some of the remarks he makes thereafter. He starts by saying: "We must suppose that the perception of sense-objects is for the soul or the living being an act of apprehension, in which the soul understands the quality

attaching to bodies and takes the impression of their *forms"* (lines
1–3, my italics). In chapter 25 he makes the point that the soul must
direct itself toward sense-objects: the soul must be so disposed as to
incline toward sense-objects (lines 2–3).[22] Sense perception is essentially an activity of the soul when it is in the body, and when it uses
the body (23.47–8). In other words we are quite clearly dealing with
the part of the soul whose operations are a function of its close
connection with the body, and so of what those who made this
distinction would call the irrational soul.

Things become less clear when we move up to the faculty of
imagination. At first sight there is no special problem about this
faculty, traditionally called "imagination" but perhaps better described by a neologism like "imaging" to stress the fact that it deals
with some sort of images and avoid the modern connotations of
imagination, for this faculty (*phantasia* or *to phantastikon*) is not
normally the source of presentations which have no basis in reality.
It can, however, recall images which are not currently being presented by the senses, and so forms the basis of memory. Memory, of
course, deals not only with the products of sense-perception, that is
with visual images, but also with other matters, and it is in that area
of its activity that particular difficulties arise for Plotinus. These
difficulties, however, relate to his belief in survival after death and
subsequent reincarnation, matters which are perhaps unlikely to be
of great interest to those who want to know about Plotinus as a
philosopher. Let us be content with saying that the consequences of
that belief led him to duplicate the faculty of imagination, so as to
enable it to remember things which were not needed hereafter while
being able to retain things which were not, or at least were not seen
as, incompatible with life without a body (IV.4.1.1–11). He does,
however, claim that this duplication does not appear during the
course of our normal life, arguing that one of the two faculties is
simply subsumed in the other (IV.3.31.8–16).[23]

What is of more interest in the area of memory is his, at first
encounter, surprisingly modern view that our personality can be
affected by unconscious memories, and indeed claims that it is such
unconscious memories that have the greatest influence on the soul
(IV.4.4.7–14). Whether or not such memories are acquired by perceiving things which we are not at the time aware of perceiving is unfortunately not clear. Nor does Plotinus spell out in detail just how

these memories affect us: he merely says that the imagination is involved not by possession of something but by being such as the things it sees (IV.4.3.7–8).[24]

Before leaving imagination we should note that it does not *start* with images arising from sense-perception as its Greek name might suggest. Even before this it, or at least a lower form of it, is responsible for transmitting to higher levels of soul the feelings that arise in the subsensitive area of the soul, such as the urges associated with physiological drives and the pleasant or uncomfortable sensations that may occur in the body. At this level Plotinus describes it as a sort of faint or vague opinion not subjected to judgment, no longer the opinion which we use as a name for the higher imagination (III.6.4.18–21), an interesting description in view of the fact that there was considerable vacillation among later Neoplatonists about whether imagination and opinion were separate or identical.

One of the more difficult aspects of Neoplatonic psychology is the distinction, corresponding to that between Soul and Intellect in the universal intelligible hierarchy, between reason and intellect, a clear distinction though one sometimes obscured by the fact that Plotinus will use the word *nous* for both (cf., e.g., V.9.8.21–2).[25] The distinction is one that has its origins in Plato insofar as he distinguished two activities of his thinking part of the soul, namely, *noêsis,* a form of thinking relating for Forms alone, and *dianoia,* reason in a narrower sense, which refers to whatever is represented by the second section of the Divided Line in the *Republic* (511d–e) and corresponds roughly to Aristotle's discursive reason, but may also include the cognition and handling of some kinds of Forms. In Plato, however, the activities differ in relation to the objects of cognition: they are both performed by a single part of the soul, and we are given very little information about how they are performed. In Plotinus that is no longer the case. Each activity has its own faculty, and Plotinus shows some concern to ensure that we are aware of the differences, a concern that is perhaps heightened by the awkward fact that the two hypostases, Soul and Intellect, are so difficult to keep apart and do at times appear equipped with each other's functions and characteristics:[26] we shall have to consider, at least briefly, why Plotinus maintained that both existed.

That problem is less acute when we consider the individual soul. Several factors combined to reinforce the idea that the two kinds of apprehension were to be found among the activities of the higher soul. Once that idea is present, Plotinus, who already showed signs of the later Neoplatonic tendency to excessive realism, had no hesitation in seeing them as activities of sections of the soul specifically devoted to them, or rather defined by these very activities. We have already noted the *Republic* distinction between intellection and reasoning. No less important for Plotinus was Aristotle's repeated suggestion in the *De anima* that there was a part of the soul which he called intellect which was somehow different from all the other faculties, in that it might be separate from the body–soul entity to which all the other faculties wholly belonged. For Plotinus that separation was no longer a tentative hypothesis but a firm conviction. It was one for which he could find support in Aristotle, but not in the Platonic tradition, and indeed he presents it as an unorthodox view. It was moreover one which most if not all of his successors rejected on philosophical grounds. So Plotinus tells us that a part of the soul does not come down to body with the rest: "And, if one ought to dare to express one's own view more clearly, contradicting the opinion of others, even our soul does not altogether come down, but there is always something of it in the intelligible" (IV.8.8.1–3). Just where in the intelligible that something is located is sometimes problematic,[27] but the mere fact of its separateness means that it requires a different mode of operation from the reason which is firmly linked to the other faculties and functions in cooperation with them, to the extent that it is reason which receives information and requests for action from the lower soul and then either processes the information or makes decisions about action. This individual intellect might be described as an image of which the hypostasis Intellect is the original, just as Soul as a whole is an image of Intellect (V.1.6.46–7), and Intellect of the One (V.4.2.23–6). It has sometimes been assumed that reason and intellect are the same, and this is an assumption that is easy enough to make because Plotinus's language sometimes fails to distinguish them. That is mainly because, as we have alread mentioned, he will use the word for intellect (*nous*) to stand for reason as well. Usually, however, it is quite clear which of the two faculties he is talking about even when he does not, as he more often does, distinguish them by qualifying the word *nous* when it refers to the reason with words like *logizomenon*, reasoning discursively (VI.9.5.7–9),[28] or *merizôn*, dividing (V.9.8.21).

The second of these qualifications may serve to highlight what for Plotinus was the crucial difference between the two modes of apprehension. The intellect sees its object, or objects – whether they are singular or plural does not matter – all at once and as a whole. Reason, on the other hand, deals with them part by part, moves from one object to another, works from premise to conclusion. It is when that process stops and we, so to speak, arrive at the top end of it, that we move from reasoning to intellection: ". . . it busies itself no more but contemplates, having arrived at unity. It leaves what is called logical activity, about propositions and syllogisms . . . " (I.3.4.17– 19). Other ways in which Plotinus will describe the procedures of this discursive reason are by saying that it moves from one object, for which we may generally substitute premise, to another, and that it deals with objects characterized by division, that is which are separate and discrete entities and remain so. Further its operations take place in time, which appears in the system at the level of Soul and is absent above it (III.7.11.23–35). In addition, even if Plotinus does not often say so, the reason deals, as we have just seen, with propositions. Herein lies perhaps its most striking difference from intellect which either sees the truths which are its objects or does not (I.1.9.12–13): it does not arrive at them by cogitation.

There has been considerable discussion in recent years about what the intellect does when it thinks. Before we look at that we should stop to consider some characteristics of the hypostasis *Nous*. Normally it is seen as composed of Forms of – at least – every species in this world and all the moral and mathematical Forms one would expect a Platonist to establish in his intellectual world. These Forms, and here Plotinus's starting point is Plato's *Sophist* (248e– 249a), are not simply self-subsistent universals but beings which think:[29] that follows from the identifications of Intellect with the Forms (V.1.4.26–9) and of individual Forms with individual intellects (V.9.8.3–7). Thus each Form is capable of thinking and of being the object of thought, realizing that identity of thought and its objects which Aristotle presented as a feature of pure thought in the *De anima* (431a1).[30] That is true both of the individual "components" of Intellect, but also of the hypostasis as a whole. So the hypostasis, and the individual Form/intellects of which it consists and which it is, also correspond to the divine intellect of *Metaphysics* Λ 9, differing importantly in that the thinking of Plotinus's Intellect is not simply a "thinking of thinking" (cf. 1074b34–5) but a thinking of proper intellectual objects, namely its own contents, thereby amalgamating the highest principles of both Plato and Aristotle in the highest form of existence in Plotinus's system.[31]

That is the kind of thinking that the human intellect may do when the soul is free from the interference which Plotinus sees in attention to the sensible world, or even in reasoning about it. It may access it simply by turning its attention in that direction, and away from any distraction offered at lower levels of being (V.3.3.27–9, cf. 42–3 and IV.3.30.11–16). We then do as *Nous* does, insofar as it thinks and is thought, thus becoming like *Nous* in those activities which do not concern its production, and perhaps sometimes regulation, of what is below it. That access is comparable quite simply to seeing something which one did not see at a previous instant, though in this case something is everything, what has been called a *totum simul*. Plotinus illustrates this with a reference to hieroglyphics which he thought, wrongly, were always simply ideograms and never represented sounds, and therefore showed how intellection did not involve process from one thing to the next (V.8.6.1–9). So the intellect's thinking is not a matter of arriving at the truth by means of considering propositions, or even looking at a truth which consists of them. Difficult though this idea may be for those accustomed to translating thought into logical argument, it was once generally accepted that Plotinus's intellection was nonpropositional: what was required was sufficient imagination to see that there could be such a thing.[32] That is perhaps no more difficult than the search for propositions suitable to be the objects of intellection by those who think that even this form of thinking cannot be conceived as happening without some sort of propositions.[33] We may add that if this thinking is propositional it would be difficult to explain how it differed from ordinary discursive reasoning: one would be driven to the unsatisfactory answer that it differs solely by difference, an explanation to which Plotinus does resort when faced with the difficulty of distinguishing between the corresponding hypostases of Intellect and Soul (V.1.3.20–1).[34]

It was primarily the need to explain how one could have knowledge of transcendent reality as constituted by the Forms that moved Plotinus to the view that a part of our souls was a permanent resident in that reality itself, thus "solving" a problem that had troubled

Plato in the *Parmenides* (133b–134b): how can we, in the sensible world, have knowledge of the Forms which are in the intelligible. Those who are interested in Plotinus as a mystic might wish to argue that only by having a part of soul at the level of undivided if not undifferentiated unity are we enabled to take the final step to union with the undifferentiated unity which is the One. What is interesting from the point of view of explaining Plotinus's concept of intellection is that it was the careful consideration of how far intellect could be seen as a unity that led him to require a higher entity which lay above the duality entailed in the difference between knower and known, even if these are in the end taken to be identical: even that kind of difference is absent from the One. Yet intellection is an experience – to avoid the word "process" – which requires the sort of direct contact which might be misunderstood as a manifestation of mysticism. That is exactly what has happened to one of the most frequently cited of Plotinus's alleged pronouncements on his mystic experience, of which the paucity cannot be overemphasized, namely the opening words of IV.8, where he writes:

Often I have woken up out of the body to myself and have entered into myself, going out from all other things; I have seen a beauty wonderfully great and felt assurance that then most of all I belonged to the better part; I have actually lived the best life and come to identify with the divine. . . . setting myself above all the rest of that which, is in the intelligible. (IV.8.1.1–7)[35]

As some recent writers on Plotinus have seen, this passage is really about what happens when we attain to Intellect.[36] There is nothing in it that cannot refer to intellection, and references to beauty, normally a characteristic of the second Hypostasis (cf., e.g., V.8.8),[37] and "the better part," a standard way of talking about the intellect and its activity as opposed to the soul or reason (so, e.g., I.1.13.6; cf. III.5.8.11–15),[38] are strong indications that it is about Intellect and not the One. What is clear here, and in most texts where Plotinus discusses intellection, is that by raising ourselves to the level of Intellect we are in no sense losing our identity. There are two ways in which this retention of individuality follows from other notions of Plotinus. Firstly, and perhaps obviously, because everything that exists in Intellect remains discrete, *qua* both subject and object, notwithstanding the identity of knower and known which is characteristic of this level of cognition, so too must the individual mind which has a place in that structure. Secondly, Plotinus frequently maintains that our intellect is our truest self,[39] a position that would make no sense if our intellect were merely, as Aristotle's may have been and Alexander's was, a single universal and common intellect of the kind which reappears in Averroes and those who thought like him. Both these arguments would work even if, as is possible, Plotinus decided at the end of his career, as he may have done,[40] that the highest part of our soul exists only at the level of the hypostasis Soul, that is in the intelligible in the broad sense in which he some-times, most conspicuously in the treatise "On the omnipresence of being" (VI.4–5),[41] uses the term *noêton* to cover both Intellect and Soul. He does so because the contents of Soul are a manifestation of the movement from the unity of Intellect to the diversity of the physical world and so are similar to, but more discrete than, those of intellect (cf. IV.3.5.8–11). They are nevertheless still part of the intelligible. Thus, our identity would be more clearly marked there and the possibility that our highest faculty is part of a shared one would disappear. If he did make this change a consequence would be that the normal goal of the soul's ascent would have been the hypostasis Soul: that would not preclude occasional ascents to the higher level of Intellect any more than having our highest part in Intellect, with that Intellect as the normal goal of our ascent, precluded the occasional ascent to the One itself.

In the same way the hypostasis Intellect was necessary to provide for various requirements both inherited from Plotinus's predecessors and inherent in his concept of the intelligible world. If we take Plotinus's starting point to have been Plato, he had to find a place for the Forms,[42] entities which were essentially transcendent and in no way involved in the structuring or governance of the physical world which depended for its existence on theirs. At the same time there had to be, for a realist like Plotinus, an ontological level correspond-ing to the psychological state of the knower's identity with the known which he accepted from Aristotle by way of some refinements and clarifications made by Alexander of Aphrodisias.[43] The mutual relations of what existed at that level would be characterized by the corresponding degree of unity between its "components." So this level had to be below that of the One from which it was separated by an otherness consisting in the duality inherent in having a distinction between knower and known, or the objects which populated the

world of Forms. At the same time, at least when Plotinus was concerned to set out the formal structure of his intelligible world rather
than merely emphasize the differences between it and the physical
world, Intellect had to be separate from Soul. While Intellect was
close to being a unit, Soul's responsibility for the physical world, as
well as its role of mediating the unity of Intellect to the diffuse existence of our world, entailed a loss of unity. With this went the substi-
tution of transition and process for immediate cognition and eternal
rest, and of time for eternity. Plotinus does not seem to have dealt
with the difficulties this last difference raises when one is confronted
with the fact that in his system Soul exists eternally no less than
Intellect and the One.[44] His explanation that time comes into existence with soul because it is linked with the process and transition
involved in Soul's peculiar mode of cognition (III.7.11.20–30) does
not seem to betray an awareness of, let alone provide a solution for,
the problem produced by his view that Soul is both eternal and also
linked to time, which is "created" with it (cf. III.7.11 passim). On the
other hand this very problem may have been what allowed Plotinus to
consider locating his individual intellect at the level of Soul, a position indicated by certain texts in the late treatises I.1 and V.3 which
are not, however, conclusive. In any case it should not be forgotten
that when Plotinus treats Soul as virtually identical with intellect in
an intelligible world which is opposed to the sensible, he will name
intellect among the ingredients of that level of being.

We have departed from the ascending order of exposition to look at
Plotinus's reasons for having an intellect other and higher than the
discursive reason. We must now return to consider the functions of
that reason. It has, in common with imagination, an intermediate
position which gives it two kinds of premises to work with. That is
to say it has one function in relation to what is above, another to
material presented to it by, or from, the lower faculties of the soul. In
fact Plotinus quite explicitly describes the soul as an intermediate
entity "occupying a middle position among the things that exist,
being at one end of the intelligible ... sharing a border with the
sensible world" (IV.8.7.5–9), and will even speak of it as living on a
boundary (IV.4.3.11–12). This description fits both Soul as a whole
and also the human reason which is that one of our faculties whose
operations, dividing in its reasoning what is united in intellect and
taking a part in the management of what is below, are closest to and

most characteristic of Soul as a hypostasis, a similarity which was to become even more important for the later Platonists in spite of the fact that they abandoned Plotinus's undescended intellect.[45]

Let us now look at these two functions of the reason. In the management of the lower soul and its requirements it approximates to Aristotle's practical reason, though Plotinus does not set out the processes by which it makes those decisions which are in its province. We are told in general that the imagination will present to reason images of urges in the lower soul, and that the reason will then deal with these. It has a further role in dealing with material from below, namely responsibility for the inferential parts of perception. Thus when we perceive something through the senses it can be referred to a standard which reason has be virtue of its juxtaposition with intellect. When impressions (tupoi) are produced by the senses reason will compare these with the impressions which it already has, in an appropriate dematerialized form, and thereby be able to pronounce on their identity: this is seen as a process of recognition (cf. V.3.2.11–13).[46] Similarly reason will decide whether or not something which appears to be a case of X will fit the standard of X that it has within it (V.3.4.13–17). Plotinus talks of fitting something to the form within, using that as a means of making a perceptual judgment in the same way as one may judge straightness by using a ruler (I.6.3.1–5; cf. VI.7.6.2–7).[47] As in all such passages we are faced with a problem about the exact meaning of the word usually translated as "judging" (krinein): recent writers have tended to translate it as "discriminate" rather than "judge."[48] In any case, it is clear that in the present context we are concerned with making perceptual identifications against a set of standards which are located in our mind by virtue of our relation with higher reality rather than as a result of some inductive process which leads to a concept based on accumulated sense-data alone.

This, then, is how reason deals with information about the sensible world, using what are ultimately the contents of Soul and Intellect to enable it to do so. It will also handle these in a way which enables us to think about them rather than merely having the immediate, but in the strictest sense supra-rational – because intuitive rather than discursive – knowledge of them which we have already discussed. This it is able to do with the help of the imagination, which makes the Forms available, in the form of images, as material

for reasoning just as it presents sense-data to the reason for processing; it also causes us to be aware of the existence of the Forms and
intellection directed to them. Plotinus conceives this as a kind of
reflection (cf. IV.3.30 passim). In fact Plotinus uses the same word,
impressions, qualified by "something like" (*hoion*), that he uses of
data presented to reason from the senses (V.3.2.9–11). Whatever the
source of its material, reason deals with it in a way that seems more
familiar than many of the operations of Plotinus's soul. It starts from
premises and moves through them to a conclusion (cf., e.g., I.3.5.1–
4), and is able to produce knowledge that is synthetic rather than
merely analytic. Contrasting the real intellect with what Plotinus
often calls "the so-called intellect" or "the intellect of the soul" he
writes "our so-called intellects which get their content from premises and are able to understand what is said, and reason discursively
and observe what follows, contemplating reality as the result of a
process of reasoning since they did not have it before but were empty
before they learnt, though they were intellects" (I.8.2.10–15). Nevertheless the purpose of the reasoning process, as Plotinus sees it, is to
arrive at the sort of truth that is available in Intellect by virtue of its
very nature (cf., e.g., V.3.5.25–8), and so he thinks of successful
reasoning achieving that kind of knowledge. When it does so it has
completed its task (IV.4.12.5–10; cf. I.3.4.9–20).

We have already mentioned the way in which more than one
Neoplatonist thought of reason as corresponding most closely to the
macrocosmic soul, a middle being between the sensible world and
the world of intellect. That view of reason should be borne in mind
when we consider that it is at the level of discursive reason that
Plotinus often thought our self, what he often calls "the we," is to be
found. That view contrasts with another, by which we are really our
intellects. It requires some explanation insofar as his doctrine of the
undescended soul, with a part of us permanently in intellect, and
also the object of our aspirations, would suggest that the undescended intellect, and not the reason which operates below it, is
what we really are.

That raises the question whether or not what we derive our existence from, or even what we are at the highest level identical with,
is our own individual Form. That is a question that has received
considerable if still inconclusive discussion, with the majority favor-
ing the existence of such a Form largely on the grounds that Plotinus

attached a special importance to the individual.[49] Even if we concede
the motivation, the expression of such an attitude does not require
the existence of a Form for each of us since Plotinus's system of ever
increasing plurality in proportion to distance from the One, but with
everything below ultimately derived from what is above, provides
for an intelligible basis for everything that exists either at a lower
level of the intelligible than that basis or even in the sensible world
itself. Thus, all individual souls are dependent on an intellect but
exist in a more diffuse state (IV.3.5.8–11), a text which unfortunately
does not show decisively whether each soul depends on a separate
intellect, or whether there are clusters of souls attached to all the
intellects in the intelligible. "Intelligible" is crucial: one cannot
simply say, clearly and decisively, "Intellect." That is because, as we
have already seen, Plotinus will sometimes talk about Soul and Intellect as if they were one rather than two of the separate levels of
intelligible being which he strictly maintains that there are: neither
more nor fewer than three (cf., e.g., V.1.10.1–4).

This tendency not to keep the hypostases clearly separate at all
times aggravates the difficulty of answering our question. It is clear
that intellects exist in the intelligible. So the highest part of our
soul, being an intellect, must be in the intelligible: the intelligible
may, however, be Soul rather than Intellect (VI.4.14.2–3). Reuniting
ourselves with this intellect of ours, and ultimately transcending it,
by union, or reunion, with whatever lies "above," be it the One or
the One and Intellect, remains a fundamental aspiration for Neoplatonists. This is so whether that reunion means turning ourselves
away from other preoccupations to our intellect's perpetual activity,
as for Plotinus himself, or rising to it as for Iamblichus and those
who came after him. Since, however, all entities are able, and seek,
to rise to a higher level than the one where they usually are, our
ability to be at the level of Intellect does not in itself show that the
highest part of our soul actually resides there rather than in Soul. If
it did we should have an individual Form, because that is what the
contents of Intellect are. Moreover, there can be no question of us
having our highest soul permanently in the One, since it cannot be
there at all. Thus any argument that seeks to maintain that we are
where we can go must fail. So we can only conclude that we cannot
determine where Plotinus eventually decided that the highest part
of our soul is to be found. If he did not himself make up his mind on

a question so important for a Platonist we might take that as impressive evidence for the open-minded way in which Plotinus is increasingly recognized as having done his philosophy.[50]

NOTES

1 This is also true of other aspects of Plotinus's philosophy, cf., e.g., Gerson 1990, 186 and 191–201.

2 A critique of Stoic materialist accounts of the soul is to be found in IV.7, chapters 3–8[3]. Some of the material in this treatise is traditional, but there is no reason to think that it does not represent Plotinus's own views too. On this critique cf. Blumenthal 1971b, 10–11; O'Meara 1985, 252–5; Emilsson 1991, 151–8.

3 For a recent summary of some such views and modern argumentation against them cf. Robinson 1993, 1–25.

4 "Which acquires it," because Plotinus, following hints in Plato's Timaeus (34b and 36e), thought of body as being somehow contained in soul (IV.3.22.7–11).

5 These matters are discussed in Blumenthal 1971a: its conclusions have been generally accepted.

6 The fullest treatment is in VI.4–5, *On the Presence of Being, One and the Same, Everywhere as a Whole.*

7 An explanation that would not have been open to Plato, since the nerves and their function were not discovered for another century after his death.

8 For an extended commentary on these chapters cf. Hellemen-Elgersma 1980.

9 It is not clear from these texts on their own whether the world soul is included in the one that is being discussed, but other texts show that it is; cf. Blumenthal 1971a.

10 For an attack on this view which precedes most of the recent debate cf. Lloyd 1981, esp. 1–48. See also Irwin 1988, 248–68. If these interpretations are correct, then Plotinus's belief in formal principles, and possibly Forms (see below), of individuals may reflect another case of his understanding Aristotle better than many of his subsequent interpreters.

11 Cf. 99–100 below.

12 A subject he found sufficiently difficult to devote a three day discussion to it in response to questions from Porphyry, cf. Porphyry, *Life of Plotinus* 13.10–11. Though it has been asserted that this discussion is recorded in IV.3–5, there is no evidence to substantiate this claim. For some opinions cf. now L. Brisson in Brisson 1992, 261.

13 Some of this discussion draws on the Peripatetic tradition, and Alexander of Aphrodisias in particular, cf. Blumenthal 1968.

14 Cf. Blumenthal 1971b, 18–19.

15 *NE* 1102a23–8. Cf. 1094b11–14.

16 Plotinus uses the word *logizomenon*, which certainly usually means discursive reason, but the context suggests that he is using it as the equivalent of Plato's usual word for the top section of the soul, *logistikon*, a term Plotinus normally avoids.

17 Here again Plotinus uses a word other than the normal tripartition term. i.e., *thumoumenon* as opposed to the standard *thumoeides*.

18 Cf. Alcinous (a.k.a. Albinus), *Didaskalikos* XXIX, 58 Whittaker (with French translation, and title *Enseignement des doctrines de Platon*) = 182.19–31 Hermann.

19 Anger is the translation most often used for the word *thumos* which forms the first part of *thumoeides*, Plato's word for this section of the soul, conventionally rendered the "spirited" or "passionate" part. Plotinus himself will use *thumos* for the "part" as well.

20 On this see further Blumenthal 1971b, 58–62.

21 The noun corresponding to this concept (*apatheia*) is very rare in Plotinus and, when it does occur, refers only once (I.2.6.25) to the soul.

22 On the active nature of sense perception in Plotinus cf. Blumenthal 1971b, 69–75; Emilsson 1988, 126–37; Wagner 1993, 36–47.

23 For further discussion of imagination see Blumenthal 1971b, 86–94; Watson 1988, 98–103. I do not, however, see what grounds Watson has for his claim that Plotinus – and other Neoplatonists – had a negative and suspicious attitude to imagination.

24 A notion neatly encapsulated in Trouillard 1955a, 38: "Dis-moi ce dont tu te souviens, et je te dirai qui tu es."

25 It is, however, generally clear from the context in which sense Plotinus is using the word, since he usually supplies descriptions indicating the definition or activity of one or the other, or both, as at I.1.8.1–3, VI.9.5.7–9.

26 Cf. Armstrong 1971; Blumenthal 1974.

27 Cf. 96, 97, 100–1 below.

28 See above 86–7, with note 16.

29 It has been argued that being and thinking entail, or are equivalent to, life, cf., e.g., Hadot 1960.

30 And also implicit in the original meanings of the words used of Intellect and intellection: in Homer they meant simply to see, and this sense of immediate apprehension of an object was never entirely lost.

31 That contributes in no small measure to Plotinus's conviction that Intellect must have such contents, one that the opening lines of V.9.3 suggest

was not shared by all of his possible audience: whether he was referring to Peripatetics or others one cannot tell.

32 On nonpropositional thought in Plotinus see esp. Lloyd 1970, 1986, and 1990, 164–6: here Lloyd suggests that the whole which is the object of intellection "occupies the place of the genus of existence or being" and that "its non-complexity belongs to it as a phenomenological or intentional object while its complexity belongs to it as an extensional object." Cf. also Alfino 1988, directed in the first place against Sorabji 1982.

33 For this approach cf. Sorabji 1980, 217–19; 1982; 310–14; and 1983 152–6.

34 On Plotinus's use of "other" and "otherness" for such purposes cf. Blumenthal 1974, 207.

35 I have altered Armstrong's translation in the last sentence: *huper pan to noêton* need not mean, as he translates "above all else in Intellect."

36 Cf. Schroeder 1992, 4–5; O'Meara 1993, 104–5. For the traditional view cf., e.g., Rist 1967, 56 with n4, on which one might comment that the Arabic version cannot show that the Greek refers to the One, but only that the translator so understood it; Hadot 1993, 25–6.

37 Cf. Rist 1967, 53–65; O'Meara 1993, 94–7.

38 The latter passage depends on the identification of Zeus with Intellect and Aphrodite with Soul: on this cf. Hadot 1990 ad. loc.

39 But not always, since there are a number of texts where it is located at the level of reason, cf. Blumenthal 1971b, 109–111; O'Daly 1973, chs. 2 and 3. Gerson 1992, 254–7 thinks that the real self is always at the level of intellect.

40 See Blumenthal 1974, 217–19.

41 On this cf. Blumenthal 1974, 211–12.

42 Plotinus shows no sign of modern suspicions, based largely if not entirely on G. E. L. Owen's attempt to redate the *Timaeus* (Owen 1953), that Plato abandoned the Forms after the *Parmenides* or relegated them to the slowest of back burners. (A recent summary of the problem may be found in the introductory chapter to *The Cambridge Companion to Plato*, Kraut 1992, 14–19.) Notions of development did not complicate Plotinus's or the other Neoplatonists' reading of fourth-century philosophy.

43 On these see still Armstrong 1960, 405–11. For a later and more skeptical discussion cf. Szlezák 1979, 135–43.

44 Except by sometimes attributing to Soul the very characteristics that normally differentiate Intellect from it. On this cf. Blumenthal 1974, 209–16.

45 On this way of looking at soul in Plotinus's successors see Blumenthal 1988, 109–18.

46 In his new commentary on V.3 W. Beierwaltes distinguishes between

reason (*dianoia*) and the soul's *nous* in this area: most would regard them as different ways of referring to the same thing; cf. Beierwaltes 1991a, 103–6.

47 The "other soul" in this passage is clearly the level of reason as opposed to that of sensation.

48 This is not, of course, a problem peculiar to Plotinus: it already arises over the *De anima* where there is no question of standards derived from "above." Cf., e.g., Ebert 1983. For Plotinus see now Emilsson 1988, 121–2 and the comments of Wagner 1993, 38 n2.

49 Cf. Rist 1963 and 1970; Blumenthal 1966; Armstrong 1977a.

50 I should like to thank Professor Gerson for his comments on the penultimate version of this article which enabled me to make a number of improvements and clarify some obscurities. I should add that I have not always followed his suggestions!

5 Essence and existence in the *Enneads*

I

An explicit distinction between essence and existence is first attributed to the Arabic philosophers Al Farabi (c. 870–950) and
Avicenna (c. 980–1037). The nature or essence of any finite being
can be conceived separately from its existence that appears to be a
perfection "superadded" or accidental to its nature.[1] Pierre Hadot[2]
has traced the roots of this distinction even further back to
Boethius, and later Neoplatonism, and in the latter case to two
principal sources: (1) the distinction between absolute being and
determinate being (respectively being-infinitive, *to einai*, and
being-participle, *to on*) found in the anonymous *Commentary on
the Parmenides* (ascribed to Porphyry) and in Marius Victorinus.[3]
And (2) the late Neoplatonic distinction (of Proclus, Damascius,[4]
and Victorinus) between pre-existence (*huparxis*) and substance
(*ousia*), that is, between pure being in its simplicity prior to all
things and substance as the determinate subject taken together
with all its accidents. I shall argue here that the roots of this distinction are also to be found in Plotinus.[5] The essence or substance
of every finite being is radically dependent upon the being or existence which comes to it from the Good. Plotinus's conception is
particularly important not only because it results in a new view of
the meaning of determinate being but also because it helps to cast
light on the character of the essence–existence distinction itself. Is
it a logical or a real distinction?[6] If real, what philosophical basis is
there for supposing that being should be so distinguished? I shall
argue that in the *Enneads* the distinction between determinate essence, or substance, and unrestricted existence is real, that it is to

be found in different ways in all finite beings – compound bodies, soul, and intellect – and that what we see for the first time in Plotinus is not the explicit distinction with its later logical clarity so much as a landscape of the relations of determinate being with the One which makes that later distinction possible.

II

In relation to the chronology of Plotinus's works the essence–existence distinction is most apparent in the later works, particularly in VI.7 and VI.8 (38 and 39 in the chronological order), but a similar understanding can be found as early as VI.9 (9 in the chronological order). The sophisticated nonanthropomorphic notion of divine causality worked out in the *Gross-Schrift* (III.8; V.8; V.5; II.9; 30–3 respectively in the chronological order)[7] and also in VI.7 and VI.8[8] is especially important for understanding how determinate substances, like souls or sensible compounds, are related to intellect and the One from within their own being but at the same time from above their immediate nature or composition.

III

A few words first about vocabulary. Of the many terms and phrases Plotinus employs to talk about the being of things the most common are, first, the infinitive of the verb "to be" with the neuter article, *to einai*, to signify "the being" which may be attributed to anything, intellect, soul, body, matter, even the One; second, the neuter participial form of the verb "to be," *to on*, and the plural, *ta onta*, to refer to intelligible "being" and "the real beings" which form Intellect's content, or to being as one of the all-pervading "greatest kinds" which Plotinus adapts from Plato's *Sophist* (namely, being, motion, rest, sameness, and otherness); and third, *ousia*, traditionally translated "substance" or "entity," and sometimes "essence" (equivalent to the general expression, "what it is," *ho esti*, since *ousia* can indicate not only "stuff" and individual substance, but also that in the substance which makes it real).[9] Generally, *ousia* and *to on* are coterminous, but occasionally *ousia* seems to mean something more than *to on*, as when number is referred to as "the very *ousia* of being" (VI.6.9.27).[10] However, *to einai*, *to on*, and *ousia* are frequently applied in general ways, just as the terms *hupostasis* and *huparxis* often denote the basic "reality" or "existence" of anything.[11] Plotinus comes close to an explicit distinction between essence and existence as such in a late work, VI.8.17.24–5, when he argues that the One has neither his being (*to einai*) nor his being what he is (*to hopoios estin einai*) from another.[12] But this distinction cannot strictly be applied, he argues, for the One is pure self-dependent being or existence, cause of existence for everything else, whereas all other beings are not only self-existents but "something else" too, that is, determinate substances (in the case of intellect and soul) or derivative qualities and quantities in matter (in the case of physical compounds) (cf. VI.8.21.30–3).[13] What then does it mean "to be" in the different cases of matter, body, soul, and intellect, and why should these form an ascending hierarchy?

IV

Everything has some form (or privation) of being, from the rich and varied being of Intellect to the minimal being or nonbeing of matter.[14] Matter has a sort of minimal *existence*, although it possesses no attributive "being" of any formal kind (such as substance, quality, quantity, etc.) (II.4.8–13; III.6.8–10). By comparison with the intelligible world, "the being" of matter, and of bodies founded upon it, is "the being of things which do not exist" (III.6.6.31–2).[15] Nonetheless, even if matter is deprived of formal being, its privative relation to being means that "though it is non-existent, it has a certain kind of existence in this way" (II.4.16.3). It is just "what it is, matter," nothing actual, merely potential (II.5.5.1–7) so that its "being" and its "substance" lie in its being potentially everything (II.5.5.27–33). Thus, even though matter is evil in itself, the physical universe would not exist "if matter did not exist" (I.8.7.2–4). Matter, then, may be said to consist in a minimal, deprived existence which is nonbeing because its existence implies privation of all form.

V

Body, in turn, is only a "shadow" of being, founded ultimately upon nonbeing (VI.2.7.12–14; VI.3.8.30–7). It is not true *ousia* or substance, Plotinus argues, because it is composed of elements posterior to substance, namely, qualities and matter. Individual bodily compounds are, therefore, not true subjects of predication, for they do not possess the kind of self-dependence one requires to treat them as true substances (II.6.1.42–9; 2.11–14).[16] However, this is not Plotinus's only view of body's being. In one sense, body is a compound of its constituents, composed of qualities and matter (II.7.3.1–5; VI.3.8.19–23). Thus, Plotinus can even call body a "second evil" to the degree it participates in matter's destitution of being (I.8.4.1–5).

V.1

From another perspective, body appears to be a locus of gradable being which ranges from the grosser, less interconnected or organized element, earth, to the most mobile element, fire, which is "already escaping bodily nature" (III.6.6.41).[17] In Plotinus's curious language, fire has "less" and earth "more" of body:

the more a thing is a body the more it is affected, earth more than other things, and the other elements in the same proportion, for the other elements come together into one again when they are parted, if there is no obstacle in the way, but when every kind of earthy body is cut, each part stays separate for ever; just as with things of which the natural powers are "failing" . . . so the thing which has most completely become body, since it has approached most nearly to non-being, is too weak to collect itself again into a unity. (III.6.6.53–61)

At first glance, this seems absurd. Why should any element be more real or have more being than any other? Elsewhere, Plotinus denies that participation in being admits of degrees or that there is a direct correlation between being and unity. "It is possible," he remarks at VI.2.11.15–16, "to have no less a real existence, but to be less one. For an army or a chorus has no less being than a house, but all the same it is less one." Plotinus probably refers to the Stoic notion of degrees of unity, according to which organisms are most "one" in the sense that they are "unified," whereas ships, towers, and houses are one in that they are "joined together," and finally armies and choirs are units of discrete individuals.[18] Here in III.6.6, Plotinus appears to mean not that fire and earth have more or less existence but rather that their determinate being or natures can be regarded as richer or poorer by virtue of their nearness to, or distance from, the intelligible world. In part, this view is the product of an outdated cosmology according to which fire in its upward motion borders upon the spiritual universe.[19] However, Plotinus also wants to relate degrees of determinate being to degrees of organizational complexity.[20] This is not plausible in the case of earth and fire, but may be more comprehensible if we think of the growth and dissolution of natural organisms in general, for these would seem to require a principle other than their present structure to account for their organizational complexity and unity. Greater or lesser capacity for unity, Plotinus implies, accounts for different relations to intelligible being. Earth is least intelligible, or "closer to non-being," because it is least capable of unification or of more developed organizational complexity (III.6.6.41–9). The other elements are more intelligible because of their capacity for greater unity (III.6.6.53–64). According to this perspective, then, bodies are not just their present structure of qualities and matter. They also require a higher principle to give them unity.

V.2

What is this principle and how is it related to individual compound natures? An early work, VI.9, gives a clearer picture of what Plotinus means.[21] Again, Plotinus argues that degrees of unity give rise to degrees of being (VI.9.1.27–8): "what has separate parts, like a chorus, is furthest from the One, and what is a continuous body is nearer" (1.32–3). Even the soul which is multiple, though not composed of bodily parts, has the "one" as *sumbebêkos pôs,* that is, like an attribute of its being, rather than its very essence (30–44). In VI.9.2, Plotinus goes on to argue (against Aristotle) that "one man" and "man" do not mean the same thing, since being and unity are different, and being like any multiplicity requires unity for "if an individual thing loses its one it will not exist at all" (2.15–16). A necessary distinction is, therefore, to be drawn between what a thing is, that is, its multiple "essence" ("man," "living being," and "rational" are many parts, 2.19–20) and the unity which makes it what it is and which is the cause of its existence ("And these many are bound together by the one," 2.20; "It is by the one that all beings are beings," 1.1). This unity is present in the thing's organization, but it is also the immanent principle of the organization, distinct from the organization itself, and to be traced to its external cause in the "uniform" (5.27) nature of intellect and finally to the One itself. I shall return to this below. For the present let me spell out some of the consequences of this distinction between the multiple essence and the unitary cause of existence.

Unity and being are not just conceptually but really distinct. What causes the composite thing to be one is really distinct from the composite itself, and if this unity causes the existence of the thing, then it must be virtually identical with that thing's existence.[22] To put this another way, the existence of individual things should properly be explicated by reference to the composite's unifying principle, and not simply to the composite itself. In the language of the early chapters of VI.7, what we want to see is not just what the composite is, but *why* it is the way it is, and if this is to be a proper principle of explanation, then it must not be abstractly separate from the composite, but in a special way internal to the intelligibility of composite things.[23] In other words, we have need of a broader perspective in order to grasp the potentially intelligible nature of body. What is this perspective and how does Plotinus manage to bridge the gap between the intelligible world and the physical composite?

V.3

Plotinus's theory of the *logos* (forming principle or principle of explanation) helps to bridge the gap between intelligible being and determinate physical things.[24] According to Plotinus's arguments in his treatise *On Nature and Contemplation and the One*, the *logos* is a real, objective entity at work in nature (cf. III.8.2). Just as in human craftsmen there is a principle which remains unmoved "according to which they will make their works," so too in nature there must be a similar power, he argues, which operates not by planning or reasoning, but simply by being what it is. Its being is not action or doing (*praxis*) but a creative activity which makes individual natures or *logoi* and these in turn, while remaining unmoved in themselves, give rise to the various qualities in different physical things: ". . . in animals and plants the forming principles are the makers and nature is a forming principle, which makes another principle, its own product, which gives something to the substrate, but stays unmoved itself" (III.8.2.27–30). The notion expressed here is not dissimilar from Aristotle's view in *Physics* VIII that the souls or vital principles of natural organisms function as unmoved movers,[25] an idea which has been compared recently by biologists to the DNA base, the natural unmoved mover of modern science.[26] The central point, however, for Plotinus is that these *logoi* function as productive forces in the physical world, not by reasoning or by action, but as contemplative acts, which is to say that they make and are capable of being recognized, because the vision of the whole is, as it were, encoded in their very being.[27] According to this perspective of internal causality, body is not a compound of qualities and matter, but its definition must also include a *logos* or causal principle of unity and organization which, in Plotinus's summary description in II.7.3, contains all the qualities, enters matter, and perfects body in matter, so that body is "matter and an indwelling *logos*" (12). In II.7.3 he gives no reasons, but in VI.7.4 and VI.8 it becomes clear that proper definition requires not only the fact of composite existence but the "why" something is as it is, a point also insisted upon by Aristotle.[28]

Plotinus characteristically argues that the *logos* is in matter but immaterial since it is not "composed" (IV.7.4.18–21). What he means by "immaterial" in this context is simply "not physically composed of qualities and matter," which is to say that, unlike the quality "white" in this individual compound, the *logos*, strictly speaking, is not in matter as a quality inheres in a substratum; rather it is directly what it is, that is, substance or soul.[29] For Plotinus, as for Alexander of Aphrodisias, soul is present in body, but not as a quality *in* body.[30] However, whereas Alexander or Aristotle insist that soul is the form or act *of* the body, Plotinus holds that soul and its content cannot be "of" the body as body's inseparable act, for they are substance "before" belonging to the individual body.[31] This line of explication may not look promising, but Plotinus's view of the relation of the *logos* to the individual compound is more comprehensible if we forget for a moment about immateriality and just concentrate on the extent of the *logos* function itself.

Plotinus recognizes that the *logos* tends to be identified with the compound and that as an enmattered *logos* it is "inseparable from matter" (II.7.3.12–14). The problem for him is the need to grasp its creative function, for when it is "in" the physical shape, it is the brother of the creative, immaterial *logos* and quite "dead," no longer having the power to make (III.8.2.25–34).[32] Consequently Plotinus stresses that even if the *logos* is inseparable from matter, it should be contemplated as a pure and self-dependent form if we are to understand its creative significance (II.7.3.12–14; VI.7.4.24–30). Why should this be necessary?

Plotinus gives a powerful analysis of what this means in practice in VI.7.2 in an extended discussion of the meaning of divine causality in relation to the *Timaeus's* description of the Demiurge's making of the world. Plato represents the Demiurge planning and acting like a human craftsman, but divine forethought cannot be like this, Plotinus argues, for to represent God as having to work things out by reasoning would be to impute an anthropomorphic deficiency to the intelligible world (VI.7.1). We see a part and work out laboriously its relation to the whole, but in each divine act everything is complete without reasoning and already included in the totality of intelligible being so that we can reason out the purpose in things later. At the beginning of chapter 2, Plotinus distinguishes the being of a particular object or event (i.e., the essence, *ti ên einai*, the reason why or *dioti*), and the object or fact of existence itself (*hoti*). When we look at physical objects, he argues, we generally see the fact of existence and the cause of existence as separate from one another. But this is not always the case: for instance, we find the fact and the cause identical in the understanding of what an eclipse is (2.4–12).[33] Perhaps, he suggests, we should regard each object as a cause (*dia ti*): "for what each thing is, it is because of this" (16). And this is what we mean by the "substance" (*ousia*) of the thing. In other words, when we try to understand what the meaning of intellect is from a consideration of physical objects (or for that matter the meaning of any scientific model for the understanding of individual events),[34] we have to enter into the nature of the object before us in such a way that the cause is not an abstraction.[35] What Plotinus tries to get at here is not so much the distinction between the formal essence and the thing itself as the meaning of the actual existence of the concrete object in relation to the cause of its existence which is not abstractly separate from it. He states, therefore, that when he says that the substance of each thing is its causal essence, he is referring not to the form as cause of being; rather he means that "if you unfold each form itself back upon itself, you will find the cause in it" (2.16–19). Thus, even the fact of a living thing's (and later in chapters 9–12 a nonliving thing's)[36] existence is seen to be neither accidental nor simply identical with either its matter or form, but rather to be derived from its intellectual nature, where "that it is" and "why it is" are one (2.45–6).[37] In the *logos*, in soul, and finally in intellect, then, Plotinus insists on the inner identity of the causal principle of unity and the existence of the finite being.

According to Plotinus's argument, we tend to distinguish existence and essence in our perception of physical objects and to see them as unconnected or separate from one another, whereas in fact in order to get a comprehensive, intelligible view of any object, we have to grasp their inherent connectedness in the form or *logos* of the thing. This does not appear to mean that essence *is* existence, or vice versa, in soul or intellect, only that what a thing is and the fact that a thing is are connected in the unity of the *logos* which makes the compound and keeps it in being.[38] How we are to conceive of this unity we have at this point of the argument no idea.

VI

There are several obvious difficulties with this account. The most pressing is the problem of soul itself. How is the *logos* to be fitted to soul? It is difficult to see why soul or intellect should be composite at all and if so in what sense. Why cannot soul be the ultimate principle of unity to account for the composite organization of the body? Is there any sense whatever in talking about soul as a "one nature which is many" (VI.2.4.32) or about soul having more being or existing more than physical things (cf. VI.9.9.7–13)? Furthermore, if the cause of being and the fact of existence are identical in the intelligible world, then why should there be any need for a further principle (namely, the Good) to explicate this identity? These questions have an important bearing on this enquiry since we want to see what grounds there are for an essence–existence structure in soul and intellect.

VI.1

Following Plato's *Timaeus* (35a1–4), Plotinus argues that soul must have a double substance or *ousia:* soul springs from an indivisible substance, but also has another substance "to be divided in bodies." Yet is remains indivisible in that it is present in all the parts as a whole and in any one part as a whole (IV.2.1.64–6; IV.1. passim). This duality, however, is really a function of soul's embodiment. The question still remains why should soul *itself* be multiple and admit of a composition different from, but analogous to, that of bodies; and what is distinctive about the composition of soul that renders it a substance in the true sense by contrast with the derivative unity of body?

In an early work, V.9, Plotinus insists that the analysis of physical compounds into matter and form on the analogy of art should be transposed into the intelligible universe, for soul receives its forming principles from intellect "as in the souls of artists the forming principles for their activities come from their arts" (3.32–3). In relation to intellect, soul serves as matter and its form is "the intellect in it," which is itself a duality: "one intellect being like the shape on the bronze and the other like the man who makes the shape in the bronze" (3.23–4). Soul's composition, then, is a function of its causal dependence upon a principle which operates within it but which is nonetheless distinct from it, namely, intellect. And the same in turn is true of intellect, for it too depends upon the One in a similar manner. Intellect comes from the One as an unformed potency which in turning back to its source becomes a formed substance.[39] Or, in other terms, "otherness and movement" "grew out of" the One and made matter (i.e., intelligible matter) which in turning to the One receives definition (II.4.5.28–33). The difference between intelligible and lower (sensible) matter, according to Plotinus, is that intelligible matter is perfectly formed as a thinking life, whereas the matter of the physical world "becomes something defined, but not alive or thinking, a decorated corpse" (II.4.5.15–18). The central point is this: against Aristotle's doctrine of intellect, Plotinus holds that all intellection involves duality and multiplicity, which in turn requires a unifying principle. Therefore, the duality of intelligible matter and form must exist in both soul or intellect. Otherwise, they would be pure unity (VI.2.4.24–8).

But how should we conceive this composition in concrete terms? What makes the cases of soul and body so different? Why should soul be "substance" or "real being," while body is only an imitation, something put together from matter and a spurious form (that is, qualities, quantities, etc.)? In a later work, VI.2, Plotinus tries to give an answer to this question. The soul cannot be a pure unity, because were it so, he argues, it would not have made a "discrete plurality" (*diestêkos plêthos*), that is, a plurality of distinct or non-unified bodies (5.8–9). On the basis of what soul "does to other things" (5.14–15), therefore, Plotinus concludes that the soul itself must be a "one-many," that is, a single nature which possesses a plurality of functions or powers, but not a unity compounded out of many parts (4.30–2; 6.13–20). What does this mean? Is being a soul anything like being a stone? Plotinus argues that being and soul-being are not externally related in the same way as the two terms "white" and "man," or being and stone-being are related to one another. To add soul to being is not to qualify being externally. What soul has is identical with its substance. Therefore, soul is a particular being (*ti on*) in the sense that it is an individual substance pure and simple (*tis ousia monon*). "White man" is an individual being in the sense that a qualitative addition has been made to "man" from outside its substance. Soul, then, is a compound of being and soul-being from *within* its own intelligible nature in such a way that the qualitative difference (*to toionde*) is not an external attribute but characterizes its proper nature (5.17–6.13).

Again, what does this mean in concrete terms? If the soul is a source and principle of existence and life, then it must be a one – many of existence and life, Plotinus goes on to argue, not as a single *logos* or definition, but as an underlying reality (*hupokeimenon*) which is simultaneously one and yet also the many powers it manifests "as if it cannot bear its being to be one when it is capable of being all the things it is" (VI.2.6.17–19). Thus, Plotinus concludes, being, life, movement, rest, sameness, and difference, all the "greatest kinds" of Plato's *Sophist* (248a–259d), are present in soul directly as multiple reflections of its self-identity. They are not in soul as a substratum, for soul itself is not even in body as in a substratum (VI.2.7.18; cf. IV.3.20–2). A quality inheres in substance or matter as in a subject, or is predicated of primary substance according to Aristotle's *Categories* (2a34–5), but if soul is the actualization of what it means to be a body – that is, if soul is the very reality or substance of body – then neither is soul "in" body as in a subject nor can the internal content of soul be "in" soul as its subject, for unity and multiplicity must characterize soul directly in its very substance. Movement and being taken separately may each appear to "have" or possess the other, as a compound may be said to "have" a characteristic, but in the language of substance, Plotinus argues, they mutually imply one another as essential characteristics of what it means to be soul (VI.2.7.18, 20–4). The highest pervasive *genera* of being, therefore, together with all the *logoi* which soul manifests, constitute the immediate being of soul: a one nature which is many.[40]

If it makes sense to argue that the content of soul cannot be treated in the same way as bodily qualities, then it is easier to see why soul or intellect should have more being than physical things or why "we exist more" (*mallon . . . esmen*) by being close to the Good, and less by "being far from him" (VI.9.9.7–13).[41] On the first count, that of determinate being, quality exists no less than substance, it is true, but in physical compounds quality still requires an intelligible foundation in something self-dependent. Plotinus argues that matter cannot fulfill this function, nor the composite for itself.[42] If "to be" in the full sense means to be a definite substance and this starts with the soul, then one is "closer to being" in the soul than in subsequent, derivative forms of being (i.e., qualities, quantities, etc.). On the second count, that of existence, if existence is a gift of the One, and if the existence of determinate natures is properly to be explained by reference to the principle which makes them one, then it is not unreasonable to talk about "more existence" in the context of the approach to the One.

VII

What does "existence" mean in the relation of intellect to the One? Is it just "existence" stripped of everything else or is it a rich and meaningful activity in compound intelligible natures? Plotinus's extended discussion of what makes things good in themselves in VI.7, chapters 18–23 and 31–42, provides an implicit but powerful correlation between goodness, generative power, and an *activity* of existence in determinate beings.

In emerging from the Good, intellect was first unlimited. Then, by looking back to the Good, it became a delimited life (VI.7.17.13–16). The connection between the act *of* the Good and the act *from* the Good which is intellect's own life is very close, according to Plotinus (VI.7.21.5–6: "life is the activity of the Good or rather an activity from the Good"), but "the form is in the thing shaped and the shaper is shapeless" (17.16–18). In other words, the generation of intellect is like a process of making or seeing in Aristotle. Maker and the thing made constitute a single activity in the making process, while they remain conceptually and really distinct, but the change occurs in the product not the maker.[43] This is why Plotinus is concerned to point out that what is given to intellect is "less than the giver" (17.6). The content of intellect remains distinct from the Good but intellect is organized as a totality, not piecemeal (17.21–34), simultaneously by the power of the Good and by its own vision of the Good which "seeing is the power from the Good to become all things" (17.33–4).[44] In other words, there is also a derivative creative power in intellect.[45] In looking at the Good, intellect sees it as itself, and thereby makes the Good the highest moment of its own being, while the Good itself remains distinct, just as in perception there is a similar duality, *my* seeing an *object*, but the object itself remains distinct.[46] As Plotinus says elsewhere, intellect is "shaped in one way by the One and in another by itself, like sight in its actuality; for thinking is seeing sight, and both are one" (V.1.5.17–19). It would appear, therefore, from the terms of Plotinus's analogy in VI.7.17 that intellect is not only a complete, thinking, living being; it also contains a creative power *for* thinking or seeing which is distinct from the Good only because it is *in* the thing generated. What this may be gradually becomes clearer in the subsequent argumentation.

What is it, Plotinus now asks (VI.7.18–23), which is *in* all intelligible beings and makes them good? To claim that this is accounted for simply by virtue of their derivation from the Good is not sufficient, he argues, because we are looking for a common property which is actually *in* intelligible beings (18.5–6). The difficulty is compounded by the fact that we cannot base our reasoning upon soul and its desires because we run the risk of making intelligible good in the likeness of diverse psychic goods (19.1–8), and even if we attain to a more objective perspective, that is, if we get an accurate assessment of "the excellence of each thing," this leads to an understanding of intelligible form, but gives us no clue as to what *in* that form makes it good (19.8–14). Furthermore, if the "why" and the "that" are the same in intellect, then it is difficult for reason to say *why* the forms are good in themselves (19.17–18). Finally, even if we examine intellectual operations such as judgments and oppositions, this will take us only as far as intellect itself, and will exclude many determinate beings, for "not all things desire intellect, but all things desire the Good" (20.18–19). This final blind alley, however, suggests a solution to the difficulty. Even beings which have intellect "do not stop there," but go beyond intellect to the Good "before reason" (20.20–2). "And if they also seek life, and everlasting existence and activity, what they desire is not intellect in so far as it is intellect, but in so far as it is good and from the Good and directed to the Good" (20.22–4). Life, eternal existence, and activity,[47] therefore, possess a wider extension than intellect. Irrational animals, plants, stones, and the elemental bodies trace existence and life through intellect to the Good and, according to Plotinus's argument, this is because "desire" in all its diverse forms cannot be explained solely in intellectual terms, but is fundamentally preintellectual in origin.[48]

Plotinus at this point rephrases his original question in terms of both unity and goodness: "What is it which is *one* in all these and makes each and every one of them good? What makes intelligible form good is something both present in the object and yet above it. Plotinus calls it "an intense love" (21.11–12: *erôs ho suntonos*), and a "grace" (22.24: *charis*) that comes from the Good to the intelligibles "not when they are what they are" (21.22), that is, determinate essences, but "when, already being what they are, they take something else in addition from there" (21.12–13).[49] This "something else" (*allo*), added to their natures, is described as light which, like the Idea of the Good in Plato's *Republic* (509b), is a *prior* condition of existence and visibility, a *present* activity of awakening beauty and desire in the intelligibles, and the productive sustainer of everything. Colored by the light of the Good, all things wake up, Plotinus says, and lift up what they have (22.34–6). What does the Good make now? "Now as well it preserves those things in being and makes the thinking things think and the living things live, inspiring thought, inspiring life and, if something cannot live, inspiring it to exist (*einai*)" (23.22–4).

According to these images of light, grace, and love, existence is a gift of the One which not only makes determinate essences possible, but which also continues to provide the beauty in them as well as to grant their own independence as beings. In one way, then, the problem how there can be something in created natures which is a part of their extended being if not strictly of their composite natures is plausibly solved by the image of light in the structure of perception and thought. Light "runs upon" the intelligible forms and makes them able to move us (1–3), just as in the case of material bodies, Plotinus argues, we do not love their substrates, but the beauty manifested in them (22.1–5). This light is not only "upon" the form (or material body) and different from it; it is also manifested in every form but obviously cannot be reduced to the concrete object (cf. V.5.7.4–6). All forms or substances, then, are good in virtue of this light which is inseparable but distinct from, as well as prior to, illuminated objects. Plotinus even goes so far as to say that the beauty of intelligible objects themselves is idle (*argon*) if we fail to grasp the outflow from the Good which gives value to determinate existences (22.10–17; 22–36).[50]

VII.1

To this point we can see a metaphorical connection between existence, life, love, and grace, but Plotinus has not yet explained what the intrinsic connection between existence and generative power may be. How is existence related to creativity and why is it that images of growth seem to proliferate the closer soul or intellect approaches the One?

In VI.7 chapters 32–6 Plotinus tries to show that there is a formlessness in our experience which responds to the shapeless nature of the Good. The Good cannot be a form because then it would simply be a part of intelligible being (32.5–6). Nor can it be all the intelligibles together, for then it would have "a variegated shape" (33.10). It must therefore, be shapeless like pure light (31.1–4; 35.20–7; 41.1–7). Plotinus tries to show that there is also a formlessness in human experience which responds to the nature of the Good. The Good cannot be limited because it is *the* measure, to which the unbounded depth of love in the intelligible world and all "longings" respond throughout nature (34.1). In a similar way, intelligible beauty is shapeless, but takes its shape from the determinate compound which manifests that beauty (32.36–7), just as perceptible beauty being more than the outer harmony of the parts requires an inner resonance in the soul for love to "grow" (33.29–32; V.5.7.1–16). This shapelessness is an object of experience, as light is perceptible in itself even if we perceive it in relation to the perceptible object. In V.5.7, Plotinus argues that for intellect this light is "its own" and gives rise to an experience so overwhelming that it takes away even the sense of an "outside" or an "inside" to the self, because there are no longer any boundaries to our experience (V.5.7.31–8.3; VI.7.32.24–39). By contrast in VI.7, soul or intellect's experience of union with the Good is experience of shapelessness or unified presence without distinction, an experience, Plotinus suggests, imitated by lovers in sexual intercourse (34.8–21; 31.8–17).

In subsequent chapters, Plotinus links intelligible composite nature and shapelessness to two different powers of intellect (intellect "in its right mind" and intellect "loving" or "out of its mind"): "intellect always has its thinking and always its not thinking, but looking at that Good in another way. For when it saw him it had offspring and was intimately aware of their generation and existence within it; and when it sees these it is said to think, but it sees that by the power by which it was going to think" (VI.7.35.30–4).[51] What is good in intelligible beings, then, turns out to be an inner light or beauty, shapeless like the One because it is direct vision, but in some sense generative of the beauty in all things and responsible for the existence and life even of things which do not possess intellect.

VII.2

But how could this be a generative act of existence in intellect? In the final chapters of VI.7,[52] Plotinus provides an answer to this question by means of a major criticism of Aristotle's *Nous* at the conclusion of which he tries to make his own view more comprehensible (40.4–5)[53] by transforming the Aristotelian notion that soul is the act or *energeia* of body into a theory about the nature of thought itself, for if thought is a movement, as Plotinus has already maintained it must be (35.1–3), then a theory of motion should apply primarily to intellect. Aristotle states in the *Physics* that "all motion is from something and to something" (*Phys.* V.224b1). In VI.7.40, Plotinus argues that "all thinking is from something and *of something*," (6) a small but significant change.[54] For Aristotle, soul is the form *of* the body. As we have seen above, Plotinus rejects this formulation on the grounds that soul must first be self-dependent substance before it becomes the form *of* anything.[55] Plotinus now goes on in VI.7.40 to embody this criticism of the entelechy doctrine within a reformulation of the nature of thought. Though a single *energeia* or act, thought has a doubleness to it: thought is both self-dependent and intentional (that is, it is really *of* something):

And one kind of thinking, which keeps close to that from which it comes, has as its ground (*hupokeimenon*) that of which it is the thought and itself becomes a kind of superstructure (*epikeimenon*), being its ground's actuality and fulfilling that ground's potentiality without generating anything itself, for it is only a kind of completion (*teleiôsis*) of that of which it is. (VI.7.40.6–10)

Thought is the form or completion of the intelligible matter. Just like the *logos* in the physical compound, it generates nothing (cf. III.8.2.30–2). Plotinus continues:

But the thinking which accompanies substance and has brought substance into existence (*hupostêsasa*) could not be in that from which it came be, for it would not have generated anything if it was in that. (10–13)

The thinking which is generative of substance is not *in* the Good, because otherwise nothing would have been generated. Rather this higher phase of thinking is generative of *intellectual* substance because it is a self-dependent power which accompanies and constitutes a thinking nature:

But since it was a power of generation by itself (*dunamis tou gennan eph'heautês*), it generates and its active actuality is substance, and also in substance it is there with it, and the thought and this substance are not different things. (13–15)

As an act belonging to intellect's nature, thinking is nongenerative; it perfects and fills the substrate's potentiality. As an act which has come from the One (with a strong resemblance to the One), thinking is a self-dependent power, distinct from the Good only because it is in intellect, for it gives substance existence and accompanies substance, and its activity is substance when this is fully realized (VI.7.40.10–24).

   This is a classic formulation of what will in later thought become the essence and act of existence distinction.[56] Essence and the act of existence are distinct, but not separated from one another, since together they constitute *one* movement of thought, and the act belongs to the determinate nature without being completely restricted to it, just as in learning, what one learns and the power by which one learns are one and yet different (VI.7.40.55–6). Intellect, then, is made both by the One and by itself. Eminently, this is the power of the One, but that power in *intellect's* own being is a power for the existence of thought.

Why should this higher power be generative? In the physical world, the generative power, that which gives life and existence, is the *lowest* soul-power. In Alexander of Aphrodisias,[57] for example, this lowest generative power is the only power that can subsist by itself, and it is the cause of being (*De an.* 36.19–20), whereas the rest of the soul's powers serve as the completion of the substratum (*De an.* 99.12–14). The parallels with Plotinus's language in VI.7.40 are close.[58] For Plotinus, however, the physical world is a mirror image of the intelligible world. What is highest here turns out to be lowest there (IV.6.3.5–7; III.6.14–15). This, I suggest, is why life and growth play such a prominent role in Plotinus's descriptions of the emergence of intellect from the One. They are metaphors, but they have a nonmetaphorical origination in the act of existence.[59] The existence and life of everything are the free gift of the Good itself.

I suggest, then, that from this simple understanding of the hyperintelligible significance of the most ordinary functions in nature (to take Plotinus's examples in VI.7.17–42, breathing, existing, living, desiring, loving, giving light, being illuminated, etc.) the later essence–existence distinction in Medieval Arabic and Christian philosophers takes its origin and draws perhaps some of its cogency.[60] In all determinate beings there is a real distinction between their composite natures and the principle which unites and gives them existence. As transcendent, this principle is the One; as immanent, it is a self-dependent generative act in the product. Only in the One is there no such distinction, because duality involves dependence, but the One is purely itself. In the *Enneads* there is a striking refusal to see determinate beings as self-enclosed units and a genuine attempt to work out the structure of such beings in terms of their own natures, the world of interrelations they manifest, and their dependence upon a transcendent principle whose nature is just to exist freely (VI.8.7–21). The height of the Good's transcendence can be gauged by the depth and extent of its presence in the physical world even to "those things which do not possess intellect," only existence and life; but the activation of that presence remains significantly in the free response of the product: "The Good is gentle and kindly and gracious, present to anyone when anyone (*tis*) wishes" (V.5.12.33–5).

NOTES

1 On Avicenna and the later tradition see Gilson 1952, 74–107; Owens 1958, 1–40; 1965, 1–22; Hyman and Walsh 1973, 212, 234, 283–4, 464–7; on Aristotle and Aquinas, and also for modern views from Hobbes and Locke to Sartre see further MacIntyre 1967 ("Essence and Existence"), 59–60. See also note 60.

2 See Hadot 1963, 147–53; 1970, 143–56; 1973, 101–13. Also see Festugière 1954, 6–17.

3 Hadot 1968, 2 vols.; see vol. 2, 98–112. Marius Victorinus, *Adversus Arium*, Source Chrétiennes, eds. P. Henry and P. Hadot, Paris, 1960, t.IV.19.4f.

4 Damascius, *Dubitationes et Solutiones*, ed. C. E. Ruelle (Paris, 1989), vol. 1, 120, 312, 11–21, 312, 29. Proclus, *The Elements of Theology*, ed. Dodds 1933, props. 8–10.

5 For several different assessments of this question in recent years see Corrigan 1984, 219–40; 1990, 133–8; Gerson 1990, 185–226.

6 By "logical," I mean that the distinction is only one of thought, just as I may distinguish "animal" and "rational" in defining a human being. The question what constitutes a real distinction is much harder to determine. Is this a distinction between modes of being or two "things" in a determinate being or two complementary aspects of being which in some sense are actually distinct, even though together they constitute the unity of the determinate being? On this see Gilson 1952, 99, who gives these three possibilities from a text in Suarez (*Metaphysicae Disputationes* XXI.1.3.115 G).

7 On the *Gross-Schrift* generally and also on the relation of II.9 (*Against the Gnostics*) to the work as a whole see Cilento 1971; Roloff 1971; Elsas 1975.

8 For commentary on VI.7 see Hadot 1988, and on VI.8 Leroux 1990.

9 For the sake of simplicity I shall translate *to einai* "the being," *to on* "being," and *ta onta*, "beings" or "real beings," and finally *ousia* "substance."

10 Cf. III.7.4.37–8. For this observation I am indebted to Sweeney 1992, 172–5.

11 For *hupostasis*, cf. VI.6.5.16–25, 12.1–2, 13–16; I.8.15.1–3, etc., and *huparxis*, III.7.13.49–50. For the technical sense of *hupostasis* see V.1

On The Three Primary Hypostases. Huparxis is never employed in the special sense of "existence" given to it later by Porphyry (Hadot 1968, v.2, 110–112.26) or Marius Victorinus (*existentia*), *Candidi Epistola* I.2.18–22; *Adversus Arium* I.30.20–4 (Henry, Hadot, 1960). The verbs *huparchein, sunhuparchein, prohuparchein,* are used sometimes in contexts which suggest original existence, coexistence, preexistence, and consequently some kind of basic existential attribution. See, for example, VI.6.10.39–41, 13.17.48. The one nature predicated of many "must exist first in itself" (*kath'hautên huparchein*) before being contemplated in many (VI.6.11.7–9).

12 A similar distinction is implicit at VI.8.12.16 where Plotinus argues that the One is no longer to be referred to another "in that it is" (*hê esti*) and "in that it is substance" (*hê estin ousia*).

13 For this distinction between substance and derivative compounds see Section VI.1.

14 On the topic of matter Plotinus has four important treatises: II.4 (12 in the chronological order) *On Matter;* II.5 (25) *On What Exists Potentially and What Actually;* III.6 (26) *On The Impassibility of Things Without Body;* and I.8 (51) *On What are Evils.*

15 Trans. A. H. Armstrong. All quotations from the *Enneads* will be from the Loeb translation of A. H. Armstrong.

16 In our investigations about the "something" we slip off it (*apolisthainein*) and are carried away to the qualitative (II.6.1.42–4; cf. Plato, *Seventh Letter* 343c1–6; II.6.2.11–14; cf. Aristotle, *Met.* 1029a16–19). Conversely, "whatever matter might have taken . . . slips away from it as if from an alien nature" (III.6.14.24–5; cf. II.6.2.11–13; VI.3.8). Strictly speaking, neither matter nor body is a true subject or substratum, for "the being" of both is not that of an individual subject (*kata to tode*) but only that of the specific form (*kata to eidos*) (II.1.1.25; cf. 4–40). At the same time, matter is in a sense "underlying" or "receptive" (II.4.1.1–6; 4.7; 5.19), though hardly a true subject like intellect (5.20–1). Bodies "are said to be" founded "upon" it (III.6.12.6–13), and may be said to have a specific potential existence (II.5.5), even if other forms of underlying potential existence are *formal* (II.5.1.30; 2.26). *Mutatis mutandis,* a similar story pertains to body, for it is "shadow" being (II.6.3.14–21): "sensible objects are by participation what they are said to be since their underlying nature receives its form from elsewhere" (V.9.5.36–8). True "subjectivity" by contrast, begins with *logos* (II.6.2.11–15; III.3.4.29–41) and even more so with soul (I.4.3.14; III.6.33.31–2; III.8.8.5) and intellect (II.4.5.22; V.8.4.18; 6.8; VI.7.40.7,47). The one "underlies" everything (V.6.3.7–8), but is not a *tode ti* (VI.8.9.39) nor even truly *hupostasis*

(10.37–8; cf. 13.44; 15.6–7,28), but again active *hupostasis* without substance (20.9–11,11–39), the truest subject (20.17–21,33).

17 Cf. I.6.3.19–26; IV.3.17.1–7; Pseudo-Aristotle, *De Mundo* 397 b 30 f.; Aristotle, *On Generation and Corruption*. 335a18–20; Stoics, *SVF* II.136.11–13; 155.30–40 (cf. A. Graeser 1972, 37); Alexander of Aphrodisias, *Quaestiones* 2.3.47.30–50.27 (Bruns).

18 For references and interpretation see Graeser 1972, 72–5.

19 See also Graeser 1972, 22–4 (re: II.1.7.10.20–49), Beierwaltes 1961, 334–62, and Ferwerda 1965, 62–9.

20 Cf. III. 6.6.33–64. For the continuation and development of this theme in relation to soul see Section VI below and also Porphyry, *Maxims* 40.36.9–38.20 (Mommert); for the subsequent importance of the *magis minusque esse* theme in Augustine see *De vera religione* II.22, Bibliothèque Augustinienne, 8.54 in relation to body and *Contra Secundinum* II, Bibliothèque Augustinienne, 17.574–5 in relation to soul and body.

21 On the significance of the early chapters of this treatise see Gerson 1990, 203–6.

22 On this see Gerson 1990, 206.

23 Cf. VI.7.3.16–19; 4.23–30; 5.1–5; III.8.2.30–4; V.8.2.32–4 (cf. V.8.1–5); II.7.3.7–14.

24 On the Plotinian *logos* and its sources see Müller 1917, 20–60; Witt 1931, 103–11; Schubert 1968; Früchtel 1970; Graeser 1972, 35; 41–3, also note 32 below.

25 See, for example, *Physics* VIII.259b1–3 (cf. Ross 1936, introduction, 91) and 258b12–13.

26 See Delbrück 1971, 55, cited with approval by Mayr 1988, 56–7.

27 See, for example, the conclusion of the first part of this argument at III.8.7.1–15; cf. VI.7.1.45–58; VI.8.14.16–42.

28 Compare VI.7.4.21–30 and Aristotle, *De anima* 413a13–16; *Post. An.* II.93a4–5.

29 On this see VI.2.4–8 and Section VI.

30 Cf. IV.3.20–1; Alexander of Aphrodisias, *De anima*, 13.9–15.26 (Bruns).

31 Alexander, *De an.*, 21.22–4; 103.20–1; Aristotle, *De an.* II.1.412a11–13a10; Plotinus, IV.7.8.40–3; IV.3.2.8–10.

32 III.8.2.30–4: "This forming principle, then, which operates in the visible shape, is the last, and is dead and no longer able to make another, but that which has life is the brother of that which makes the shape, and has the same power itself, and makes in that which comes into being." The close connection between the meanings "forming principle" and "discourse" or "speech" for *logos* in Plotinus's mind can readily be seen if we compare *Phaedrus* 275d–276a which Plotinus is adapting to his own

purpose in III.8.2. Plato compares written discourse, which has no real power of its own and which always needs its parent to protect it with its "brother" which "together with knowledge (*epistêmê*) is written in the soul of the learner" (276a5–6), and is "living, ensouled speech of which the written kind may justly be called an image" (276a9–10).

33 Cf. Aristotle, *Post. An.* II.2.90a15; *Met.* VIII 4.1044b14.

34 For Plotinus's use of science (*epistêmê*) as a model for understanding the nature of intellect and soul as well as the relation between the intelligible and sensible worlds see especially V.9.6.3–9; IV.9.5; III.9.2; IV.3.2.49–54; V.8.4.47–50.

35 Cf. VI.7.3.9–19; 21–2; 4.28–30; VI.8.14.20–5.

36 Plotinus argues that irrational animals in the sensible world must be conceived as forms of living thought in the intelligible world (VI.7.9) and the parts of animals (horns, claws, teeth) are a part of the completeness of intellect itself (VI.7.10). Even the elements are alive in the physical world, though they do not manifest the presence of soul in them unless we grasp their connection through the *logos* to the intelligible world (VI.7.11).

37 Cf. VI.7.2.10; 19.18; V.8.7.39.

38 Cf. VI.7.3.9–22; VI.8.14.14–29; II.7.3.9–14; III.3.4.37–40; V.8.1–6.

39 See especially V.9.8; V.4; V.1.5–7; V.2.1; V.6.5; III.8.11; VI.7.15–18; V.3.11.

40 Cf. VI.2.8.25–49; V.3.6–10; VI.7.13.16–21; V.1.4.26–43.

41 The whole passage is as follows: "For we are not cut off from him or separate, even if the nature of body has intruded and drawn us to itself, but we breathe and are preserved because that Good has not given its gifts and then gone away but is always bestowing them as long as it is what it is. But we exist more (*mallon . . . esmen*) when we turn (*neusantes*) to him and our well being is there, but being far from him is nothing less but existing less (*êtton einai*)." See also note 20 above.

42 See II.6.2.6–17; VI.3.8.

43 See Aristotle, *Physics* III.3.202a13–b22; also Lloyd 1987, 168, and 1990, 99–101, in relation also to *Physics* VIII.4.

44 *hê de horasis hê ekeithen dunamis pantôn.* For the close connection between the act of the Good and that act in intellect see VI.7.21.4–6; 35.30–3; V.5.7.29–8.5; V.5.8.21–3.

45 See, for example, VI.7.40.18–20 (on chapter 40 generally see Section VII.2); 41.18–19; VI.6.9.35–7; 13.51–4; VI.8.13.24–5; VI.2.8.16–18; V.6.4.18–20; 5.9–10.

46 Cf. V.6.2.7–13; III.8.11.1–11; V.5.7 passim; VI.7.15.18–22; 16.10–35; 17.14–21; V.3.10.7–51; 11.1–21.

47 On the importance of life, being, and thought in the *Enneads* see Trouillard 1954, 351–7; Hadot 1960; Armstrong 1971; and Lloyd 1987.

48 Cf. V.6.5.9–10; V.5.12.1–19; 33–49; V.3.11.4–6; 11–12.

49 On these chapters in VI.7 see also Corrigan 1990, 135–6.

50 Throughout this passage the influence of Plato's *Phaedrus* is evident as a glance at the list of sources in the Henry-Schwyzer *editio major*, V.3, makes clear.

51 On the importance and difficulty of this passage for Plotinus's philosophy of the self see O'Daly 1973, 88–94; and for a different view, Hadot 1988, 342–5.

52 On VI.7.40 in particular see Corrigan 1984, 234–7; also Lloyd 1987, 171–7; and for entirely different interpretation, Hadot 1988, 360–2.

53 "But necessity must have persuasion mixed with it" (cf. V.3.6.10–11).

54 Why this small change? It may well be accidental but because (1) the Peripatetic formula "every form and entelechy is of something" (Alexander of Aphrodisias, *De an.* 103.20–1; 21.22–4; *Quaestiones* 2.10.55.10 [Bruns]) is so well known to Plotinus, (2) Plotinus employs the regular "*termini*" language of Aristotle's *Physics* elsewhere (that is, the "from which" and "to where": e.g., III.8.8.39–40; VI.2.8.11–13; 11.25–6; V.3.11.16–20), (3) in IV.5.6.26–7, in his treatment of light, Plotinus states clearly that while an activity (*energeia*) comes "from some substrate" it is not "to some substrate," in the sense that it becomes a determinate affection of a substratum, but remains "an activity of soul" (6.28), and (4) if every motion must be "of something" and not simply "on its own" (VI.3.21.9–10) so that if thought is motion, one cannot have either a thought which is not of something or a "thinking of thinking" (as in the case of Aristotle's divine *Nous*) – for these four reasons, in addition to the text of VI.7.40 itself, I propose that the change from Aristotle's *Physics* formula is not accidental. Only in intellect does an *energeia* characterize the substratum completely or substantially.

55 See Section V.3 and note 31 above.

56 See note 60 below.

57 On the question of Alexander's relation to this and other passages in Plotinus see Hager 1964, 174–87; Rist 1966, 82–90; Blumenthal 1968, 254–61; Szlezák 1979, 137 and n435–6; Sharples 1987, 1220–3.

58 For Alexander, the "first soul" is cause of generation, nurture, growth, and composition (*sustasis*) and being (*to einai*) (*De an.* 36.16–21). The generative power is the perfection of the nutritive, and the act in accordance with the generative power does not contribute to its own safety and perfection but is a cause for things which are already complete of their generating something different but like themselves out of desire for immortality (36.5–8). The nutritive or first soul is alone capable of existing without the other soul powers (29.13; 105.3–29), whereas the rational power (and all the others) cannot exist on its own, for this would

mean that there are many souls in the human being (99.6–11). The person who possesses the highest power of soul must also possess the powers before this, since this power is the completion (*teleiotês*) of soul, and the perfection is in and with the subject of which it is the completion (*ep' ekeinô kai sun ekeinô estin hou esti teleiotês*). For Plotinus by contrast, the "first energeia" (VI.7.40.18–19) is the generative, self-dependent power which is together with and in substance (40.10–15), and the second is the completion (*teleiôsis*) of the subject of which it is (*ekeinou gar estin hou esti monon hoion teleiôsis*) (40.10). The two together make up thought, just as in Alexander the two powers of soul (the generative power of existence and the aesthetic power of judgment) result in a new composite activity and action (*energeia te kai praxis*) (105.20–2; 3–4: *hê men gap estin auton prôtê, hê de deutera, hê de epi tautais*). A similar application of the two powers or acts which result in a new composite intelligible activity is already indicated in VI.7.18.12–13; 41–3 where Plotinus discusses what in intelligible things makes them good: (1) The first generative act is described in three different ways. "What pertains to the first activity" (*to eis protên energeian*) (12) is equivalent to "the first activity" (41), which is "good because it is brought into being by the Good" (42–3); (2) The second act is similarly characterized as "what is given to the first activity" (12–13), "what is defined following upon it" (41–2) and what is good "because it is a *kosmos* or order from it" (43); (3) And the composite nature which unites both of these acts is "what depends on these" (42–3: *to sunamphô*). I do not insist that Plotinus must have only Alexander in mind. The term *sunhupostasis* (VI.7.40.48; cf. 2.37), for instance, does not occur in Alexander. However, it is reasonable to suppose that Plotinus has the general Aristotelian-Peripatetic doctrine of soul as a double entelechy quite firmly in mind in these passages. For a similar view in relation to other passages see Lloyd 1987, 167–70. In VI.8, written immediately after VI.7, Plotinus is clearly aware of this implicit relation between the lowest physical and the highest intelligible power, for he points out the difference between them. The "true life" we have become is self-sufficient to being (*eis to einai*), he states, and immediately goes on to qualify his statement; the "first hypostasis" cannot be "in the unsouled and in irrational life," for this is too "weak for being," whereas true life is the "root, beginning, and basis of the greatest tree" which gives the tree "to be" (VI.8.15.23–36; cf. III.8.10.1–14).

59 On the question of metaphor see Beierwaltes 1961, 334–62, and 1971, 116–7; and Ferwerda 1965, esp. 46–61. See also Corrigan 1993, 187–99, and in this volume Schroeder.

60 Plotinus's analysis of determinate being and the generative power of life

and existence is clearly very different from Avicenna's view that existence is an accident of essence or Averroes's contention that the distinction between the two is only conceptual (see note 1 above), and much
rather to be compared, I suggest, to Aquinas's theory. In Aquinas especially (but also to a much lesser degree in Proclus and Pseudo-Dionysius),
being is a simple perfection which is prior to essence or the "what is" of
the thing, which enters into composition with it and which also points
beyond itself as created *esse* to *Ipsum esse*, that is the existence or being
which is beyond being, of God (on this see Corrigan 1984, 220–8). The act
of existence is really distinct from the essence, but not separate from it,
for like an infused light it "continues to grow from above" providing a
natural creativity to a supernatural end (*Summa theologica* I.12.5.resp.).

6 Plotinus on the nature of physical reality

Plotinus adheres to the classical Greek tenet that we understand and explain something's nature by knowing and articulating its causes, and he articulates the order of causes which explains physical reality as a metaphysical procession whose first principle is his One. Here, though, I shall focus on some main features of Plotinus's analysis of physical reality which prepare the way for relating it to his metaphysical principles.

Plotinus thinks of physical reality, first and foremost, as the domain of coming-to-be (*genesis*). His analysis of coming-to-be focuses on the coming-to-be of particular things – for example, particular plants or animals or human beings and, in so doing, he intends to continue Plato's project of assuring and explaining the real existence of those particulars and of their comings-to-be. Plotinus does so, in part, by incorporating into his analysis the notion of substance (*ousia*), which Aristotle introduced to denote the proper subject(s) for assertions of real existence or ascriptions which presuppose real existence; but he considers the notion of substance to be by itself insufficient for his explanatory task. Plotinus notes that the notion of substance must, "in the case of corporeal things, . . . incorporate the notion of things constantly in flux, which in more precise language we term *coming-to-be*" (VI.3.2.2–4); and, more significantly, his analysis of the notion of substance, as it denotes the physically real particulars taken by Aristotle to be instances of substance *par excellence*, implies that it does not even have a single or "absolute" sense which might then be taken to explicate the real existence of things in coming-to-be. Indeed, Plotinus maintains that physical substance may be explicated in *four* ways.

(S1) *The form–matter composite substance.* Though not the only way to explicate physical substance, this explication is primary with respect to the other three because it most clearly satisfies the Aristotelian definition of "primary substance" as "that which neither exists in a substrate nor is designated by reference to a substrate as something distinct from it" (VI.3.5.13–16) and because the notion of forming-principle (*logos*), the principal unifying element of Plotinus's analysis of physical reality, is most closely associated with this explication inasmuch as a forming-principle causes (explains, or is the source of) a particular's real existence "in conformance with the form" of its composition (e.g., VI.3.3.13–16).[1]

(S2) *The corporeally constituted substance.* This explicates a physical substance in terms of its functional components, or parts, and their corporeal constituents. This explication also satisfies the Aristotelian definition of primary substance (VI.3.8.10–11); but it assumes that a particular substance is delineated primarily by its corporeal constituents and only secondarily by its form of composition. When explicated in this way, for example, physical substances might be distinguished into (i) *more matter-like* substances, which may be delineated directly in terms of corporeal parts whose constituents are the four "simple bodies" (air, earth, fire, and water); and (ii) *more instrument-like* substances, which may be distinguished into various sorts of "complex bodies," whose "particular configurations of parts" (functional components) explain their suitability as bodies for various sorts of living things (e.g., for plants or for animals), before they are delineated in terms of their corporeal constituents (VI.3.9 Cf. VI.3.2.5–6).

(S3) *The accidental substance* (cf. VI.3.2.7) explicates a physical substance as "a certain agglomeration of qualities and matter" (VI.3.8.20). Here, that particulars are the objects of sense experience (*aisthêsis*) becomes salient (cf. VI.3.1.8), as Plotinus associates this explication with conceiving physical reality itself as "an aggregation of particulars as they *are* relative to sense experience" (VI.3.10.16). In general, however, a particular's qualities are the various respects in which it may be distinguished from other particulars (e.g., II.6.3.6), though this surely includes so-called sensible qualities. Moreover, this explication *passively* relates a particular to its qualities – as that to which the various respects in which it is distinguishable from other particulars belong, or to which we may ascribe those qualities. But this amounts to conceiving particulars as just *matter*, since it conceives them as nothing more than substrates or subjects (*hupokeimena*) for qualities and qualitative ascriptions, and since being a *passive substrate* or *mere subject* is a characteristic of matter (*hulê*). As a result, explicating a physical substance as "an agglomerate of qualities and matter" no longer satisfies the Aristotelian definition; for, although "matter" here denotes the particular itself, qualitative existence is more properly understood, not as what merely belongs or is ascribable to particulars, but as included among those things which "come about from and because of" substances in the primary, (S1), sense (VI.3.4.35–6). The accidental substance itself thus more properly belongs to that which its qualities "come about from and because of," so to what by itself is an (S1) substance and therefore is related to the qualitative agglomerate *as* something distinct from it – that is, as something which is *not* a *mere* substrate but the cause or source of its (qualitative) existence. Indeed, this seems one of the principal payoffs for Plotinus of phrasing the second disjunct in the Aristotelian definition so that it encompasses not only something's being ascribed to something which *is* distinct from it but also its being ascribed to something *as if* it were distinct from it:[2] It allows him to maintain that the (S1) composite and the (S3) agglomerate are in reality one and the same thing (viz., some particular)[3] and yet that the composite more properly explicates its substance, since the (S3) agglomerate presupposes the (S1) composite as its cause and so requires that its own substrate be viewed *as if* it were something distinct (or, as a distinct sort of substance) from it. Also, a qualitative agglomerate is *accidental* in that the physical substance it explicates *could be otherwise* in its regard: different qualities may be ascribed to the same composite substance; or, it is not necessary that a given composite also be (or "have") a certain qualitative agglomerate. And yet, we shall see, the physical substance is the qualitative agglomerate's cause only because of its essence, in that all of its causal activites are essential to it. One and the same physical substance, then, is an "accidental" sort of thing with respect to our qualitative ascriptions regarding it and an "essential" sort of thing (an essence) with respect to its causal activities, including those which explain its qualities.

(S4) *The derivable substance* (cf. VI.3.2.7) explicates a physical substance by conceiving one or more of the qualities in the (S3) agglomerate as qualifying the (S1) substance itself – that is, by conceiving the (S1) substance, not as the cause of qualitative existence, but as having itself acquired qualitive existence, or as itself a *qualified thing*. Inasmuch as the Stoics conceived substances as qualified, not just by any or all of their qualities, but by "particularly distinctive" qualities (e.g., a certain philosopher's snub-nosedness or human beings' bipedality),[4] Plotinus suggests that this explication allows us to distinguish substances, for example, with respect to "the hot-and-dry, the dry-and-cold, the moist-and-cold, and the hot-and-moist, and compositions and mixtures from these; or, with respect to the shapes and other discernible differences among various sorts of living things" (VI.3.10.1–9). But, Plotinus does not seem generally to distinguish the qualities which delineate a derivable substance from those delineating the same particular as an accidental substance. As explicative of a physical substance, in other words, (S4) derives from (S3) for Plotinus, regardless of whatever scientific or other value the Stoic conceit of "particularly distinctive" qualities may have.[5] Accordingly, although (S4) seems to satisfy the aforementioned Aristotelian definition, it is even further removed than (S3) from (S1)'s primary explicative status (cf. II.6.2.6–8; VI.3.6.8–14). At the same time, relating particulars and qualities as (S4) does underscores the fact that explicating physical substances in ways associated with being the objects of sense experience explicates one and the same particulars which (S1) and (S2) explicate without presuming this association.[6]

The following pairs of examples illustrate Plotinus's four ways to explicate physical substance:

(S1) a statue; a human being
(S2) a bronze thing; a so-and-so configured flesh and blood thing
(S3) a such-and-such shaped bronze-colored thing; a 5′ 5″ tall snub-nosed thing
(S4) a such-and-such shaped statue; a snub-nosed human being

Two features of these examples are noteworthy. First, no explicit mention is made in the (S1) examples of the matter (e.g., the bronze or the flesh and blood) which, together with the mentioned form, would compose Aristotle's primary substances. Second, no one of the various items mentioned in these examples is explicitly mentioned in all four. I begin with the first feature.

In Plotinus's system, the matter referred to in the notion of the form–matter composite (viz., its substrate) does not contribute to a composite's real existence since it is as such nothing; or, rather, it is not anything other than or apart from the physical substance itself. In general, something is a *substrate* insofar as it is that to which something is related in such a way that we may ascribe this to it. The notion of substrate thus denotes a *function* and not a (real) thing; and what fulfills that function for the composite is just the substance, or particular, itself. Insofar as "matter" may be used to denote something real or actual as such, it does not denote the composite's substrate but another substance (what we might call a *constitutive* substance) *from* or *out of* which the composite substance has been formed.[7] To be sure, the constitutive substance does play a role in the composite inasmuch as every physical substance has certain functional components (or at least, if it is "matter-like," certain distinguishable parts) and the constitutive substance becomes the corporeal constituents of those components (or parts) within the substance that has been formed or composited from it. Whereas, the function of a substrate, we have seen, is to provide an appropriate subject to which we may ascribe things as, for example, "belonging to" or "informing" or "received by" it; and, that to which we may ascribe, in particular, a substance's form of composition is not its functional components and parts or their corporeal constituents but the thus formed substance itself. Thus, a composite substance is not two things, one denoted by "form" and another by "matter," which are now somehow related in some "composite" way but is only one thing which both is composited in a certain way ("has form") and is also the appropriate subject to which we may ascribe its being composed in that way ("is matter").

Put another way, Plotinus maintains (a) that a physically real particular is always a particular *of a certain sort* and (b) that a physically real particular also will have been constituted *from* some (one or more) other particular(s) of some constitutive sort(s). But, the particular is not those other particulars, though they may corporeally constitute its various components or distinguishable parts. The particular, rather, is a particular just *of the sort* which it is, though it also may have certain components or parts because it is a particular of that sort. Thus, (a) most properly explicates the particular and, in those terms, the notion of form in (S1) denotes that particular with respect to its being a particular of the sort which it is (e.g., a human being, a plant, a statue) while the notion of matter in (S1) denotes that same particular with respect to its being that to which we may ascribe something's being a particular of that sort. Moreover, in these terms again, this notion of matter contributes nothing towards explicating the particular itself, since the notion of form already fully explicates its being nothing other than a particular of a certain sort (i.e., of just the sort which it is), but merely highlights the fact that we may ascribe this to nothing other than that particular itself.

Plotinus's view that a physically real particular is its own substrate with respect to its form of composition as a substance also implies that by itself the form already satisfies the Aristotelian definition of primary substance. For, unlike qualities (which "belong to" it) or qualifications (which are "of" it), its form is what in its entirety it just *is*—or, rather, "is *a*" (e.g., it is a tree or it is a human being).[8] Plotinus thus argues:

If I predicate *human being* of Socrates, I am not asserting something akin to stating "the wood is white" but akin to stating "the white thing is white" since stating "Socrates is a human being" asserts regarding some particular human being that he *is a human being*, which is to say that it asserts *human being* in reference to the humanity of Socrates, and this amounts to the same thing as asserting *Socrates* in reference to Socrates. (VI.3.5.18–23. cf.VI.3.4.16–18)

The real existence of a given particular is thus explained by its form, just as its real persistence in coming-to-be is explained by its continued conformity with its form (i.e., its remaining a particular of just the sort which it is) as it comes-to-be (e.g., IV.3.8.25–8). Regarding a particular's composition (i.e., its being a particular of a certain sort), Plotinus thus argues that,

Socrates does not impart the reality of a human being to what is not a human being but, rather, humanity imparts this reality to Socrates; for, since a particular human being thereby shares in humanity, what else could Socrates be if not just the particular thing of the human being sort which he is? And, how could this *particular-of-the-human-being-sort* which he is effect any more real a substance than the existent human being does already? (VI.3.9.28–32)

But, then, surely the particular's compositional form should remain integral when (S2) explicates its substance in terms of its corporeal constituents and again when (S3) conceives it to be a substrate for qualities, which (S4) then does take to qualify its composition. That this is not the case does not indicate conceptual sloppiness on Plotinus's part, however, but reflects his further view that the compositional form which most properly explicates the particular's real existence and persistence as a substance itself requires explanation. Indeed, that a particular is primarily just the sort of particular which it is, that it remains so as it comes-to-be, that it has a certain corporeal constitution, and that certain qualities may belong to it or qualify it may all be explained by a single causal source, Plotinus believes, which therefore explicates the particular itself in an even more fundamental way than its "substance" and the compositional "form" of its substance.

For Plotinus, something's real existence may be genuinely assured and sufficiently explained only by relating it to his system of real causes proceeding from his One. The notion of substance – and especially the Aristotelian notion of substance – is by itself insufficient to do this. For this, the pivotal notion in Plotinus's understanding of physical reality is *forming-principle* (*logos*). In our current context, for example, Plotinus maintains that in the domain of coming-to-be "a real substance itself proceeds by coming-to-be from a real existing source" (III.7.4.24–5. cf. VI.3.7.6–9). For, "nothing is real which is not a unity" (VI.6.13.50), so that "whatever is not a unity in some respect must be sustained by a unity and be just what it is because of that unity since, had it not become a unity despite its many constituents, it would not now exist as just itself – as what we designate to be a *particular* thing" (V.3.15.13–14. cf. VI.6.13.55–7). Plotinus identifies this "real existing source" of unity for a particular with its forming principal; and so he explains the foregoing identification of the particular with its form of composition, and also reemphasizes the derivative status of (S3) and (S4) explications of it, by arguing:

It has been asserted regarding the qualified thing that, by intermixing and blending different qualities and in consort with matter and quantity, it effects substance for the objects of sense experience; and it has also been asserted that what common [as opposed to strict, or philosophically precise] speech designates as a "substance" is just this conglomerate of many things, so that a substance is no longer the particular thing itself but a qualified thing. Even then, however, the real existing forming-principle (e.g., of fire) would still indicate more the particular thing, while the shape it effects indicates more something qualified. Likewise, *the real forming-principle of a human being* is *the particular existing human being*, whereas the qualitative superfluance associated with corporeal nature as such is in reality an image of the forming-principle and exists rather as some qualified thing. Just as if, for example, the visible Socrates were the real human being and yet an image contrived in his likeness, and whose reality amounts to so much color and paint, was designated to be Socrates – so too, *since there exists a real forming-principle to which the real Socrates conforms, the Socrates experienced sensorially is strictly speaking* not *Socrates but so much color and configuration of parts which in reality are imitations of real existents encompassed by his forming-principle.* (VI.3.15.24–37)

Here, explicating a particular's real existence in terms of the qualities we ascribe to it (e.g., based on how it appears to our sense experience) is portrayed as akin to identifying the thus qualified particular with a painted simulation of its appearances, since the particular is the cause of its qualitative existence (e.g., of how it appears to us) and so its real existence must be explicable apart from its qualities or appearances. Unlike the painting, however, the qualified thing is in reality not anything distinct from the particular itself – nor is its compositional form, nor its forming-principle; rather, these explicate its real existence in increasingly more real, or metaphysically adequate, ways.

The foregoing gloss of Plotinus's strategy for explicating the reality of particulars suggests how Plotinus's understanding of physical substance "incorporates the notion of things in coming-to-be" insofar as it indicates that a particular's compositional form and forming-principle also explain its real persistence as it comes-to-be; and, we shall see, the character of a given Accidental or Derivable substance is partly related to the particular's comings-to-be. This, however, does not explicate coming-to-be as such; it does not assure nor explain the real existence of the comings-to-be through which a physical substance persists and which contribute to its qualitative existence. In this regard, Plotinus is particularly concerned with Aristotle's failed attempt (he believes) to assure and explain the reality of coming-to-be.

Aristotle's analysis of coming-to-be is partly a response to Eleatic arguments denying real existence to movement (*kinêsis*) – the genus of coming-to-be and, for example, of alteration and change. Aristotle summarizes Zeno of Elea's principal reason for denying the reality of movement in the so-called bisection argument that "the halfway mark would have to be reached before something could proceed towards the end-goal," and so on *ad infinitum*.[9] In response, Aristotle insists that time is correlative with magnitude (or distance) with respect to movement such that dividing one divides the other in the same way (e.g., into halves), and he distinguishes infinite quantity and infinite divisibility to argue that "while it is not possible to traverse an infinite quantity [of distance] in definite [finite] time, it is possible to traverse what is infinitely divisible in definite time; for, time is also infinite in this sense."[10] This response, however, is part of a more general strategy to explicate the real existence of movement in such a way that, not only are Eleatic logical maneuvers reduced to speculative exercises in possibility and not reality, but any description or delineation of a movement which is presumed by one who questions whether in reality it may proceed and be completed thereby assures its real existence.

To accomplish this, Aristotle makes it axiomatic to his analysis of movement that "since every change is from something to something, . . . some of it must exist in what it is from and some of it in the consequent of the change."[11] Aristotle terms a movement's "from which" and "to which" its *extremities* or *termini* and he understands the foregoing axiom to imply that a movement's reality, both as something which in reality proceeds in a certain way and which in reality is a movement of a certain sort, is explicated by its termini. This allows Aristotle to respond in more general terms to Zeno that "no change may [in reality] be infinite in any of the ways in which change may exist; for, since every change must be from something to something, a change exists because a pair of termini exists, and its termini will be related to one another as contradictories or as contraries."[12] If we presume a change from nonwhite to white, for example, this delineates the sort of change it is in terms of termini which are contradictories; and the way in which this change proceeds is also delineated by this same pair of termini. In particular, Aristotle observes that "we may call something white or nonwhite, no only if it exists entirely as just such a thing, but also when the greatest or most notable portion of it [is white or nonwhite]. . . . So too, in the case of real and nonreal and other pairs of contradictories, a thing must exist in one or the other respect even when it does not exist entirely in either."[13] Accordingly, a presumed change from nonwhite to white would proceed by something which at first is nonwhite becoming increasingly less nonwhite and then increasingly more white until it *is* white. Movements or changes whose termini are contraries (e.g., hot and cold) would be delineated similarly. Unlike contradictories, however, it need not be the case that one or the other of a given pair of contraries must exist in, or be ascribed to, something before it changes; and so, were this the case, that pair of contraries *could not* be the termini of any change we might ascribe to it (or presume for it).

But neither contradictories nor contraries can exist concurrently; and so, since Aristotle's analysis explicates the reality of movement (change, coming-to-be, etc.) in terms of contradictory and contrary termini, his analysis seems unable to assure movement's reality after all. In other words, the very things (the termini) required to delineate or explain a movement's real existence imply that it does not have real existence since at most one of them can itself exist at the movement's purported inception, conclusion, or anywhere in between, and yet the movement is purportedly explained as existing "partly in the one" and "partly in the other" of the two. Indeed, upon summarizing his analysis in his well-known definition of movement as "the realization of what is potentially real, with respect just to its potential reality"[14] (so that "everything changes from what is real potentially to what is real actually"[15]), Aristotle admits (though he waffles a bit) that his analysis implies that movement must be "an indefinite sort of thing, . . . as it belongs neither just among potential realities nor just among actually existent things; . . . perhaps movement is an actual existence, but one whose actuality is incomplete."[16] Moreover, Aristotle's termini of movement (even if they were able to assure its reality) do not explain *how* movement can begin nor *how* it can be completed (or arrive at an end), though these seem to be Zeno's principal points of attack on its real existence. Once again, Aristotle seems at first to acquiesce but then salvages a half-victory. He accepts the Eleatic conclusion that "for any given process of change, a beginning [or source] does not exist."[17] Yet he insists that the change must have arrived at its end in a way not needing explanation, namely, *instantaneously*[18]; otherwise, "something which has changed would, at the moment when it has changed, be changing into that which it has changed. But this is impossible; and so, that which has changed must already [or, in the exact same moment] attain that into which it has changed. . . . [Hence,] that first moment of its existence, when what has changed has just changed, must be indivisible."[19]

Plotinus launches his most explicit attack on Aristotle's analysis by arguing that to term movement "incompleteness in actual existence" is not to classify it as something other than a form of actual existence. Rather, Plotinus argues, "incompleteness is ascribed to it, not because in no respect is it an actuality, but because it is entirely an actuality and [one which] embraces its completeness recursively ('again and again') – and not in order finally to attain actual existence, which it entirely has already, but in order to bring about something else whose existence is consequent upon its own actual existence, . . . a state-of-affairs which it was intent to bring about" (VI.1.16.5–9). Here, Plotinus rejects Aristotle's axiom partitioning a movement's reality and placing parts of its existence in each of its termini and argues instead that movement differs from other real sorts of existence by its actuality's inherent recursivity. The Aristotelian conceit that part of Achilles' running movement remains back at the start-line and part of it has already arrived at the end-line (presumably, with numerous additional parts of it strewn along the way between the two) is absurd. Wherever and whenever Achilles is running, he is doing nothing less than entirely running and, there and then, his movement is nothing less than an entirely real or actual running-movement. Moreover, Aristotle has the relationship between a movement and its end backwards. Achilles' arriving at the end-line does not explain (even partly) his running; rather, Achilles' running-movement causes and explains his arriving at the end-line.

More precisely, Plotinus distinguishes above between a movement's actuality and various states-of-affairs whose existence is "consequent upon" the movement and its actual recursion. Achilles' arrival at his end-line is a result of his continual (recursively actual) running-movement. Such quantities as the distance he runs and the time it takes him to run it are also states-of-affairs that are consequent upon his running-movement – effects brought about by its actual existence and continuance (recursion) therein and not causes, sources, or delineations of its real existence or of the actual sort of movement it is. Using an example of someone who intends to walk one complete lap around a stadium, Plotinus thus argues that his movement is (entirely) actual walking "from its beginning [or source]," so that "if he intended to complete a stadium lap but did not, the deficiency did not exist in his walking – in the walking-movement itself – but [given his intent] in the distance that he walked. For, walking, even with respect to distance of any given smallness whatsoever, is still walking, and is already [actual walking-]movement" (VI.1.16.10–14).

Plotinus calls special attention to the "foolish discussion" wherein Aristotle argues that "there does not exist a beginning [of movement] relating to some time at which or after which the movement proceeded, so that nor is there any [actual, real] source even for the movement itself" (VI.1.16.21–3). Aristotle's acquiescence to Zeno's denial of a beginning or source (archê) for movement is tantamount to denying that its reality is explicable, since something's real existence is explicable primarily in terms of its source. For now, though Plotinus emphasizes the logical muddle Aristotle makes of a movement's relation to time when Aristotle maintains, for example, both that "the actuality of a movement [as Aristotle understands this] comes-to-be timelessly" (it arrives at its end instantaneously) and yet also that "the [actual] movement itself requires time, and not just some [temporal] duration or other . . . but a definite quantity of time" (VI.1.16.26–8). Rather, not only are all temporal (or, e.g., spatial and other quantitative) states-of-affairs relating to a given movement consequent upon its reality[20] but, Plotinus explains further, all such states-of-affairs may thereupon be ascribed to the movement itself only accidentally (kata sumbebêkos) (VI.1.16.29–30), as opposed to ascribing things essentially (kath'hauto). When Plotinus's lap-walker ceases walking, for example, she will have walked for one hour or two hours or some other definite time, and she will have completed one lap or one-half of one lap or some other definite distance. These states-of-affairs will be consequent upon her movement because they will coincide with the cessation of her walking and they will be explicable (caused) by the walking she will have done. Yet, she will have actually walked (continually, recursively) – indeed lap-walked – no matter the elapsed time or the completed distance, or whether this was the time or the distance she may have intended. As in qualities' accidental relation to composite substances, a movement would remain just the sort of movement it is and would proceed just the way in which a movement of that sort proceeds were it to bring about different states-of-affairs (or, were the states-of-affairs brought about by it different).

In response to Aristotle, then, Plotinus maintains that a movement's reality is not explicated by its termini or any other such accidental states-of-affairs, all of which are instead consequent upon *it*, so that it is rather the source or cause of *their* reality. To develop further his analysis of movement (or coming-to-be) Plotinus analyzes *productivity* and *passivity* in coming-to-be, adapts and incorporates Aristotle's conceit of *potentiality* into his analysis, and critiques the Aristotelian notion of *essence* and its relation to qualities and (or) accidents. In so doing, he relates comings-to-be to his primary explication of physical substance (viz., the form–matter composite) and to his notion of the primary causes of reality in the natural universe (viz., forming-principles) in such a way that these are more clearly understood as the sources or causes of coming-to-be in physical reality. His explication of productivity and passivity initiates these developments inasmuch as characterizing movement in one of these two ways seems to require relating its actuality to some one or another particular that is either moving or being moved; and it ends up associating passivity with movements ascribed to corporeal things as such – for example, with (S2) substances or with the constitutive substances which then constitute their corporeal components or parts – and productivity with movements ascribed to forms, or forming-principles – for example, with (S1) substances or with the forming-principles that cause their composition and compositional forms.

Plotinus suggests several ways one might distinguish productivity and passivity with respect to movement; but the formulation which instigates his own analysis states that "movements which proceed from the moving things themselves are productive," whereas "movements which proceed from others [into the moved thing] are passive" (VI.1.19.11–12). Plotinus evaluates this formulation by considering, first, whether passivity is thereby characteristic of movements which could also be productive from another (opposite) viewpoint and, second, the relevance of a movement's source to whether it is productive or passive. He introduces the former consideration by observing that if movements which proceed from others are thereby passive, then these same movements could also be denoted as "movements which proceed into others"; for example, "cutting, both as proceeding from what is cutting and as proceeding into what is being cut, is one movement" (VI.1.19.14–16). Cutting, as what proceeds into what is being cut, is not merely "from another" but proceeds in other words from the cutter itself (or himself), and so it would be productive from its (or his) viewpoint. Plotinus suggests two ways to avoid having the identically same movement be both passive and productive. The first considers such movements to be in reality successive pairs of movement, so that, for example, "cutting occurs when, from a certain sort of actuality and movement ascribed to the cutter, another succeeding movement comes to be in what is cut" (VI.1.19.16–18). The second considers the cutting movement as such to be a single (and productive) movement proceeding from the cutter into what is cut, and then it utilizes the notion that one existence may be different from yet consequent upon another to maintain that "the difference may not pertain to being cut as such but to a distinct movement which comes to be [in the recipient or 'patient'] consequent upon being cut: for example, being in pain, which is a clear case of something that is undergone passively" (VI.1.19.18–21).

Plotinus prefers this second way, presumably because it conforms to clear cases of passivity, as when a sentient being suffers pain consequent upon being cut. He concludes from this that, when no such distinct movement is passively undergone by the patient, there is no passivity but only the fact that when movement proceeds from one thing into another "productive movement has a double existence: first, without regard for its existing in another thing, when this is intended by it, and, second, as existing also in that other thing" (VI.1.19.23–5). Plotinus also concludes from this that "passivity" denotes "what comes to be consequent upon a productive movement, where this does not mean its opposite (as being burnt is the opposite of burning) but denotes something that comes to be consequent upon the one real movement of being burnt and burning – namely, pain or something else, for example, shrivelling-up" (VI.1.19.35–9). Plotinus's second consideration, the relevance of a movement's source to its productivity or passivity, is not so readily resolved.

Plotinus first considers whether a source of movement could not also passively undergo something consequent upon its own movement – or, in terms of the original formulation, whether passive movements must proceed from others or, now, be consequent only

upon movements which proceed from others. He cites an example of
one thing rubbing against another (e.g., so that the latter is left scarred
in some way) and he suggests that the former might also passively
undergo in some way (e.g., become scarred as well): "Are we to
say that somehow two [productive] movements exist in relation to
the one thing [viz., the one rubbing]? But how could there be two
movements, when the rubbing-movement is only one movement?"
(VI.1.20.10–12). Or, for an example involving only one thing from the
beginning (and which also begins relating his analysis to physical
substance), Plotinus suggests a maturing swan whose feathers undergo "being whitened" because of productive movement by its own
forming-principle; but he adds that here there may be some question
whether it is proper even to presume that its feathers being whitened
may be a passive movement: "If the forming-principle of the swan
includes whiteness and a swan which is coming-to-be is whitened,
shall we say that the swan passively undergoes being whitened if it is
being whitened while proceeding to-be a substance? Shall we say this
if, instead, its being whitened is consequent upon its having come-to-
be a substance?" (VI.1.20.18–21). Finally, Plotinus complicates matters even more with an example where one thing is being moved by
another yet seems involved in bringing about what it consequently
undergoes, observing that when a student learns something which his
teacher has been intent on teaching him, "neither does it seem that
the student himself will not have been actively involved in his coming to know; for, learning is not like being struck, inasmuch as it
includes a real understanding and becoming cognizant of what is
learned" (VI.1.20.30–2). Plotinus, secondly, also questions the original formulation of productivity as movement whose source is the
moving thing itself. Desire, for example, seems a productive movement; after all, we say "*I* desire so-and-so" or "*she* desires such-and-
such," just as we say "I hit so-and-so" or "she pushed such-and-such."
Yet, it also seems that "desire moves because of the [external] object
of desire" (VI.1.21.14). Plotinus responds, however, that desirous
movement "does not result from some productivity proceeding from
the object towards which desire moves, but from desire rousing itself
in response to that object" (VI.1.21.14–15). Nevertheless, Plotinus
seems to think that the possibility of other-sourced productive movement is sufficient for concern, even if desire is not a particularly good
example of it.

Plotinus attempts to synthesize the salient features of all these (counter) examples by proposing that "passivity does not exist based on whether movement is from another or from oneself – e.g., something may rot on its own; rather, it exists when something, without part of itself being involved in the production, endures an alteration which is not involved in bringing about its substance" (VI.1.21.18–21). Thus, if some "part" of human beings is productively involved in our becoming desirous or becoming knowledgeable, then these are not passive movements; but if not, then they are. The case of one thing rubbing against another would seem to depend on whether the former's also becoming scarred is for it analogous to fruit rotting or whether it must have an analogous aetiology to the scarring undergone by the latter. In either case, its own scarring would not be due to a productive movement from another thing; but fruit's rotting seems sufficiently explained as due to inherent weaknesses in fruit's corporeal constitution rather than as a state-of-affairs which fruit produces as such, and the scarring undergone by the thing doing the rubbing might be explicable in a similar way. This proposal's bearing on the maturing swan case may seem equally clear: If the feathers whitening were consequent upon its coming-to-be-a-swan-substance, the whitening would not be involved in bringing about its substance; but, since whiteness was presumed to be contained in its forming-principle, it would seem that "part" of the swan is involved in producing that whitening. Plotinus raises a potential counterexample to the current proposal, however, which further complicates the swan case as well.

Plotinus focuses on the stricture that movement involved in the coming-to-be of a substance does not qualify for passivity, and supposes that a statue's remaining hot consequent upon the bronze being heated during production of the statue thereby involves its hotness in the bringing about of a substance (viz., the statue); whereas, there also are many cases where something's being hot is not consequent upon any substance-producing movement. Hence, it may seem that being hot sometimes is and sometimes is not a passivity (VI.1.21.23–6). In response to this suggestion, Plotinus distinguishes the substance (the statue) from the matter (the bronze) and argues that, since the statue is not what was heated during its production (the bronze was), strictly speaking the statue is also not what remains hot as a result of that heating (the bronze is); consequently, the hotness ascribed to the statue in the example's initial supposition could not be the hotness involved in bringing it about, nor a remnant of *that* hotness as such (VI.1.21.26–9). In the maturing swan case, of course, whiteness was presumed to be contained in its forming-principle, and this might or might not have an analog in how hotness may or may not relate to statue-forming. However, the swan's feathers (and other corporeal components and constituents) *are* analogs to the statue's bronze. So, if the feathers whitening is strictly speaking not an alteration endured by the swan-substance then it would qualify for passivity, whether or not the whiteness contained in the swan's forming-principle would thereby involve "part" of the swan in producing that whitening.

Strictly speaking, too, "alteration" most typically denotes movement with respect to contrary qualities (e.g., hot and cold, wet and dry, light and dark); but there is no obvious reason why passive movement should be similarly restricted (e.g., being in pain need not be preceded by feeling pleasure), nor why it should be restricted to qualitative delineations of such movements insofar as they may be ascribed to composites or to corporeally constituted substances as such. Plotinus may have this in mind when he summarizes his analysis by concluding that "passivity comes-to-be when something has within itself a movement whereby it is altered *in any way*; whereas productivity exists either when something has within itself a self-contained movement arising from itself, or else when a movement arising from itself proceeds to its end within another" (VI.1.22.1–5). Or, as he restates it without mentioning the restrictive term "alteration" at all:

Passivity resides in something's being disposed [ordered, or inclined] *differently than before.* The substance of what passively undergoes gains nothing whatsoever that pertains to substance; and, when a substance does come-to-be, what passively undergoes is another reality [than the substance as such: viz., its corporeal constituents]. (VI.1.22.8–10. cf. III.6.19.8–11)

Plotinus thus associates passivity with movements ascribed to bodies (e.g., to constitutive substances, or to the corporeal components of physical substances), either as such or with respect to features of qualitative existence that are closely associated with bodies. He maintains that *corporeal things are as such always and only passive* with respect to movement (III.6.6.50–2), and he associates productivity and passivity also with a distinction between soul-like movements and corporeal movements (VI.1.19.9). He thus argues, for example, that a presumably soul-like movement such as remembering should not be explicated as an alteration because "passive undergoing is associated with an activity of this sort only because of the composite substance's relationship with matter [i.e., corporeality or its being corporeally constituted] . . . as, for example, is also the case with sight, where the seeing is in reality an active process but the eye is concurrently subjected to passive movement" (III.6.2.49–54).

Alteration, or passive coming-to-be, must still conform to Plotinus's initial analysis of movement *contra* Aristotle: it must as such be just a certain sort of actual movement, even if one that always is passively undergone by corporeal things. That is, Plotinus observes, "alteration" (and also "change") may be understood "to signify something that is different and in opposition to something else" (e.g., something hot, as this would differ from something cold, its "opposite"); but, the sort of actual *movement* it denotes is one wherein things actually move in certain ways, even if passively and not productively: "Hence, alteration is indeed a certain form of movement: movement wherein *something departs from how it itself was*" (VI.3.21.46–7). Aristotle's analysis implied that an alterative movement's actuality is delineated by ("exists in"), for example, the hotness of the thing which has been altered and the thing's contrary coldness before it was altered. But, Plotinus's analysis implies that these qualitative states-of-affairs are only accidentally related to the alterative movement as such. As something "departs from how it was" in a certain way, if this is regarding its temperature and it was cold, then the qualitative state-of-affairs related to the onset of its alterative movement would, consequently, be coldness; and it may also be the case that the qualitative state-of-affairs related to the cessation of its alterative movement is hotness, if this is the quality we would ascribe to something which has departed from its previously cold condition precisely as this thing had when its alterative movement ceased. The actual movement, however, is as such neither of these two accidental consequents (nor somehow both of them) but is just its actually departing from what it was in a certain way (here, regarding its temperature), and this was entirely the movement's actuality at its onset and continually (or, recursively) until it ceased.

In physical reality, moreover, an alteration of some sort or other (i.e., some passively undergone alterative movement or other) accompanies every movement. In physical reality, in other words, movement always moves something and what it moves is always something corporeal or which is corporeally constituted. And it is in this regard, Plotinus believes, that the language of potentiality is appropriate and useful to analyzing movement. Aristotle's understanding of his own notion that movement is a sort of incompleteness in actual existence (viz., that its actuality is somehow incomplete) was misguided; insofar as a movement of a certain sort actually exists at all, it entirely exists as in actuality a movement of just that sort. The foregoing distinction between productive movements and passive movements, however, begins detailing how actual movement relates to physically real particulars or, more precisely, to physical substances and their forming-principles. The notion of passivity with respect to movement seems particularly ripe for further investigation regarding its relation to the notion of passivity with respect to substance, for example, regarding the passive role of "matter" as substrate.

Plotinus states that we can give "an impression" (a useful, even if not strictly proper or perspicuous, indication) of what movement is by characterizing it as "the passage of something from potentiality to that which it is said potentially to be" (VI.3.22.4–5); and, he avers that when explicated this way movement may be distinguished into those whereby something potential comes-to-be a real thing of a certain sort and those whereby something potential comes-to-be a real thing with respect just to the movement itself: "For, something may be potentially a real thing in that it can attain a certain form (e.g., it may be potentially a statue) and another in that it can attain an activity (e.g., it is able to walk), and when the former proceeds to become a statue, this procession is its movement; whereas, when the latter proceeds to walk, the walking is the movement," for example, so that the thing becomes something-walking (VI.3.22.5–9). But, in either sort of case, since movement differs from other actualities by its recursivity, "so long as movement is present the thing has a continual urge towards another – to be different, not to remain in sameness" (VI.3.22.40–1). To incorporate into Plotinus's analysis, then, the notion that some sort of "passage" occurs in these two sorts of cases that is indicative of movement must, rather, itself be explicable in terms of the actuality of the movement itself, for example, so that for what goes through this "passage" the movement itself is from its onset "a restlessly awake form" (VI.3.22.14) and not itself a potential existence. Likewise, what it means for what goes through this "passage" to be initially a potentially real thing must also conform to Plotinus's stricture that only actually existing or real things can be real causes or provide real explanation. Plotinus thus argues that in cases where this actual existence is something other than the movement itself, as in the example of the statue,

> one must speak of some potentially real thing as "already another thing," as something and able to be another thing subsequently to being itself, either in such a way that it nonetheless survives the production of that other thing or else meaning that by admitting its own destruction it sacrifices itself for the sake of that other thing. The former is the sense of saying "bronze is potentially a statue," whereas water is potentially bronze and air is potentially fire in the latter sense. (II.5.1.17–22)

But, then, what *were* we saying when we initially ascribed potential existence, or a potentiality, to something (e.g., the bronze)?

One response might be that "potentiality" denotes a potency (or power) which something has to generate, produce, or do something, so that articulating something's potentialities delineates the extent or range of its potency. Plotinus rejects this approach (II.5.1.22–6). It certainly seems off-the-mark to suppose, for example, in the case of the bronze which is potentially a statue, that bronze has the potency to produce statues. Another response would be that something's potentialities delimit it with respect to the sorts of comings-to-be or movements in which it may become involved. This second response seems to be Plotinus's own intent in maintaining that, "rather, *potential existence*, in our sense, designates some such thing as a certain substrate for passive undergoings and shapes and forms which it is meant to receive in that it is disposed by nature to be receptive of them" (II.5.1.29–32). Here, Plotinus also implies that a potentially real thing's involvement or role in coming-to-be must as such be entirely passive; its potentialities delimit, in particular, the sorts of passive movements (also forms, etc.) which may be ascribed to it as their substrate when it becomes involved or implicated in some movement or coming-to-be. Accordingly, Plotinus reasons further:

> If this is so, then it is not that the potential thing comes-to-be an actual thing but rather that the subsequent actual thing comes-to-be from the preceding potential thing. Moreover, the actual reality is the composite –

not just the matter nor just the form imposing on it. This includes cases where a different substance comes-to-be, as the statue comes-to-be from the bronze; for, it is a different substance just in that now the composite is the statue. Whereas, when things are considered entirely not to persist, it is evident that the potential thing was different in every respect from the subsequent actual thing. (II.5.2.8–15)

Plotinus's disavowal in his current context of potentiality as potency thus renders matter also passive with respect to the actual compositing of a physical substance from it (i.e., when the relevant "matter" is a constitutive substance), in that *it* does not as such come-to-be what exists from it at all. Rather, what comes-to-be is the actual (composite) substance and this coming-to-be does not occur, for example, because a potential existence or potentiality becomes otherwise (e.g., becomes itself a real existence, or a realization or actuality). Rather, whereas previously there was potentiality or a potential existence (e.g., bronze) there now exists, because of the actual coming-to-be of a real thing (e.g., a *statue*-producing movement, if you will, or a movement productive *of a statue*), an actual substance (e.g., a statue). Strictly speaking, then, the matter is not involved in the actual coming-to-be of a substance, though one consequence of this coming-to-be is that the matter is now related to the composite as the substrate or "recipient," for example, of its passive undergoings. At least with respect to this consequence, though, the matter *has* undergone an alteration of sorts, and so must in some sense be "differently disposed than before."

This last, and the preceding notion that matter or corporeal things cannot as such be involved in the actual coming-to-be of a composite substance (since this is a productive form of movement and matter is entirely passive with respect to movement) become clearer when we also recognize that the actuality or real existence of movement generally, far from being an abstraction from our observations of movement in physical reality, is rather itself the explanatory cause of the observable phenomena with which we commonly identify it:

We must not suppose that things which are in movement are the existent movements. For, walking is not the feet but an actuality proceeding from a potency to encompass the feet. Since the potency cannot be seen in the authentic condition in which it exists [as a potency], however, it is necessary to look at the activity of the feet, that is, not simply the feet as when they were at rest but as they are now encompassed by another [prior] existence. This cannot as such be seen but by its association with something else [the feet] it can be seen accidentally (*kata sumbebêkos*) when one looks at the feet as first one assumes a certain position and then the other one does and they are not still. But the alternating bipedal movement one thus sees is a consequence of the alternating feet whereas the walking-movement itself is not something qualitative regarding the feet. (VI.3.23.5–13)

Here, Plotinus explicates observable movement, or movement as seemingly engaged in by observable (corporeal) things, in terms of the actuality of movement as such and its use ("encompassing") of corporeal things (e.g., a substance's bodily components) to manifest itself in observable ways, which may then be ascribed *accidentally* to its real source or cause. In this way, the corporeal things utilized by actual movement in manifesting itself in observable ways may as such be involved in movement only passively and not productively; and so, "movement comes into sensible [corporeal] things from another which stirs and prods and innervates and pushes those which participate in it so that they do not pause nor exist successively in the exact same condition" (VI.3.23.1–4). Hence, corporeal things cannot as such be real sources or causes of movement; rather, movement causes corporeal things to move because it proceeds from a potent source to utilize or "encompass" them "as a breath of air proceeds into another. And so, when the potency for movement is the capacity to walk it pushes, as it were, and it productively moves the walker's feet continually to assume one position after another; and when it is the capacity to heat it heats something; and when the potency brings matter together into a natural assemblage it is the generative capacity for natural growth . . . " (VI.3.23.20–5).

Plotinus's adaptation and incorporation of the language of potentiality into his analysis of coming-to-be, we have seen, also focuses that analysis on the coming-to-be of physical substances as form–matter composites (cf. VI.3.3–5). In those terms, however, physical *substances* do have a means for causative involvement in movement inasmuch as they have (indeed, strictly speaking, are) compositional forms and, unlike matter,

no form of any kind can admit disorder or be at all passive but must be itself undisturbed while the matter has become passively related to it so that

when there is coming-to-be the form, because of its presence in the composition, sets the matter in movement. . . . And so, this is the manner in which
actual form exists in nature: such that it produces coming-to-be because of
its presence in a composite substance – just as if the harmony existing in a
lyre, by proceeding from itself, plucked the lyre's strings. (III.6.4.35–44)

But explicating the productive capabilities of physical substances
this way may seem most apropos comings-to-be which presume an
already existing substance – for example, walking or growing. On
the contrary, explicating the production or actual coming-to-be of a
composite in terms, for example, of form "coming to" matter and
compositing a substance from it, or of matter "receiving" compositional form so that an actual substance exists where previously there
was only matter, may *primarily* emphasize and characterize matter's passivity with respect to the coming-to-be of substances; but
Plotinus maintains along with this that the real causes of all movement or coming-to-be in physical reality are just the potencies
which compositional forms bring to physical reality (i.e., we shall
see, which exist in the forming-principles that "bring," for example,
cause, compositional form).

Plotinus's distinction between a statue coming-to-be from bronze
and the bronze coming-to-be from water or fire coming-to-be from
air, for example, was not meant to distinguish between the coming-
to-be of substances and some other wholly different sort of coming-
to-be. Rather, the coming-to-be of bronze from water and of fire
from air are examples of the coming-to-be of some *elemental* constitutive substance from another *elemental* constitutive substance.
Plotinus insists that elemental fire, for example, must come-to-be
just as other physical substances do (e.g., by matter receiving the
form of fire or, more fundamentally, by a forming-principle configuring matter in a certain way);[21] or, if someone obstinately insists
that matter instead is, say, set on fire when elemental fire comes-
to-be: " 'set on fire' is not being used in its usual sense but here
means that matter has come-to-be fire. For, it is not the same for
something to come-to-be fire and for something to be set on
fire; . . . and, how could that which is itself a part of [elemental
substance] fire be set on fire?" (III.6.12.37–42). For, as themselves
substances, constitutive substances (including elemental ones)
must have their own compositional forms (and so also potencies).
As *constitutive* substances, however, they differ from one another

in what we might term their *constitutive potentials*. Plotinus's subsequent characterization of the coming-to-be of elemental constitutive substance in terms of what comes-to-be differing from the substance whence it came "in every respect" thus means that, in whatever other respects they may or may not differ,[22] they at least differ in their constitutive potentials; whereas, when a nonelemental substance comes-to-be, the potentially real thing "persists in the coming-to-be" in that the constitutive potentials of the constitutive substance whence it came remain the same. For example, the bronze, as now the corporeal constituency of a statue, retains the exact same constitutive potentials it had before the onset of the productive movement(s) wherein the statue actually came-to-be. Were other productive movements to occur wherein another substance (e.g., a sword) came-to-be from the same bronze, and so replaced the statue-substance, or were the bronze to become an inchoate mass of bronze once again, it would not need somehow to regain its constitutive potential regarding statues; for, it had never lost it or had it transform into something other than a constitutive potential.

But, then, in what sense *does* the bronze as "matter" become differently disposed as a consequence of its passivity with respect to the actual coming-to-be of a statue? The statue's shape would seem to belong to the statue and the hotness which earlier was presumed to remain in the bronze would belong, respectively, to the statue and to the bronze insofar as these may be explicated as Accidental or Derivable substances, and so these qualities would not pertain to them as substances in the more proper, (S1) or (S2), sense presumed by the current discussion. We have, however, in effect seen yet another way in which matter may be passive: for example, as in Plotinus's example of the potency for walking-movement utilizing a human being's feet to observably manifest the actuality of the walking-movement it produces. To generalize, Plotinus sometimes terms the productive source of movement in physical substances *soul*, and he maintains that "the potency of soul's substance, as ruler over corporeal things, moves things to come-to-be and to do so just as it moves them" (IV.3.10.20–1). Matter, as constitutive substance and then as the corporeal constituents of composite substances, is thus passive also as an *instrument* (or, an *instrumentality*) for the productive movements of soul, form-in-nature, or whatever notion we use to denote the potent source of movement in physical reality.

A bronze sword may be a clearer example here, inasmuch as the bronze is not merely the sword's corporeal constituency but it is thereby also a capable instrument for cutting; whereas, an inchoate mass of bronze, for example, is incapable of being used to cut anything. Analogously, the corporeal constitution of an organic animal-substance is a capable instrumentality for growth, local-movement, or the like. In various such ways and respects, then, a substance's corporeal constituents are relied upon for capabilities or potentials not in those constituents as such, or as just the constitutive substance from which the physical substance was composed, so that it (or they) is (are) now "differently disposed than before" regarding what we might term its (or their) *instrumental potential(ities)*.

Plotinus adds crucial detail for explicating how his analysis extends to comings-to-be or movements by already existing substances when, *pace* treating potentiality and actuality as contraries, he queries: "When one who is potentially learned comes to be actually learned, how could it not be the case that what potentially existed and the actually existing thing are the same thing? For, the potentially wise Socrates is the same Socrates as the actually wise Socrates" (II.5.2.15–17). In response, Plotinus argues that a composite's coming-to-be in a certain condition must (whether or not this is a qualitative state-of-affairs) be *accidental* to the substance itself and yet be explicable by something in the substance which has an *essential potential* for that condition, or for coming-to-be in that condition. Thus, in his recent example:

The uneducated person comes-to-be knowledgeable accidentally. For, it was not due to being uneducated that a person was potentially knowledgeable but it also was accidental to him that he was uneducated; rather, his soul, having the prior disposition for knowledge essentially, was the potential thing because of which he came to be knowledgeable. (II.5.2.19–23)

Moreover, the composite's accidental potentials (delimiting in what ways or what else it may come-to-be) and the essential potentials of what in it causes (is the source of) its comings-to-be both are unaffected by its subsequent, actual comings-to-be. For example, "does the potential for knowledge survive the coming-to-be and the potential to be learned remain after he becomes learned? Indeed, nothing prevents this, and we can describe it in another way: Previously there was the potential only, whereas now the form of knowledge also exists in the potential thing" (II.5.2.23–7). Plotinus adds that the form of a statue likewise "supervenes upon" its substrate (II.5.2.27–8), rather than somehow replacing or displacing its statue-potential, so that the composite may concurrently both be actual in a certain respect (because of its form) and also remain potential in that same respect (because of its matter). Similarly, something in a substance may be (and remain) essentially potential in a certain respect concurrently with (and still after) it actually comes-to-be in that same respect. To be sure, Plotinus argues his point here from considering the paradigmatically soul-like movement of coming-to-know; but, we have seen, all productive movement is in reality soul-like movement. Any physical substance which (unlike an artifact, e.g., a statue) may causatively or productively involve itself in actual coming-to-be may do so, in other words, only because it or some "part" of it has the requisite essential potential, which (unlike accidental, instrumental, and constitutive potentials and also mere or material potentials) is indeed a *potency,* or *power.*

Of course, an already existing substance also may come-to-be consequent upon productive movement by another thing or substance. Such cases would seem to divide into the following sorts. In some cases, the substance might in fact not come-to-be at all. Its movement is just the productive movement proceeding from its source into that substance. In such cases, the movement will cease in the recipient substance when its source ceases producing it. At the other end of the spectrum, a productive movement may affect it, or alter its matter (its corporeal constitution or constituents), such that the substance is in fact perishing rather than coming-to-be. In between these two extremes are cases where the substance is indeed consequently coming-to-be and not perishing. One way in which this could happen is on the model mentioned earlier for desire, wherein it comes-to-be because of a potency within it but as this responds to a stimulus or other condition effected by another source. Another way would be for the productive movement to affect it, or alter its matter, but in a manner that is insufficient to bring about its demise. In such cases, however, it would seem that either the substance must respond potently to the passive movement it consequently undergoes and return to its proper condition, or else it will be diminished to some extent. It seems most consistent with Plotinus's analysis, in other words, to consider any purported coming-to-be of a substance which is neither directly con-

sequent upon (or caused by) its own potencies nor indirectly consequent upon its potencies, as these sufficiently respond to invasive
movements from other sources, to be in reality involved in the contrary of coming-to-be, namely perishing, destruction, or at least the
diminution of substance.

Plotinus most commonly identifies that "part" of a physically
real particular that has the essential potentials (potencies) associated with its compositional form as its forming-principle, so that:
"we term that *form* which is capable of producing a substance and
forming-principle that which in the domain of [physical] substance
productively moves it in conformity with its form" (VI.3.3.15–16).
Consistent with our discussion of essential potentials, moreover,
Plotinus thus further relates the coming-to-be of substances to his
more metaphysically real or explanatory notion of forming-
principles in arguing:

When the form proceeds to matter it brings everything along with it, since
the form encompasses everything – even magnitude, and everything else, in
accordance with the forming-principle and what proceeds from it. Magnitude is thus delineated for each sort of natural thing because of its form; for,
the magnitude [or dimensions] of a human being differs from a bird's, and it
also differs among various sorts of birds. . . . Likewise, a particular thing,
insofar as whiteness may be present in it, comes-to-be white because that
[forming-principle] within this living being produces a white-colored thing,
just as various other colors may be present in a variegated thing not because
there exists some sort of variegated color but, if you please, because it has a
variegated forming-principle. (II.4.8.23–8 and 9.8–10. Cf. III.6.16.1–10 and
17.27–31)

Heavily influenced by the Stoics' understanding of *logoi* (forming-
principles) as generative causes existing within nature, Plotinus
objects especially to their conceiving these as themselves instrumentalities of a single causative source for all nature which preordains
"what is necessary for everything in every respect" (III.1.7).[23] Nonetheless, Plotinus utilizes their understanding of *logoi* as the primary
productive causes in nature to explain not only the real existence and
compositional forms of particulars but also all movement and everything that a physical substance shall come-to-be or that is consequent upon its movements or comings-to-be. Thus, regarding even
physical substances' corporeal constitutions and related qualities,
Plotinus maintains that "although corporeal things (e.g., animal bod-

ies and vegetal bodies) exist, each one of them, as a plurality because of their colors and configurations and magnitudes and their various bodily parts and in whatever else may differ among them, this entire plurality derives from some one thing . . . [so that] corporeal substance exists because of the potency of forming-principles" (VI.2.5.1–5 and 14. cf. VI.6.13.55–7). Plotinus argues even further that the notion of "corporeality" itself, in reference to the corporeal constitutions or "bodies" of physical substances, does not denote just "an assemblage of everything associated with corporeal things" but "a certain kind of form and forming-principle: one which by relating itself to matter produces the corporeal thing"; and so, since the forming-principle of a corporeal thing is therefore "not nothing more than a definition denoting an existing thing by reference to a certain essence [as it is for Aristotle] but a forming-principle which produced the existing thing itself," he concludes that it must "encompass everything which delineates a thing with respect to the qualities distinctive of corporeal things" (II.7.3).[24] Plotinus's notion of forming-principles is, however, pivotal in his own understanding of physical *essence*. That is, his foregoing objection to Aristotle's understanding of *logoi* as definitional formulae, rather than real causes, is meant to complement his rejection as well (cf. II.7.5) of Aristotle's understanding of essence as what is designated regarding a substance by a definitional formula mentioning its genus and providing it a specific difference (e.g., "a human being is a rational animal"). Rather, the essences of physical substances, Plotinus maintains, are identical to their forming-principles (VI.3.7.6–9). Plotinus's own understanding of essences, accordingly, may be viewed either as a denial of (Aristotelian) essentialism, or as a *super-essentialism* in its own right inasmuch as it implies (*pace* Aristotle's genus/differentia formulae) that "you therefore must state *everything* pertinent to existing things in your causal accounts (*aitiologoi*) of them" (VI.7.3.13–14).

More precisely, Aristotle understood the "what something was meant to be" (*to ti en einai*) or the "what it is to be something" (*to ti estin*) – his principal Greek locutions for what is commonly translated as *essence* – to be what is designated by a definitional formula which "conforms to the thing itself (*kath'hauto*)."[25] In explanation, Aristotle suggests that the essence of a thing is designated in response to concerns of the form "Why is it that a thing is what it is [and not something else]?" – for example, "Why is it that a human being is a human being [and not, e.g., a rutabaga]?" Such concerns, Aristotle argues, cannot be about something's "fundamental existence" since (as in his strategy *contra* Zeno on movement) if this were not already evident, such concerns could not be raised or investigated regarding it. They must therefore be concerns about why something is itself, rather than something else; and, such concerns are most surely answered by designating "just the thing itself" – or, playing off Aristotle's Greek locutions, by recognizing that a thing is what it is because it is-what-it-is to be that thing, or because it is what it was meant to be.[26]

Plotinus's adaptation of Aristotle's locutions and narrative vocabulary contrasts his own understanding of essence with Aristotle's in two subtle, yet significant, ways. First, Plotinus *does* link the *dia ti* (in the Aristotelian context, the "why a thing is") to discerning *"the cause, within the thing itself, of its fundamental existence"* (VI.7.2.27). Whereas Aristotle characterized the essence of a thing as just the "why a thing is itself," Plotinus's analogous characterization asserts that "the essence for each thing is that because of which it exists" (VI.7.2.16). Second, Plotinus is sure *initially* that a thing and its essence coincide only in the case of his authentic-realities – forms as they exist in and proceed immediately from his metaphysical principle of intelligibility, *Nous* (Intellect). Thus, Plotinus foreshadows his insistence that we state "everything pertinent" in articulating a (complete or sufficient) causal accounting of something's real existence when he observes that "there [in intellect] everything exists in unity, so that the existing thing and its because-of-which [cause] are the same. Here below, too, often the existing thing and its because-of-which [cause] are the same, for example, regarding "What is an eclipse?" (VI.7.2.11–13). Thus, for instance, Luna intercepting Sol's rays is both the cause of a solar eclipse and the solar eclipse itself. But, it may not be initially evident that this holds for everything in the natural universe. In particular, insofar as "a thing is inert and lifeless it does not at all possess that because-of-which it exists" (VI.7.2.20–1). Here, "inert" and "lifeless" is Plotinian argot for lacking a forming-principle. Plotinus's response to his own remark here, though, is that *there are no* corporeal things which are inert and lifeless; or, *nothing* in physical reality *is* inert and lifeless. Rather, some things may be less self-actuating (or potent) and alive (or lively) than others, and so may in that sense be considered to have comparatively weak or deficient forming-principles:

All resistant things and those which impact forcefully when they strike against others are indicative of physical substances. . . . But, I propose, those which are more self-sufficient interfere less with others and are less troublesome for them. Thus, the more solid and earth-like things are (that is, the more they are deficient in life, and are downward-tending and incapable of lifting themselves upwards)[27] the more destructive and violent are their impacts on any slower or weaker bodies they happen to strike against . . . whereas, ensouled things, which means things that participate in reality, the more they participate in reality the more congenial and cooperative they are when relating to their fellow beings. Indeed, movement is but a certain mode of life existing in corporeal things and, for those which possess it, it is an image of that life which seems stronger in things the less corporeal they are – as if the deficit in reality of something lacking in life rendered it more corporeal. And this is even clearer from those movements termed "passive undergoings": for, the more corporeal something is, the more passive its existence – earth more than the other elements, and other things in like proportion to their constitutive elements; whence the other elements coalesce once more into a single body after being divided (if no partition is placed between the divided portions) whereas, when any sort of earth-like body is cut apart, each part remains permanently sundered from every other part. . . . Likewise, something which has become most utterly corporeal, since it has descended most nearly to what is not at all real, becomes too deficient even to reconstitute itself as a [corporeal] unity; and its impacts against others become more forceful and violent, so that they crumble it into numerous pieces because, when one deficient body impacts against another, the force is strong in relation to it as well. (III.6.6.35–64)

By extending reality and life (i.e., forms and forming-principles) even to the most elemental or body-like of things in physical reality,[28] Plotinus thereby relates all physical substances to the authentic-reality of Intellect so that it "gives to every one of them . . . the cause of their existence" (VI.7.2.30–1). Intelligible humanity, for instance, has "the entirety of a human being immanent within it . . . and so, since everything it has it has concurrently from its inception, it thereby contains its essence absolutely and immediately" (VI.7.2.31–3). But, the same entire form of humanity also exists in nature because of the causality of human beings' forming-principles, so that human beings in the natural universe conform to the same principle of intelligibility that partly defines authentic-reality for Plotinus, namely, that "substance and essence and the cause of existence are one" (VI.7.3.22). And this is the case for every other sort of physical substance as well.

Plotinus also critiques the Aristotelian understanding of essence by investigating the notion of specific difference, or differentia, and in so doing relates his treatment of essences to our preceding identification of forming principles' potencies as the real causes of all movement and consequent (including qualitative) states-of-affairs in physical reality. He begins with two problematic suppositions: first, that some qualities, for example, bipedal and quadrapedal, differentiate composite substances while others are "only qualities" and not also differentia; and, second, that there are qualities which for some substances are differentiae – for example, whiteness, which in a swan or in white-lead "brings about its completeness as a substance" – while for others they are accidents of the already existing substance (II.6.1.17–22). Either supposition would allow Plotinus to develop his key points. He chooses to focus on the second, and indicates two approaches to resolving it. The first maintains that, for example, "the whiteness existing in something's forming-principle would indeed be involved in bringing about its completeness but this whiteness would not be a quality; whereas, the whiteness existing because of something's sensible appearance is a quality," and so not a differentia (II.6.1.22–4). The second just distinguishes two sorts of qualities: "those which are also distinctively characteristic of particular existing substances of a certain sort, and those which are only qualities" (II.6.1.24–5). Plotinus proceeds by criticizing this second approach.

Both Aristotelian and Stoic influences converge in Plotinus's critique of the second approach. In the former regard, Plotinus accepts that a differentia must, for instance, be something without which a particular would not be the sort of thing it is (e.g., the rationality in human beings). He thus observes that whiteness could not be a differentia of swans "because there may be swans which are not white" (II.6.1.32). Regarding the latter, Plotinus supposes that a differentia must be something "particularly distinctive" or "distinctively characteristic" of particulars of a given sort *as we sensorially experience them*; and so he argues against the second approach that "it is not reasonable to consider qualities existing in those they bring to completion to be one sort of quality and to consider qualities existing in those they do not bring to completion to be a different sort of quality, since they are the same [in both cases] when considered in the natural course of their own existence" (II.6.1.39–41). The whiteness we sensorially experience in corporeal things, for example, is the same qualitative whiteness whether we observe it in a swan or in white lead or in a coffee-cup or in an autumn snowfall; there is nothing distinctive about the whiteness merely because we observe it in one rather than another sort of thing. Plotinus implies that the supposition that "heat would seem to be what brings fire, *as a substance visible to us*, to completeness," for example, should be treated similarly (II.6.1.35–6).

Indeed, Plotinus begins to show, no qualities could be differentiae of proper (composite) substances because they are not properly "parts" of those substances at all – hence, they could not be parts which "complete" them; rather, qualities are entirely associated with the less proper Accidental or Derivable substance (the "qualified thing"):

The things we denote as being particular existing substances of a given sort are entirely forming-principles, which produce the qualities we then associate with those particulars; and so, if we subsequently investigate what in this respect some one particular substance from among those forming-principles has produced as if it were now itself the completed substance, what we would now be considering is the qualified thing and no longer the particular substance itself. Indeed, this is how we always become misled when, while investigating the particular substance, we back away from it and conform our investigation to the qualified thing instead. For, the real existing fire, for instance, is not what we are asserting it to be when we delineate it in terms which pertain to the qualified thing. The fire itself is a real existing substance; whereas, what we are seeing right now – as we gaze intently at what we are now considering the fire to be – this diverts our investigation from the particular substance, and so what would end up getting defined this way is the qualified thing [and not the fire substance itself]. (II.6.1.41–8)

But, even if qualities as such could not differentiate real physical substances, perhaps they could be sensible envoys of certain real "parts" of forming-principles which therefore *could* differentiate them. This sounds very much like the first of the two approaches introduced at the outset of Plotinus's investigation of differentia; and, indeed, Plotinus does conclude from the foregoing that we should not term those things "qualities" which designate what brings substances to completeness, inasmuch as these are *actualities* proceeding from forming-principles and from potencies indigenous to existing substances of a given sort; whereas, qualities exist outside [proper] substance altogether. They do not appear in the guise of qualities in some cases and not as qualities in other cases but exist amid the superfluant things which are derivatively designated as being substances. (II.6.2.20–5)

But, Aristotelian and Stoic influences again converge, this time in Plotinus's understanding of qualities themselves, to challenge the first approach as well. Thus, in Aristotelian terms, Plotinus avers: "*all* that are *accidental* to things, and so are not actualities and forms of substances, . . . are qualitative" (II.6.3.21–2). The qualities most typically associated with sensible appearances, even if paradigmatic examples of quality, do not exhaust the qualitative domain and nor do they delineate what it is. For this, and so to delineate the accidental domain as well, Plotinus embraces another feature of the Stoics' understanding of qualities and, indeed, generalizes on it[29] when he argues that, "among the forming-principles, every term we use to designate a quality can be taken to denote an actuality, in concordance with our doctrine that the qualities which may be distinguished for each existing thing are *those ways in which substances may be demarcated in relation to one another*" (II.6.3.3–6).

This suggests that at least one reason why "all that are accidental to things" *are* accidental to them is that, since the terms we use to ascribe qualities to corporeal things really designate ways in which they "may be demarcated in relation to one another," if something were related differently or to different things then its qualities would also be different – or, perhaps, then it would have different qualities. More significant for our current discussion, though, is that any attempt to relate qualities (even indirectly) to Aristotelian differentiae (e.g., as qualitative representations of them) seems doomed by this feature of qualities because it implies that "while a quality is entirely a characteristic of some particular thing, it is *not* a characteristic of it because of its being a substance *of a certain sort*" (VI.1.10.54–5). For, although every quality or qualitative state-of-affairs is consequent upon a real "part" of a forming-principle, it is not thereby a condition, characteristic, state-of-affairs, or the like, just of the substance itself – hence, it cannot be qualitatively representative of the thing it characterizes as being just a substance of that sort; rather, as Plotinus also expresses it, the quality "derives from it *as it relates to some state-of-affairs external to it*" (II.6.1.28–9). Moreover, Plotinus has rejected the feature of the Stoics' understanding of qualities alleging that certain qualities are discernibly "distinctive" when we observe them in certain sorts of things; and so, nor can they be discernibly distinctive (or qualitatively representative) as deriving from substances of a certain sort *as they relate to* other things or to certain (sorts of) external states-of-affairs.

The gambit of having terms for qualities designate (in the qualitative domain) sensible envoys, or some analogous sort of qualitative representations, of actual "parts" of real substances must be emended to propose that "the same quality-term is used to designate both . . . something existing in a particular substance, for example, a certain actuality of it, and also something consequent upon the preceding but existing in the one substance *as it relates to some other substance*" (VI.1.10.55–9). Moreover, every "part" of a real substance is related to every other part and to the substance itself such that "cause and caused are concurrent" (VI.7.2.35–8); and so, *every* such "part" of a forming-principle is *essential* to it – its "parts" thus being *essential* potentials and the actual (productive) movements that those essential potentials (potencies) cause – and so, in that sense, every such "part" of a forming-principle differentiates it. In the qualitative domain, however, every quality ascribable to a physical substance is accidental to it and differentiates it, not in the manner of an Aristotelian specific difference, but in the emended Stoic Manner of "marking it off" as one among many particulars by virtue of its relations to the external states-of-affairs which other particulars comprise (in relation to it) or produce (as, in reality, forming-principles also).

Of special interest to understanding coming-to-be, of course, are relations among corporeal things wherein one seems to move another or to interact with it, or which are relational states-of-affairs that are consequent upon such dynamic relations among corporeal things. In the derivative domain of qualified things – whose reality is vindicated by the fact that its source *is* the real causality of forming-principles, even if as their effects relate to "external states-of-affairs" in delineating its derivative reality – such classical notions as understanding alteration as an exchange of contrary qualities provide one sort of framework for analyzing corporeal comings-to-be; so too would, for example, supposing that "when qualities intermingle with respect to matter many of them will interact productively with one another, especially those which exist in contrariety to one another, . . . [and so] that which passively moves is altered with respect to contraries by what is contrary to it" (III.6.9.25–8 and 33–4). Similarly, insofar as a qualified thing is viewed as lifeless, such a framework might analyze its seeming potency to move others in terms of its facility to "render what is apt to passively undergo qualitatively like itself . . . to prod others into likeness with itself" (IV.3.10.33–6). Or, viewed in an even more corporeal and less soul-like manner, a purportedly lifeless thing's dynamic relations with others might be analyzed in terms of such notions as local-movement, impact, force, and the like. In these terms, for example, perishing may be analyzed in terms of the fact that, insofar as corporeal things are deficient in life, "they destroy one another because of their irregular and unrestrained movements" (I.8.4.4).

To be sure, when explicating the real existence of particulars themselves or of their particular movements and comings-to-be, their dynamic (inter)relations with one another are also more properly explicated in the more authentic framework of potencies and productive movements, forms and forming-principles, passive undergoings and corporeal instrumentalities, and the like. Even at the most corporeal level of elemental constitutive substances, however, although they are distinguished as such by their constitutive potentials, they must also have their own potencies inasmuch as they *are* actual substances and, "for a potentially existing thing, its own actuality is its ability to move as this proceeds from it itself" (II.5.2.34). Likewise, as we have seen, even the most corporeal of things may be viewed as soulless or lifeless only in comparison with things whose potency or life is more evident: "But how is the Earth living? . . . The expansion and shaping of rocks and the visible formation of mountains and their growing upwards from within themselves: all such things as these indicate the presence within the Earth of a productively craft-like ensouling forming-principle of some sort" (VI.7.11.18–26). But, insofar as coming-to-be may also be analyzed in a less authentic or less proper framework (e.g., in some qualitative or accidental framework), Plotinus considers quantitative qualities (or, qualitative quantities) to be the most suitable. He does object to some Stoics identifying corporeality and matter with geometric and mathematic quantity as such (VI.1.26.20–7); and, similarly, against some Stoic notions regarding elemental substances, Plotinus argues:

What, in the case of fire, then, is the substance that precedes the qualified substance? Is it the body? The genus – body – will then be the substance of fire, and then fire as such will be just the hot body and not even the entire qualified body will be the substance of fire. Or else, the heat will be in the fire in the way that snub-nosedness is in you. But, if we then took away the heat, and also the brightness and the lightness – as these also seem to be qualitative existences – the body's three-dimensional extension is all that remains, and then this matter will itself be the elemental substance. But this does not seem correct; for, the form of a thing more properly designates its substance. But, the form of fire seems to be something qualitative. Not at all; the form of fire is not a fiery quality but a forming-principle. (II.6.2.8–16)

But, in the qualitative domain itself, quantifiable extension's primacy is evident from the fact that, as Plotinus has just intimated, it seems to function as itself a sort-of substrate in relation to all other corporeal qualities (cf. II.4.12.1–7). Plotinus argues in various contexts that matter as such, or as "primal" (II.4.6.15), is entirely a passive substrate with respect to every substance or form or actuality (including the elements) and likewise with respect to every quality or qualified thing whatsoever (including extension, magnitude, or mass).[30] Moreover, we have seen, anything ascribable to a passive substrate (i.e., matter) may only be ascribed to it accidentally. It would therefore be a mistake, in Plotinus's view, to suppose that extension, mass, quantity, or the like may be itself a proper differentia or an essence of some sort (say, of some purported "material" substance or reality, as purportedly differentiated thereby from some immaterial substance or reality). Nevertheless, extension and other such quantifiable notions or qualities do seem to be in a way distinctive of physical substances (as the Stoics maintained) inasmuch as, Plotinus observes, it does seem that "whatever matter receives, it accepts *in an extended form*" (II.4.11.18); for, "that which is receptive of every form cannot itself even be mass. But, concurrently with receiving any other quality, it is as though it becomes a certain mass; it thus has the appearance of being mass since its most primal inclination, as it were, is for this [viz., mass, or magnitude]" (II.4.11.25–7).

As coming-to-be relates by way of forming-principles to the authentic order of real causes as well, extension or place seems the most primal of all qualities. Plotinus thus argues, regarding the reality of corporeal things, that "if corporeal things were not real existing things, soul could not proceed, since it is not predisposed to exist in any other sort of place. But, since soul must proceed, it generates place for itself, and therein corporeal things" (IV.3.9.21–4). Quantifiable extension even seems the primary representation in the qualitative domain of the causative potency inherent in authentic-reality itself, including in the intelligible archetypes of physical substances. When souls (forming-principles) proceed, Plotinus maintains, they do not merely "generate place" but they "generate a magnitude in accordance with the intelligible form . . . so that what has come-to-be will be proportionately equal by virtue of its magnitude to the potency of its unextended archetype" (II.9.17.8–10). Moreover, that physical reality as a whole is generated by its forming-principles so that physical substances are functionally related to one another and also have functional components of their own may likewise be represented primally in the qualitative domain by supposing that the causative procession of souls (forming-principles) generates a universe "so filled with magnitude . . . that it is not deficient at all with respect to magnitude, and it is not scattered randomly about but has interrelated parts and is not incomplete in any parts" (III.6.18.9–14).

Plotinus sometimes subjects this supposition that souls' generative procession "fills" physical reality with magnitude to a more geometric characterization which may also provide a framework for more rigorous sorts of quantitative analyses of physical reality and its coming-to-be.[31] For example, he divides the work of generating physical substances between a universal soul which administers the natural universe as a whole and the many souls which administer particular things, and he avers:

For, what is there to prevent us from saying that the potency of the soul of the entire universe, since it is the universal forming-principle, produces the universe as a sort of preliminary sketch before the [many] soul-like potencies subsequently proceed as well, and that this sketch is something like preconditioning luminations existing in matter so that a soul which continues the work by following a given sort of tracings produces a corporeal thing by detailing the tracing part by part so that each such soul becomes a forming-principle in relation to that corporeal thing to which it then properly proceeds by configuring it to itself – as a dancer assumes a role which has been suitably adapted to her. (VI.7.7.9–17)

In generating such a geometric universe, Plotinus supposes, soul(s) proceed in accordance with its intelligible archetype inasmuch as Intellect itself may be understood as such that there exist "in the singular configuration (schêmati) of Intellect something like measured sketches (perigraphas) and measured sketches within measured sketches, the configurations of all things being thusly constituted within it by its potencies and intellections" (VI.7.14.13–15). And, Plotinus also suggests, in such a universe the movements of its "greater parts" (e.g., the planets and heavens) seem ready models for analyzing dynamic relations more generally inasmuch as they intimate a universe which

actively moves its parts in relation to itself, forever reconfiguring its greater parts, as the relationships of its parts to one another and to the whole and their differing consequent dispositions towards one another bring about all the rest [of coming-to-be]. . . . Each part thus moves in conformity to numbers – like the choreographic parts of a living being – so that the activities of the existing universe must be completely rational in two ways: both regarding the configured things which come-to-be within it and regarding configurations among these parts [of the universe] – and also regarding whatever these bring about and the manners in which they do so. (IV.4.33.28–31 and 35.13–17. cf. IV.3.13.1–4)

Of course, a rigorously geometric or mathematic science of nature and natural movement would still be analyzing and investigating physical reality in a derivative (qualitative, or accidental) manner. Its appropriateness and legitimacy would still depend upon a metaphysical system of real causes wherein the sort of physical reality presumed by such a science may be explicated or explained in terms of its primary causes – for Plotinus, forming-principles: principles which explicate the formation of physical reality and the particulars which come-to-be within it, on the one hand, with respect to "everything pertinent" to it (and them) and, on the other hand, so that its formation (and theirs) conforms to his metaphysical principles of real existence by virtue of those formation principles being themselves derivable from these "higher" principles.

NOTES

1 The composite is not typically considered to be Plotinus's primary explication of physical substance: see Rist 1967, 103–11. For related discus-

sion of "substance" in Plotinus, see Evangeliou 1988, 144–50; Lloyd 1990, 85–95.

2 For Aristotle's own statement of the definition, see *Categories* 5.2a11–13.

3 Whereas, some Stoics were alleged to hold that corporeal things really are identical with (at least) two distinct existences – one which is substance properly speaking, the other a "qualified" doppelgänger of some substance: see Long and Sedley 1987a, 166–7 (fr. 28A, C). Cf. Long and Sedley 1987b, 169–71 (fr. 28A, C). To be sure, it is by no means clear that such accounts of the Stoic position (e.g., Plutarch's) are not failures to distinguish ontological from conceptual, methodological, or epistemological distinctions in other philosophers. Thus, in contrast, Nemesius describes the Stoics as accounting for the real existence of particulars by a "tensile movement" whose outward-directedness brings about their magnitudes and qualities, and whose concurrent inward-directedness brings about their unifications and substances: Long and Sedley 1987a, 283 (fr. 47J). Cf. Long and Sedley 1987b, 282 (fr. 47J).

4 See, e.g., Long and Sedley 1987a, 166–9 (fr. 28A-D-G, H). Cf. Long and Sedley 1987b, 169–73 (fr. 28A-D-G, H).

5 In this regard, Plotinus seems to share his elder contemporary Sextus Empiricus's skepticism regarding Stoic attempts to draw epistemically significant distinctions between sorts of qualities, or sensorial appearances. He thus implies, for example, that insofar as we differentiate substances by their apparent existence in relation to sense experiences of them, it is most reasonable to take the entirety of what we sensorially experience regarding them into account (VI.3.10.12–17). For Sextus Empiricus's own spin on the issue, of course, see *Outlines of Pyrrhonism* II.72–9: Bury 1933, 196–201.

6 In short, "the objects of sense experience" (*aisthêta*) does not name an ontological category for Plotinus: see Wagner 1982b.

7 In addition to denoting a substrate or subject and to denoting constitutive substance or corporeal constituents, a third main use of "matter" by Plotinus in regards to physical reality is for denoting what in or about something renders it deficient or defective in a certain respect, most typically in comparison with what would be ideal or "intelligible" for something of that sort or in relation to some one or another metaphysical principle of reality as such. For more general discussion of Plotinus's notion of matter in his metaphysical system, see Rist 1961 and Rist 1962.

8 In the case of human beings, however, there is the additional complication of the unique nature of human souls or forming-principles in virtue

of which we are not just physical substances but, in more contemporary terms, persons: see, e.g., Armstrong 1977a.

9 *Physics* VI.9.239b10–13.

10 *Physics* VI.2.233a13–30. For Plotinus's critique of Aristotle's understanding of time and for the outlines of his own understanding, see *Ennead* III.7.8–12. For discussion of Plotinus's notion of time, see Manchester 1978; Simons 1985; Strange 1994.

11 *Physics* VI.4.234b10–16.

12 *Physics* VI.10.241a26–30.

13 *Physics* VI.9.240a23–9.

14 *Physics* III.1.201a10–11.

15 *Metaphysics* XII.2.1069b15–16.

16 *Physics* III.2.201b24–32. Cf. *Metaphysics* XI.9.1066a13–22.

17 *Physics* VI.5.236a14.

18 This also despite otherwise criticizing the notion of indivisible moments (instants) of time: *Physics* VI.1.231a21–231b20; VI.10.240b30–241a6.

19 *Physics* VI.5.235b21–33.

20 E.g., III.6.17.8–35; III.7.11; IV.3.9.21–4, 46–9.

21 E.g., II.4.6.14–19; III.6.12.43–5; V.9.3.25–31.

22 They will, for example, also differ as actual substances (cf. II.5.2.34); but any two substances, elemental or not, will differ in this respect.

23 For Plotinus's more detailed criticism of Stoic determinism, see III.1.7.1–22; III.1.8.5–9; IV.4.33.15–19. For related discussion of Plotinus's doctrines of universal causality and *sumpatheia*, see Gurtler 1988, 90–137; Graeser 1972, 105–11. Two of Plotinus's main criticisms of materialism generally are, first, that not all phenomena, even regarding corporeal things as such, can be fully explicated in terms of some elemental material(s) and its potentials or qualities (IV.4.31.33–40; VI.3.25.30–42) and, second, that the elements of corporeal matter (and their characteristics, relations, and movements) are themselves to be included among the things which an account of the universal natural order should explain (see II.4.8.12–13; IV.4.10.5–13).

24 Cf. *Ennead* VI.2.4.1–11; VI.2.5.1–10; VI.7.3.10–13. For discussion of pertinent features of the Stoics' understanding of corporeal things, see Hahm 1977.

25 *Metaphysics* VII.4.1029b14.

26 Cf. *Metaphysics* VII.17.1041a14–18.

27 Galen explains birds' ability to remain aloft (fly) in terms of their ability to counterbalance the downward inclinations of their bodies by the upward inclination of their soul's tension [Galen's life principle] as their

particular musculatures allow them to extend this throughout their bodies: Long and Sedley 1987a, 283 (fr. 47K).

28 For the analogous viewpoint in Stoicism, see Long and Sedley 1987a, 284–5 (fr. 47M-N-O-P, Q). Cf. Long and Sedley 1987b, 283–5 (fr. 47M-N-O-P, Q).

29 E.g., Long and Sedley 1987a, 33–6 (fr.7B, D), 176 (fr. 29C, D). Cf. Long and Sedley 1987b, 26–30 (fr. 7B, D), 178–89 (fr. 29C, D).

30 E.g., *Ennead* I.8.10.2–4; II.4.6.2–8; II.4.8.3–8; II.4.13.26–8; II.5.4.4–5; II.5.5.6–17; III.6.11.16–19. In addition to emphasizing that all ascriptions regarding corporeal things as such are accidental ascriptions, this suggests that matter as substrate is the primary sense of "matter" in regards to physical reality (see note 7 above). We have also seen, for example, that constitutive substances and the corporeal constituents of composites are delineated, respectively, by constitutive potentials and instrumental potentials; and these, too, seem to delineate certain ways in which something to which they belong (i.e., may be ascribed) may function. At the same time, though, what they denote are not merely certain roles or functions which may or may not be fulfilled by any actuality or real existing thing; rather, anything which has a constitutive or instrumental sort of potential existence must also be real or actual in its own right (e.g., II.5.2.34). Whereas, this is not the case for the more basic notion of matter as just (passive) substrate or (mere) subject, which encompasses the matterlike character of such derivative notions of matter as the foregoing but need not also implicitly denote anything actual or in reality existent. Regarding the semantic value of ascriptive assertions, for example, inasmuch as attempting to ascribe something to a nonexistent subject can serve as a model (or paradigm case) for explaining falsehood in general, in this respect (and, for Plotinus, only in such respects as this) matter may be considered a cause (viz., the cause of falsehood). It is not thereby a real cause (or, a cause that in reality exists), however, inasmuch as what it "explains" (viz., falsehood) is not itself something real or actual but a failure, lack, deficiency, or the like with respect to actuality in the relevant domain – where, in this case, truth ("semantic actuality," as it were) would be explained by an ascriptive assertion conforming with (*kata*) Plotinus's order of real causes and existence as it proceeds from them, including physical reality (particulars, comings-to-be, qualities, etc., as these in reality exist, or *are*). For a more general discussion of the disappearing role of corporeal matter in Plotinus's metaphysical system, see Wagner 1986.

31 See Wagner 1985.

7 Plotinus on matter and evil

Plotinus describes matter as "evil itself" (I.8.8.37–44; I.8.13.7–14) and as source of evil in the soul (I.8.14). However, those two apparently straightforward statements lead at once to paradox when we learn that matter is nonetheless derived from the One, through the mediation of soul (III.9.3.7–16; III.4.1). And that paradox is only heightened by Plotinus's repeated claim that matter, "primary evil" and "evil *per se*" (I.8.3.35–40), is also "non-being" (II.4.16.3; II.5.4–5; III.6.7.1–19).

Various attempts have been made to eliminate one or other element in the paradox. Thus Schwyzer claims that matter exists independently of soul and of the One.[1] Rist allows that matter is a product of the soul, but claims that the soul's production of matter is itself an evil act; from which it should follow that at least one evil act is performed by the soul, independently of the presence of matter.[2] While Pistorius claims that matter, according to Plotinus, simply does not exist at all.[3]

None of those interpretations can survive close confrontation with the text of Plotinus. And, conceptually, none of them does justice to the intricacies of Plotinus's thinking.[4]

My own conclusion will be that a production of the non-being that is matter through the agency of one of the lower manifestations of soul is essential to Plotinus's explanation of evil in the world and of evil in the soul. It is true that, here as elsewhere, Plotinus's arguments are highly elliptical, and rely for their cogency on concepts and categories that are alien to modern ways of thinking and that have often only a tenuous relation to the writings of Plato and of Aristotle that are quoted, tacitly or explicitly, in their support. Nonetheless, a careful reading of the text of the *Enneads* will, I believe, be found to yield a consistent and a subtle answer to the question *What are evils and where do they come from?*[5]

Matter as non-being

I take first Plotinus's description of matter as non-being. For the modern reader, the point to appreciate is that, when Plotinus says that matter is "non-being," he does not mean that matter does not exist. To discover what he does mean, we have to go back to Plato's *Sophist.*

Admittedly, by working back from Plotinus to Plato, we may seem to be condemned to explaining *obscurum per obscurius.* For the burden of the Stranger's proof of the existence of non-being in the *Sophist* is commonly misrepresented in modern studies of that dialogue. In particular, the Stranger of Plato's dialogue is commonly presented as seeking to refute Parmenides' denial of the very possibility of any conception of "what is not," whereas in fact Plato's argument is considerably more complex. For the Stranger concedes to Parmenides that we cannot speak, nor even think, of "what is not in any way at all" (*to mêdamôs on,* 237b7–8), of "non-being in and by itself" (*to mê on auto kath'hauto,* 238c9). What the Stranger seeks to prove is that that concession does not, as Parmenides thought it did, make a plural world, and rational discourse, impossible.

In order to restore the existence of a plural world and the possibility of rational discourse, the Stranger seeks to prove, against Parmenides, that non-being (but not "non-being in and by itself") is an essential condition of the existence of any object, since all objects, except only being itself, participate in otherness in relation to being, and in so far as they are "other than being" must therefore be counted as "non-being." The Stranger's point is that movement and rest and all other "forms," with the sole exception of being itself, are "non-beings," not because they do not participate in being, but because, although they participate in being, they participate also in otherness in relation to being, and are therefore not identical to being.[6]

This part of the Stranger's argument concludes with two definitions of "non-being." Both definitions turn on the existence of a form of otherness. Non-being is first defined as an opposition between the form of being and that part of the form of otherness that is opposed to being (258a11–b4). A second definition identifies non-being as "that part of the form of otherness which is opposed to the being of each thing" (258d7–e3). The difference between the two definitions lies in the difference between "being" as form and as particular: the form or "nature" of being which is one of the two opposed terms in the first definition is replaced by "the being of each thing" in the Stranger's second definition.

Plotinus takes the second of Plato's two definitions (258d7–e3) as a definition of matter. He does so, however, by following a reading of the text which is not that of our manuscripts, but which is nonetheless known to us from quotations of the Sophist given by Simplicius in his commentary on Aristotle's Physics. In Simplicius's version of the Stranger's second definition (in Phys. 238.26), the opposition lies between a part of the form of otherness and "each being" (as distinct from "the being of each thing" which is how the Stranger's definition is worded in the extant manuscripts). Plotinus clearly refers to (what will be) Simplicius's version of the Sophist in the concluding chapter of his treatise On Matter. In the penultimate chapter of the treatise, Plotinus has considered whether matter is identical to "the infinite" (II.4.15). In the opening lines of his final chapter, Plotinus asks: "Is matter then also identical to otherness?" (II.4.16.1). And he replies: "Or rather not; matter is instead identical to that part of otherness which is opposed to the beings properly so-called, the beings which are forms" (II.4.16.1–3).

It is true that there is no overt reference to the Sophist in this passage. But Plotinus's allusion to a "part of otherness" (II.4.16.1–2) is unmistakably a reference to the Stranger's account of the "parts" of otherness in his definition of non-being in the Sophist (257c5–258e5). And it is also clear that Plotinus follows (or conceivably inaugurates) the text of Plato that will be recorded by Simplicius (in Phys. 238.26; Soph. 258d7–e3). For Plotinus's designation of the second term in the opposition as "the beings properly so-called" unmistakably picks up, not "the being of each thing" (the text of the Stranger's second definition given in the extant manuscripts), but "each being" (the text of the Stranger's second definition recorded in Simplicius's commentary on the Physics).[7]

Plotinus's identification of matter with (an emended form of) the Stranger's second definition of non-being will prove essential to Plotinus's conception of matter as evil. But for the moment it is worth pausing simply to appreciate that it is only by reference to Plato's *Sophist*, and to the criticism contained therein of Parmenides, that the several distinctions which Plotinus makes in his description of matter as "non-being" can have meaning.

To take only the example most pertinent to Plotinus's analysis of matter as evil: in chapter three of his treatise *What are evils and where do they come from?* Plotinus's conclusion that evil must be found, not among beings, but among non-beings (I.8.3.1–6) is followed by a two-sided distinction. The non-being that is evil, and that will be identified with matter as the treatise progresses, is not "absolute non-being" (*to pantelôs mê on*), and it is not non-being in the way in which movement and rest can be said to be non-being (I.8.3.6–9). It is, instead, "a form which is of what is not" (*eidos ti tou mê ontos on*, I.8.3.4–5). That curious expression is taken from the preliminaries to the Stranger's second definition of non-being in the *Sophist* (258d5–7). The description of the form of non-being as a form "which is" (or a form "which happens to be," in the text of the *Sophist*) is designed precisely to distinguish the non-being which the Stranger has isolated at the conclusion of his analysis, and which participates in being, from the "absolute" non-being ("what is not in any way at all," "non-being in and by itself") which has been condemned by Parmenides, while equally the mention of "form," by Plato and by Plotinus, is designed to distinguish the non-being defined by the Stranger at the end of his analysis from the non-being attaching to movement and rest and all other "forms," which, in the *Sophist*, are "non-beings" only because they participate in the form of otherness in relation to being, and not because they are themselves "opposed" to being.[8]

At the same time, the non-being which Plotinus identifies with matter is not a simple restatement of the "form" of non-being which has been isolated by the Stranger in the course of his argument. The difference between the Stranger's definition of non-being as a part of otherness opposed to "the being of each thing" (*Soph.* 258d7–e3) and Plotinus's definition of the non-being that is matter as a part of otherness opposed to "the beings properly so called" (II.4.16.1–3) may seem nugatory. It is in fact crucial to Plotinus's conception of matter as non-being, and to his description of matter as "evil itself" and "evil *per se*," as we shall now see.

Matter as evil

There is no indication in the *Sophist* that the "form" of non-being is evil. It is true that, in the following pages of Plato's dialogue, the Stranger's definitions of non-being will be adapted to prove the possibility of falsity in opinion and in speech (260a–264b). It is true also that, in the preceding pages of the dialogue (257b1–258a10), the Stranger has introduced a whole series of "negative" forms: the non-large, the non-beautiful, the non-just, all of which are constituted by a "part" of the form of otherness that is opposed to largeness, to beauty and to justice (in the same way, or so the Stranger would have us believe, in the first of his two definitions, 258a11–b4, that non-being is constituted by the opposition between a "part" of otherness and the form of being). But, as the Stranger has carefully pointed out in his analysis of "what is not large," the negation of large is not coextensive with the contrary of large, since "not large" will cover the equal no less than the small (257b6–c4). Following the same line of reasoning, what is not beautiful will not be coextensive with what is ugly, nor will what is not just necessarily be coextensive with what is unjust.[9] How then is Plotinus able to claim as he does, in chapter 6 of his treatise *On What are Evils*, that the "form" of non-being which he had spoken of in chapter three of his treatise, and which in the intervening chapters has been explicitly identified with matter, is not merely a negation of substance, but the contrary of substance, so that if substance is identified with goodness, matter, as the contrary of substance, is identified with evil?

To arrive at that conclusion, Plotinus has to take issue with Aristotle's refusal, in the *Categories*, to allow that there can be any contrary to substance (*Cat.* 5.3b24–32). Plotinus introduces a distinction. He agrees that, in the world as we know it, there is no contrary to individual substances. But he argues that there can nonetheless be a contrary to substance as such (I.8.6.28–36). Plotinus therefore emends Aristotle's definition of contraries as "things which stand furthest apart within the same genus" (*Cat.* 6.6a17–18). Contrariety, Plotinus claims, can designate things which stand "furthest apart" and which are not in the same genus (I.8.6.36–41).

To further his point, Plotinus argues that even individual substances could be so constituted as to allow contrariety. Fire and

water, in the world as we know it, are made up from contrary qualities (fire from hot and dry, water from cold and wet), but are not
themselves contraries, since those qualities adhere in a common
substrate. If fire and water were not joined by a common substrate
(matter), if instead they existed "by themselves" and were "independently constitutive of their substance," without the presence of any
common substrate, then they too, or so Plotinus argues, could be
contraries (I.8.6.49–54).[10]

Plotinus's point is apparently that the qualities themselves count
as contraries when they remain as qualities present in a common
substrate (my hands are hot or cold; my hair is wet or dry), because
in that case the presence of a common substrate (my hands, my hair)
does not hamper their contrariety. But when, as in Aristotle's theory
of the elements (cf. *On Generation and Corruption* II.3), hot and dry
or cold and wet are joined with a common substrate (matter) so as to
constitute the very substance of the elements, then the presence of a
common substrate excludes contrariety. For the elements themselves to count as contraries, they would have to exist as substances
independently of the material substrate which allows for their mutual transformation. If that were so, if fire and water were made up
from opposite qualities with no common substrate, then fire and
water would count as contraries, despite their being substances.[11]
And that same conclusion, or so Plotinus claims, will hold for the
opposition between substance and the non-substance that is matter.
Substance and matter have no common substrate, and since therefore matter as non-substance is at the furthest possible remove from
substance, Plotinus concludes that matter is the contrary of substance (cf. 1.8.6.54–9).

Since matter is the contrary of substance, Plotinus argues, in chapter 10 of the same treatise, that it is the contrary of form, and therefore not merely lacking in all quality, but evil (1.8.10).

This radical transformation of ideas taken from Plato and from
Aristotle is typical of the author of the *Enneads*. The simple opposition which Plato had established in the *Sophist* between a part of
otherness and the being of each thing (258d7–e3) has been transformed by Plotinus into an opposition between a part of otherness
and the forms (II.4.16.1–3), and that opposition has itself been transformed, through a modification of the doctrine of Aristotle's *Categories*, into a contrariety (I.8.6.28–59), a contrariety which establishes

the "form of non-being," since it is contrary to all the positive characterizations of substance, as not merely not beautiful, but ugly, as not merely not good, but bad (I.8.10).[12]

Matter and contrariety: Summary

Admittedly, Plotinus's argument on the possible contrariety of the elements in chapter 6 of his treatise On What are Evils is more than usually elliptical. I hope that I have understood his argument aright, and that my account of it is clear. The argument, as I have understood it, turns on a difference between qualities and the elements (I.8.6.49–54).[13]

Qualities. Since the substrate of the qualities is not constitutive of the qualities as such (even though the presence of a substrate is essential to their instantiation), the qualities hot and cold can represent "things furthest removed from each other," and can therefore be counted as contraries.

The elements. The elements, by contrast, being bound by a common substrate which is constitutive of their existence as elements, cannot be counted as "furthest removed from each other," and cannot therefore be counted as contraries. For the elements to exist as contraries, they would have to exist as elements independently of any common substrate.

Matter. Substance (the forms) and non-substance (matter) do not have a common substrate (since existence as such is not a substrate), and do therefore count as contraries, since the negation ("non-substance") does here indicate that the two terms in the opposition are as far removed from each other as possible. For the only term, other than matter, which could, so to speak, be even further removed from the substance of the forms would be "absolute" non-existence, which has already been excluded, as impossible and inconceivable, by both Plato and Parmenides.

Plato, Aristotle, Plotinus. Plato's Eleatic Stranger, at the end of his argument, had in fact dismissed Parmenides's "absolute" non-being as an – impossible and inconceivable – "contrary" to being (*Soph.*

258e6–259a1). Plotinus has so to speak rescued non-being as a "contrary," by circumventing Aristotle's *Categories* and by establishing matter as the contrary, not of being as such, but of substance.[14]

Matter and privation

Plotinus's account of matter as evil is reinforced by his identification of matter and privation. Here again, Plotinus is deliberately drawing on Aristotelian ideas, which he nonetheless radically transforms to answer to his own purposes. Aristotle's criticism of his predecessors, and notably of Parmenides and of Plato, had turned on a distinction between matter and privation. In rejecting that distinction, Plotinus will establish matter not only as evil, but as eternally and irretrievably evil.

The account of privation which Plotinus seeks both to appropriate and to subvert is that given in the final chapters (7–9) of the first book of Aristotle's *Physics*. Aristotle's initial argument is linguistical (*Phys.* I.7.189b32–191a3). He constructs two strings of sentences describing how a man "becomes educated." The first string takes as subject of the sentence the *terminus a quo* of change, while in the second string of sentences that same *terminus a quo* is put in an oblique case and preceded by a preposition ("out of"/"from"). Where the subject of the sentence is the *terminus a quo*, we can say: (1) "A man becomes educated," (2) "The uneducated becomes educated," and (3) "The uneducated man becomes an educated man." Where the same *terminus a quo* is put in an oblique case, we can say: (2a) "From being uneducated, he becomes educated" and (3a) "From being an uneducated man, he becomes educated." But we cannot similarly convert the first sentence of the first string. For we cannot say (1a) that "from being a man, he becomes educated," since that form of expression would imply that the man, in becoming educated, ceased to exist.[15]

From this very simple linguistic exercise, Aristotle concludes that we must distinguish between substrate and privation. The substrate (in the example given, the man) persists through change. The privation (his lack of education) does not. Hence (according to Aristotle) the difference in the expressions quoted. "From x, he becomes y" implies the disappearance of x, and that formula can therefore be used only where x describes, or includes, the privation. "A man becomes educated" cannot therefore be rewritten as "from being a man, he becomes educated."

In the final chapter of the first book of the *Physics*, Aristotle thinks to clinch his argument by giving as an example the desire of what is ugly to become beautiful (*Phys.* I.9.192a16–25). "The ugly" as such (he tells us) cannot desire to become beautiful, for it would then be desiring its own extinction. The desire must be a desire of the substrate, characterized accidentally by the privation, and the object of its desire will be the form that is opposed to that privation. Hence the need to recognize no less than three factors in any analysis of change or of "coming-into-being": privation, substrate and form.

Recognition of these three factors, Aristotle tells us (*Phys.* I.8), will provide an escape from the Eleatic claim that whatever comes into being would have to do so from what is not (and that coming-into-being is therefore impossible). Aristotle replies that the Eleatic claim is true, and that coming-into-being does take place from what is not in so far as the *terminus a quo* of change is a privation. But the Eleatic claim is not therefore true absolutely, since all coming-into-being is from a pre-existing substrate. Change (or coming-into-being) is precisely the replacement, within a continuing substrate, of privation by form.

The sublime triviality of Aristotle's argument and of his conclusion would hardly seem to leave room for correction or for emendation. But there is one striking anomaly when, at the end of his analysis, Aristotle quotes a second example in illustration of his thesis: the desire of the female for the male (*Phys.* I.9.192a22–3). If we follow the model of the ugly and the beautiful, then we should be able to distinguish, in the *terminus a quo* of change or of desire, between substrate and privation, while in the *terminus ad quem* we should somehow discover the same substrate characterized now, not by privation, but by the corresponding form. But how can this possibly work out in practice? What is the substrate, characterized by "female," which will end up being "male"? On the face of it, Aristotle's example would seem to mean that a female animal, in her desire for the male, desires to become male, and would indeed do so if that desire were not somehow frustrated. But could even Aristotle have thought that?

Whatever Aristotle might have thought (and it is tempting to suppose that at this point he perhaps did not think at all), Plotinus seizes on this Achilles' heel in Aristotle's argument in order to subvert the whole reasoning which would make of privation something other than the substrate (II.4.14 and 16).[16] According to Plotinus, when the female desires the male, or when she is inseminated by the male (maddeningly, the manuscripts let us down at precisely that point), she does not therefore somehow cease to be female (II.4.16.13–16). On the contrary, she "becomes more female" (*mallon thêlunetai*, a *hapax* in the vocabulary of the *Enneads*).[17] Drawing on that example, Plotinus concludes that the advent of form confirms, paradoxically, the absence of form. The arrival of form, far from ousting the privation, "preserves" the privation "in its existence" (II.4.16.11–12). The privation achieves "actualisation" and "perfection" by the very presence of the form of which it is – and remains – the privation (II.4.16.12–13).

Aristotle would obviously have objected that such an identification of matter (or substrate) and privation would make any real change impossible. If the object which is ugly is not divested of its privation (Aristotle would have said), then it cannot become beautiful. If the object which "becomes" beautiful remains characterized by the privation of beauty, then it would be, impossibly, both beautiful and ugly at the same time. . . . And Plotinus would reply: exactly so. The beauty of the sensible world, Plotinus holds, is a mere charade (cf. 1.8.15.23–8). In the sensible world, matter and form are never united, as they are in the intelligible world (II.4.5.12–23; II.5.3–5). Matter, in the sensible world, remains forever deprived of form, precisely because matter and privation are the same thing, with the result that the "participation" of matter in form fails to produce any real transformation of matter. The ugly remains ugly, even when the presence of form covers it with the appearance of beauty (III.6.11–14). In the eyes of the philosopher, the body of the sensible world remains forever a mere "corpse adorned" (II.4.5.18).

The rejection of Aristotle's distinction between matter and privation is thus a crucial element in Plotinus's whole conception of the sensible world, and in his attempted solution to the problem of evil. Aristotle, in the *Physics*, had charged Plato (and Parmenides) with failing to distinguish, in change, the substrate, which persists and which is "in a way substance," from privation, which is not substance "in any way at all," and which is annihilated in the process of change (*Phys.* I.9.192a3–6).[18] Although he rejects that distinction, Plotinus does not therefore return to the position which Aristotle attributes to Plato (*Phys.* I.9.191b35–192a34), whereby matter and form are the only factors in change and no account at all is taken of (Aristotle's new concept of) privation. On the contrary Plotinus gives pride of place to Aristotle's innovation. But the use which Plotinus makes of the concept of privation is entirely different from the purpose for which that concept had been introduced by Aristotle.[19] For Plotinus rejects Aristotle's claim that the substrate, since it persists, cannot be privation, and claims instead that what persists *is* privation (II.4.12.16). With the shattering consequence that matter, the contrary of substance and "evil itself," remains evil, even when covered by soul with the appearance of form.[20]

The origin of matter

Matter as evil, and as irretrievably evil, poses an immediate and obvious threat to Plotinus's belief in emanation. For how can evil be derived from the One which is the sovereign good?

The modern reader is not alone in being startled by that conjunction of ideas. Numenius, an earlier contemporary of Plotinus and someone whose philosophy in many ways foreshadowed that of Plotinus, claimed emphatically that matter was not derived from the supreme principle.[21] The reason why Plotinus should have diverged on this point from Numenius and refused to allow that matter could exist independently of the One is probably to be found in the preliminaries to his account of intelligible matter. Plotinus there tells us that, if matter were not derived from any principle prior to itself, then there would be more than one first principle, and the relationship of the first principles would be the product of chance (II.4.2.9–10). To avoid such dualism, and to maintain the dependence of the universe on a single first principle, Plotinus is prepared to maintain that even matter, utter evil, is ultimately derived from the One. But the way in which matter derives from the One will be most carefully circumscribed.

Matter is generated by a "partial" soul, the soul "which comes to be in plants." Complementary descriptions are given, in nearly successive treatises (III.9.3.7–16; III.4.1), of how this is done. In the first passage (III.9.3.7–16), we are told that the "partial" soul is illuminated when she turns toward the principle prior to herself, whereas, when she turns toward herself, "as it were walking on emptiness" and "becoming more indefinite," she makes "what comes after her." This "what comes after her" is an "image" of soul, but an image which is "without definition" (since it is the product of the soul's own increasing lack of definition) and "non-being" (in the technical sense, defined above). In the companion passage (III.4.1), the soul "which comes to be in plants," generates something "totally other than herself," which is again described as "totally lacking in definition."

Some scholars have resisted the conclusion that, in these two passages, the product of soul is matter.[22] But any doubts are dispelled when, in the second passage, we learn that the offspring of soul "becomes body" by its reception of "form" and, as body, "provides a receptacle for the principle that has brought it to birth" (III.4.1.14–16). For the "form" by which what is totally without definition "becomes body," will be the form of body, or "bodilyness," while the "receptacle" that is thus provided will answer to the soul's need to "generate for herself place and therefore also body," when she issues forth from the intelligible world (IV.3.9.22–3). The object which is generated by soul and which is "without definition" prior to the advent of form as body, – what could this possibly be, other than matter?

But if the soul has generated matter, the way in which she has done so is utterly different from the way in which Intellect or Soul or even intelligible matter have been generated, directly or indirectly, from the One. The One is "complete" (V.2.1.7); the soul generates matter, not because she is complete, but, on the contrary, by becoming "more indefinite" (III.9.3.11–12). The One does not generate because of any need (V.2.1.7–8); the soul generates matter, because, without place and body to receive her, she cannot enter the sensible world (IV.3.9.22–3; cf. IV.8.5.27–37). The One is "overfull," and "as it were overflows" (V.2.1.8–9); but both those expressions are metaphorical: neither the One nor Intellect generates by being in movement (V.2.1.16–18). Just the opposite is true of soul: the soul's act of generation is accompanied by movement (V.2.1.18–19); III.4.1.1–3). And, in the case of her generation of matter, the movement of soul is movement "towards herself" and towards "what comes after her" (III.9.3.7–12).

The differences continue *ex parte prolis*. Intellect, Soul and intelligible matter, when they are generated, turn back of their own accord towards the principle from which they have issued, and intelligible matter, when it does this, "is defined" (V.2.1.9–13 and 19–20; II.4.5.33–5). None of this is true of the matter of the sensible world. The matter generated by the lower soul is "lifeless" (III.4.1.7), and has no power to turn back of itself toward the principle from which it has sprung. When matter receives form and "becomes body" (III.4.1.14–16), she does so, only because the soul, "by a second initiative," "looks again" at the object she has made, and herself "invests it with form" (III.9.3.14–16).

Even matter's reception of form, as we know already, is less than it might seem to be. For the matter of the sensible world, in being identified with privation, is incapable of being truly united with form (III.6.11–14). Thus when Plotinus asks how matter can "participate without participating" (III.6.14.21–2; cf. II.5.5), his answer is that, in the sensible world, the participation of matter in form is an appearance only (III.6.14.22–36). The decoration of matter is a mere cloak cast over the destitution of matter (cf. III.6.11.20–1). Even when the soul has covered it with form, and when it has "become body" (III.9.3.14–16; III.4.1.14–16), matter remains a "corpse adorned" (II.4.5.18), a corpse that has never known the breath of life (III.4.1.7).

Matter and soul

The question cries out: how can something so impotent become cause of evil in the soul? The answer to that question is already implicit in the account that Plotinus has given of the soul's relation to matter. When the soul has both generated matter and invested matter with form (III.9.3.14–16; III.4.1.14–16), she enters into the object she has made (the bodies of the sensible world), "rejoicing" (III.9.3.16).[23] But there are then two possibilities. If the soul "makes haste to escape," then "she will come to no harm" (IV.8.5.27–33). But if the soul enters into relation with body "with too much eagerness," then she will be unable to avoid "taking back something" from the body "in return" (IV.8.7.1–14). By being thus contaminated by matter, the soul will herself become "evil" (I.8.14).

But the soul's becoming evil is subject to two essential restrictions. Firstly, the soul cannot be, or become, intrinsically evil

(I.8.11). The soul becomes evil, when she does so, only "accidentally" (I.8.12), and, even then, only through the presence of matter (I.8.14). And the second restriction is even more crucial: for although the soul becomes evil through the presence of matter (I.8.14), and although the presence of matter is, in that sense, a necessary cause of evil in the soul, nonetheless the presence of matter is not a sufficient cause of the soul's being evil (cf. I.8.5.26–34). I take both points in turn, and the first point first.

To prove that the soul cannot be evil of herself, and independently of the presence of matter, Plotinus has recourse to another tightly compressed argument which turns on the question of contrariety (I.8.11). In the course of this argument, he abandons the Platonic formula by which matter is a "form" of non-being, and states plainly, what had been implicit in his description of matter as non-substance, that matter, the contrary of substance, is not form, but contrary to form (I.8.10.11–16; I.8.11.1–4). Since evil is the contrary of form, therefore, if the soul were evil of herself, she would be deprived of form. But since the soul, by her very definition, possesses life, which is a form, the soul cannot be deprived of form. The soul cannot therefore be evil of herself, without ceasing to be soul (I.8.11.10–16). Evil can be no more than an accident of soul. The soul is not intrinsically evil (I.8.11–12).

The force of this argument is apparent only if it is seen as an extension and an adaptation of the final argument of Plato's *Phaedo* for the immortality of soul. Socrates, in the *Phaedo*, argues that the soul is characterized by life, in the way that fire is characterized by heat, or snow by cold, "four" by even, or "three" by odd. Fire cannot be fire and cold; snow cannot be snow and hot. Snow, "at the approach of" heat must either "withdraw," in which case it will continue to be snow and to be cold, or it must "stay behind" and "perish," that is, melt. But the soul, at the approach of death, can only "withdraw," for the additional form which characterizes soul, the form of life, makes it impossible for the soul to "stay behind" and "admit" death. It is as impossible for the soul to "admit" death and to die as it would be for fire to be cold, for snow to be hot, or for "three" to be even (*Phaedo* 102a10 – 107a1).[24]

This is the argument which Plotinus refers to when he tells us, in his treatise *On What are Evils*, that the soul possesses life "by her very definition" (I.8.11.15). From this it follows (we now move to Plotinus's extension and adaptation of Plato's argument) that, if evil is defined as total privation, then the soul cannot be evil "of herself" (par'hautês, I.8.11.16), since, were she to be evil of herself, she would be deprived of form. And that Plato had shown to be impossible. The soul possesses life "by her very definition." A soul that *per impossibile* was intrinsically evil would therefore no longer be a soul (I.8.11.14).

The causes of human evil

Granted that the soul is evil only *per accidens*, how does she become so? Answer: by the presence of matter. Nonetheless, the presence of matter is not sufficient cause of evil in the soul. For Plotinus explicitly states that "the perceptible gods" (i.e., the stars), despite the presence of matter, are innocent of evil (I.8.5.30–1). He continues (I.8.5.31–4):

There is (sc. among the perceptible gods) nothing of the sin which men have, seeing that not even all men have sin. For the sensibly perceptible gods control their matter – although those are better which have no matter – and they control it with that in them which is not in matter.

This text should be taken in conjunction with a passage later in the same treatise, where Plotinus writes (I.8.14.49–54):

Matter is therefore both cause of weakness in the soul and cause of sin. It is therefore itself antecedently evil and primary evil. For even if the soul, by being subject to some affection, herself generated matter, and if the soul then shared in matter and became evil, matter is still the cause of evil by its presence. For soul would not have come to be in matter, if the presence of matter had not provided soul with the opportunity of coming to be in it.[25]

At first glance, we might think that it was contradictory to claim both that matter is cause of evil in the soul (I.8.14.49–54), and yet that souls (human and divine), where matter is present, may not be evil (I.8.5.30–4). For we might think to conclude, from the admission that some souls are related to matter and yet are free from evil (cf. I.8.5.30–4), that the difference between sinful and sinless souls can lie only within the soul itself, and that the soul is therefore herself responsible for the fault which makes her evil, independently of the presence of matter. And yet that conclusion would be contrary to Plotinus's explicit insistence, later in the same treatise (I.8.14.49–54), that matter is cause of evil in the soul.

But the theory need not be inconsistent. For the souls which enter-tain too intimate a relation with matter are not therefore evil of themselves. An excessive eagerness in their care for the body will admittedly divide souls which are, or which become, evil, from souls which are sinless. But the souls which are "too eager" become evil, not because their excessive eagerness is in itself a sufficient cause of evil, but because the matter which arouses their excess of eagerness is itself antecedently evil.

Expressed more formally: the soul's excessive eagerness will not be a sufficient cause of evil, although it will be a necessary cause, since, if the soul did not display an excess of eagerness, she would not be evil. Similarly, matter, as antecedently evil, will also be a necessary cause of evil in the soul, since without matter the soul would not be evil. But again matter is not a sufficient cause of evil in the soul, for, if it were, no soul where matter was present could be free from evil. It is only the conjunction of the soul's own excessive eagerness and of the presence of matter that will prove to be suffi-cient cause of evil in the soul. Even though each of those two ele-ments on its own is causally necessary, it is only in conjunction that they are causally sufficient.

Admittedly, souls which have too intimate a relation with matter will inevitably be evil. For if we count the presence of matter and the soul's excessive eagerness as part causes of evil in the soul, then the excessive eagerness of the soul, even though it is not a sufficient *cause* of evil, will nonetheless be a sufficient *condition* of evil in the soul. For the soul will inevitably become evil if she allows herself too close a proximity to matter. Of the two causes which are neces-sary but not sufficient as an explanation of evil in the soul (the presence of matter and the soul's own excessive eagerness), one (the soul's excess of eagerness) is a sufficient condition, even if, taken alone, it is not causally sufficient.

I sometime allow myself, in moments of excessive extroversion, to engage in idle gossip with my concierge. This does not happen every time I see the concierge, so the presence of the concierge cannot be counted as a sufficient cause of our idle chatter. Our idle chatter is dependent on two part causes: the presence of the concierge and my mood of excessive extroversion. When both part causes are activated, our idle conversation will take place, and not otherwise.

But the relation of those two part causes is not symmetrical. Sometimes when I meet the concierge, I refuse to engage in idle conversation. But my concierge does not exercise a similar constraint. She always has the time and inclination to engage in idle gossip. My mood of excessive extroversion therefore becomes a sufficient condition of our having an idle conversation, since every time I see the concierge she will engage me in idle gossip, if I let her. But even though my excessive extroversion is a sufficient *condition* of our having an idle conversation, it is nonetheless not a sufficient *cause*. For I would not engage in idle conversation, unless the concierge was there, waiting to exploit my mood of excessive extroversion.[26]

Plotinus and the Gnostics

The preceding pages give the bones – the logical and the metaphysical bones – of Plotinus's solution to the problem of evil. Nonetheless, Plotinus's theories of contrariety and of privation, although I would not for one moment suggest that he did not believe in them, are singularly uninformative on the motivation for Plotinus's belief in matter as "evil itself" and as source of evil in the soul. Why did Plotinus think as he did?

That question might well have been an impossible one, were it not for the inclusion, in Porphyry's edition of the *Enneads*, of one treatise (II.9) which is wholly untypical both in its tone and in its subject matter. This is the treatise entitled variously *Against the Gnostics* and *Against those who say that the maker of the world is evil and that the world is evil*. This is the only treatise in the *Enneads* where Plotinus explicitly criticizes his contemporaries.[27] And the ferocity with which he does so is unparalleled in the tense but good-tempered pages which make up the rest of the *Enneads*.[28] However, the interest of Plotinus's treatise *Against the Gnostics* is not merely a historical and a human one. Philosophically, the treatise is of the first importance in making clear to us that Plotinus's theory of matter as evil is only incidentally designed to correct Aristotle's theories of contrariety and of privation. Plotinus's main philosophical target lies elsewhere, in the Gnostic beliefs which were prevalent in third-century Rome, and which had found adherents even among the well-to-do men and women who frequented Plotinus's lecture hall in the fifties and sixties of the century.[29]

Take, for example, the following passage, where Plotinus is defending his own view of a universe without beginning or end in time, against the Gnostic view that the world as we know it will one day come to an end. Plotinus writes (II.9.3.14–21):

> Only those things will perish which have things which they can perish into. What does not have anything which it can perish into, will not perish.
>
> But if someone objects that things perish into matter, then why not say that matter too will perish?
>
> But if someone is going to say that, yes, matter too will perish, then we shall ask: what necessity was there for matter to come into existence in the first place?
>
> And if they are going to reply that it was necessary for matter to come into existence as a consequence of principles prior to matter, then we shall say: the same necessity holds now as well.
>
> But if matter is one day going to be left naked and alone, then the divine beings will not be everywhere; they will be instead in some place apart, and as it were walled off.
>
> But if that is not possible, then matter will be illuminated.[30]

In this passage, Plotinus supposes that his anonymous interlocutor (who changes from singular to plural in the space of a couple of lines) will concede that matter follows as a necessary consequence from principles prior to matter, a thesis which will coincide, nearly enough, with Plotinus's own belief in a generation of matter by the soul. What Plotinus's unnamed adversaries fail to appreciate is that that concession must carry with it both the impossibility that matter should ever cease to be present and, no less, the impossibility that matter should ever be left "naked and alone." For if matter has come into existence as a consequence of principles prior to matter, then those same principles (or so Plotinus argues) cannot be supposed to have been "shut off" from the object whose appearance follows of necessity from their own prior existence. On the contrary, the matter that has come into existence "will be illuminated" (the "light" of the forms being here contrasted, implicitly, with the "darkness" of matter). The necessity which has brought matter into existence (we are intended to conclude) will not only continue for evermore; that same necessity will also require matter to be forever covered by form.

Plotinus returns to the "illumination" of matter later in the same treatise, in the course of a long critique of Gnostic views on the formation of the cosmos. Plotinus confronts his adversaries with a choice (II.9.12.33): "The illumination must be either according to nature, or contrary to nature." He continues (II.9.12.34–8):

If the illumination is according to nature, then things will be always as they are now.

Whereas, if the illumination is contrary to nature, then what is contrary to nature will find its place among the intelligible realities. Things evil will exist prior to this world. This world will not be cause of evils; instead the intelligible beings will be cause of evil to this world. Evils will not come from here below to the soul; instead they will come from the soul to the world we live in.[31]

Plotinus's own belief is that the "illumination" of matter (its being covered by form) is an activity that is "according to nature" and is therefore eternal. But Plotinus does not here imply merely that an illumination which came to an end would be an illumination that was "contrary to nature." He also supposes that an activity that was "contrary to nature" would be evil. Since "illumination" (the imposition of form) must come from the higher realities, an illumination that was contrary to nature would therefore imply that the activity of the higher realities was evil. And that would lead to a complete reversal of Plotinus's own belief: the evils which we see in this world would have their origin in the higher realities, contrary to Plotinus's own conviction, as stated in his treatise *On What are Evils* (I.8.14), whereby matter is source of evil for the soul.

In both passages, therefore, the eternal "illumination" of matter is intended to disprove the possibility that evils in this world could result either from the presence of evil in the world of forms (II.9.12.33–8), or from an incapacity on the part of the divine realities to cover with form the object whose appearance derives inevitably from their own prior existence (II.9.3.14–21).[32]

Plotinus's "theodicy"

And that conclusion provides a neat reversal of what might otherwise have seemed Plotinus's main preoccupation in his treatise *On What are Evils*. For Plotinus's arguments in that treatise are largely directed to establishing matter as "primary evil" and as "evil *per se.*" What we discover from Plotinus's treatise *Against the Gnostics* is that the designation of matter as evil is intended to be not so much a condemnation of matter as a means of protecting the realities of the higher world from any immediate responsibility for the evils which we see in this world.

Hence the paradox whereby Plotinus's "theodicy" is founded on the theory of a generation of matter. Matter does depend on principles prior to itself, and matter is utter evil. Nonetheless, responsibility for evil cannot be laid to the charge of the higher realities. For even though a "partial" soul has made matter, nonetheless she has not made matter to be evil. The product of a partial soul is evil, not because the soul has willed it to be so, but because the soul's own increasing lack of definition produces what is utterly lacking in definition (cf. III.9.3.7–16; III.4.1), and because what is utterly lacking in definition cannot fail to be identified with privation, cannot fail to be the contrary of substance, and therefore cannot fail to be evil.

The soul in fact does all she can to palliate the inevitable consequence of her own increasing lack of definition. For although the matter produced by soul is intrinsically and irremediably evil, nonetheless it will never, as the Gnostics claim, be left naked and alone. For soul will forever cover with form the formlessness and the disfigurement of the object whose appearance is a consequence of her own movement away from the higher principles and "towards herself" (cf. III.9.3.7–16).

Not that that movement was itself evil. The soul becomes evil, not in the making of matter, but only as a possible consequence of her activity in covering with form the object to which she has given birth. For the soul's activity in caring for the objects of the sensible world exposes her to contamination by the matter from which they are constituted. But even that potential contamination does not place soul at the mercy of matter. For the presence of matter is not a sufficient cause of evil in the soul. The soul will be contaminated by matter only if she abandons herself with too great a desire to the care of the object that she has herself brought to birth.

Even so, the soul does not become evil of her own volition. Her "sin" is not the expression of any will for evil. The soul's excessive absorption in caring for the things of this world has the tragic consequence that the soul herself becomes evil, because of the nature of the object that she cares for. The soul becomes evil, when she does so, because the object of her care is "evil itself."[33]

NOTES

1 Schwyzer 1973, 275–8.
2 Rist 1967, 123–4. Rist varies his interpretation in later publications. These are reviewed in O'Brien 1993, 29–35 and 69–77.
3 Pistorius 1952, 117–33. Pistorius writes, for example, of matter as "Absolute Non-Being" (p. 121) and as "the negation of all possibility of being" (p. 118).
4 For a general review of earlier interpretations, see O'Brien 1969.
5 This is one of the titles attached to the 51st treatise in Porphyry's chronological ordering of Plotinus's writings. This treatise was written therefore in the years 269–70, when Plotinus was living alone in Campania, in the throes of the illness that was soon to lead (in 270) to his departure from this mortal life.
6 For this interpretation of the *Sophist*, see O'Brien 1992a, 1995.
7 For the difference in reading (*to on hekastou*, in our manuscripts of *Soph.* 258e2; *to on hekaston*, in Simplicius's quotation of the passage, *Phys.* 238.26), see O'Brien 1991a.
8 These inevitably rather sibylline utterances are given clearer expression in O'Brien 1991b.
9 What is not just will not *necessarily* be coextensive with what is unjust. If there is no intermediate term, then the negation ("not-just") will be coterminous with the contrary ("unjust"), in the same way that, if things were either beautiful or ugly, and if there were no middle term (e.g., "plain"), then "not-beautiful" would be coterminous with "ugly."
10 At I.8.6.51–2, Armstrong takes *epi* with the genitive (*ep' autôn*) to indicate possession. He translates: "If they only had the things which go to make up their substantial forms without what they have in common . . ." I take the preposition in the sense given by L.S.J. (s.v. *epi*, A I, 2, c): "If the elements existed by themselves (*ei d' ep' autôn ên*), alone making up the fullness of their substance (*mona tên ousian autôn sumplêrounta*), without what is common (*aneu tou koinou*) . . ."
11 "Fire and water would count as contraries." This is, in fact, more or less how fire and water had traditionally been spoken of (see, for example, Aeschylus, *Agamemnon*, 650–2, where fire and sea are said to be "most hostile," *echthistoi*), and is indeed how Aristotle himself writes of the elements at more than one point in *On Generation and Corruption* (II.3.331a1–3; II.8.335a3–6). Plotinus's *ousia ousiai enantion* (I.8.6.53–4) may even be a reminiscence of Aristotle's *ousian ousiai enantian* at I.8.335a6.
12 Matter, in being identified with the non-being that is contrary to sub-

stance, is therefore discovered to be not merely "unformed" (*aneideon*, I.8.3.14), but "ill formed" (*duseides*, II.4.16.23). Cf. O'Brien 1969, 116.

13 For help in understanding this tricky passage (I.8.6.49–54), I am much indebted to Ysabel de Andia and to Wilfried Kühn.

14 In this summary, I use "absolute" non-being as a convenient term to cover both Plotinus's expression when he denies that matter is *to pantelôs mê on* (I.8.3.6–7) and the two expressions used in the *Sophist:* "what is not in any way at all" (*to mêdamôs on*, 237b7–8) and "non-being in and by itself" (*to me on auto kath'hauto*, 238c9).

15 I have translated Aristotle's opposition of *mousikos* and *amousos* (*Phys.* I.7.189b32–191a3) as "educated" and "uneducated," and not as "musical" and "unmusical" (the translation usually adopted).

16 The question whether matter is identical to *sterêsis* is raised at II.4.14. The discussion may seem to end aporematically; but the question asked at the end of the chapter (II.4.14.28–30) is rhetorical, and the answer intended is an affirmative one. For when Plotinus takes up the point in the final chapter of the treatise, he writes explicitly that matter is "non-being" and "the same thing as *sterêsis*" (II.4.16.3). In this latter passage, the *kai* is not concessive. Armstrong, following Harder, translates (II.4.16.3): "Therefore (*dio*), though it is non-existent (*kai mê on*), it has a certain sort of existence in this way (*houtô ti on*), and is the same thing as privation (*kai sterêsei tauton*)." The meaning is rather: "And that is exactly why (*dio kai*), being in this way something (*houtô ti on*), it is non-being (*mê on*), and is identical to privation (*kai sterêsei tauton*)." "Being in this way something" (II.4.16.3: *houtô ti on*) picks up from Plotinus's rewriting of Plato's second definition of a "form" of non-being in the sentence preceding (II.4.16.1–3). For Plato, all the "parts" of otherness "are" (*Soph.* 258a7–10), even the part which is opposed to being. Similarly, for Plotinus, those are wrong who wish to assert that matter simply does not exist at all (I.8.15.1–3).

17 The sentence which follows in the text of the *Enneads* is utterly banal (II.4.16.15–16: "'That is: it becomes more what it is"), and reads exactly like a gloss. Which is presumably just what it is (though not recognized as such by Henry and Schwyzer, in their edition). The apparent lacuna in the manuscripts at *Enn.* II.4.16.15 would be happily filled by *ephietai*, the verb which is "understood" at Aristotle, *Phys.* I.9.192a23 (cf. a20: *ephiesthai*).

18 Matter is "in a way substance." At *Phys.* I.9.192a6, Aristotle writes that matter is *eggus kai ousian pôs.* W. D. Ross translates (ad loc.): "almost even substance, in a sense." Others take *kai* to be copulative: matter is "nearly substance" (*eggus* sc. *ousias*), "and it is, in a way, substance" (*kai ousian pôs*). I find it difficult to choose between these two transla-

tions. (Ross's alleged parallel from Plato's *Meno*, 91e6–7, is inconclusive, since the use of *kai* preceding numerals is well attested. When Plato writes that Protagoras died *eggus kai hebdomêkonta etê gegnota*, the meaning is that he died when he was "nearly all of seventy years old.") Fortunately, Aristotle's argument makes his intentions clear. Matter is "nearly substance," because it acts as substrate both to privation and to form. But it can be substance only "in a way," since, taken in abstraction from form, matter cannot be a concrete particular (a *tode ti*). The distinction between matter which is "nearly substance," or "in a way substance," and *sterêsis* which is not substance "in any way at all" (*oudamôs*) nicely highlights Plotinus's innovation: by refusing Aristotle's distinction (II.4.14), and by making matter identical to privation (II.16.3–4), Plotinus is able to claim matter, no less than privation, as "non-being" (II.4.16.1–3).

19 "The use which Plotinus makes of the concept of privation is entirely different from the purpose for which that concept has been introduced by Aristotle." One might of course object that a concept is indistinguishable from the use made of it: in that case, one will have to say that Plotinus has introduced a new concept of *sterêsis*.

20 In his commentary on the *Physics*, Simplicius takes account of Plotinus's attempted identification of matter and privation (*in Phys.* 251.32–252.6; the anonymous *tis* introduced at *Phys.* 251.32 is almost certainly Plotinus). In particular, Simplicius attempts to take up Plotinus's challenge (II.4.14) that anyone attempting to distinguish matter and privation should define each one of those two terms without any reference to the other. Simplicius replies that the "otherness" by which form is distinct from matter, and vice versa, is not the same as simple "absence" of form. Matter, he implies, remains forever "other" than form (all forms, any form), whereas privation, defined as the absence of some specific form, cannot persist once that form has come to be present in matter.

21 As recorded by Chalcidius, *in Tim.* cap. 295, pp. 297.7–298.9 ed. Waszink (= fr. 52 ed. Des Places), Numenius declared that belief in the generation of matter was unworthy of anyone claiming to be philosophically literate (. . . *ne mediocriter quidem institutis hominibus competit*).

22 See Schwyzer 1973, 275–8; cf. Schwyzer 1970, 249. For a review of Schwyzer's interpretation, see O'Brien 1991c.

23 The juxtaposition of these two passages (III.9.3.14–16; III.4.1.14–16) supposes that the form which is given to her offspring by a "partial" soul in the *first* passage (III.9.3.14–16) is the same as the form which, in the *second* passage (III.4.1.14–16), is received by the offspring of "the soul which comes to be in plants," and the same as the form by which that offspring "becomes body."

24 For this interpretation of Plato's "last argument," see O'Brien 1967–8. For Plato's metaphor ("withdraw," "stay behind"), see also O'Brien 1977a.

25 For a more detailed analysis of these two passages (I.8.5.30–4; I.8.14.49–54), see O'Brien 1969, 129–30 and 135–9; 1993, 64–7 and 69–75.

26 Blumenthal 1987, 559, finds the causal structure that I suggest for the *Enneads* too "systematic," and prefers to think that, in the *Enneads*, "inconsistencies and contradictions are inevitable." I hope my rather heavy-handed analogy (with apologies to my present concierge, who is particularly taciturn) will make it clear just how simple in fact is the underlying causal structure that I suggest for the relation between matter and soul in the production of evil.

27 Plotinus does criticize his contemporaries at other points in the *Enneads*, but without naming names. For a couple of examples (Numenius, Longinus, and very probably the pagan Origen), see O'Brien 1992b.

28 Plotinus even suggests at one point (II.9.10.6–7) that the Gnostics he knows are not sincere in their beliefs.

29 This we know from chapter 16 of Porphyry's *Life of Plotinus*. For details, see Tardieu 1992.

30 The English text I have given is not a translation, but an expanded paraphrase. For example, the whole phrase "come into existence as a consequence of principles prior to matter" is represented in the Greek by the single verb *parakolouthein* (II.9.3.18). (Neither Plotinus's original expression nor my paraphrase is intended to imply that the "consequence" here spoken of entails any temporal priority). Again, I paraphrase as "naked and alone" the simple *monê* at II.9.3.18, if only to avoid the colloquial meaning of "leave alone." It is true that "naked and alone" gives the sentence a rather emotive overtone, but that overtone is in fact not out of place. For a couple of chapters later Plotinus refers to the Gnostic belief that matter will one day be "stripped of form," where the verb used (*aposulesas*, II.9.5.34–5) could well suggest a corpse lying naked on the battlefield because it has been plucked of its armour.

31 This is again an extended paraphrase and not a translation proper. For example, when I write "then things will be always as they are now," Plotinus writes simply *aei houtos* (II.9.12.34). And where I write of "intelligible realities" and of "the world we live in," Plotinus has recourse to his usual shorthand, and writes simply of "things there" (II.9.12.35), and of "here" (II.9.12.38). I have even changed the syntax of the sentence: Plotinus's string of conjunctions (no less than four occurrences of *kai*) has been replaced by a series of three full stops. This gives the English a staccato effect, which is lacking in the Greek. But the English nonetheless suggests, as does the Greek, that Plotinus is hammering his point home.

32 For both the passages quoted above (II.9.3.14–21; II.9.12.33–8), see O'Brien 1993, esp. 78–86. For Gnostic beliefs used as a foil to Plotinus's own ideas, see also O'Brien 1981 and 1990.

33 I have to stop there. But two crucial topics are hovering in the wings, and can only with difficulty be kept from coming on stage. It is central to Plotinus's theory that only souls which enter the sensible world are potentially subject to the evil influence of matter (I.8.14); however, the division of labor between a "partial" soul, individual souls, the world soul and what I have called "the higher realities" is a complex question, and one which I have had to leave entirely out of account in this sketch of Plotinus's theory of evil. And I have also had to leave entirely aside the vexed question of the soul's "volition." In the earlier of the two passages quoted in my last section but one (II.9.3.14–21), Plotinus several times speaks of "necessity." But Plotinian "necessity," when applied to the activity of soul, is a slippery concept, and one which often leads modern commentators astray. "Necessity," as understood by Plotinus, excludes both choice and constraint. But it does not follow that a soul, subjected to necessity, is "unwilling." On this latter problem, see O'Brien 1977b.

Important Note. The original printing of this chapter (1996) contained numerous and significant errors for which I am in no way responsible.

8 Eternity and time

In the treatise devoted to eternity and time (III.7) Plotinus begins by reflecting on his own style of philosophizing. These reflections are one of the most important sources for understanding Plotinus's method in general, but it is worth considering them closely in the context of this particular treatise and its topic, for an understanding of Plotinus's approach will help us to follow and better evaluate the general direction of his argument. Plotinus presents us with six aspects. We begin our enquiry (1) with the general notions and presuppositions which will have formed in us a concept of time and of eternity. For Plotinus himself one important and central element of this is the linking of eternity with the unchanging and transcendent intelligible world and time with the physical world of becoming. Clearly Plato lies partly behind this. But what influences may have been at work in the formation of this preliminary concept are of no significance at this stage. Now (2) when we look at our ideas more closely we become more and more puzzled as objections and difficulties arise. In fact Aristotle's discussion of time in *Physics* IV.10–14, a passage of great importance for Plotinus, begins from exactly such puzzlement. The next step (3) is to look at what the ancients have said, which is precisely what Plotinus does in this treatise. But we should also look at how they have been interpreted. In this treatise, this will be of particular relevance with respect to Plato whose interpreters are quietly corrected on a number of points and for Aristotle too in whose case the commentators produce interpretations which Plotinus finds fruitful for further development. We should then (4) become clear about our own interpretation of the ancients (III.7.1.10–13) so that we can confidently say what their opinions are. We should then (5) realize that some of these philosophers have hit on the truth; but we must be careful to "investigate which of them have attained it (truth) most completely" (III.7.1.14–15). It is important to notice the plural here and that no philosopher is said to have reached *the complete* truth. In this treatise Plotinus makes Plato his primary authority, but Aristotle's views provide an important and positive foundation both for his enquiries and for the notion of time in this world. Moreover even Plato is not in possession of the *whole* truth. There is still much for the philosopher to work out for himself. Plotinus is thus aware that he is to some extent moving on from Plato.[1] Lastly (6) we must search for ourselves, which Plotinus does in this treatise in which he builds on Plato and to some extent on Aristotle.

Apart from the initially expressed assumption relating eternity and time respectively to the Intelligible and physical realms Plotinus also regards the concepts as intimately linked, a presupposition equally founded on Plato. While the treatise begins with the assertion that one may approach eternity from time or time from eternity, in fact the dominant approach is the latter. In Plotinian terms then we determine the image from the archetype. After exploring and defining eternity Plotinus turns to time in chapter 7. But this turning to time is seen not merely as changing from one (metaphysically higher) subject to a lower but in terms of the soul's descent – "so then we must go down from eternity to the enquiry into time, and to time" (III.7.7.7–8). We descend, that is, not merely to a lower epistemological level but "to time," to a lower level of being.

The exploration of time begins with the examination on their own terms of ideas of other philosophers culminating in those of Aristotle, at which point Plotinus first begins to introduce elements of his own theory of time. The doctrine of Aristotle is deemed inadequate precisely because it commences from and does not rise above an empirical analysis of time, an attempt to find an adequate account of how time operates rather than to ask what it *is* – a question which can be answered only by an account which begins above with eternity and which clarifies the implications of Plato's definition of time as the "moving image of eternity" (*Timaeus* 37d6–7). Thus time may be adequately described only in the context of eternity. It is the life of the soul. Plotinus's interest in time then ends not with the solution of the sort of aporiae which he mentions at the outset of his enquiries and which were the starting point of Aristotle's enquiry but with the nature of the soul, its activity and destiny, which are central concerns of Plotinus's philosophy as a whole. The structure of this treatise is a clear witness to the dynamic of Plotinus's philosophical method and reflects the general structure of his metaphysical system and the close connection of philosophical reasoning with the moral and spiritual progress of the individual.

I ETERNITY

Plotinus's discussion of eternity is a dynamic exploration. Although the entire discussion centers on Plato and in particular the *Timaeus* and to that extent is clearly circumscribed, there is nevertheless a strong element of open enquiry. It is interesting that Proclus and Damascius both criticize Plotinus for identifying eternity and Intellect.[2] In fact Plotinus rejects such a simple equation right from the start. Proclus has either misunderstood the subtlety of Plotinus's discussion or thinks that it has not worked. In chapter 2 of this treatise Plotinus begins his discussion of eternity by raising some basic problems involved in a simple identification of eternity with Intellect or with "rest," chosen as the most relevant characteristic of the intelligible world. Although he appears in chapter 6 in a broad sense to make such an identification he searches in chapters 3 to 6 for a more nuanced solution as we will see.

It seems likely that the two attempts to identify eternity respectively with Intellect and with rest do not represent the doctrines of any particular predecessors but are invented by Plotinus[3] to introduce his exploration. This is quite different from the later exploratory "definitions" in the following chapters which reflect the ideas of previous thinkers. Nevertheless they may both be taken as fairly obvious and general interpretations of Plato. The identification of eternity with the intelligible substance may be seen as rooted in Plato's "living being" which is contemplated by the demiurge. This is described as "eternal" (*Timaeus* 37d1) and as "always existing in the same state" (28a6). That eternity also "remains in unity" (37d6) could also suggest "rest." Rest and substance (*ousia*) are also two of the five concepts in the *Sophist* (254d–e) which Plotinus raised to the level of exhaustive categories of the intelligible world.[4]

The identification of eternity with the intelligible substance is seen

as a counterpart to the identification of time with the whole heaven
and the universal order (cosmos). This latter idea, which is brought up
again in the discussion of time,[5] is of Pythagorean origin and one
might just speculate that the eternity equation was a doctrine of some
now lost Neopythagorean treatise. Two main arguments are put forward to support this thesis and are in turn criticized. We consider
eternity to be something very majestic; the intelligible is the most
majestic (interestingly he excludes the One, which must be the most
majestic of all, since the One transcends all speech and we are concerned with what we can speak about); therefore eternity is the intelligible. The second argument begins from the claim that eternity and
the intelligible are both inclusive of the same things. If they have the
same content they must be identical. But this argument is quickly
refuted by appealing to the concept of "being *in* eternity" which suggests that eternity is different from what is in it and secondly from our
saying that the intelligibles are eternal, for the predicate cannot be
identical with the subject of predication. This last argument clearly
demonstrates the ground on which Plotinus bases all his discussion
and his chosen starting point since it is obviously taken from *Timaeus* 37d3 where "the nature of the living being" is said to be "eternal." The consideration of predication now prompts Plotinus to return to the criticism of the first argument, which may be rejected on
the grounds that a common predicate does not signify identity of a
subject.

Despite the rejection of both arguments and thus of the simple
identity of eternity and intelligible substance two positive observations are made which will be carried forward to the subsequent
analysis of the problem. The first is that although eternity is not the
intelligible we may still say that is has something to do (*peri*) with it
or that it is *in* it or that it is present to it (*para*). And secondly that
the inclusiveness of the intelligible and of eternity are to be understood differently. While the intelligible includes everything as a
whole includes its parts, eternity includes the whole all at once
(*homou*), that is, simultaneously and not as parts.

The second part of this chapter now concentrates on "rest." As
with substance so here a counterpart in time is given. Rest corresponds to eternity as motion does to time. Rest is viewed in turn in
its simple meaning as rest in the intelligible. Two arguments and an
aporia are raised against the former identification. If rest is eternity,

it is not eternal, just as eternity is not eternal for it would then participate in itself. Presumably this argument presupposes that we already accept that rest is eternal, an idea provided by Plato's reference to resting in unity (*Timaeus* 37d6). The next criticism argues that motion cannot be eternal if rest is eternal. Once again it is Plato who provides one of the basic premises, that motion (or a certain type of motion) is eternal (*Timaeus* 37d6). If eternity is rest and if motion is eternal, then motion is at-rest. Plotinus's last point is an aporia: how can we accommodate the idea of the "always" in the concept of rest? The notion of rest in the intelligible to which he now turns introduces us more precisely to the metaphysical level in which Plotinus wishes to locate eternity and at the same time to some central ideas. Four objections are made against identifying eternity with intelligible rest: (1) It would exclude the other four Platonic "categories" of the intelligible world as derived from the *Sophist* (254d–e) – substance, motion, the other, the same. Once again the Platonic basis for the objection is clear and we note how the five *genera* are brought back into the account again in chapter 3. (2) Rest must involve unity – again appealing to *Timaeus* (37d6). (3) Eternity must be without extension so as to differentiate it from time. But rest does not of itself include the notion of lack of extension. (4) "Remaining in unity" is predicated of eternity (Plato again). Therefore eternity participates in rest but is not rest.

The results of the enquiry so far have been negative but a number of markers have been laid down. Chapter 3 begins with virtually the same question again but by its end we have reached a partial working definition of eternity which is more than a simple identification. Succeeding chapters will add to this definition by approaches from different viewpoints. Although Plato provides Plotinus with the outlines at least of a fairly clear goal for his enquiry we have the distinct impression (and it is, I think, more than just an impression) of spontaneity in the way in which the enquiry proceeds. The conclusion is not all neatly determined and clear for Plotinus from the beginning.[6] This spontaneity is achieved by two features which provide the essential characteristics of Plotinus's philosophizing and which are finely displayed in this chapter: (1) a genuine exploratory and aporetic procedure which does not pretend to solve all problems and (2) the direct experience of reality (here eternity) itself that it is possible for a philosopher to have when his intellect is one with the universal Intellect.

The positive exploration of eternity follows a distinctive method of Plotinian philosophizing – of circling around an issue, viewing it from different sides.[7] Only in this perspective may one attempt to reconcile apparent contradictions. One may note the following characteristics:

1 The tension between the search for identifying eternity with some already established feature or level of reality in the Plotinian intelligible world and the giving of a "definition" of it.

2 The significance of our own epistemological experience at different levels of reality.

3 The repetition of key expressions.

4 The presentation of a multifaceted description or series of definitions which do not necessarily combine to form one single coherent whole.

The first definition, that eternity is "the life which belongs to that which exists and is in being" relates eternity to the totality of the Intelligible. But it is not to be identified with it as a whole nor to any part of it. The approach to eternity is to be a dynamic one. Employing the Platonic dialectic of division and synthesis we first see the Intelligible in its various aspects – the five genera excluded from the concept of eternity by its alleged identification with "rest" are now reintroduced as aspects of the Intelligible. But it is only when these aspects are "put together again" that eternity is seen in them as "life that abides in the same." This life which eternity is, is not identical with the Intelligible itself but is something "seen" in it, a manifestation of it. "Eternity is not the substrate, but something which, as it were, shines out from the substrate itself." The emphasis is against identifying eternity with the Intelligible and expressing its separate but dependent nature. It is "around" (peri) Being and is seen in it. It manifests itself from Being, like light caused by something else, dependent on and attached to its cause but different from it.

But this separateness needs some correction (chapter 4). Eternity does not come to the Intelligible "from outside," but it is that nature and from it and with it" (1-2). "But it is that nature" cannot be taken literally for it would be a clear contradiction of the former denial of the identification of eternity with the Intelligible. It is intended rather to underline the very close connection of the two. When Plotinus does come very near to identifying them at the end of this discussion in chapter five that too is to be taken in the same way – for in the end the sort of unity in diversity of the Intelligible world cannot be adequately expressed in human language or concepts. The reality of the situation can only be pointed to and often lies between expressions, as it were.

The relationship is expressed in terms already familiar to us. "The nature of eternity is *contemplated in* the Intelligible nature existing *in* it as originated *from* it because we see all the other things, too, which we say are There existing *in* it, and say that they all come *from* its substance and are *with* its substance" (III.7.4.3–5). It is an aspect of the Intelligible world as much as Beauty or Truth. In this sense it comes very close to being like a Plotinian Form at the Intelligible level. But although eternity may be of similar status to these it is not them but rather the "state (*diathêsis*) and nature (*phusis*)" of complete reality. And this state and nature is one that is "deficient in nothing" with neither past nor future – for if something has become or will become it was or must now be deficient in some way. Reality is something which "is always existing" – from "always existing (*aei on*)" is derived eternity (*aiôn*).[8] Plotinus has narrowly negotiated the thin line between giving eternity a precise and distinct ontological status and seeing it as a quality.

He now brings out completely into the open the basic difficulty of capturing "eternity" in thought. It may be comprehended only by its like within us. The most perfect form of knowing is found at the level of eternity and Intellect where we become one with the object of knowledge (V.3.4.10–13) by means of our intellect (V.1.10.5–6).

The possible difference between "everlastingness" and "eternity," which had been raised though not taken any further at the beginning of the enquiry in chapter 3, is now invoked again. Eternity is now regarded as the substrate from which everlastingness manifests itself. This looks very much like a contradiction of the earlier statement that eternity is not the substrate but comes *from* the substrate. But Plotinus does not apply the term "substrate" to the same reality here. Earlier he used it to refer to the Intelligible. Here it is used to refer to eternity as the object of contemplation and, as such, a real

existent. This is surely meant more as a counterbalance to any impression we might have had from the previous chapter that eternity
is simply a manifestation. In fact, eternity is not simply the substrate to everlastingness (the manifestation), but rather it is the "substrate *with* the corresponding condition manifested." Plotinus has
then added substance to the idea of manifestation so that he can
finally claim that eternity is a "god proclaiming and manifesting
himself" where the term "god" is the substantial element.⁹ We may
see in "god" a half-reference to the Intelligible; for despite the fact
that Plotinus has ruled out the simple identification of eternity with
the Intelligible, he applies to it many of the attributes which are the
mark of the Intelligible as a whole – plurality in unity and "unend-
ing (*apeiron*) power." But the final definition offered, it should be
noticed, is still only an approximation: "and if someone were in
their way to speak of eternity as a life which is here and now endless
because it is total and expends nothing of itself, since it has not past
or future . . . he would be near to defining it" (III.7.5.25–8).

Two final points are now made. Firstly the relationship of eternity
to the One is established. Since eternity is the life of real being and
real being is from, in, around and directed toward the One, eternity
too is related to the One in the same way. The very activity of
abiding by the One is eternity. And secondly a possible misunderstanding is removed; for although it has been made clear that eternity like being is unchanging, there remains the possibility of regarding eternity as an enduring present. The word "always" in "always
is" might tempt us to imagine an enduring and therefore extended
unchanging state. "Always," which has been included in the description of eternity (and the etymology *aei on* for *aiôn* has already been
noted) to aid our rather time-bound thoughts toward a better understanding of what eternity might be, is really redundant and even
misleading.¹⁰ Here Plotinus is also resolving a problem which had
been touched on at the beginning of the whole enquiry.¹¹ The consequences of this concept of eternity are elsewhere fully exploited by
Plotinus for the life of the individual, whose real self is to be located
at the level of Intellect. The traditional philosophical goal of "well-
being" Plotinus also places here. "Well-being must not be counted
by time but by eternity; and this is neither more nor less nor of any
extension, but is a 'this here,' unextended and timeless" (I.5.7.22–6).
The good man enjoys the life of the true self, the level of Intellect

and true Being, outside time, just as his real self remains unaffected when the lower self feels the pain of being roasted alive in the bronze "bull of Phalaris" (I.4.13.5–12).[12]

II TIME

We can make statements about eternity only because we have a share in eternity ourselves. But how can we have a share in eternity if we are in time?[13] This central problem of Neoplatonism is not, of course, to be solved in this treatise alone, but provides the immediate reason for now looking at time. Despite the impression we may have given that eternity is more important for Plotinus and that time is subordinate to it in that it may be understood properly only in the context of eternity, nevertheless the puzzles over time and the examination of other philosophers' theories of time are not just an interesting but ultimately redundant school exercise. The details of the theories of time which he examines are drawn largely from Aristotle's treatment of time in the *Physics*, but they include theories later than those of Aristotle (Stoics, Epicureans), and the whole discussion reflects also the ongoing consideration of these issues particularly in the Aristotelian school.[14] Plotinus's framework, borrowed from Aristotle, is supplemented with later views. Theories of time are divided in chapter seven into three categories: time is

(a) movement
(b) what is moved
(c) something belonging to movement

This is based on Aristotle who discusses candidates for the first two categories (*Phys.* 218b1–20). Aristotle's own view that time is number of motion would provide Plotinus with his third category. Plotinus can add into these the views of the Stoics which he places in both (a) and (c), as well as of the Epicureans. The more common Stoic view of time as extension, which falls in (c) he treats at length in chapter 8, Aristotle himself in 9, and the Epicureans in 10. But there can be little doubt that the dominant influence is Aristotle both because of the long discussion devoted to him and the acceptance of his basic framework for the critical presentation of concepts of time. It should be emphasized that Plotinus is not simply presenting us with a collection of views for their purely historical interest, but rather preparing the ground for the exposition of his own view of time by showing the inadequacies of previous accounts as well as their possibilities which point in his view inevitably to his own solution. Moreover, since we are ourselves time-bound to a large extent and particularly in our reasoning it makes sense to have as full an understanding as we can of our human situation. Despite the fact that the real self may be located at the level of Intellect and eternity, the empirical self, the self which philosophizes discursively, is vested in the reasoning powers of the soul (V.3.3.35–6) whose life is time. To this extent the transcendent world may be, if not illuminated by, at least indicated from the time realm of reason. Hence the importance of time as well as eternity.

He begins by rejecting the claim that time is movement. It is interesting to note that in fact Plotinus will later accept that time is a kind of movement, the movement of the soul. But the criterion for the examination of received views is restricted, as are the views themselves, to physical motion. To that extent he can use the ideas of Aristotle whom he follows closely.

The first counterargument is based on the premise that motion is in time (and must therefore differ from it). But the premise is not argued for and we must assume that Aristotle's discussion is to be taken for granted (*Phys.* 221aff.). The second counterargument is that motion can cease, but time cannot. This is not found in precisely this form in Aristotle. In fact Aristotle argues that there must be change for there to be time ("But neither does time exist without change," *Phys.* 218b21). But presumably Plotinus means not the absence of all motion, but cessation of motion in a particular object. Aristotle conceives of such a situation as "rest in time" (*Phys.* 221b7–12). While these two arguments may be regarded as distillations from Aristotle,[15] it is also possible to discern a certain originality in them.[16]

Having stressed, more so than Aristotle, as an argument against the identification of time and motion, that motion may lapse but time does not, he naturally airs the objection that the movement of the all (or of the heavenly circuit) does not cease and presumably may be a serious candidate for identification with time. He uses once again against this the argument that this movement is "in time" since (1) one can distinguish in time a full circuit of the heavens from a half circuit which takes half the time to complete,

(2) the fast and slow speeds of the outer and inner spheres respectively, a fact admitted by proponents of the theory, who themselves point to their being in time, since speed is distance covered in a certain period of time. Aristotle does not adduce this argument about the movement of the heavens although the elements of it are to be found in his works.[17] It is found in Plotinus because for him the movement of the heavens presents a greater problem for two reasons: (1) as already noted he has stressed more than Aristotle the idea of lapse of motion and (2) the issue was probably more important in his time. Eudemus, Theophrastus, and Alexander all seem to have interpreted Plato as identifying time with the movement of the heavens.[18] The idea was still current in the fourth and fifth centuries.[19] Finally the identification of time and the sphere is dismissed by Plotinus as summarily as it is by Aristotle presumably since the arguments against motion in general should suffice.

He now turns to what can be broadly recognized as the Stoic definition of time as extension of motion. This is firstly conceived as spatial distance. If the distance covered is time, he argues, then since not all movements are at the same speed different movements will cover different distances and there would then have to be a standard means of comparison which would be time. But which of the many distances would provide the standard? Even if we can pin it down to one standard, for example the distance traversed by the movement of the universe, it may still be objected that the distance is measured as space rather than as time. He then considers the movement itself as extension. But this would be either sheer bulk or magnitude, for example, a great mass of heat or bulk in repetition like water flowing which comes "again and again." This repetition of "again" and "again" can be expressed by abstract number which allows us to count repeated magnitude, but does not in itself convey a sense of time. In fact all this activity of motion takes place "in time"; otherwise time would not be everywhere but would be located in a particular substratum (motion). This examination of Stoic doctrine prepares us for the critical exploration of Aristotle which is to follow, where some of the same themes reappear: the inadequacy of number as an explanation of time, the emphasis on the need to search for "what time essentially is" (III.7.8.58–9), and the importance of the concept of being "in time." A further stimulus to the examination of the Stoic theory must surely have been that many Middle Platonists

accepted as an interpretation of *Timaeus* 37d5–7 Chrysippus's definition of time as the extension of the motion to the cosmos.[20]

In chapter 9 Plotinus examines Aristotle's own definition of time
as the "number or measure of motion." His criticism of Aristotle is
not intended in any sense to be an exhaustive refutation but rather a
critical exploration in which he highlights the problems and inadequacies of Aristotle's account which he hopes his own account of
time in chapters 11 to 13 will avoid. In the course of this criticism
indirect allusions to his own preferred approach surface constantly.
Moreover, Plotinus follows and builds on a long tradition of critical
reflection on Aristotle's ideas by Peripatetics themselves. Indeed,
Plotinus is so far from a rejection of Aristotle that he attempts to
accommodate Aristotle's theory to his own view of time in the
universe, complaining only that the Aristotelians lacked sufficient
clarity because they were addressing their ideas to an internal school
audience (III.7.13.9–18).[21]

Plotinus begins by looking at what is measured and making the
distinction, as he had already done with the Stoic theory, of regular
and irregular motion. How is it possible to number or measure what
is irregular? The same difficulty had already been raised by Aristotle's pupil Eudemus.[22] Aristotle would, in the end, probably answer as Plotinus (III.7.9.32–5) that irregular motion is measured
against regular motion and that it is the continuous regular motion
of the outer heavenly sphere which is the primary directly measured
motion. The same solution could also suffice for Plotinus's other
criticism that there are many different kinds even of regular motion
and the same type of measure would not be appropriate for each. But
there is a deeper objection here. Even if we are dealing with only a
single motion we need to know not only what is being measured
(motion) but what the measure is. If number is the measure when it
is abstracted from what is measured we are left with an abstract
number, for example, ten without the horses. In the case of counting
objects "it is possible to think," he says, "of the number." It has a
certain "nature" of its own apart from the objects enumerated.
Time, too, then, if it is a measure or number, should have its own
nature. As a Platonist Plotinus has a natural inclination to giving
prominence and independent existence to arithmetical number, but
he is also building on a problem already identified within the Aristotelian tradition. Although Aristotle himself on several occasions

makes it clear that "number" in his definition of time refers to "number that is numbered" rather than number that numbers, that is, concrete as opposed to abstract or arithmetical number, this presented difficulties to his later followers. Aspasius and Alexander both want him to refer to abstract numbers,[23] for if number is concrete each motion will have its own time (cf. III.7.9.20–1).

If the measure/number is conceived as a continuous measure like a ruler other problems ensue (III.7.9.17–31). It will be like a line running alongside what it measures. Then it will measure only what it runs with. But why then should one measure the other rather than the reverse? And what determines the measure in the measuring "ruler"? (III.7.9.40–1). We have thus returned to our original question – what *is* the number/measure? Supposing time is abstract number (III.7.9.51–5) and has its own nature like ten apart from the horses, what then according to Aristotle is it before it measures? Although Aristotle seems in general to regard time as something independent of the soul and objective, he occasionally gives a leading role to soul. He says, for example, that time cannot exist without a soul to number it (*Phys.* 223a21–9) and even that we can be aware of time-motion within ourselves, independently of any outside motion (*Phys.* 219a4–8). Plotinus seems to pick out and emphasize these Aristotelian comments so as to suggest that the notion of ideal time and soul as cause of time is to be found in Aristotle. Aristotle failed however according to Plotinus to explain the nature of this pre-existent measuring number. His attempts to attribute the discernment of "before" and "after" to number[24] are not satisfactory since "before" and "after" are either spatial concepts or if used with a temporal meaning this very temporal content in turn needs to be explained. Time therefore is something other than "before" and "after." Then time is either present in the spatial world independently of the measure – but this makes little sense of Aristotle's claim that time is number or measure – or time depends in some way on soul. It is this idea which he will exploit in the presentation of his own view.

But before doing so he briefly completes his survey with the Epicurean definition of time as accompaniment of motion. It is left to the end for summary dismissal because in Plotinus's view it says nothing; for it does not answer the question *what* it is that accompanies motion (II.7.10.1–4). In any case the concept also begs the

question of what time is because it itself contains a temporal concept, whether what accompanies comes before, after, or simultaneously, that is, what accompanies is "in time" (III.7.10.4–6). This
is after all a philosophical and not a historical enquiry (III.7.10.10–
12) and there is, therefore, no need to give full details of philosophically unhelpful theories.

III PLOTINUS'S OWN THEORY OF TIME

In the end, however, we will not discover what time is simply
from an examination of its manifestations in this world. Sufficient
pointers to a transcendent cause have already emerged from the ex-
plorations of his predecessors' views. In this sense Plotinus's own
view of time both emerges from the views of his predecessors and
stands in strong contrast to them as receiving its substantiating
context from the Intelligible world and from eternity. Hence the
return in chapter eleven to that world. The world of time is illuminated both by stressing its origin from the Intelligible and by contrasting the two.

We are asked firstly to imagine how time would itself describe its
"origin."[25] The "generation" of time is, of course, properly to be
conceived of in terms of causal rather than temporal sequence. The
procession of time from the transcendence of Intellect is expounded
within the familiar framework of procession of Hypostases. Not that
time is in any way a separate Hypostasis; Time and Soul are intimately linked, for time is the life of the Soul. Plotinus takes care to
mention them both but marks the subordinate position of time.
When "Soul" or what is to become Soul becomes restless in Intellect
and seeks to proceed from it, time also moves. It is significant that
time is mentioned after Soul.[26] Plotinus now changes the subject to
"we" – "we made a long stretch of our journey and constructed time
as an image of eternity." The significance of "we" has been dis-
puted.[27] If, as I am inclined to think, it has a metaphysical significance rather than being simply expository it suggests the doctrine
that we, individual souls, are "part" of the Hypostasis Soul. Thus,
time, the life of soul which is to be identified with discursive reason
(dianoia), is very much our life. Understanding what time is helps us
to understand what we are, at least at the level of discursive reason.
This does not mean that we, as humans, determine time (i.e., a

subjectivist view of time as found in St. Augustine), since time in this world is at a still lower level, as we shall see, and "we" as individual souls are in any case subsumed in the totality of soul and time is directly communicated to the world through the World Soul.

The descent of soul from Intellect is described in terms familiar to us from the Plotinian system. Indeed the parallel is made explicitly (III.7.11.47–8). Immanence in the higher in a state of "quietness," the restless activity which wants to be master of itself and be its own, leads to movement from the prior to independent existence on a lower level. This restlessness and self-assertion, sometimes termed *tolma*,[28] represents one of the tensions in Plotinus's system, for this critical assessment of procession as a descent to the inferior is balanced though perhaps never fully reconciled with clearly positive descriptions of procession as arising from the generous nature of the highest Hypostases (IV.8.6.7–16; cf. III.2.1.20–6; VI.7.8.13–14). And just as soul constitutes itself as an image of its prior and then produces the physical world as an image of itself, so too soul in the context of time constitutes its own life as an image of eternity and in turn creates as an image of itself the physical world *in time*. Time exists then on two levels – as the life of soul, and here Plotinus uses the verbal form of "time," apparently coined by him expressly for this purpose, "soul *temporalized* itself" – and as the time perceived in the physical world where things are "in time." Thus, soul is not "in time." Rather the physical world is in soul and since the life of soul is time, the physical world is "in time," much as when Plotinus prefers us to say that the world is in soul rather than the reverse, like the net which is in the sea of soul.[29]

The life of soul is the life of discursive reason in which soul presents one activity after another. This life is seen not simply as activity in a fixed spot as it were, but as activity in a linear progression from eternity, that is, the very procession from eternity is the time-life of Soul – "time is the life of soul in a movement of passage from one way of life (eternity) to another" (III.7.11.44–5; cf. the "long stretch of our journey" at III.7.11.19). We may wish to ask ourselves at this point just what sort of time condition, if any, Plotinus attaches to soul if it is not "in time." The discursive reason is seen as something "extended" as it were,[30] as "unfolding itself" (III.7.11.24). Movement is made from one idea to another. We might think that this involves time in the same way as movement in this world. But far from involving time its time status is not even to be imagined as similar to that of physical rest; for according to Plotinus if the heavenly circuit should cease to move (and hence all physical movement cease) even its rest would be in time (III.7.12.15–19) and could be measured (by soul). Time at soul level transcends even this notion of rest in time. One of the other important marks of time is the notion of "before" and "after." Now Plotinus sees this element not only in the things that are "in time" but in time itself. It is foolish, he says (III.7.13.30–40), to take the "before" and "after" in movement in this world as time and deny that there is "before" and "after" in the "truer" and more real movement of soul.[31] But elsewhere Plotinus suggests that this "before" and "after" are present even in Intellect which in its eternity is divorced from time altogether. Their presence in Intellect provides the model for their significance in time at soul level. These are indicators not of temporal sequence but of order of importance or causality. "And, as the prior and the subsequent in the species forms are not temporal, so neither will the soul make its acts of intelligence of the prior and the subsequent in temporal sequence" (IV.4.1.26–8). "Before" and "after" signify order (taxis) rather than time just as in a plant the order begins from the root and extends to the top; for the observer who sees the whole plant at once this is an order of ranking rather than of time (IV.4.1.29–31). There is then a form of discursive reason on a lower level than Intellect in which there is movement and change from one thing to another but which is not measurable by time in the sense of our concept of time drawn from the physical world.

But it is likely that he does think of our normal discursive state as being often dependent on and restricted by physical concepts. This may express itself simply in the need to employ language to express ideas (V.3.17.23–8).[32] Discursive thought is here contrasted with Intellect in its need to express its ideas in words. It is this that brings about sequence.[33] But discursive reason is not always so impeded. After all, the soul before embodiment is differentiated from Intellect; and the Hypostasis Soul, even if ultimately linked to the body of the universe through the World Soul, has a cognitive life distinct from that of Intellect and unencumbered by external distractions. Evidently because of the nature of soul as discursive thought in process there was a great temptation to regard and describe its movement in temporal terms. But Plotinus strives constantly to correct this impression.

These problems exercised him in the context of the question whether souls when "separated" from body have memory (IV.4.15). If soul is connected with time, he argues, will it not have memory? Will the World Soul have memory? But, he counters, the World Soul is not "in time" but generates time. Even individual souls are not "in time" but their affections and activities are. In fact souls are everlasting and time is later than them. What is "in time" is less than time itself. That soul is everlasting does not mean that it is at the level of Intellect or eternity. Plotinus can apply the same description to discursive reason itself ("everlasting progression," III.7.13.43–4). Indeed, in giving this emphasis and stressing the subordinate relation of time to soul (we recall that he does precisely this in III.7.11)[34] he is saying neither more nor less than his claim in III.7 that soul is not "in time" but in a sense *is* time. It is true that in the chapter following this (IV.4.17) he has a rather pessimistic view of the individual's life as time-bound and impeded, but in the end he claims the good man can allow his ruling power and higher soul to dominate. There is more than one type of discursive reason. The lowest operates in time, but at the higher level Plotinus seeks to accommodate movement and timelessness, a sort of thinking whose stages cannot be measured in time intervals. In a way this concept of discursive reason brings with it as many problems as the concept of intellectual activity in the eternal and unchanging present of Intellect.

We return now to III.7. In chapter 12 Plotinus asks us to imagine a reversal of procession (which cannot in fact occur since all the Hypostases are ever active) with soul returning to Intellect so that time would be abolished. Therefore, it is the procession of soul which "generates" time. We note here that the withdrawal is seen initially as one process in which the dependence of the physical world in time on the soul is intimately connected with its own activity as soul – "an activity which is not directed to itself or in itself but lies in making and production" (III.7.12.7–8). A few lines later, however, the process of withdrawal is seen as having two stages, from the physical world (15–19) and from the world of soul itself back to Intellect (19–20). This difference suggests that the levels of soul and World Soul (which is directly concerned with creating) are continuous.[35] It is important to be aware of the flexibility Plotinus shows in the vantage points he adopts, in this case looking at souls now as the

Hypostasis Soul, now as World Soul or both or including individual souls.

Time proper then is the life of the soul. This universe is "in time" and although Plato may seem to have equated the heavenly sphere with time, if he is interpreted precisely it will be seen that what he really means is that the sphere and the planets "manifest" time (III.7.12.25–8). Time as we know it is time manifested. Whether we consider it as that which measures or as measure or as what is measured these are all accidental attributes of time (III.7.12.42; 12.55; 13.11–12). Thus, manifested time may be considered as manifest to us as a distinct interval *measured* by the movement of the heavens (e.g., from sunrise to sunset) which may in turn be used as a *measure* (which may also seem to be *measuring*). But none of these is time itself. We can then be aware of time without knowing what time itself is; for we take intervals *of* time and employ them as measures just as when we measure length by a cubit in the sense of measuring specific lengths but without knowing what we mean by "length itself." The manifestation does not itself produce time but indicates it to us so that we have a concept (*ennoia*) of time; but this concept is not time itself. The major instrument in gaining this concept is what is measured, that is, the measured interval. It is better to call time what is measured than to call it the measure of movement, the Aristotelian definition. But he tries to accommodate Aristotle by suggesting that the Aristotelians may really have meant what is measured (III.7.13.13–18). Be that as it may Aristotle has still not defined time itself. It remains to invoke Plato again who never describes time itself in these Aristotelian terms but as the "moving image of eternity."

The treatise ends with a number of arguments pointing to the substantial and real nature of time as life of soul (III.7.13.28–69), commencing with a reference back to the argument based on imagining a withdrawal of soul-life from the universe with which he had tried to establish the dependence of time in this world on a transcendent cause (12.4–23). That he ends with this stress on time or life of the soul need not surprise us, for it is a conscious corrective to the opening of the whole treatise in which eternity and time are assigned respectively to the unchanging Intelligible world and to the physical universe. Time we have now discovered lies properly, that is, in its essence, between the two; and the life of soul, of course, forms the focal point of the individual in his median role between two worlds. As so often in Plotinus theory is rooted in and serves experience.

NOTES

1 Cf. V.1.8.10–14 with a different emphasis: "These statements of ours are not new; they do not belong to the present time, but were made long ago, not explicitly, and what we have said in this discussion has been an interpretation of them, relying on Plato's own writings for evidence that these views are ancient."

2 Proclus in Tim. III.12.9–12; Damascius in Simplicius Phys. 791.32f.

3 So Beutler and Theiler in their commentary IVb511.

4 Theodorus of Asine also identified eternity and rest (Test 24 Deuse = Proclus Theol. Plat. V.30 p.311.30f). It is not however clear whether this was a simple identification of the kind criticized by Plotinus or whether any qualifications have been lost to us.

5 III.7.7.19.

6 The impression given by Beierwaltes's (1967) analysis.

7 Smith 1992, 26.

8 Cf. Aristotle, De caelo 279a25–8.

9 Armstrong (1966–88 ad loc.) understands "god" as referring to the "Intellect or Real Being, the Second Hypostasis." Beierwaltes (1967 ad loc.) is inclined to exclude this.

10 Boethius sees the same problem in De trinitate 4.67–77 "Philosophers say that 'ever' may be applied to the life of the heavens and other immortal bodies. But as applied to God it has a different meaning. He is ever, because 'ever' is with him a term of present time, and there is this great difference between 'now,' which is our present, and the divine present. Our present connotes changing time and sempiternity; God's present, abiding, unmoved, and immoveable, connotes eternity. Add ever (semper) to eternity and you get the constant, incessant and thereby perpetual course of our present time, that is to say, semipiternity."

11 III.7.2.27–9.

12 Cf. Smith 1974, 25, 74–5.

13 Cf. IV.8.1.1–11.

14 See pp. 207–8 what is said on Plotinus III.7.9. The systematic collection and comparision of ideas on time is reflected in Diels, Doxographi graeci, 318.

15 Callahan 1979, 98–101.

16 Strange 1994, 41: "apparently original." Strange notes that Plotinus (III.7.8.45–7; 10.6) appears to take the notion that things are "in time" as part of our common conception of time and suggests that the premise of the second argument (motion may cease, but time not) may have been similarly regarded.

17 The movement of the all is endless, *Phys.* 222b6f; *De caelo* 284a9. He rejects identification of all and time, *Phys.* 218a33f. Slow and fast movements depend on time, *Phys.* 218b13–14; *De caelo* 287a23. For the latter the reference in *Phys.* is to movement in general. Nor does it seem that Plotinus is precisely following Aristotle in the rejection of the identification of time and the movement of the all since he is more specific than Aristotle, and whereas Aristotle argues from an assumption that a section of the circuit "is a time" Plotinus argues that a section is "in a certain time."

18 Cf. Simplicius, *Phys.* 700.17f.

19 Cf. Aug. *Conf.* XI 23 probably referring to the Arian Eunomius. Cf. Basilius, *Adv. Eunomium* I.21 and Callahan 1958, 439f.,

20 Philo, *Opif.* 26f; Alcinous, *Did.* 14.6 (170.21f. Hermann); Apuleius, *De Plat.* 10.

21 This statement reminds us of Plotinus's debt to Aristotle as recorded by Porphyry (*Life* 14.5–7) and to the commentators (*ibid.* 12–14).

22 Simplicius, *Phys.* 717.6–14.

23 They even emended the text of *Phys.* 219b7–8 from "Time obviously is what is counted, not that with which we count" to "Time obviously is not what is counted, but that with which we count."

24 *Phys.* 219b1–2: "For time is just this – the number of motion in respect of 'before' and 'after.'"

25 In a similarly vivid way "nature" (*phusis*) describes how it creates in III.8.4.

26 By Soul here Plotinus means not the World Soul but the Hypostasis Soul. In III.7.13.65–8 he locates time in us and in the Soul of the all in the context of the unity of souls and Soul ("all are one"). Earlier however in chapter 11 he seems to include the World Soul as part of the continuum of soul which "begins" with the Hypostasis Soul. There is nothing unusual for Plotinus in this flexible use of terms.

27 E.g., Beierwaltes (1967, ad loc.) argues that it refers to Plotinus and his colleagues.

28 Cf. especially V.1.1.4 and Armstrong's note (1966–88 ad loc.)

29 IV.3.9.36–42.

30 "An unextended extension," IV.4.16.22.

31 Also in III.7.12.12 "before" and "after" are attributed to soul.

32 So too in IV.4.16.12–16 where he distinguishes speaking and doing.
33 In IV.4.17 he speaks even more strongly of our being bound "in time," that our reasonings are subjected to external influence through images.
34 See p. 210.
35 The simultaneity of the two movements, the "generation" of time as life and soul and the "generation" of the universe, is stressed in III.7.13.26–8 since the universe no less than Soul has always existed. Moreover Plotinus needs to take into account (III.7.12.22–3) Plato's stress on the simultaneity of time and creation (*Timaeus* 38b6: "Time and the heavens came into being at the same instant").

9 Cognition and its object

In this essay I shall address some philosophical issues that have to do with the relationship between cognition and its objects in Plotinus. This involves inquiring into the connection between Plotinus's epistemology and psychology, on the one hand, and his ontology, on the other. Interesting questions arise with respect to Plotinus's views both as regards the relation between sense perception and the sensible object and that of thinking and the intelligible object. One set of questions concerns realism versus idealism and subjectivism: Is there in general an essential connection between cognition and object in Plotinus such that the mode of cognition in some sense determines the object? This would imply idealism of some sort. One may also ask whether the immediate object of cognition is always something belonging to the subject of cognition as opposed to something extra-mental. Such a subjectivist position would place the extra-mental beyond the direct reach of cognition and might involve radical skepticism about it. Or is Plotinus neither an idealist nor a subjectivist and objects appear to be such and such because they are such as they appear independently of the mode of apprehension? Different stories may of course have to be told about intelligibles and sensibles with respect to these questions. So I shall in fact argue. Still it is interesting to inquire whether there are any common principles underlying Plotinus's views on both sensibles and intelligibles in this regard. This too I shall take up here.

I THE NATURE OF SENSE PERCEPTION

Plotinus normally speaks as a nonrepresentational realist about the objects of sense perception: what we perceive are qualities of exter-

217

nal objects, qualities that exist out there independent of us.¹ He even
makes a point of insisting that what we see is an external object out
there, rejecting certain theories about vision on the ground that the
theories would entail that we do not see the objects themselves
(IV.5.3.21–2). Against a view that holds that we see by receiving
physical impressions of the objects we see, he writes that "if we
received impressions (*tupos*) of what we see, there will be no possibility of looking at the actual things we see, but we shall look at images
and shadows of the objects of sight, so that the objects themselves
will be different from the things we see"² (IV.6.1.29–32). And there
are several other remarks that clearly point to direct realism.³ Nevertheless, there are also some indications to the contrary. First, certain
features of Plotinus's theory of sense perception may be difficult to
reconcile with direct realism. Second, there are some passages that
at first glance at least speak against perceptual realism. Third, there
are considerations speaking for the view that Plotinus holds that
what is out there, if anything at all, is quite different from what
appears to our senses. I shall now take up these issues in turn.

Before proceeding, however, let us have an outline of Plotinus's
views on sense perception. The elements involved in sense perception are the following: an external qualified object (or the quality of
such an object) is what is perceived. The subject of sense perception
is the individual soul and its role is described either as judging
(*krisis*) or the reception of the form (*eidos*) of the object (I take these
to be different descriptions of the same phenomenon). For perception to occur the soul must come into contact with the external
object. The soul by itself, being an intelligible thing, cannot do this:
alone, it only grasps intelligibles and in any case it cannot be affected by sensibles. But to perceive through the senses is to apprehend sensibles, extended spatial phenomena, and the soul must
somehow come into contact with these. This it does by means of
ensouled sense organs: these are affected by the object of perception.
This sensory affection, which Plotinus also describes as "assimilation," is transmitted to the soul. By the stage at which it reaches the
soul, it is no longer an affection (*pathos*) but a form or judgment.
Plotinus's usual story about sense perception is along these lines.⁴
One question that obviously arises is how Plotinus reconciles the
realism which he insists on with the role he assigns to sensory

affections. It is for instance hard to see how he could be a realist if he also holds that what we immediately perceive is the sensory affections and that the sensory affections are different from the external objects of sense perception. In my book, *Plotinus on Sense-Perception*, I discuss the insides of Plotinus's account of sense perception and argue for an overall interpretation which seeks to do justice to his realistic intuitions.

Now I shall not repeat the details of my previous account here, only summarize the points that are of direct concern to us now. (1) The affection (or assimilation) in sense perception is a sensation, a nonconceptual, phenomenal presence of the external quality to the senses. (2) This phenomenal quality is in a way identical to, in a way different from, the quality as it exists in the external corporeal object. It is the same quality without the matter or bulk, and hence it is not the quality in its normal corporeal mode. The phenomenal quality is not a purely intelligible item, however, since it retains the spatial features of the corporeal – we do perceive things extended in space. We can perhaps describe this by saying that the quality the sense organ takes on is the quality of the object but in a hybrid mode of being in between the corporeal and the intelligible, having some features in common with each. There is some evidence that Plotinus actually held such a view, even if he does not express it explicitly in terms of different modes of being.5 (3) The judgment attributed to the soul is a judgment about the external object, not about the affection. So the idea is that Plotinus can with some plausibility retain his realism: even if the soul is immediately aware of the affection, the judgment (the perception itself) is about what is external, and the affection, the quality the organ takes on, is in the way indicated above identical with the external quality.

I still think that an interpretation along these lines is the best available one. Certain difficulties however deserve a fuller treatment than I gave in my previous account and it should be admitted that Plotinus's is a vulnerable sort of realism: a skeptic would jump with a wedge in hand at the distinction between the affection and the external corporeal quality. In the next section we shall inquire whether Plotinus himself gets into such a skeptical mood in the first chapter of the celebrated treatise "That the intelligibles are not outside the Intellect and on the Good" (V.5).

II POSSIBLE EVIDENCE FOR SUBJECTIVISM
OR IDEALISM

I mentioned above that there are some Plotinian passages that may seem to state or imply antirealism about sense perception. For instance Plotinus writes in one place: "And soul's power of perception (aisthêsis) need not be of sensibles, but rather it must be receptive of the impressions produced by sense perception (aisthêsis) on the living being; these are already intelligible entities" (I.1.7.9–14). Obviously, there are two kinds of aisthêsis at stake in this passage: the soul's perception and that of the living being. It has been suggested that the aisthêsis attributed to the organism is a mere sensation and that of the soul fully fledged sense perception.[6] In that case, the passage would affirm antirealism or at least a denial of direct realism. It is also possible, however, to take the aisthêsis attributed to the living being to be simply sense perception (including, but being more than, sensation), and that of the soul to be a nonsensory apprehension of mental representations, the kind involved in memory and in discursive thinking, the highest stage of the human soul. There are ample instances in Plotinus of aisthêsis being used to refer to nonsensory apprehension.[7] In my view the latter interpretation gives a better sense to the passage in its context and has the advantage of acquitting Plotinus of the charge of holding that sense perception is an apprehension of intelligible things, which is both counterintuitive and contrary to his normal teaching. For even if in Plotinus's view sense perception, qua judgment and form in the soul, involves intelligible forms or impressions, it need not thereby be necessary to ascribe to him the claim that it is *of* something intelligible. Moreover, this latter interpretation is easily harmonized with other significant passages about sense perception: he elsewhere clearly attributes sense perception as a whole, the sensory affection and the judgment or reception of intelligible form in the soul, to the organism or, which is the same, compound of soul and body.[8]

The passage which is by far the most worrisome for a realist interpretation is V.5.1. I shall now consider it at some length.[9] As will become clear, its examination will lead us beyond the theory of sense perception to the theory of Intellect and questions of metaphysics.

Plotinus's original concern in V.5.1 is the question of the conditions for ascribing perfect infallible knowledge of what is real to the

universal, divine Intellect. He will argue that only if the objects of
Intellect's thought – the Forms, what is ontologically primary – are
internal to Intellect itself, will it have such knowledge of them. We
shall come to this doctrine in its own right later on. But in the first
chapter Plotinus remarks that Intellect's knowledge cannot be
founded on demonstration. For even supposing that some of Intellect's knowledge is founded on demonstration, not all of it can be so
founded. Some at least must be immediately evident. This is of
course just a statement of the familiar point that not everything can
be demonstrated, something must be assumed; and if the demonstration is supposed to yield knowledge, what is assumed must be
known to be true without any further proof. Then Plotinus goes on
to ask from where "they" (these are some unnamed philosophers)
suppose Intellect comes to have the self-evidence (*to enarges*) about
that which they admit to be immediately known.[10] He then continues with the passage containing the crucial remark for our concerns:

But anyhow, what they admit to be immediate, whence do they say its self-
evidence comes to it? From where will it get the confidence that things are
so? For it may even be doubted about that which seems clearest in sense-
perception, whether it has its apparent existence not in the substrates but in
the affections, and intellect and reason are needed as judges. For also if it is
admitted that what sense-perception is to grasp is in sensible substrates,
what is known through sense-perception is an image (*eidôlon*) of the thing,
and sense-perception does not grasp the thing itself: for that remains outside. (V.5.1.12–19)

What does Plotinus mean by the claim that the senses know only
an image[11] of the object? And what does he mean by "the thing
itself" which he says remains external? At first sight the point of
Plotinus's remark may seem to be that in sense perception we grasp
only a *subjective* representation, something that pertains to us as
perceivers, and that this is contrasted with the object as it exists
externally independently of us. What we are directly aware of in
sense perception would then be a representation in the sense of an
image, existing in our sense organs, of the external object. Furthermore, it seems to speak for such an antirealist interpretation of our
passage that in this same chapter, V.5.1, Plotinus argues along the
following lines: If the intelligibles are external to Intellect, Intellect
must receive an impression of them if it is to know them at all; it

would in that case be just like sense perception; what Intellect would then know is a mere impression (or representation) and not the intelligibles themselves; but Intellect does know the intelligibles themselves, which, therefore, must be internal to Intellect. The implication seems to be that a power of cognition that does not contain the objects it knows, must somehow acquire them. But it cannot acquire these objects themselves, and must therefore make do with representations that pertain to it, the power of cognition. Given that this is the line of argument for the internality of the intelligibles, one naturally takes the "image" in the passage quoted above to be an image pertaining to the faculty of sense.

However, not everything is as it seems here. Such antirealist reading of the passage quoted above also runs into difficulties on examination: Plotinus seems in fact to be making two points in denial of the supposition that Intellect gets its self-evident premises from sense perception: first, considering sense perception alone, it may be doubted whether what is perceived is external or just in the affections; reason and intellect are needed as judges; secondly, *granting* that what it apprehends is external, it is nevertheless an image.[12] So one would suppose that the image mentioned here is in fact something external. But what would then the "thing itself" which remains external be? A natural answer not involving antirealism is provided by the first lines of chapter 2 of the same treatise. Here Plotinus summarizes the main points established in chapter 1 and it becomes clear that by the "image" (*eidôlon*) that sense perception grasps he means the qualitative features of each thing as opposed to the essence or quiddity of which these are an expression.[13] So one would expect that "the thing itself" in our original passage from chapter 1 is the imperceivable and separate essence of the thing, as opposed to the qualified matter which constitutes the sensible object.[14]

Such a view, according to which the perceptible qualities of an object are representations or images of an intelligible essence, which is the real thing, is a standard Plotinian view as is the claim that sense perception fails to grasp essences.[15] The following passage shows this particularly well:

[So called sensible substance] is not an essence (*ti*) but rather a quale; and the formative principle (*logos*), of fire for instance, indicates rather the essence, but the shape it produces is rather a quale. And the formative principle is the essence, but its product in the nature of body, being an image (*eidôlon*) of the form, is rather a quale. It is as if, the visible Socrates being a man, his painted picture, being colours and painter's stuff, was called Socrates. (VI.3.15.27–33)

Sensible qualities are just this: expressions in matter of the action of an imperceptible and separate inner nature or essence (*logos, to ti*).[16] There is another passage from the early treatise V.9.(5), where Plotinus deals with the internality of the intelligibles to Intellect as in V.5, which supports this understanding of "image." He has affirmed that Intellect thinks the real beings (*ta onta*) and raises the question whether it thinks them "somewhere else." In response to this he says:

[It will] surely not [think them] in sensible objects, as they suppose. For the primary object of each kind is not the sensible object: for the form on matter in the things of sense is an image (*eidôlon*) of the real form, and every form which is in something else comes to it from something else and is a likeness (*eikôn*) of that from which it comes. (V.9.5.16–19)

The treatise V.9 is less sophisticated than V.5, but it presents the same general doctrine about the internality of the intelligibles to Intellect. Here the sensible object is rejected as the ontologically primary object and Plotinus explains its image character in terms of its being "in something else," that is in some matter which takes on the form, and "from something else," that is the intelligible cause, without a word about the nature of sense perception or antirealism about the cognition of external objects. Thus, the word "image" here has clearly the meaning I have suggested for V.5.1 in a similar context.

So there are difficulties on internal grounds for an antirealist reading of our passage: such a reading squares badly with Plotinus's regular position, and another interpretation naturally suggests itself. Nevertheless, there remains the difficulty of the contrast between intellection and sense perception in Plotinus's argument for the internality of the object of intellection: this still counts in favor of an antirealist reading. So let us ask: Is there a way of interpreting Plotinus's contrast between intellection and sense perception in V.5.1 without attributing to him an antirealist view on the latter? It should give us ground for pause before attributing such a position to him on this account that in V.3, where he also argues for the internality of the objects of thought to Intellect and contrasts intellection with sense perception, there is no suggestion of this sort of subjectivism. In fact, the sense of "internal" Plotinus seems to be after here for the objects of Intellect is a stronger sense than the one in which sensory images can be said to be internal to the faculty that apprehends them. For the apprehension of such images counts for him as cognition of something external too.[17]

I believe there is a plausible interpretation that avoids subjectivism while doing justice to the contrast Plotinus wishes to draw between thinking at the level of Intellect and sense perception. This is basically an expansion of the interpretation cursorily stated above which identifies the contrast between the representation and the thing itself in our passage with the contrast between sensible qualities and the nature or essence of the thing which is the immediate intelligible cause of sensible qualities. As a preliminary to the full statement of this interpretation, we must recall some aspects of Plotinus's metaphysics.

Plotinus distinguishes between two kinds of act or activity (energeia): an inner act and an outer act. This distinction, whose primary function is to account for progression from a higher to a lower stage in the Plotinian hierarchy, pervades his thought. Even if Plotinus nowhere describes it explicitly and systematically, a schema along the following lines suggests itself: The One has a totally self-contained internal activity[18] and an inchoate Intellect as an external act, which is an image of the One itself; this inchoate Intellect reverts to its source, whereby it becomes informed; this is Intellect's inner activity, identical with Intellect's substance. This internal activity in turn has Soul as an external act. Plotinus frequently describes the inner act as the real thing itself, and the outer act as its image or representation.[19]

This process continues at soul-levels below the hypostasis soul until we reach immanent sensible forms and matter which have no external activity and progression comes to an end. So, not only is the relationship between sensible qualities and the underlying nature that produces them that of image and original, the image–original relation here is a part of the double activity schema. This is quite clear for instance from chapters 1 to 7 of III.8. Formative principles produce sensible qualities and shapes (outer activity) as a result of reverting to and contemplating their immediate cause (inner activity).

Let us now consider what we have just ascertained together with one tenet of Plotinus's realism: (1) The internal activity of the formative principle is the cause of sensible qualities; the qualities are external acts and, thereby, images of formative principles. (2) In sense perception the quality taken on by the sense organ is the same quality as the one that exists externally (though in a different mode of being; cf. p. 219). It follows from these two premises that in sense perception there is no further activity from the object side in addition to the activity of the formative principle: it is not as if the formative principle first causes the external quality which then in turn acts separately on the senses; rather, there is just one activity: the internal act of the formative principle with a sensible quality as a concomitant byproduct. So, metaphysically speaking, the quality the sense organs take on is still the external act of the object's formative principle.

Now, I suggest we ascribe to Plotinus the following principle: A power of cognition that does not by itself possess the internal activity of its objects can at most apprehend these objects through their external activity, that is, their images. This is because "not possessing the internal activity" implies in Plotinus's view that the power must be affected by the objects; and to affect is to have an effect in something else, which by definition is the work of an external, as opposed to an internal, activity. Plotinus does not explicitly state such a principle. It seems plausible to suppose, however, that a principle along these lines is what underlies many of his arguments for the internality of the intelligibles in V.5.1 and arguments to the same effect elsewhere. I shall come back to that issue later on. In any case, if Plotinus adheres to such a principle, he has good reasons for contrasting sense perception and intellection in the way he does in V.5.1: the faculty of sense does not possess the intelligible causes of sensible objects, that is, it does not possess the internal activity that constitutes the intelligible essence of these objects. What these objects are in themselves is external to the faculty of sense. The faculty can be acted on by these objects, however, in such a way as to come to share in their external activity. Or to use a more Plotinian language, the objects themselves, that is, the imperceptible *logos*, may act externally in the sense organ of a sentient being. To hold this is not to deny that the same external act may exist as an objective quality or quantity of a body.

Objections

I have maintained that through sensing the faculty of sense comes to apprehend the external qualities themselves, whereas it cannot apprehend the internal nature of the sense object. Isn't this a violation of the principle just stated that a cognitive power can at most apprehend images of what is external to it, for indeed we have said that the senses apprehend the external qualities themselves? For doesn't this principle dictate that we know images of the qualities? And secondly, if the senses can know something external to themselves by taking on or sharing in that very thing itself, why shouldn't Intellect be able to know the intelligibles themselves in an analogous manner, even if they are originally external to it?

These questions would, I think, be based on a misunderstanding. Responding to them may however clarify the position I am urging. The first question presupposes that qualities in their turn have a sort of inner and outer activity, and that by the principle their inner activity is beyond our reach; what we grasp through sense perception, then, is the outer activity of the qualities, not the outer activity of the object's formative principle. I see no reason for supposing this to be Plotinus's view. To my knowledge, Plotinus nowhere explicitly discusses what is the real agent in sense perception, whether it is the quality itself or the underlying formative principle. He does say, however, that the perceptible manifestations of (the last) formative principles are dead, by which he means that the cycle of inner and outer activity has come to an end: "This forming principle, then, which operates in the visible shape, is the last, and is dead and no longer able to make another" (III.8.2.30–2). Qualities, I should think, are not active in their own right according to Plotinus. It is true that he does say that opposite qualities in matter affect one another (III.6.9). However, this is compatible with holding that the real agent in such cases is a formative principle, a view he also expresses in the same treatise (III.6.16). This is also what is suggested by the mirror analogy he invokes and makes much use of in III.6 to explain the relations between matter, sensible corporeal forms and their intelligible causes: these relations are to be seen on analogy with a mirror, the image that appears in it and the real object reflected in the mirror (see p. 233). Furthermore, Plotinus has a peculiar theory about the transmission from object to percipient in sight and hearing, a theory which holds that such transmission takes place through *sumpatheia*. Many details of this theory are obscure, but it is clear that *sumpatheia* is a process involving psychic agency and is not a mechanical process.[20] So, even if the evidence is meager, what there is suggests that qualities are not active in their own right in sense perception.

Let us turn to the second question: Why shouldn't Intellect be able to know the intelligibles themselves even if they were external to it, if the senses can know something external to themselves by taking on that very same thing itself. Let us suppose for the sake of argument that Intellect were in a similar situation as the faculty of sense. It might in that case know the intelligibles by participating directly in their external activity. Intellect would in that case know this external activity itself as opposed to an image of it (just like sight knows the objective color itself rather than an image of it). Presumably the cognition the soul has of Intellect is of this sort: it knows the primary intelligibles at the level of Intellect by sharing in (in fact by being) the external activity of the primary intelligibles (cf. V.1.3; V.3.4). But on the present hypothesis in another sense Intellect would not know the intelligibles themselves at all, since it would fail to know them through their internal activity. Given an account along the lines suggested here of how in a sense we perceive an external item itself and how in another sense that external item is not "the thing itself," Plotinus has indeed a reason to contrast sense perception and intellection: sense perception turns out to be of what is external to it, and we have explained how the object of sense perception is bound to be an image because it is of what is external.

If the preceding account holds, Plotinus's celebrated doctrine that the intelligibles are internal to Intellect should be interpreted as the claim that Intellect's primary activity and that of the intelligibles is one and the same activity. In other words, Intellect knows the intelligibles by their internal activity and this could not be the case unless Intellect and this activity were identical.[21] It is tempting to elaborate on this. The claim that a given form of cognition is of an object internal to the cognizing subject means that the object's inner activity and that of the subject are the same. Likewise, the claim that a form of cognition is of something external means that the activity which is the object is not identical with the activity of the cognizing power in question. So, this latter type of cognition is bound to be of the external act of the object, and hence of an image of it. Since subject and object coincide only in Intellect's cognition of the intelligibles, every other form of cognition is of images.

We have arrived at this position through fairly abstract reasoning that has taken place well above the texts. But in fact Plotinus says as explicitly as one can expect from him that the activity of the intelligibles and that of Intellect are the same: "But being is activity: so both [being and Intellect] have one activity, or rather both are one thing" (V.9.8.15–16). In the same vein he claims in V.3.5 that the intelligible is a kind of activity and that life and thinking are not imposed upon it from the outside. And he continues: "If then it is activity, and the first activity and fairest, it is the first intellection and substantial intellection: for it is the truest; but an intellection of this kind which is primary and primarily intellection will be the first Intellect" (36–9). Plotinus is claiming here that the intelligibles are essentially active, that their activity is intellection and that this intellection is the universal Intellect. In other words the activity of the intelligibles and that of the Intellect are identical. The same doctrine underlies Plotinus's beautiful analogy of sight seeing itself and light mingling with light that he uses to illustrate Intellect's thinking (V.3.8).

What about the second aspect of the claim above, that cognition of what is external is cognition of the external activity of the object? Can we see evidence for such a view elsewhere in Plotinus's thought? Plotinus's primary use of the double activity model is to account for the generation of the hypostases and his accounts of this are the obvious place to look. In this context our question becomes the question of whether, for example, Intellect (or inchoate Intellect, which does not "yet" think) by reverting and "looking" towards its source apprehends the One through the latter's external activity. And a parallel question may be raised about the generation of Soul from Intellect. Unfortunately, Plotinus is notoriously obscure about this whole subject and there are significant differences between his several accounts of this process.[22] The subject of ontological generation is too large and too far off our main scope to be addressed in detail here. Some remarks are nevertheless in order.

A typical account of the generation of Intellect from the One is along the following lines: In addition to its own totally self-contained inner activity, the One also has an external activity or power.[23] This external activity is inchoate Intellect or Intellect before it becomes a thinking Intellect. Inchoate Intellect, which is described in Aristotelian terms as potential vision, "looks" toward the One and becomes filled with it. "It strived for it not as Intellect, but as vision not yet seeing, and emerged possessing what the vision itself multiplied" (V.3.11.4–6). Thus, the "vision" of the One emerges as the thinking of Intellect, Intellect thinking itself.

Plotinus writes as if this were a fairly straightforward matter, but few of his readers share that view. A part of the problem is that Plotinus's discourse here abounds in visual and other psychological terms that cannot be literally true of the subject matter. However, these metaphors are so congenital with Plotinus's thought here that the reader has no other choice than to accept them and pursue their import. The most relevant question for our purposes is this: What precisely is the immediate object of inchoate Intellect's "vision" when it "looks" toward the One? Does it "see" (a) the One itself as it is in its own inner activity and "hyper-noesis," (b) the One as it reveals itself through its external activity (which corresponds to the version of realism I have been advocating), or (c) an image of the One which appears in and is known as a constituent of Intellect itself (which corresponds to a subjectivist interpretation)? We can dispose of (a) right away: Plotinus has indeed a notion of vision of the One itself. This is what is often referred to as the mystical experience of union with the One.[24] It is clear, however, that inchoate Intellect's vision of the One is different from the mystical union.[25] Judging between alternatives (b) and (c) is more precarious. It speaks for (b) that Plotinus sometimes says that Intellect sees an image of the One (V.3.11.8–9, etc.), but quite often he simply says that it sees the One (V.1.6.41, etc.). This can be taken as variation in expression rather than an inconsistency in doctrine, if we suppose that seeing (both in the metaphorical sense involved here and the ordinary sense) is of the external activity of its object and hence, ontologically speaking, of an image of it, and that as in the case of ordinary vision, here too it is normal usage to call seeing such an image "seeing the thing." Interestingly, in the context of Intellect's cognition of the One Plotinus uses visual metaphors without modifying the notion of vision. By contrast, when he uses visual metaphors to describe internal cognition such as Intellect's self-knowledge or mystical, hyper-intellectual "vision" of the

One, he has to modify the ordinary notion, since it implies a polarity of subject and object. On the other hand, the identification of Intellect's vision of the One with Intellect's self-thinking suggested by passages such as V.6.5.17, where Plotinus says that "it is in looking to the Good that it [Intellect] knows itself" may seem to speak for (c): if Intellect knows the One by knowing an image of the One which exists in it, Intellect, we can make some sense of the claim that its seeing the One and knowing itself is the same thing. However, there is evidence showing that Plotinus wishes to distinguish between Intellect's vision of the One and Intellect's self-thinking which produces being. This is noted in a recent illuminating study by A. C. Lloyd and accepted by Bussanich.[26] Perhaps one may think of Intellect's vision of the One as analogous to a mere visual sensation. At any rate, a mere ordinary sensation is of something external to the subject and, I have claimed, thereby of the external activity of the object. What fails in Intellect's vision of the One is the transformation of this sensation into a fully fledged perception of the One. This fails because the sensation qua "sensation" of the One cannot be conceptualized. What Plotinus describes as Intellect's actualized vision and identifies with Intellect's self-thinking is not a direct apprehension of the One, but the thoughts Intellect ends up with internal to itself when trying to apprehend the One, trying to conceptualize its sensation. (This may be compared with trying to see the instant position of the blades of a fast-moving fan: I may end up with a mental picture of them in a certain position, and seeing the fan in motion may be crucial for forming that picture, but no picture I come up with would count as seeing the actual blades in that position.)

So, to summarize, there is some evidence to be gained from the accounts of hypostatic generation in support of the claim that cognition of something external is cognition of the external act of the object known in the way I indicated for ordinary sense perception above. Unfortunately, this evidence is too poor and too unclear to count as decisive, but I have not found anything here that refutes my hypothesis. There is indeed abundant evidence that what a lower level grasps is the external as opposed to the internal act of the higher level – if it really grasped the internal act it would be identical with it and hence no longer "lower" (cf. V.3.4.20–31). But the evidence is slippery in respect of deciding between a subjectivist view and the kind of view I have been advocating. One reason for this is that in the context of hypostatic generation what is apprehended and the subject of the apprehension are both external acts of the level above. Inchoate Intellect itself, for instance, is an external act of the One. I do not think Plotinus holds that there are two different external acts, one constituting the subject, the other constituting what the subject apprehends. Rather, this is a question of which way the "look" is directed in one and the same act. The relevance of this for our present concerns is that an apprehension of a higher hypostasis may well be an objective apprehension of its external activity and at the same time of something pertaining to the lower hypostasis itself, because the lower hypostasis is the external activity of the higher.

So far I have argued that Plotinus is not a subjectivist in the sense that what we apprehend in sense perception are subjective images of the external world. Subjectivism should be kept distinct from subjective idealism. An idealist maintains that there is no external world independent of us. A subjectivist holds that what we perceive are images that pertain to us and he is liable to say that the external world as it is in itself is unknowable. So the subjectivist is likely to be a skeptic about the nature of objects as they are independently of being perceived; he may even doubt the existence of the external world; but as I use the term "subjectivist" he is not one who denies the meaningfulness of the notion of an independently existing external world.

If my contentions about V.5.1 above are correct, Plotinus never sustains doubt about the general adequacy of sense perception as cognition of external qualities or objects. He does not skeptically contrast what is given in sense perception with physical objects as they are, independent of being perceived. He does hold, nevertheless, that sensibles (physical objects) are not the sorts of things one can have knowledge about. But the reasons for this have more to do with the nature of sensibles as such than with the faculty of sense perception. The sensible object is a conglomerate of qualities in matter (cf. VI.3.15, p. 222 above). This conglomeration is indeed an image of an intelligible archetype. However, the archetype is not given in the conglomerate as such. The archetype and the image are only homonymous: they have only the name in common in the same way as a house and a picture of that house can both be called houses. A pictuie of a house is hardly intelligible as a picture of a house without prior knowledge of real houses. Similarly the intelligible Socrates, Socrates' soul, is not given in Socrates' perceptible image. Furthermore, a sensible conglomerate, albeit an expression of an intelligible essence, does not have any essence itself: the object which is the sensible Socrates is no more essentially a man than something warm or something pale.[27] All this disqualifies the sensible object as an object of knowledge. To this we may add that Plotinus frequently contrasts the togetherness of everything in the intelligible realm – often quoting Anaxagoras's phrase "everything together" – with the dispersion in the sensible realm (II.6.1; III.2.2). Such remarks indicate the spatiality of sensibles and contrast it with the nonspatiality of intelligibles, but they also have a bearing on epistemology. The togetherness in Intellect turns up in accounts of how Intellect can grasp the intelligibles and their connections all at once (V.8.6). The dispersion characteristic of sensibles also means that there can be no understanding of the connections between sensibles and sensible features. There are only separate particular facts (VI.4.1.18–28) and the sensible object as such does not contain any explanation of the relations between these particulars (cf. II.6; VI.7.2.9–13). One must inquire into their intelligible causes for the explanation to the extent it is to be had.

If the preceding account holds, Plotinus is not an idealist about the sensible world either: if perception reveals to us objective features of the world, there is an objective world and the world we sense is not a creation of our senses. Unless, of course Plotinus is a very subtle idealist of the Kantian type who redefines the notions of objectivity and externality in some such way that the sensible world is somehow constituted by, or defined in terms of, our cognitive faculties, perception or thought or both, but is still external and objective. I can see no hints of such a line of thought in Plotinus, however.

Nevertheless, there are scholars who think that Plotinus is some sort of idealist about the sensible realm.[28] And it must be admitted that Plotinus himself often uses the kind of language germane to idealism. So let us consider the matter. Plotinus holds and in fact emphasizes that the qualities and quantities in matter, that is, the directly perceptible features of things, are in some sense unreal. He

for instance writes: "[Sensible substance] is a shadow, and upon what
is itself a shadow, a picture and a seeming."[29] Such language may
suggest idealism in the sense that trees and houses only appear to be
out there but really they are not there at all. Our previous remarks
about Plotinus's notion of an image should however keep us from
hastily jumping to such a conclusion. At least a part of the explanation
of the language suggesting nonreality is that in such passages the
sensible is contrasted with the intelligible. The latter is of course what
is real and original, and the sensible, being a mere dependent image of
the intelligible, is a shadow and an appearance of it. The passages that
suggest the nonreality of the sensible are usually also associated with
a certain view of the relationship between matter and sensible features: the features that appear in matter are not genuine properties of
it for matter has no proper form of its own. Indeed Plotinus goes as far
as inviting us to see the relationship between the intelligible archetypes, their sensible images, and matter on analogy with an ordinary
physical object, a mirror image of that object, and the mirror.[30] The
features that appear in matter fail to belong to matter in a similar way
as the colors appearing in a mirror fail to be genuine properties of the
mirror. However we are to understand Plotinus's views here in detail,
two facts seem evident: first that by itself the mirror analogy does not
suggest that the features which appear in matter are unreal in the
sense of being somehow the products of our senses and, second, that
the analysis of what is involved in the use of the mirror image explains
the language of shadows and unreality without necessitating idealism. So it seems that we can make sense of his claim that the external
sensible world is unreal without attributing to him any sort of idealism about the sensible world.

So we have come to the conclusion that sensible features are objective in the sense of being there independently of us as perceivers,
even if they are somehow unreal, mere appearances of reality. It
would be desirable to be able to give an account of their lack of
reality that goes beyond Plotinus's mirror analogy. This is not the
occasion to penetrate into this question, and I shall only give the gist
of the answer that seems most promising: On scrutiny the sensible
object breaks down, fails to be a genuine object at all. There is just
matter, which turns out to be nothing positive at all, and features in
it which cannot be *its* features since matter is no determinate object,

and hence, trivially, there is no object there to have the features. Nevertheless, it may seem to us that there is a real object out there with the features that appear to us. But this would be a mistake similar to mistaking a mirror image for a real object.[31]

III THE OBJECTS OF THOUGHT

We have already mentioned Plotinus's famous thesis that the intelligibles are internal to Intellect – the Internality Thesis, as I shall hereafter call it.[32] We saw that in V.5.1 this claim about the intelligibles was contrasted with the externality of the objects of sense perception. The Internality Thesis is in V.5 connected with the claim that Intellect knows the things themselves as opposed to images of these things (cf. V.3.5; V.8.4–5). According to the line of interpretation suggested above, knowing "the things themselves" implies that the activity constituting the object of Intellect's cognition and the activity constituting the subject are identical. We have seen that this is indeed Plotinus's view. Further, knowing the things themselves in this sense is described by Plotinus as Intellect's self-knowledge and as its self-thinking (V.3.5.45–6; V.9.5.14–16). In fact the universal Intellect is the only stage in the Plotinian hierarchy where identity of subject and object of cognition, knowledge of the things themselves and self-knowledge, obtain. It remains to consider more closely what this means. Before I proceed to do so I shall dispose of some preliminary difficulties that Plotinus's position here involves.

One may ask why Intellect's knowledge isn't knowledge of images since Intellect knows the One's external activity and the One's external activity is an image of the One itself. The answer is that with respect to the One, Intellect's knowledge is indeed knowledge of an image, as Plotinus in fact clearly asserts.[33] This does not prevent this cognition from being knowledge of the things themselves because the things Plotinus calls real or ontologically primary beings (*ta onta*) – the paradigms of all other existences – first come about at the stage of Intellect. Intellect's cognition is knowledge of *these* objects themselves. Secondly, given my account of apprehension of images and of the things themselves in terms of apprehension of external and internal activity, one may wonder why cognition at the level of soul does not qualify as apprehension of the things themselves: surely there are internal activities constituting the levels of soul and these activities are forms of cognition; why aren't these self-knowledge and knowledge of their objects themselves? I believe the answer is that the kind of relation we described just above between Intellect and the One holds in these cases: what is known at the level of soul is not the internal activities constituting the objects known, which are items at the level of Intellect, but external activities, that is, images, of these objects. So even if there is an internal cognitive activity constituting soul, identity of subject and object does not hold in this activity.

So according to Plotinus there exists a type of cognition that is identical with its object or, in other words, cognition in which the activity constituting the object of cognition and the one constituting the subject are one and the same. Moreover, the objects known in this cognition are what Plotinus considers the real beings. Thus, in this doctrine Plotinian metaphysics, psychology, and epistemology come together, actually merge. I shall now address this fusion. One might approach this subject via several routes. A complete account would for instance involve considering Plotinian texts about the genesis and structure of Intellect. I shall not take this route in the present study. Instead I shall focus on some passages where Plotinus insists on and argues for the identity of subject and object of Intellect's thought in particular in V.3.

In chapter 5 of this treatise Plotinus argues that Intellect and the intelligible are one and the same. Unfortunately, crucial steps in the argument are obscurely stated. It is clear, however, that he wishes to combine three prominent ideas: that of Intellect's complete self-knowledge; the notion of the intelligibles as the ontologically primary beings as opposed to mere images or representations; and the unity of subject and object in intellection. First he establishes that if Intellect is to have genuine self-knowledge, it cannot be the case that it knows itself in the sense that one part, the subject side, knows the other, the object side of thought. In that case Intellect as a whole would not know itself completely, for the subject side would not know itself at all (1–15). The subsequent lines (16–22) are the most obscure bit and I am far from certain about the following paraphrastic exegesis, which however seems to make sense and to be compatible with the text: Intellect knows certain objects, intelligibles. If it is to have genuine self-knowledge, we must in addition attribute to it a reflexive act whereby it apprehends itself as subject. But this apprehension will include apprehending the objects of this subject's thought. These objects that Intellect apprehends in apprehending itself as subject are either ontologically primary beings or images of such. If images, Intellect's knowledge was not knowledge of primary beings (since it was only of images of such). But Intellect does have knowledge of the intelligibles and the intelligibles are the primary beings. So in apprehending itself as subject Intellect apprehends the primary beings which it must have contained all along. From this Plotinus concludes that if what Intellect knows are the ontologically primary beings, it cannot be divided into a subject side which does not contain these objects and an object side which does, since such a division would lead to the unacceptable conclusion that it knew only images or impressions (*tupoi*). This, he says, would imply that truth in Intellect was truth about something else. I shall return to this last point shortly. In the remainder of the chapter Plotinus proceeds to give an account of how Intellect is one with its object and knows itself. The crucial aspect of this account is the abolition of the notions of mind and objects of thought as something existing prior to and independently of thought, in favor of an account in terms of thinking activity: Intellect is nothing but acts of thought and the intelligibles are constituted in such thinking activity.[34]

This chapter shows that for Plotinus Intellect's genuine self-knowledge (the notion he starts from) and the claim that Intellect's knowledge is of ontologically primary beings are intimately connected. How is this so? The answer is, I believe, that genuine self-knowledge (self-knowledge in Plotinus's strong sense which excludes knowledge of part by part) and knowledge of the ontologically primary must satisfy similar conditions: neither can be a relation between different things. In terms of Plotinus's activity theory, self-knowledge and knowledge of the ontologically primary each requires that the activity constituting the knower is identical with that constituting the known; what is known in each case cannot be other than the knowing subject. The structure of his argument is to establish first the identity of activity for subject and object in knowledge of the ontologically primary and then show that such identity also qualifies as Intellect's self-knowledge or self-thinking.

Let us now consider more closely the part of the chapter where Plotinus insists that truth in Intellect must not be of something else. He says:

For, if [Intellect and the intelligible] are not the same, there will be no truth; for the one who is trying to possess realities (*ta onta*) will possess an impression different from the realities, and this is not truth. For truth ought not to be truth of something else, but to be what it says. (23–6)

The expression "truth ought to be what it says" is particularly noteworthy (cf. also V.3.6.23–4). This is of course metaphorical, for literally speaking, truth in Intellect says nothing at all. But what is it that truth "says" and why this choice of figurative expression? There is a similar but fuller statement of the same point in V.5.2.18–20, where Plotinus is in fact stating his answer to the question about the source of Intellect's certainty with which he begins V.5 (cf. pp. 221–2 above):

And then again, it [Intellect] will need no demonstration and no confirmation that this is so, for itself is so and itself is manifest (*enargês*) to itself. . . . So that [in Intellect] there is also the real truth, which does not agree with something else, but with itself, and says nothing other than itself, but it is what it says and it says what it is.[35] (V.5.2.15–20)

Thus we have here that truth in Intellect "says what it is" in addition to being what it says. The expression "does not agree with something else" corresponds to the claim that "truth ought not to be truth of something else" in the former passage. In both cases Plotinus is contrasting truth at the level of Intellect with other, ordinary kind of truth, which evidently does "agree with something else" and is "of something else." But what sort of truth is it that agrees with itself? Now, the regular Greek word for truth, *alêtheia*, may also mean "reality," and one may wonder whether this isn't its meaning here. Surely, it is true that reality does not agree with something else and it would be quite proper for Plotinus to assert that Intellect contains reality. Indeed, the notion of *alêtheia* Plotinus wishes to attribute to Intellect is in part that of reality: this "truth" is not merely supposed to say something, but to be something. However, there is more to Plotinus's notion of *alêtheia* here. To put it simply: truth in Intellect is not merely supposed to be but also to "say." This is the feature that truth in Intellect has in common with ordinary truth and suggests that *alêtheia* in Intellect belongs not merely to the order of reality but also to the order of significance or meaning.

The notion Plotinus is after here is a notion of something in which reality and signification converge: the real is the content of the thoughts in Intellect. These thoughts are not thoughts of something else nor are they true because they agree with some other reality against which they may be tested. On the contrary, they constitute reality. Hence, they are not true in the ordinary sense which takes truth to consist in a correspondence between a proposition or thought and reality. Nevertheless, these thoughts may also be said to be true in the sense that through them something is known, namely these thoughts themselves. So if forced to explicate what these thoughts "say" and "to whom," the answer must be that they make their own content known to Intellect. But Intellect, we have seen, is just these thought acts. So the conclusion is that thoughts in Intellect are self-conscious. Plotinus indeed indicates this himself, for in the first part of the passage just quoted he says that Intellect is manifest to itself. This I take to be the point of the claim that truth in Intellect "is what it says" and "says what it is."

Several further comments on this are in order: first, about the sources of Plotinus's Internality Thesis. It is clear and well known that this thesis of Plotinus owes much to Aristotle and his followers: Basically, Plotinus follows Alexander of Aphrodisias in unifying the account of God as a pure thinker in *Metaphysics* 12 and that of the active intellect in *De anima* 3.[36] The Platonic Forms become for him acts of thought which constitute the universal divine Intellect.[37] This means that, say, the Platonic Form of beauty is for Plotinus a certain act of thought which has the characteristics we have been describing: it is beauty and says so, that is, it is the thought which has beauty in general as its content. And this is the primary beauty both in the sense that it is the cause of beauty on all lower stages in the Plotinian hierarchy and in the sense that it is the original beauty: there is no prior beauty on which this thought depends; beauty is, one might say, created in this act of thought (cf. V.9.5.12–13). Plotinus's debt to Aristotle in this area actually cuts quite deep also in certain details:[38] for instance, the Aristotelian view that the divine mind is substance, and hence ontologically primary in a fuller sense than material objects because it is pure thought and pure thought is pure activity/actuality, is at play in the doctrine we have been considering in V.3.5.

There is however an epistemological strain in Plotinus's Internality Thesis which is absent or at least not prominent in Aristotle. As noted above, Plotinus's original concern in V.5, where he most explicitly argues for the Internality Thesis, is how to answer the question why Intellect will never "be in error and believe what is untrue." He also says that if the intelligibles are external and Intellect "only receives in itself images of the truth, it will have falsities and nothing true" (V.5.1.56–8). What is Plotinus's epistemological worry here? Is it just that anything less than direct knowledge of the ontologically primary is not good enough for the universal Intellect as this would violate the Platonic principle that knowledge is of the fully real? Or is there something about images in addition to failing to be primary that makes them epistemically suspect or inadequate?

In Plotinus's view, there is, especially when the knower is Intellect. First, let us note that image-making in Plotinus's metaphysical sense of the term is not exact copying but always involves a loss. Images have their intelligible content, and hence their identity, entirely in virtue of their archetypes. On a purely ontological level this means "remove the archetype and the image will perish" (III.6.13.37–8; VI.4.9.38–41). On an epistemological level it means that for a mind without access to the archetype everything it encounters becomes entirely void of meaning. We can see the germs of such a view in Plotinus's famous first treatise *On Beauty*. Recognition of sensible forms depends on the prior possession of these forms in the soul of the person who judges. The architect pronounces the external house before him beautiful by using the form of beauty he has in his soul "as we use a ruler for judging straightness" (I.6.3.4–5). In V.5 this view is quite explicit and used as an argument for the Internality Thesis. Plotinus is exposing the consequences of the view that the intelligibles are external and Intellect receives images of them:

But how, also, will it know that it really grasped them? And how will it know that this is good or beautiful or just? For each of these will be other than it, and the principles of judgement on which it will rely will not be in itself, but these too will be outside, and that is where truth will be. (V.5.1.28–32)

So, as all Platonists will agree, the Forms are the principles of judgment, and if the divine Intellect does not already possess these principles, it would not recognize images of these Forms for what they are, that is, images of just these Forms. This argument evidently assumes that no image contains the principle for what it is – is self-evident, "says what it is." I should think that according to

Plotinus no image – no external activity – says what it is. Presumably this is so because Plotinus holds that just as it is a defining characteristic of images that they depend on their causes for their being, recognition of their intelligible content refers to and presupposes knowledge of something else, namely the originals. So to receive a mere image of the intelligibles in the absence of the intelligibles themselves would be like hearing a foreign language one does not understand. Plotinus's view here may perhaps be summarized as follows: The intelligibility of any image depends on the thinker's possession of a primary intelligible which the image expresses. The image necessarily expresses the primary intelligible "in something else," that is, some matter or potentiality which expresses but is not identical with the intelligible content of the image.[39] This does not mean that we always ascend to Intellect in every mundane cognitive activity. We normally understand the world around us by means of concepts or images belonging to the order of soul.[40] But the question can be raised about the concepts belonging to the soul themselves, how a thinking subject recognizes the intelligible content of his concepts. It turns out that these concepts are themselves images that express through something else, words or mental pictures, some intelligible content (cf. note 40). They are not intelligible in virtue of themselves. This leads to the postulation of a level of intelligible content in itself, not expressed through anything else. This is a thought which constitutes the intelligible content there is. This is also "the ontologically primary" because such intelligible content involves no potentiality.

Plotinus's epistemological concerns we have been considering here are likely to be modified by the skeptical tradition. The dilemma he set out to solve in V.3.5 and we considered above about Intcllect's self-knowledge parallels a dilemma mentioned by Sextus Empiricus, where Sextus argues that Man's self-knowledge is impossible.[41] The argument in V.5.1 we just considered and the notion of truth in Intellect which "says what it is and is what it says" is probably also prompted by skeptical considerations: it may be an attempt to block the kind of skeptical move which consists in insisting on a criterion for the validity of any proposed criterion.[42] Plotinus's theory of divine thoughts is clearly meant to make such thoughts self-validating. In general, it seems to be instructive to see Plotinus's epistemological concerns – his contrast between knowl-

edge of images or impressions and knowledge of the things themselves as well as his insistence that genuine knowledge is identical
with its object and true just in virtue of itself – in the light of skeptical considerations. His theory is so construed that it is impossible to
put any wedge between Intellect and the object of its cognition.

Let us briefly mention the notion of nondiscursive thought which
often is associated with the Plotinian Intellect. The characteristics
usually ascribed to this kind of thought are the following: subject
and object of nondiscursive thought are identical; nondiscursive
thought is supposed to be intuitive, that is, not based on reasoning;
it is nonpropositional and a grasp of the whole at once, *totum
simul*.[43] Now, with the possible exception of nonpropositionality,
thinking on the level of Intellect in Plotinus has indeed all these
characteristics. However, one significant feature of nondiscursive
thought in Plotinus is missing, namely that such thoughts are not
representational: the vehicles of these thoughts are not representations of the things they are thoughts about, but rather, somehow, the
things themselves are the vehicles of the thoughts. This is of course
just the doctrine we have been discussing. It may be said that nonrepresentationality in this sense follows from, or even is another way of
asserting, the identity of thinker and object of thought. But if so,
nonrepresentationality nevertheless points to an important feature
of Plotinus's version of the identity claim. For not every version of
the identity claim will maintain that the vehicles of thought must
be the very objects thought of.

There is some tendency to confuse this feature of nonrepresentationality with that of nonpropositionality. The very point of some
passages such as V.8.5–6 and V.5.1.38–42 that have been taken as
evidence for nondiscursive thought and its nonpropositional character is in fact to assert its nonrepresentational character. The two
features are also easily confused but they are not the same: it requires a certain philosophical view on propositions to hold that all
propositions are necessarily representations. I take it, however, that
according to Plotinus Intellect's thought is not propositional, at
least not in the ordinary sense, because it is supposed to be intuition
of many truths at once. Thus, nonpropositionality probably follows
from the *totum simul* requirement. This is why Plotinus finds it
useful and appropriate to liken such thought with vision: we may
see several facts at once in a single vision without unfolding in our

minds in temporal succession the corresponding propositions. But even if nondiscursive thought is not propositional in this sense, it does not follow that it involves no variation, that it abolishes the distinctions between concepts or objects.

It is enlightening to compare Plotinus's account of Intellect's perfect knowledge with some later ideas in the history of philosophy. Wilfrid Sellars launched an attack on what he called "The Myth of the Given."[44] In particular he has traced in the tradition of empiricism a notion, mostly implicit rather than explicit, of items which are at once supposed to be items of a certain kind and instances of knowledge of that kind. That is to say, in the empiricist tradition a given sensation (sense datum, impression, sensum, phenomenal quality, or whatever it is called) is supposed to be at once, say, something green and an awareness of or knowledge of something green. Such items may seem to provide a solid foundation of meaning and knowledge, for they seem to bridge the gap between what is and what is within the reach of our minds: the very same thing is an F and our direct awareness of F. Plotinus's notion of the intelligible as something which "says what it is and is what it says" shares the formal features of Sellars's notion of the given: The Plotinian intelligible is at the same time something (e.g., Beauty) and the thought of (awareness of) what it is. It must be said in Plotinus's praise that he shows a keen understanding of what it takes for there to be a given and, as opposed to the empiricists' view, his account of it cannot be rejected on the ground that the proposed givens (the intelligibles) fail to be so. Sensual images or impressions of qualities must have a conceptual or "intelligible" content in order to function as givens in an epistemologically relevant sense. As Sellars has shown, it is however most unlikely that any such conceptual content is given in virtue of a mere sense impression. Plotinus, on the contrary, designs his account of divine thoughts in such a way that this kind of attack would not succeed. As we have seen, the epistemic principle or criterion of, say once more, beauty must at once be that very thing of which it is the principle, namely beauty, and in being beauty it must somehow "say" that which it is. Plotinus sees to it that it is not possible to separate the intelligible content from the thing which has the intelligible content in question or from the "mind" which grasps it. One might say that his program is precisely to reduce both the thing and the mind to the content as thought.

Plotinus's doctrine of the givenness of the contents of Intellect and the problems he hopes to solve by it have a parallel in another modern philosophical issue (which ultimately is closely related to the question of the given):[45] recent discussions of skepticism about meaning and self-knowledge prompted primarily by Saul Kripke's *Wittgenstein on Rules and Private Language.* The main contention of this skepticism is that there do not seem to be any facts about us that determine the meaning of the expressions we use, whether in mental or in spoken language. In surveying candidates for determinants of meaning Kripke briefly mentions Platonism in connection with Frege's views. Frege's Platonism is, of course, the sort of Platonism according to which mathematical objects exist as Platonic "Ideas" independent of any mind. Expressions have a certain "sense" associated with them that is likewise an objective nonmental thing. This sense determines the reference of a sign, which in the case of mathematics is a "Platonic" objective mathematical entity, for example, the plus function. But for people to grasp the sense associated with a sign, they must have appropriate ideas in their minds associated with the sign. According to Kripke it is in relation to the alleged function of these mental ideas that Wittgenstein's skeptical problem about meaning sneaks in for a Platonist of the Fregean sort:

[The skeptical problem] arises precisely in the question how the existence in my mind of any mental entity or idea can constitute "grasping" any particular sense rather than another. . . . For Wittgenstein, Platonism is largely an unhelpful evasion of the problem of how our finite minds can give rules that are supposed to apply to an infinity of cases. Platonic objects may be self-interpreting, or rather, they may need no interpretation; but ultimately there must be some mental entity involved that raises the sceptical problem.[46]

Suppose one is willing to go along with Platonism in holding that Platonic objects are in themselves self-explanatory (or need no interpretation), while insisting that what anybody, including God, can have access to is at best certain representations of them. Suppose in addition that one believes that no representation (image, impression) is self-authenticating. This is very much the position Plotinus finds himself in with respect to skepticism about Intellect's knowledge. Given the availability of the Aristotelian doctrine of divine thought, the natural move would be to maintain that the Forms, the ontologically primary beings, are in fact internal to Intellect, are its thoughts which it immediately knows.

In saying this I am not suggesting that Plotinus saw right through the skeptical problem about meaning that preoccupied Kripke's Wittgenstein and other contemporary philosophers, and proposed a solution to it. However, there are interesting common features. First of all, Kripke's point against Fregean Platonism is analogous to one objection Plotinus raises against classical "objective" Platonism, according to which the ideas are extra-mental. Plotinus seems to have held that no representation (image) of F, whether a mental representation or expression of it or a material embodiment of it in nature, can show the general nature it represents in such a way that one could read off what is represented from the representation alone. This is evident for instance from his remarks in V.5.1.28–33 considered above that if Intellect had mere representations of the intelligibles, it would not be able to recognize the just for the just or the beautiful for the beautiful (cf. also lines 49–50 and p. 239 above): Intellect would have no way of knowing what the representation it received represented unless it had independent access to what it represents as a self-authenticating criterion. In Plotinian language this is so because no representation "is what it says and says what it is." The self-authenticating aspect of Intellect's thought functions in Plotinus to preclude any kind of skepticism and indeterminacy as to what is what. Nothing less is required if Intellect is to be able to have knowledge of the real and, which is the same, of the content of its own thought. To what extent this might provide solid grounds for the thought of lesser, human minds is a different issue that I shall leave untouched here.

IV PLOTINUS'S IDEALISM

While the sensible object is in no way defined in terms of sense perception, the faculty by which we apprehend such objects, the intelligible object is defined in terms of thinking. Since the intelligible object is also the ontologically primary object, Plotinus becomes a kind of idealist after all.[47] As we saw in Section III there are epistemological reasons for this: Plotinus believes that divine knowledge is infallible and self-authenticating and he thinks that this requires the identity of the objects of this kind of knowledge with the acts of thinking these objects. So far this sounds as if the Internality Thesis results merely from the request for secure knowledge on behalf of the divine mind. This is however only one half of the story. Plotinus is of course not only concerned with showing that there can be something given in an epistemological sense; he is also and no less concerned about showing that there can be real things, substances or essences, that is, things that satisfy traditional Greek criteria of ontological priority. The most important of these is self-sufficiency: that which stands in need of nothing for being what it is is ontologically primary. From the account above we can see that in Plotinus's view thoughts at the level of Intellect satisfy the conditions: each of them is fully actual, fully is what it is, and in general they satisfy all the important conditions of Platonic Forms. They are self-sufficient and essentially active things. So divine thoughts have both the required epistemological properties and satisfy the conditions of being. Is this sheer metaphysical luck?

This is a large and difficult topic about which I shall only make a few cursory remarks here. One way to put our question is to ask: Given Plotinus's general outlook, might there be something which satisfies the conditions of the ontologically primary without being epistemically primary? Does Plotinus give us any arguments for the view that the ontologically primary must be a mind of the sort of his Intellect? We can indeed extract the following kind of Aristotelian argument: the intelligibles, that is, the ontologically primary, must be identical with some inner activity which constitutes it; that activity must not involve any potentiality for otherwise this would not be the ontologically primary activity, and the only activity which does not is a thinking activity of the kind we have described. An argument along these lines seems to lie behind for instance V.3.5.31–48. One premise here is of course that the only conceivable pure activity is thinking, and for this we do not get much explicit argument. I suspect that behind Plotinus's view there lies an intuition which connects the notions being, meaning or intelligibility, and mind: what a thing is is what is intelligible about it and the source of intelligibility must be a thought. The primacy of thinking for Plotinus lies already in the quasi–intellectual attributes of the One and in the fact that the external activity of the One is an inchoate intellect.

NOTES

1 See e.g., IV.6.1.23–32; cf. IV.5.1.10–13. See also Emilsson 1988, chs. 4, 6, and 8.

2 Plotinus argues forcefully against accounts of sense perception and memory on the model of impression on wax and the like; however, he is himself willing to use the terms *tupos* and *tupôsis* in the context of perception and memory, but he insists that the *tupos* is not to be interpreted physically: see III.6.1.7–14; III.6.3.27–30; and IV.3.26–33.

3 See IV.5.1.10–13 where he says that through the sense organs the soul must somehow become one with the sensible objects themselves (*eis hen pôs pros auta ta aisthêta ienai*); cf. IV.4.23.16–19.

4 See in particular Plotinus's fullest account of sense perception in general in chapter 23 of IV.4.

5 See especially IV.4.23.20–9, where Plotinus says that sensory affections must be in between the sensible and the intelligible. For a discussion of the passage and support of the present reading of it see Emilsson 1988, 90–1.

6 Blumenthal 1971b, pp. 71–2 and 1976, 47.

7 See Sleeman and Pollet 1980, under *aisthêsis* b.

8 See IV.3.26 and IV.4.23 and Emilsson 1988, 91.

9 I also discuss the question of antirealism in V.5.1 in Emilsson 1994. The treatment there is however considerably less elaborate than here.

10 It is a widespread opinion that Plotinus's target here is Epicurus and his followers. I find this doubtful, see Emilsson 1988 118–19. The Peripatetic school or Platonists influenced by it seem to be a better hypothesis. We can see Plotinus as making the following point against the Aristotelians: "If you think this knowledge is based on deduction from self-evident premisses and the premisses are ultimately founded on sense perception (cf. Aristotle, *Posterior Analytics* II.19), you are in trouble because sense perception itself is always suspect."

11 I usually render *eidôlon* and its synonyms as "image," but sometimes as "representation" or "expression."

12 There is no need to take the *epei kai* ("for also") in V.5.1.15, with which Plotinus begins the sentence where he claims that sense perception grasps an image, to introduce a reason for the immediately preceding statement, i.e., the statement that intellect and reason are needed as judges of the objectivity of sensory affections. Plotinus is apt to write several *epei*-sentences one after another stating independent grounds for something stated earlier or to explain a previously stated problem, cf. *epei* in ll. 9, 12 and 15 in IV.3.23 and II.9.7.22 and 24.

13 The relevant lines run as follows: "But since we must bring in knowl-

edge and truth and watchfully preserve being and the knowledge of the essence (*to ti*) of each thing and not of its quality, since then we would have a image (*eidôlon*) and trace of it. . . ." (V.5.2.5–8).

14 When Plotinus contrasts quality and essence as he does here we are not to understand "quality" in a strict Aristotelian sense according to which a quality is an accidental as opposed to a substantial feature of an object. Rather "quality" here is the conglomerate of qualities that constitute the sensible object, which as such has no essence (see p. 231).

15 In general Plotinus calls the forms perceptible in matter representations (*eidôla*, sometimes *mimêmata* or *eikones* or uses other words meaning "image," "trace," or "shadow"). Thus, the general sense of "representation" in Plotinus is "ontologically derivative." All this is just standard Platonism based on such passages as *Rep.* VII.516a7; 520c4; *Phdr.* 250b2–d5; *Soph.* 239d4ff. *Epist.* VII.342b2, etc.

16 See also e.g., II.4.9.7–15; III.8.2.; IV.4.29.32–8.

17 Cf. V.3.1–4 and V.6.1. Plotinus claims that neither sensation of what goes on within our bodies nor discursive thinking is knowledge of what is internal to the cognitive faculties in question.

18 For the One as activity see Gerson 1994, 22–41.

19 For the doctrine of inner and outer acts see e.g., II.9.8.22ff.; IV.3.10.31ff.; IV.5.7.17ff.; V.1.3.6–12; V.4.2.27–30; VI.2.22.26ff.

20 See IV.5 especially 3.35–8. See Emilsson 1988, 47–62. On *sumpatheia* in Plotinus more generally see Gurtler 1984, 395–406; and 1988, ch. 3.

21 Plotinus holds that even if subject and object are identical at the level of Intellect, thinking nevertheless involves a duality of subject and object, cf. V.1.4.27ff.; V.2.10.8–14; V.6.1.

22 The most important passages bearing on the generation of Intellect from the One are discussed by Bussanich (1988).

23 Plotinus, however, sometimes denies that the One acts. See e.g., V.6.5.3. and the commentary and references in Bussanich 1988, pp. 66–70.

24. See especially VI.9.9–10. Cf. also VI.8.16.19–21 where self-vision is attributed to the One.

25 See Bussanich 1988, commentary on V.3.11.15–16, 231–6.

26 Lloyd 1987, especially 171–8; Bussanich 1988, 227–31.

27 Cf. Gerson 1994, 104–15.

28 Cf. Wagner 1982a, 59ff. and A. H. Armstrong's remark that "we are left with the very strong impression that for Plotinus there are not two worlds but one real world apprehended in different ways on different levels" (introductory note to VI.7, *Plotinus* VII, 79).

29 VI.3.8. See also III.6.6–19 passim and II.4 passim.

30 III.6.7.22–44; 9.16–19; 13.32–55; VI.2.22.29–36.

31 For a somewhat different account of this same problem see Strange 1992, 493–5.

32 Many of the issues dealt with in this section are also treated by Emilsson (1994).

33 V.6.5.12–16; V.3.11.7–8. Plotinus also calls Intellect as a whole an image of the One, cf. V.1.6.46–7 and VI.8.18.35.

34 Cf. V.1.4.27–8; VI.7.40.10–12. It does not follow from this that thought is prior to being. We should take Plotinus's word for it that they are equivalent (V.9.8.16–23). It is, I believe, a misunderstanding that Plotinus rejects the view that being is constituted by thinking in V.9.8.11 and 7.12ff. (cf. Atkinson 1983, 93; and Oosthout 1991, 63–5. In V.9.7.12ff. he is denying that Intellect creates individual Forms by individual thought acts, i.e., he is making a point about the unity or togetherness of the Forms in Intellect (cf. l.12 homou panta). The latter passage does indeed assert that we must conceive of being before Intellect (to on tou nou proepinoein). But this can hardly mean that metaphysically speaking being as such precedes Intellect, for Plotinus carefully explains in the next few lines that in reality being and thought are equivalent and that it is we humans, with our partitioning minds, who conceive of the one before the other (epinoeitai thatera pro tôn heterôn).

35 Armstrong's Loeb translation modified. The translation is based on a slight emendation proposed by Theiler and followed by H-S₂ and Armstrong.

36 For Plotinus's debt to Alexander of Aphrodisias here see Armstrong 1960, cf. Szlezák 1979, 135–43.

37 On Middle Platonic precursors to Plotinus here see Jones 1926 and Rich 1954. It is important to note however that the identification of the realm of Forms (being) with Intellect is not merely an Aristotelizing trait in Plotinus: he thought he had Platonic support for this in Soph. 248e8–249a9, where being is endowed with intelligence (nous) and life. See Hadot 1960 and Szlezák 1979, especially 122–5.

38 Porphyry remarks in Life of Plotinus 13 that Aristotle's Metaphysics is concentrated in Plotinus's writings. The use Plotinus makes of Aristotle in his theory of Intellect is systematically laid out by Szlezák (1979).

39 Plotinus's view that images are always "in something else" (en allôi; en heterôi) seems based on Plato's Tim. 52c, cf. V.3.8.13–14.

40 Plotinus does not have any one word he systematically uses to refer to such concepts in the soul, but chooses an expression according to the context. He often uses logos, cf. V.1.3.7–8; I.2.3.27, IV.3.30.9, but also "form" (eidos) in the soul, cf. I.1.8.7–8, "impression" (tupos), cf. I.1.7.12 and p. 220 above, and "representation" (eidôlon, eikonisma, phantasia, etc.) of Intellect, cf. I.4.10.

41 *Against the Dogmatists* 7.284–6, cf. Wallis 1989, 917–25.

42 See *The Outlines of Pyrrhonism* 1.166.

43. Cf. Lloyd (1970), 261–74. For further discussion of nonpropositional thought in Plotinus see Sorabji 1982 and 1983, 152–6; Lloyd 1986 and Alfino 1988.

44 See Sellars 1963, 69–70, 129–34 and 156–61.

45 The givens of the empiricist tradition are, according to Kripke, one main set of candidates Wittgenstein considers and rejects as items to which we can refer in order to determine meaning. This is what the famous private language argument is meant to show, cf. Kripke 1982, 41–53.

46 Kripke 1982, 54.

47 Burnyeat 1982, 16–18 attempts to cast doubt on the view that Plotinus was an idealist in "any interesting sense." He gives two grounds for this doubt: (1) matter really is independent of form, like preexisting darkness which is illuminated. (2) With respect to Plotinus's notion of the One's self-knowledge, (if he had such a notion, Burnyeat leaves the question open) Burnyeat claims that "it would be misleading and partial to describe the ultimate monism as of a mind." I disagree on both points. As to (1) see O'Brien 1991 who very convincingly shows that matter is indeed caused by the One. As to (2), even if may be conceded that it would be misleading to call Plotinus's view "a monism of mind," since "mind" may suggest something like the Plotinian Intellect, it would hardly be misleading to call it a "monism of the spiritual." More importantly, however, in his inquiry into the presence of idealism in antiquity Burnyeat does not consider Plotinus's identification of primary being with acts of thought – what should count as idealism if not that doctrine? Interestingly, he also ignores as a possible germ of idealism the Aristotelian view of God as at once an Intellect and a substance in the most primary sense. This does not give us idealism in the sense that everything that in some way exists is mental nor even the weaker thesis that absolutely everything has a mental cause. However, Aristotle's views here connect the notions of being or substance and that of thought in a remarkable way and were, as we have seen, developed by Plotinus and other Platonists in an idealistic direction: for Plotinus absolutely everything has a mental cause and everything that deserves the name of "being" is thinking of some sort, cf. III.8. This whole Platonic–Aristotelian idealistic tradition in turn greatly inspired the main philosophical movement that goes under the name of idealism in modern times, i.e., German idealism, cf. Beierwaltes 1972 and Vieillard-Baron 1979.

10 Self-knowledge and subjectivity in the *Enneads*

Plotinus anticipates Descartes in arguing both that the soul as sub-ject of perception cannot be an extended substance, as well as in arguing that the mind necessarily knows itself.[1] Like Descartes, Plotinus also invokes an introspective or subjective stance within his dialectical procedure.[2] Methodologically, it will be seen, Plotinus shares along with Descartes in a tradition of philosophy of mind that employs thought experiments as a method of persuasion.[3] The spe-cial nature of this persuasion is effected through the textual represen-tation of a highly structured subjectivity as if it were immediately available within the reader's own consciousness.

In this chapter, I will be looking at what might be called a Carte-sian method of self-representation, that is, at the philosophical ap-peal to subjective states, and asking whether and how it informs the contemplative pedagogy of Plotinus. In particular, I will concentrate upon Plotinus's use of thought experiments, in order to discuss his views about self-consciousness and subjectivity.

I SUBJECTIVITY AND SELF-CONSCIOUSNESS

What does it mean to for someone to be a person – what is the essence of the human self? In the modern, Cartesian tradition, one answer to this question is that the self is the mind, whereas the mind in its turn is a substance uniquely endowed with both reflex-ive consciousness and with subjectivity.[4] Recently, historicist chal-lenges to this mentalistic conception of personhood have argued that the ancient Greek philosophers managed their psychology and epistemology quite well without the concept of consciousness.

Richard Rorty in his book *Philosophy and the Mirror of Nature*[5] claims that Descartes invented the modern notion of mind. Prior to Descartes, people had intellects capable of grasping immaterial, universal truths, but ever since Descartes, people have had minds. The Cartesian mind's great virtue consists in its incorrigibility: it is indubitably aware of any given experience as evidenced within consciousness.

This concept of personhood privileges two features of the mental life, namely, the mind's self-transparency and the privacy of mental states. For any state that the mind is in, the subject of consciousness, upon introspection, cannot doubt the existence of that state. Moreover, the access that the subject of consciousness enjoys with regard to her own inner states is private: only the subject can know with certainty that she is in a particular mental state.[6] Cartesian subjectivity and self-consciousness are the two pillars upon which epistemology in the modern era has been reconstructed: along with this privileging of the subjective point of view, coincides the invention of subjective truth.[7]

Prior to Descartes, the ancient skeptical tradition capitalized upon strategies that maximized the opacity of the the external world *vís-à-vís* the perceiving subject. In their ad hoc replies to the positivistic epistemological constructions of the Stoa, academic skeptics regularly argued as follows: how each of the external objects appears we can perhaps say, but how it is in its nature we cannot assert.[8] Descartes's *Meditations*, for the first time in history, present us a text in which the isolation of the perceiving subject from the cognized object became a locus of epistemological certainty. The way to *remove* epistemological doubt was discovered via the method of subjective truth: how things *seemed* counted as instance of the way things actually *were:*

> I am the same who feels, that is to say, who perceives certain things, as by organs of sense, since in truth I see light, I hear noise, I feel heat. But it will be said that these phenomena are false and that I am dreaming. Let it be so: still it is at least quite certain that it seems to me that I see light, that I hear noise, and that I feel heat. This cannot be false, properly speaking it is what in me is called feeling; and used in this precise sense that is no other than thinking.[9]

As one scholar, trying to account for the notion of subjective truth, perspicuously puts the matter:

This permits a novel response to arguments which conclude that we know nothing from the fact that we are fallible about the external world. Whatever such arguments show about knowledge of external reality, we can retreat to the newly recognized inner reality, and refute the claim that we know nothing on the ground that at least we know these newly recognized facts about subjective appearances.[10]

For modern critics of the Cartesian project, Descartes's problem lay in his confusion between employing the criterion of incorrigibility (that is, using the *cogito*) in order to prove the existence of the person and employing this same criterion to determine the essence of the person as mental.

We also find that in the Neoplatonic tradition, the possibility of self-knowledge is treated as a proof or demonstration that the self is incorporeal. For example, Proposition 15 of Proclus's *Elements of Theology* states that "everything that is capable of reverting upon itself is incorporeal." Now despite the parallelism of this text to the Cartesian distinction between *res extensa* and *res cogitans* as resting upon the criterion of self-transparency, the meaning of "reversion" in the Neoplatonic tradition does not share the Cartesian conceit of mental states that are incorrigibly transparent.

Plotinus does think that, at the highest level of identity, self-knowledge is not only certain, but actually necessary. But unlike the case of Descartes's *res cogitans*, this subjective certainty does not hold for any act of cognition: instead, it only holds in extraordinary circumstances at the highest summit of intellectual absorption.

This disparity in the epistemological valuation of mental states occurs for two reasons. First, Plotinus is sensitive to the empirical falsity of the claim that mental states are apprehended incorrigibly within consciousness; he recognizes that there can be a fairly wide gulf between mental processes and the conscious awareness of those processes.[11] Secondly, for Plotinus, Cartesian incorrigibility would be fundamentally representational in nature, since all discursive activity of the mind, such as thought or perception, introduces a representational gap between the knower and the object known.

The intellect, as the subject or seat of all such representations, cannot fathom itself as an object of thought or of perception: self-awareness does not constitute self-knowledge *eo ipso*.[12] If self-knowledge is to be valid, it must be able to circumvent the intentional structure in which objects are normally represented to consciousness. For Plotinus, any *conceptual* representation of the self or subject of consciousness can never be complete and can never succeed in conveying the self that it purports to represent. The fallibilism of any such conveyance is a consequence of Plotinus's more general theory of knowledge according to which truth cannot be ascertained by means of linguistic or conceptual representations. It can be apprehended only when there is an identity between the knower and the known.[13]

Of course the major problem with such a theory is that it appears necessarily to elude both verification and experience. Plotinus attempts to bring this theory of noetic self-identity into the sphere of experience through a detailed investigation of human subjectivity. He makes use of thought experiments in order to represent some features of consciousness that exhibit, more or less perfectly, a degree of unity between the knowing subject and the object known. His thought experiments are intended to guide the reader to a better understanding of what knowing in the most proper sense both is and is like.

II INCORRIGIBLE ARGUMENTS

In the last section, I considered incorrigibility as the foundation of Cartesian epistemology. Descartes triumphs over skeptical doubt concerning the existence of the self by resorting to an ancient strategy: he insists upon the self-evidence of the thing in question. According to Descartes, if we are aware of our states of mind, then we are aware of or know ourselves. I also suggested that Plotinus does not invoke the incorrigibility of self-awareness in order to sustain a *conception* of the immaterial self,[14] since the self cannot be known discursively. In what follows I will show that, contrary to the opinion of many scholars, Plotinus does develop an argument from incorrigibility in defending the possibility of self-knowledge, although he does not do so for the sake of an epistemological project. In fact, Plotinus's interest in subjectivity stems more from the aspiration for self-realization, than from the aspiration for certainty.[15]

The problem for Plotinus is not simply whether the self can be known, but more importantly, how can the self be known? If the mind attempts to represent itself to itself, then it is still trading in an epistemological distance brought about by the distinction between mind as subject and any of its possible objects. This is a problem that Plotinus explores in his treatise V.3 *On the Knowing Hypostases and That Which is Beyond.*

The very first line of the treatise begins by asking whether or not a simple entity can know itself; and this is a loaded question. It looks forward to Plotinus's theory of noetic unity, but it also is couched as a reply to skeptical arguments against the possibility of self-knowledge. Thus it is that Plotinus willingly lets certain skeptical strategies in the front door, only to usher them out the back door, after using them to bolster his own theories. In chapter 2, lines 2–5, for example, we encounter the familiar skeptical complaint that sensation encounters only the external world. Plotinus here would admit that mental states such as perception are subject to correction, since perceptual objects are outside of the perceiving faculty. But what is especially interesting is that the body now becomes quite explicitly a part of the external world: for even when soul perceives the body's internal processes, these are still external to the perceiving subject.

This delineation of the person as the soul, and more specifically, as the subject of awareness, is in keeping with Plotinus's enunciation elsewhere of what belongs properly to the individual human being, and what belongs properly to the body of the world soul, the physical universe. Plotinus clearly states that the individual ensouled body is a part of the cosmos whose growth and decay are controlled by the soul of nature, of by the world soul. For example, the nutritive power of the soul is actually a contribution to the embodied human being from the world soul, whereas sensory perception when accompanied by intellect "is a [faculty] of the individual."[16]

Now the ancient skeptics not only denied that there could be knowledge of the external world, they also denied the possibility of self-knowledge as well. We find in Sextus Empiricus a series of arguments designed to impugn the possibility of self-knowledge: the soul cannot know itself as a whole or as a part, for either the subjective side or the objective side would have to disappear.[17] Plotinus,[18] in refuting these arguments, proceeds by means of a hierarchy of increasing self-awareness, beginning from sense perception, and ending with intellectual self-knowledge. Can the faculty of discursive thought have knowledge of itself? Is the thinker, *qua* thinker, self-transparent? This question is of great importance if we want to know whether or not Plotinus thinks that we can construct an argument which proves that the self can know itself. Can we use reason in order to demonstrate that we are by nature rational beings, that we are, in Descartes's words, "things that think"?

Definitely not, according to Plotinus. Self-knowledge, if it exists at all, must be prior to the deliverances of discursive thought. Here we find Plotinus enlarging upon the representational gap that he admits in the case of sense perception by extending it to all modes of mental representation whatsoever: "[Intellect's thoughts] are certainly not premises or theorems or propositions. These are about things other [than themselves] and are not identical with the realities [that they signify]" (V.5.1.30).

Thought, in representing states of affairs, may specify exactly which states of affairs are necessary for the veridicality of its assertions, although it obviously fails as a guarantor for such conditions. Of course thinking that things are thus-and-so is not identical to their being thus-and-so, in most circumstances. The point seems almost too obvious to belabor, and yet it is a point that Plotinus repeatedly stresses when discussing the ontological concomitants of discursive thought. Apparently, what crucially distinguishes mental states from acts of the intellect is that the former are directed toward particulars in the world, while the latter are not. To borrow a bit of modern jargon, one might say that one of the most salient characteristics of discursive thought is its intentionality, the fact that it is about objects that are other than itself.[19]

Actually when Plotinus describes discursive thinking he associates it with two distinctive modes of alterity: conceptual alterity, or transition from one concept to another, and ontological alterity, or the nonidentity of the thinking subject with the object of thought. The latter dominates his discussion of the topic. In III.8.6.23 for example, Plotinus again contrasts intellectual knowledge, in which the identity between knower and known prevails, with discursive thinking: "[Soul] is other than its object, and has a discursive awareness that sees as if it were one thing gazing at another."

As has been frequently pointed out, Plotinus borrows the language of Aristotle's discussion at De anima III.8 concerning the identity of knowledge and its objects,[20] where Aristotle delineates two possible ways in which the mind can be identical with its objects. It can be identical with the object itself qua hylomorphic compound, or it can be identical with the Form, abstracted from the composite substance. Aristotle chooses the latter possibility.[21] He further stipulates that the mind "thinks the forms by means of mental images"[22] in order to represent its objects (whether they be perceptual or conceptual).

Plotinus, following Aristotle, agrees that thinking in the ordinary sense involves mental representations of the Forms: "The discursive mind making a judgment about sense-impressions has a simultaneous awareness of the Forms. . . ." (I.1.9.17–21). Nevertheless, Plotinus's account of epistemic identity diverges from Aristotle's: according to Plotinus, the mind's ability to entertain a representation of the Form does not render the mind identical with its intelligible object. Discursive thought still sees its objects as substantively distinct from itself. It gazes outside at the world and discovers the sensible object, or gazes within toward the Forms and discovers the conceptual object. At its best, to be sure, the mind provides, in Plotinus's words, a kind of "partnership" between the inner and the outer,[23] but discursive thinking is always inherently directed toward some object.

In treatise V.3.1, Plotinus denies that this same discursive structure is present when the intellect knows its objects. The question then becomes, does intellect know only its objects, or does it also (necessarily) know itself?[24] Plotinus's answer to this question is a resounding yes but our task is to trace the path by which he arrives at it.

Initially it seems that Plotinus has just raised more problems than he is able to solve. We have already seen how eager Plotinus is to admit the skeptical strategy of denying that there can be knowledge of an object that is external to the knower. In chapters 1 and 3 of our treatise, we learn that the intellect does not have these problems: it is aware of "what is in it," and, presumably, whatever is in intellect, is intellect.[25] There is every reason to believe that intellect *can* know itself, given that its objects are internal. But why, one could insist, is it *necessary* that it know itself? Plotinus takes up this question in a very early treatise, (V.9.8.15) where, according to one commentator, he invokes an Aristotelian conception of *energeia* in order to demonstrate the necessity for the mind's self-knowledge. Intellect *is* pure intellectual activity; hence, intellect necessarily engages in knowing.

So far, this dialectical approach to Plotinus's arguments for self-knowledge has yielded a structure that rests upon formal ontological principles.[26] There do not appear to be any ancestral traces of Cartesian incorrigibility, which rests upon an appeal to the self-evidence of the *cogito*. Nevertheless, it is generally accepted that a hallmark of Plotinus's procedure for solving epistemological questions especially, is the largely introspective nature of his arguments.[27]

At V.3.7, Plotinus associates his demonstration of the mind's self-knowledge with some form of philosophical necessity: "Has then our argument demonstrated something of a kind which has the power to inspire confidence? No, it has necessity, not persuasive force, for necessity is in intellect but persuasion in the soul." How can he think he has succeeded in an argument that has the force of necessity? It is a question of how one follows the argument.[28] The argument takes the form of a *reductio:* he first assumes that the intellect can be in contact, not with reality directly, but only with an impression of some kind. Plotinus then goes on to say that if this is the case, the same doubts about intellectual knowledge will arise as arise in the case of sense perception. But if we have an intellect that cannot vouchsafe that it knows, then we will have to posit another intellect to oversee the first, and so on. Either we lack knowledge entirely, or we are capable of knowing that we know. Intellect must be the primary instance of self-knowledge.

Plotinus has pointed out the necessity of self-knowledge, and also that soul knows by means of intellect. So if soul knows anything, it participates in a kind of subsidiary self-knowledge: in knowing that knowledge is present, the mind recognizes that its knowledge is owing to the self-knowledge present in intellect, that is, the mind affirms its own ability to know. This very affirmation is a partial self-knowledge that constitutes a demonstration of the principle of intellect, whose very nature is to know itself. Otherwise we would have intellect that is unintelligent, and this is sheer impossibility.

It hardly seems plausible that this counts as a demonstration at all, much less as an irrefutable one, for it seems merely to beg the question. The skeptic's riposte will be, "That's just what I mean; there is an infinite regress of knowers, and intellect, the very principle of knowledge, can't guarantee anything, since it doesn't even know itself."

This demonstration of the principle of self-knowledge, if it is one, cannot be said to be a formal account. Instead its purpose is to ready the student for an intellectual affirmation on her own part. Plotinus is convinced that it is not by rational argument that the principle of knowledge can be established, but only by a self-recognition on the part of the soul of this indubitable fact of awareness itself.[29]

> One is not really apprehending it [sc. nous] through an image, but it is like taking a piece of gold as a sample of all gold, and if the piece taken is not pure, purifying it in act or word by showing that not all this sample is gold, but only this particular portion of the whole mass; here it is from the intellect in ourselves when it has been purified, that we apprehend what the intellect is . . . like. (V.8.3.12ff.)

Likewise, in treatise I.4 *On Well-Being* we find a description of self-reflexive awareness, in which thought, projected back onto itself, is likened to a calm reflective surface, a *katoptron*. Because its focus is upon the self as self-reflexive consciousness, and not upon the self as discursive thinker, there is both a continuity as well as a divergence from the Cartesian argument from incorrigibility.

Direct insight into the nature of the cognitive moment as such is the method that Plotinus employs. The mind attains self-knowledge, not by developing a conception of what it is to be a knower, but rather by uncovering self-knowledge through a process of gradual detachment from the objects of consciousness:

> If someone is unable to discover the soul in this detached state, first let him grasp the discursive soul, and then ascend from there. But if he cannot even do this, then [let him grasp] the faculty of sense-perception that conveys the intelligibles still more distantly, since sense-perception in itself is actually bound up with the forms. (V.3.9.28–32)

To summarize this section, we can say that self-knowledge involves the realization that the mind or self is not an object of any kind. In this sense, self-awareness does not automatically yield self-knowledge. Rather, the mind can *become* self-transparent by concentration upon itself, and the self that it thereby discovers will no longer be any of the intentional structures that occupy the mind when directed toward an external object. Nevertheless, Plotinus is not content to let this rest as an item of doctrine. He makes use of thought experiments as a means of illustrating his recommended method for cultivating self-knowledge. These experiments also convey his radical insistence upon a specific orientation to the truth under consideration: the student must not consider herself as separate from the reality which she seeks to comprehend.

III THOUGHT EXPERIMENTS

It has been argued that Descartes, writing in the tradition of the meditation manual, a genre designed for an introspective audience, uses his provisional doubt as a cathartic method, thus imitating the progression of a penitential meditation, in which his soul is purged of the error of doubt by undergoing sensory deprivation.[30] Descartes writes in the meditative tradition previously shared by authors whose intention was to foster a mental state that could become receptive to divine grace, or to the light of divine knowledge. In the *Meditations*, these exercises are also coupled with a theoretical approach to epistemology, intended to be illustrated by the self-reflective practice of the reader. As Gary Hatfield writes of the *cogito:* The briefly sketched argument to the conclusion "that the proposition 'I am,' 'I exist,' is necessarily true" is ultimately presented as resting on the direct apprehension of the meditator's own thinking.[31]

Hatfield stresses that Descartes is keenly aware of his selection of the meditative mode of discourse. He insists upon the need for a practical basis for the metaphysical inquiry whose conclusions often run counter to the testimony of the senses and the ontological assumptions fostered by long habit. Descartes writes concerning the primary notions of metaphysics, that "though in their own nature they are as intelligible as, or even more intelligible than those the geometricians study, yet, being contradicted by the preconceptions of the senses to which we have since our earliest years been accustomed, they cannot be perfectly apprehended except by those who give strenuous attention to them." And in the reply to the second set of objections, he writes: "I counsel no one to read this work, except those who are willing to meditate seriously with me."

The notion of the subjective self that Plotinus shares with the modern world is the self that presents itself in the introspective stance. Plotinus, for the development of this introspective communication between author and reader, relies upon a series of thought experiments embedded within the text, whose purpose is to foster the potential for self-awareness and so orient the student upon a path of self-knowledge.

At the opening of V.8.1 there is an extended meditation upon the relationship between wisdom and the products whose creation it governs. Real beauty is not discovered within the artifact, but within the productive knowledge that conceives it. The beauty of our cosmos, Plotinus tells us, can best be appreciated if we conceive of the cosmos as transparent. We can only see the beauty of the world if we are capable of seeing through the world. Although the remarks in chapter 1 may seem elusive, falling somewhere in between metaphor and cosmological speculation, it quickly becomes apparent that Plotinus expects the reader/audience to be following very closely indeed.

He offers us nothing less than instruction in how to recreate this image of the transparent world for ourselves, describing an exercise involving visualization of the world as situated within a diaphanous sphere. The center and the circumference of the sphere become metaphors for the perceiving subject and the visual object respectively. The success of the analogy is due in part to the rhetorical stealth with which this passage is constructed, as Plotinus inculcates the impression that this image is a literal description of the way that any of us, qua knower, actually confronts the world: "So far as possible, try to conceive of this world as one unified whole, with each of its parts remaining self-identical and distinct. . . ." (V.8.9.1–3).

Here Plotinus suggests that the reader try to perceive the world as unified within thought, to think of the world as a single object of thought, yet as retaining all of the features of its different members. Consider, he tells the reader, how any conditions of awareness whatsoever are confronted by you, the knower. These directions are a way of calling attention to the most general features involved in any encounter with the world, any possible object of awareness. We might paraphrase them as follows: Consider the total possible field of objects of awareness – that same field is simply what I mean by "world."

It is fair to call this passage a meditation because it involves two features often employed in meditation techniques: the active but directed use of the imagination, and the sustained presence of this imaginative construction as a method of changing habitual modes of thought of self-awareness: "So that whatever part of, for example, the outer sphere is shown forth, there immediately follows the image of the sun together with all of the other stars, and earth and sea and all sentient beings are seen, as if upon a transparent sphere" (V.8.9.3–7; trans. Armstrong).

This meditation involves a very careful direction of the mind and imagination of the student. Holding the simple image, the sphere, before the mind's eye, the reader is to fill up the space of that image entirely, exerting herself to the utmost to picture the entire universe of sentient and nonsentient beings in all of their diversity. Certainly one would need at least a certain amount of practice and effort in order to carry out all of the conditions of the meditation successfully.

All of these components of the picture must be held in an even gaze. All sentient beings are visible within the diaphanous sphere at a single glance: *euthus*. An important feature of the meditation is the training of the student's concentration and attention. The practice of this exercise leads both to a focusing capacity, an intense direction of the mind's eye to a single object, without letting any feature of that object dominate in the moment, and to a detachment. None of the beings, either animate or inanimate, either human or nonhuman, is to have priority within the meditation. All are equally and completely subsumed within the general category of content of the sphere. All are, we might say, equidistant from the center. This equidistance is what Plotinus is hinting at by saying that the elements are, as it were, upon the surface of the sphere.

The practice of concentration upon an object by means of the inner vision of imagination steadies the mind by withdrawing it from the vertiginous whirl of sensory experience. This withdrawal, while not a goal in itself, begins to enable the student to direct her attention inward: "It would in fact be possible to see all things within [the sphere or mind]." At the end of the meditation, the student has before the mind's eye a vast field consisting in the panoramic sweep of the entire cosmos which is simultaneously intricate in its detail and specification. The purpose of this interior visualization is to call attention to the quality of interior vision itself, and in particular, its capacity to be at once unitary and multifaceted in a way that exterior vision is not.

Actually, the passage we have just examined is one of numerous texts in which Plotinus uses the symbolism of the sphere to illustrate the relationship between consciousness and its contents. We find these texts broadly divided into two different types, one macrocosmic, the other microcosmic. Under the first type, the vision is described as planetary, and the contents of the vision include an enumeration of the parts of the cosmos and their respective inhabitants.[32] Under the second type, Plotinus uses a more abstract description of a geometrical object, a simple illuminated sphere, although at times, this shape can represent an individual head, or a head peering out by means of the faces of all sentient beings.[33]

This variation between the microcosmic and macrocosmic perspectives is Plotinus's way of illustrating two different ways of conceiving the world. The macrocosm is a publicly available world, inhabited and experienced by countless sentient beings, each with a diverse perspective. The microcosm is that same world, seen from within the confines of an individual consciousness. Above all, these texts suggest that Plotinus was grappling with the issue of how to represent subjectivity as a philosophical construct, as well as with the methodological issue of how to couch a dialectical appeal to the subjective.

At this point it is time to recap and to take stock of where we are in terms of the historical question with which we began. Starting with the general question, what use does Plotinus make of the appeal to incorrigibility in arguing for the necessity of self-knowledge, we found that there were texts in which the self-evidence of consciousness formed the last step of a dialectical progression. Furthermore, these texts were complemented by a series of thought experiments in which a highly structured form of subjectivity was represented as immediately present to the reader. In effect, the thought experiments offer the reader a mirror in which to observe his own inner life. These texts provide a reply to the historical question, "When and why did philosophers first lay claim to knowledge of their own subjective states?"[34] even as they raise other questions. First, can we compare any of the tenets or implications of Cartesian subjectivity with elements of Plotinus's appeal to the subjectivity of consciousness? Second, what philosophical work are his thought experiments designed to do? Are they an elaboration of Plotinus's arguments or are they supposed to provide an element of persuasion quite apart from the metaphysical assumptions upon which they rely?

IV INTERNALISM, PHENOMENALISM, AND THE LIMITATIONS OF THE SUBJECTIVE

Plotinus begins VI.5.9 with a kind of psychological experiment: let us say that someone imagines a given number of elements as forming a sphere within his thought. Now Plotinus wants us to look at the relationship between the "maker of the sphere," *to poioun*, and the content of that sphere, *ta merê*.

Suppose the hypothetical thinker in our passage to be considering any group of *stoicheia*, any possible content for the sphere, for the purposes of argument. No matter how diverse the causes that initially produced these elements in the external world, as for the contents of the sphere considered solely as objects of thought, it is true to say that their productive cause is singular, namely, the hypothetical thinker himself.

This thought experiment relies crucially upon an appeal to the introspective stance in order to secure the strong form of internalism expressed in the conclusion to the argument, a conclusion that bears close comparison to the internalist position of contemporary philosophy: "An individual person or animal's mental state and event kinds – including the individual's intentional or representational kinds – can in principle be individuated in complete independence of the natures of empirical objects, properties, or relations."[35] In our passage, the contents of the sphere or, as we might say, the contents of consciousness (consisting in simultaneous mental events or states) have only one unique cause at the time in which they are thought, namely, the hypothetical thinker. Now since the thinker is not a separate substance apart from his own thoughts, the mental events/states of this thinker are in some sense a part of the thinker. Therefore, the contents of consciousness belong to a mental (intelligent), not a physical, substance. This conclusion both resembles Cartesian internalism and rests upon a methodology that recalls Descartes's: the argument turns upon an appeal to introspection. Only the thinker as he is thinking can confirm that he is the cause of his thoughts. Someone else, to whom the perceiver is reporting his thoughts, might have occasion to remark that the cause of a particular perception was, for example, the man, Socrates.[36]

To this argument is appended a brief attempt to address the problem of intersubjectivity, that is, the public availability of a self-consistent world to a plurality of knowers. The causal independence of mental states from the physical environment must now be treated as an analogy: just as the mind is the source and cause of its own contents, so the world soul is the source and cause of *its* own contents. Hence, the world soul contains the physical cosmos, while universal soul contains the plurality of individual souls.[37]

The question is, what justifies this transition from treating the individual mind as an example of the causal independence of the mental with respect to the physical, to the larger inference, that there must be some universal mind that exercises causal independence with respect to the physical macrocosm? And more importantly for our purposes, how does Plotinus's appeal to introspection enter into the structure of the argument? On the surface, this appeal seems a crudely deceptive attempt at persuasion. Starting from an internalist position, Plotinus ends by invoking the metaphysical principle that underlies his experiment, the doctrine of panpsychism. In fact, however, Plotinus needs his doctrine of panpsychism in order to account for the intersubjective consistency of the world. The argument appears to exhibit a circularity masked by the ingenuity of an appeal to the immediacy of consciousness.

In order to understand this transition, we turn to another thought experiment. Here we consider the analogies between Plotinus's exploration of subjectivity and the *esse est percipi* variety of idealism upon which modern-day philosophers heap so much scorn. The passage we are about to consider seems to introduce a form of phenomenalism as a step in the argument, which is intended to show that there are Forms for all sentient beings, or that all sentient beings exist within the hypostasis, *nous.*

In this text, the bodies of living beings, by means of which they express their individuality, are envisioned as a unity, objectively, as constituting one world body, and subjectively, as constituting one phenomenal presentation. What happens in the next step of the experiment is that the qualities that are known to comprise, on the Neoplatonist's account, the sum reality of the individual,[38] are shown to be no longer capable of doing the work of presenting attributes by which an individual might be discriminated from another individual. Instead, the individual's qualities are to be apprehended as elements within one unified field of sense presentations, while it is the consciousness of the apprehender to which these presentations belong:

> They all flow, in a way, from a single spring, not like one particular breath or one warmth, but as if there was one quality which held and kept intact all the qualities in itself, of sweetness along with fragrance, and was at once the quality of wine and the characters of all tastes, the sights of colours and all the awarenesses of touch. (VI.7.12.23–8; trans. Armstrong)

Thus, the progress of the passage is from the objective description of the quality, as sweetness or smell, to its fundamental nature as a kind of awareness on the part of the perceiver.

This text presents a thought experiment in which the objective world dissolves before the mind, leaving in its wake what might literally be described as a stream of consciousness. In our passage, individual substances are shown to consist in *qualia* and these *qualia* in turn are simply modifications of consciousness, or *nous*, which, I take it, is the "single source" described in the text. In both of these experiments, Plotinus shows us how the soul constructs a contracted sense of self when it conceives the world as outside of the self; this notion of externality is a result of habitually identifying with the body. The thought experiments reveal a way of conceiving the world as not external to the self. Gradually the boundary that separates self and world is erased, when the demarcations of selfhood are no longer around the body, but around the totality of any given phenomenal presentation.

So far, we have encountered thought experiments in which the subjective stance has been used as a support for some very weighty metaphysical tenets, including the doctrine of panpsychism, and the doctrine of the Platonic world exemplar. In both passages, a structural puzzle crops up. A supposedly unmediated and hence, unbiased appeal to consciousness becomes a method of securing credibility for what are obviously entrenched dogmas within the Platonic school. Why bother to employ such a circuitous method? Do we stand in danger of being fooled by the text and its rhetoric of immediacy? Persuasion is not the final goal of this experiment; participation is. The success of the thought experiment means for Plotinus a validation of the contemplative journey.

In fact, one of the strongest motivations that Plotinus has for approaching subjectivity by means of these thought experiments is

to point out the limitations of the subjective. The appeal to introspection invites a scrutiny of the assumptions which the knower
makes about himself. Instead of singling oneself out as possessing a
privileged epistemic status, these texts instead encourage the reader
to doubt both his own identity and to recognize his own cognitive
limitations.

In the thought experiments we have discussed, one of the most
important configurations presented is the relationship between the
sphere and its contents. The person, qua knower, or subject of consciousness, will identify with the sphere, rather than with any of its
contents. Immediately, definitions of the self which are appropriate
for the knower considered as a sensible particular are no longer
appropriate for the person undergoing the exercise. The purpose of
this exercise is to sustain an insight into the nature of the individual
insofar as he is a knower, by suggesting a contrast between his
knowledge of himself qua individual, and his identity as a knower,
qua knower. The very stance that is assumed if one identifies, not
with the contents of consciousness, but with consciousness apart
from its contents, immediately begins to erode the identity of the
knower. The center of consciousness is infinitely expansive, including within itself any individual identity which the knower may
possess as an unremarkable feature of the total interior landscape.
That is, every cognizable fact about the knower's identity as subject
is converted to the status of an external condition: body, personality,
life history, passions, and so forth. This detachment from the narrow
confines of a historical selfhood, while it does not consist in a denial
of the empirical self, allows the larger selfhood of soul to emerge
from behind the veil of the objective domain.

V SUBJECTIVITY AND ITS TRANSCENDENCE

In chapter 18 of the *Life*, Porphyry relates how he had once tried to
"show that the object of thought existed outside the intellect"[39] and
that this belief formed the chief obstacle to his embracing the teaching of Plotinus,[40] who taught that the intelligibles, or forms, existed
within *nous*. Porphyry's difficulty seems to be founded upon an
assumption which characterizes ordinary as opposed to intellective
cognition, namely, that the world, or real being, must exist outside
of the knower. This assumption is in turn founded upon the need to

withstand the subjectivism which would apparently result from saying that intellect cannot discover an object that exists prior to it.

Porphyry's objections may serve as an introduction to a key difficulty in the conception of self-knowledge that I have been developing here. The path of introspection should result in the belief that the empirical self is not the true self. But it is hard to see how the individual subject of consciousness, which contains but is not identical to any of its contents, can ever overcome the solipsism which threatens to engulf it. The creations of the individual mind are entirely subjective; the objects of intellect, *nous*, are preeminently objective.

The problem of discontinuity between the individual mind together with the individual's thinking, and the intellect as such, together with its extensionality as the eternal forms, formed the basis of "worst difficulty" argument already in the Platonic *Parmenides*, which is generated from the subjectivist implications of treating the ideas as the *noêmata*, or thought objects, of an individual mind.

But, Parmenides, said Socrates, may it not be that each of these forms is a thought, which cannot properly exist anywhere but in a mind . . . (132c7). And besides, said Parmenides, according to the way in which you assert that the other things have a share in the forms, must you not hold either that each of those things consists of thoughts, so that all things think, or else that they are thoughts which nevertheless do not think? (132b3)

So far from continuing in the thought productions which serve to limit and condition the knower with an overlay of opinion, however true, or scientific knowledge, however coherent, there must be some use of the human intelligence which can lead to an insight that frees the knower from the narrow confines of her own thought, from the confines of her own intellect, and permits access to intellect as such.

Plotinus's methodology attempts to stand outside of the conditions of particular thought, and to grasp the total occasion of awareness which includes both subject and object of intellection as its terms of reference. He expects that this fundamental condition of conscious experience, the reality of the knower as engaged in the confrontation with the world as given to consciousness, will provide the best opportunity for an exploration of the nature of intelligible reality.

Plotinus relies upon a method of directly pointing to the very primacy of cognition or awareness in its most general aspect, the very consciousness which is the basis for any mode of cognition. This method assumes at the outset that intellect in us is intellect as such, but we do not yet recognize it. Plotinus tells us "And to put it another way, *nous* does not belong to the individual, but it is rather universal" (III.8.8.41).

The soul attains to identification with intellect through the practice of concentration, but not concentration upon anything external to it, for this attachment to and distraction by the conception of an external, ontologically separate reality, is precisely the habit that obstructs the mind's progression in knowledge.

VI CONCLUSION

One of the questions we started with when undertaking this study of Plotinus's presentation of subjectivity was, "what is it to be a person?" In the thought experiments considered, Plotinus treats the empirical self as an object of consciousness:

If you first of all separated the body from man (and, obviously, from yourself), and then the soul which forms it and, very thoroughly, sense-perception and desires and passions . . . what remains of soul is this which we said was an image of Intellect. . . . (V.3.9.1–10; trans. Armstrong)

The empirical self is no longer the self with which the knower identifies, whereas the authentic self emerges as the pure subject of awareness, only uncovered when the various modes and objects of cognition are progressively shed.[41] What gives the person in this experiment the right to demarcate her selfhood as if it existed outside of the boundaries of any mode of cognition or any of the psychological parameters that normally characterize a personality or possessor of a life history? The detachment recommended here seems at odds with a requisite self-honesty which would admit passions, sense experiences, and bodily states as all belonging to the self.

In order to put this issue into sharper focus, we borrow from a complaint lodged against the Cartesian *res cogitans*, the pure subject of consciousness enshrined within the empiricist tradition:

For empiricism, the self is an unobjectifiable subject, just as the eye is an invisible organ. But . . . the empiricist self vanishes when subjected to empiricist scrutiny. The self is not discoverable by any sense, whether inner or outer; and therefore it is to be rejected as a metaphysical monster.[42]

The thought experiments that Plotinus engages in continually refer the reader to this self which can never be grasped as a definite object, as this or as that. Indeed, the most that such a "witness" self, or subject of consciousness, would have to say for itself would be, "am, am," or "I, I."[43]

This speculative self, the watchful fleshless eye that has been repeatedly denounced in the postmodern era as an artificial attempt to reify a linguistic convention,[44] is easily discoverable within the premodern tradition. But for the modern tradition, this self was part of an elaborate epistemological construction that introduced an enormous amount of excess metaphysical baggage, to wit, Cartesian dualism and its internalist consequences.

Plotinus's motivations lay in another direction entirely. In fact, it would be hard to overemphasize the affinities that Plotinus shares with Descartes in terms of textual allusions to a religious tradition. The most significant feature of Plotinus's thought experiments is their association with prayer or invocation, a usage we can see by returning to the treatise, *On the Intelligible Beauty:*

Keeping watch over this image, place another next to it, taking away its mass. Remove both space and the imaginary conception of matter in you [altogether]; do not simply try to get hold of another sphere, smaller in mass than [the first]. *And calling upon the god whose imaginary conception you have, pray for him to come.* (V.8.9.11; trans. Armstrong)

Here the sphere is obviously treated as an icon of deity. But more than the sphere itself, the world as a whole, since it is contained within the sphere, is conceived as an icon, a sacred image of the god who can be encountered face to face within his shrine.[45] This meditation then is also a Cletic prayer, an invocation which depends upon making the world as a whole both one's offering and one's object of worship. The exercise helps the student to treat the world as a theophany, as an image of the deity whose real presence is yet to be recognized.[46] This recognition is best attained, according to Plotinus, within an introspective search: Plotinian prayers employ the formula, "alone to the alone."[47]

This introspective practice involves simplifying and clarifying the relationship that the soul as knower has with all possible objects of awareness. One of the consequences of this clarification is the restoration of the soul's proper fullness, an appreciation of the rich and creative intellectual potential which is available to every human being as a birthright. No longer circumscribed by its historical, temporal, and emotional limitations, the Plotinian self embraces a vast domain whose boundaries extend to the fullness of what is encountered in every knowing moment. In this respect, the reconstructed self of Plotinus is met with in a moment of attention that can be reenacted at any point within history.[48]

NOTES

1 For possible historical or philosophical connections between the thought of Plotinus and Descartes in regard to the issue of self-knowledge, see Lloyd 1964 and Emilsson 1991.

2 The seminal work on the issue of whether or not there was anything like a notion of the subjective and whether or not there was any claim to knowledge of subjective states is of course Burnyeat 1982. See also Everson 1991b for a rejoinder to Burnyeat's discussion of Cyrenaic subjectivity.

3 On Cartesian thought experiments, see Wilkes 1988, ch. 1 and also McDowell 1986. For the Cartesian method of self-representation, see Judovitz 1988.

4 For these two criteria as the defining attributes of personhood see Gill. See also David Wiggens, "Locke, Butler, and the Stream of Consciousness," in Rorty 1976.

5 Rorty 1986.

6 This is a summary of Gill 1991.

7 On the notion of subjective truth and its invention see Burnyeat 1982 and McDowell 1986.

8 On Skeptical strategies the literature is vast. Primary sources are of course Cicero's *Lucullus* and Sextus Empiricus, *Against the Dogmatists*, for the debate between Skeptics and Stoics on the criterion of truth. For an excellent summary of this debate, see Frede 1987.

9 Descartes, *Meditatio Secunda*, paragraph 9.

10 McDowell 1986.

11 This is a topic that I will not be exploring in this paper, since much excellent work on the ideas of consciousness and quasiconsciousness has been done by Warren. But cf. IV.9.21 for an instance of Plotinus

pointing out that self-consciousness does not necessarily attend the various thoughts of experiences that the mind might entertain at a given time.

12 On the association of incorrigibility with the Cartesian subject of consciousness, see Gill 1991 and Wilkes 1991.

13 An interesting parallel to the critique of self-representation as equivalent to self-knowledge developed here may be found in Kant: ". . . the simple representation I, for itself empty of all content, which can never be said to be a concept, but only a pure consciousness which accompanies all concepts" (*Critique of Pure Reason*, A346; quoted in Marion 1993, 57).

14 On the association of incorrigibility with the Cartesian subject of consciousness, see Gill 1991 and Wilkes 1991.

15 Commentators often acknowledge Lloyd (1964) in their footnotes when they wish to dismiss Plotinus as a progenitor of the modern mental person, but in doing so, they often fail to notice that Lloyd rightly distinguishes between two different notions of self-knowledge: one of them he calls the doctrine of *conscientia*, which is a formal account or proof of the incorrigibility of consciousness. Thus Descartes, according to Lloyd, would have us believe that: "the proposition that I know I am sad and the proposition that I am aware it is I who am sad are deducible from the proposition that I am sad." Now Lloyd differentiates this from another notion of self-knowledge, self-knowledge as a kind of inner sense, which primarily has psychological force. This second notion is associated in the Platonic tradition with *gnôthi seauton*, and is tied to the doctrine of the "god within," in religious texts. The upshot is this: philosophical reasoning would like to present us with a formal, reasoned, demonstration for self-knowledge, while religion would like us to dive within and find ourselves or god, or both.

16 IV.9.3.27. On this passage, see Blumenthal 1971, 29.

17 Sextus Empiricus, *Against the Dogmatists* I.310,311. Wallis 1989 was the first scholar to call attention to V.2 as a response to the Skeptical attack on the possibility of self-knowledge.

18 Here I am very much indebted to the work of Wallis 1989 on Skepticism and Neoplatonism.

19 Cf. Searle 1983, 1: "Intentionality is that property of many mental states and events by which they are directed at or about or of objects and states of affairs in the world."

20 *De an.* 431a1.

21 *De an.* 431b26–8.

22 *De an.* 431b1–2: "It is the forms which the faculty of thought thinks in mental images."

23 I.1.9.21–2: "[We are talking about the] discursive intelligence proper, which belongs to the genuine soul. Genuine discursive intelligence in fact is an actualization of the intelligibles and often a samenesss or partnership of the inner and the outer."

24 "Nous has knowledge of as many things as are objects of intellect. But does the intellect that knows these objects also know itself?" V.3.1.22.

25 For this strategy, see Lloyd 1964: Neoplatonists argued regularly that the mind or thought can think of itself because the identity of nous and noêton implies that every nous is also an on or noêton; and they were only repeating Aristotle's unsatisfactory solution in De anima III of the traditional aporia.

26 According to Lloyd, the Neoplatonic demonstration of the necessity for mind's self-knowledge rests upon the metaphysical commitment that thought and its object are one in intellect and so is a formal account.

27 See Smith 1981, 104–5: Smith discusses the concept of enhorasis, an intuitive approach to metaphysical thinking, and in particular the appeal to intuition in III.7.5 "The verb enhoratai is a favorite with Plotinus to express the way in which we may find the relationship of elements within the intelligible. It may be found in the treatise 'On Eternity and Time' where too we are told the normal reasoning will not adequately grasp the nature of the eternal and its relationship to Being. We must employ 'the eternal in us.' "

See also Warren 1964, an article which cites numerous examples of introspection as a method of philosophic investigation. Warren raises the issue of whether or not the many instances Plotinus cites of human conscious activity are actually intended to represent the states Plotinus is investigating. Such examples as the lack of self-consciousness associated with either intense concentration or with habitual actions are often appealed to as evidence for questions concerning the origins of perception, memory, and imagination within the human soul.

28 For a detailed discussion of the dialectical context of V.2.2ff., see Wallis 1989. Wallis identifies this passage as a response to standard Pyrrhonist strategies which attempted to eliminate both of the disjuncts, that the self knows itself either as a whole or as a part. In either case, according to the skeptics, the subjective or objective side must disappear in the moment of self-apprehension.

29 Armstrong's translation.

30 Rorty, "The Structure of Descartes' Meditations," in Rorty 1986.

31 Hatfield 1986, 4–10.

32 Cf. V.8.9.4–10; VI.7.12.4–30; V.1.2.28–40.

33 Cf. VI.4.7.22–37; VI.5.9.1–10; VI.7.15.25–6.

34 Burnyeat 1982.

35 Burge 1986, 118–19. He continues: "The mental natures of all an individual's mental states and events are such that there is no necessary or other deep individuative relation between the individual's being in states, or undergoing events, with those natures, and the nature of the individuals' physical and social environments."

36 Cf. V.3.3.5.

37 For an extremely thorough discussion of the causal relations between the individual embodied soul and the world soul, see Helleman-Elgersma 1980, 42–52. There is a distinction between the hypostasis, soul (universal soul), and the world soul, which governs the cosmos as a whole. Elgersma calls attention to the work of Blumenthal, who demonstrates the inadequacy of the prevailing assumption in scholarship, introduced by Zeller, that these two souls should be equated. If the individual soul is simply a part of the world soul, and not directly related to the universal hypostatis, soul, then the cosmos would entirely subsume the autonomy of the individual.

38 II.6.3. On the purely qualitative existence of the individual see the extensive discussion of Wurm 1973.

39 Porphyry, *Life of Plotinus* 18.10

40 Many scholars have done an exemplary job in pointing to the connections between this central tenet and the historical developments of the Stoic, Peripatetic, and Middle Platonic interpretations of the Demiurgic creation combined with the self-thinking Aristotelian divinity. One of the most interesting treatments of the problem is that of Rich 1954, 123–33, who discusses the Platonic forms as thoughts in a human mind, a pattern evidenced already in the *Parmenides*, as part of the "worst difficulty" *aporia*.

41 Cf. the acute study of Plotinus's recommendations for contemplative detachment from the empirical self by Schroeder 1989.

42 Kenny 1992.

43 V.3.10.36.

44 That is, reifying the first person pronoun, which, as subject of all self-referring predicates, is a linguistic device to indicate the presence of an ego substance, but is, according to some theorists, a metaphysical cipher. See Kenny 1992.

45 There are many passages in the *Enneads* where the image of the sphere is associated with the activity of contemplative meditation or prayer. Often Plotinus uses the language of solar worship to discuss this kind of meditation, but as often he uses the language of cult and celebration, employing dance imagery as an application of the same spherical model. Cf. especially V.5.8.3-7, Armstrong's translation: "So one must not chase after it, [the One] but wait quietly till it appears, preparing oneself

to contemplate it, as the eye awaits the rising of the sun; and the sun rising over the horizon ("from Ocean," the poets say) gives itself to the eyes to see."

Or again, VI.9.8.35ff. for dance imagery. For explicit uses of shrine imagery see VI.9.11.19–30 and V.1.6.10. This last passage is again a very pointed discussion of prayer and invocation.

46 For an excellent discussion of the worship of the cosmos as either itself divine or an image of the divine, see Pépin 1986.

47 Dodds 1960, 16–17, discusses the history of this phrase and cites evidence that Numenius, who seems to have employed it in fragment 11 of his *Peri Agathou*, and whether or not the phrase was actually part of an Egyptian cult formula.

48 Many thanks to the editor, Lloyd Gerson, for his helpful suggestions. Nevertheless all the views as well as any errors expressed here are entirely the responsibility of the author.

11 Plotinus: Body and soul

Porphyry tells us that he "once went on asking Plotinus for three days about the soul's connection with the body, and [Plotinus] kept on explaining to him. A man called Thaumasius came in who was interested in general statements and said that he wanted to hear Plotinus speaking in the manner of a set treatise, but could not stand Porphyry's questions and answers. Plotinus said, 'But if when Porphyry asks questions we do not solve his difficulties we shall not be able to say anything at all to put into the treatise' " (*Life of Plotinus* 13.11–18). Porphyry further claims that the works of Plotinus's "middle period" ([22] to [45]), written while Porphyry was with him, were the greatest (*Life* 6.31–7), but it is difficult to identify any special difference that his questions made (unless that Plotinus wrote at greater length, and yet more tortuously). Plotinus may have reached his convictions by argument, and been prepared to defend them, but what he says at the beginning, in the discourse *On Beauty* (I.6), is very much what he says at the end, *On the Primal Good and the Other Goods* (I.7), "When [we] see the beauty in bodies [we] must not run after them; we must know that they are images, traces, shadows and hurry away to that which they image. . . . Shut your eyes and change to and wake another way of seeing, which everyone has but few use" (I.6.8.7–9, 25–7). "We must say that life in a body is an evil in itself, but the soul comes into good by its virtue, by not living the life of the compound but separating itself even now" (I.7.3.20–3).

The separation of dissociation that Plotinus asks of us is not, of course, "a journey for the feet" (I.6.8.23–5): the Other World is not a place apart from Here, beyond the moon or past the vault of heaven. "If you are looking for the place where the soul is [once it has left the body], you must look for the place where [substance and reality and the divine] are; but in looking you must not look for it with your eyes or in the way you look for bodies" (IV.3.24.27–9). The soul is not another sort of body, briefly interfused with flesh and blood but destined to outlive that union – though Plotinus does seem to give some weight to the idea of "astral bodies," acquired in the soul's "passage" through the vault of heaven (IV.3.15.1–4). Without soul there could be no bodies – and therefore no body separate from soul. René Descartes's insistence that there are two separate and unrelated sorts of substance (namely extension[1] and thought) is not something that any Platonist could accept. Nor did Plotinus, unlike Descartes, suppose that we could easily "know" our "inner" or "mental" being: " 'Know Yourself' is said to those who because of their selves' multiplicity have the business of counting themselves up and learning that they do not know all the numbers and kinds of things they are, or do not know any one of them, nor what their ruling principle is, or by what they are themselves" (VI.7.41.22–6). But it would be pedantic to deny that Plotinus was, in another sense, a dualist. "For every man is double, one of him is the sort of compound being and one of him is himself" (II.3.9.31–2). It is these two "dualisms," one apparent and one real, that need exposition here. The second, which requires that each of us has an "inner" or an "upper" self, already distinguishable from the matter-entrapped "outer" self, is a doctrine that perhaps receives a little more emphasis after Porphyry's arrival, but it would be rash to suppose that it was therefore an innovation.

Porphyry included most of the treatises dealing with the soul in Book Four of the *Enneads*, and that can, despite its chronological disorder, serve as a good introduction to the present topic. But Plotinus's arguments, and aphorisms, on the subject may be found throughout the *Enneads*. I shall myself make most reference to the treatises *On the Immortality of the Soul* (IV.7), *On the Essence of the Soul* (IV.1), *On the Descent of the Soul into Bodies* (IV.8), *If All Souls are One* (IV.9), *On the Three Primary Hypostases* (V.1), *On our Allotted Guardian Spirit* (III.4),[2] *On the Presence of Being* (VI.4–5), *On Difficulties About the Soul* (IV.3–5), *Against the Gnostics* (II.9),[3] *How the Multitude of Forms Came into Being, and on the Good* (VI.7), *On Well-Being* (I.4), *On Providence* (III.2–3), *On Whether the Stars are Causes* (II.3), and *What is the Living Being and What is Man?* (I.1). We have Porphyry's word for it (*Life* 8.1–12) that Plotinus neither revised his treatises nor wrote preliminary drafts of any parts of them. Nor did he give them titles, or arrange them in the order that is now canonical (*Life* 4.17–18; 24.5–16). What he says of the soul is also true of his work: "it is like a long life stretched out at length; each part is different from that which comes next in order, but the whole is continuous with itself, but with one part differentiated from another, and the earlier does not perish in the later" (V.2.2.26–30).

I THE BODY'S NEED OF SOUL

That Plotinus did argue for his conclusions may come as a surprise to those who think of him as poet and mystic. It would not have been irrational of him to rely upon experience and lively intuition for his doctrine. My own conviction that I have a name and human ancestry is not one that I could prove was true to someone eager to doubt it. Why should I attempt to prove (what may be just as obvious to me) that "[my] birth is but a sleep and a forgetting"?[4] Plotinus nonetheless did argue, and what he had to say against alternative conceptions of human being still has force.

"Man could not be a simple thing, but there is in him a soul, and he has a body as well" (IV.7.1.4–6). If that soul were itself corporeal it would be divisible, and whatever part of it gave life to the composite "soul" would be the real soul (IV.7.2.9–11). What sort of body could it be that was, by its own nature, living? Fire, air, earth and water, and any other corporeal element, are "lifeless of themselves": how could they, singly, or collectively, produce life? The soul cannot, in brief, be a body, both because bodies are always composites (and so in need of an ordering principle), and because no available bodily stuff is essentially life-giving. "How could the composition of the elements have any sort of life?" (IV.9.5.18–19). To explain the fact that some things are alive at all there must be something that is essentially alive, to which we give the name of soul.

For certainly all things cannot have a borrowed life: or it will go on to infinity; but there must be some nature which is primarily alive, which must be indestructible and immortal of necessity since it is also the origin of life to others. . . . This then which is primarily and always existent cannot be dead, like a stone or wood, but must be alive. (IV.7.9.7–25)

No corporeal stuff will do – though any such stuff, it turns out later, must also be alive (VI.7.10.44–6). The apparent contradiction can be avoided: nothing extended and divisible is alive in virtue of its corporeal properties, but anything that is identifiable as something is, to that extent, a unity – and alive (since what makes it a unity also makes it living). Stones, qua separated stones, are only fragments, broken from the living earth (IV.4.27.9–12).

Nothing, moreover, that is "united with itself in community of feeling can come from bodies which are without feeling and unable to be united" (IV.7.3.4–6). In the absence of such an indivisible unifying principle "there would be many souls directing each one of us," without any shared perception (IV.1.2.9–10). In fact, it is one and the same soul that is "present in" both foot and hand "as perceptions show" (VI.4.1.25–7). Bodies can only exist alongside each other, and cannot penetrate each other "whole through whole": souls are present throughout the relevant bodies, and so are not themselves corporeal (IV.7.8^2.21–3). Similarly, when a body is cut (and the living being feels that pain) this is precisely because the soul itself has not been cut (IV.4.19.9f). "Pain is consciousness of withdrawal of a body which is being deprived of the image of soul" (IV.4.19.2–3). If the withdrawal were complete, there could be no remaining pain. "The image," or trace, or shadow, or soul which, as it were, warms the body of an animal or plant, is what constitutes it as a unit (IV.4.18.4–8). There is "another soul," of which I shall speak below, "the dominant or essential part of us" (IV.4.18.15–16), but the distinction Plotinus draws is not between "the soul" and the soulless body. There can be no single body that is not informed and regulated by the unifying principle, nor any perception that is not the perception of the soul. "If anything is going to perceive anything, it must itself be one and perceive every object by one and the same means. . . . For there is not one perception of the nose and another of the eyes, but one and the same perception of all together" (IV.7.6.3–9).

Later philosophers, faced by the difficulty of explaining "life" or "sentience" or "thought," have sometimes appealed to the notion of "emergent" properties. Even if the parts of which an entity is wholly composed are "dead" (insentient, unthinking), they say, the entity itself may still, predictably, be living, sentient, and thoughtful. The other supposedly emergent properties they instance to make this magical event more plausible (as that atoms of oxygen and hydrogen are not wet, but water is) are no help at all. Insofar as "being wet" is a phenomenal property it is an example of exactly the sort of thing whose existence in a dead, unthinking universe is puzzling. Insofar as its "emergence" is not puzzling, this is because "being wet" only means being in a certain, mathematically predictable relationship with other atoms. Others have hoped to analyze the "higher" properties entirely into properties possessed by the parts (as could perhaps be done with physical wetness). On those latter terms a "living" thing is only an aggregate the movement of whose parts add up in a particular way which have given an evolutionary advantage. Since neither subjective sentience nor (as Plotinus pointed out: I.4.2.31–43) reason itself can be shown to give such an advantage, there have even been determined evolutionists who have denied the very existence of what is most obvious, our own powers of thought and feeling. Neither "emergence" nor "reduction" offers much by way of explanation; emergentists rely on magic, and reductionists on our credulity. Plotinus argues that any composite thing must be made up either of homogeneous or of heterogeneous parts. But a composite soul would therefore be made of soulless things (things unlike each other, and the whole), or else be quantifiably larger than the lesser "souls" that make it up: either alternative is absurd (IV.3.2.29–35). Pure materialism is founded on an extraordinary error: we first postulate a world devoid of all phenomenal or subjective properties, and then find with surprise that such a world contains nothing to explain the existence of those properties. Plotinus was wiser.

This rejection of both emergentism and reductionism may seem to make him an ally of Cartesian dualism, the belief (as above) that there are *two* sorts of substance, body and soul. The truth is more subtle: there can be no body at all, not even the smallest visible unit, without soul. But, *pace* the panpsychists, the soul, the livingness, of each larger whole is not compounded from the souls of all its parts. The explanation runs the other way: there are lesser beings because the soul forgets more and more of its own being, involving itself perpetually in tinier events.

When a soul does this for a long time, flying from the All and standing apart in distinctness, and does not look towards the intelligible, it has become a part and is isolated and weak and fusses and looks towards a part and in its separation from the whole it embarks on one single thing and flies from everything else. . . . It is by now applying itself to and caring for things outside and is present and sinks deep into the individual part. (IV.8.4.13–22)

On which more hereafter.

"Neither any of the parts of the soul nor the whole soul are in body as in a place. . . . It is certainly not in the body as in a receptacle either" (IV.3.20.10–12, 15–16). Neither is the soul a property of the underlying material (IV.3.20.28). Even the analogy of a steersman and a ship is inadequate: "this is a good comparison as far as the soul's ability to be separate from the body goes, but would not supply very satisfactorily the manner of its presence" (IV.3.21.6–8). Oddly, Plotinus actually uses the comparison, a few chapters earlier, to describe the dangers of too great an absorption in bodily concerns: just so "the steersmen of ships in a storm concentrate more and more on the care of their ships and are unaware that they are forgetting themselves, that they are in danger of being dragged down with the wreck of their ships" (IV.3.17.23–6). But in both chapters the point is that the soul's or steersman's "presence" is not spatial. "If the soul was altogether one, in the sense of being altogether indivisible and a self-contained unity . . . then nothing soul took hold of would ever be ensouled as a whole: but soul would set itself, so to speak, at the centre of each living being and leave the whole mass of it soulless" (IV.1.2.35–40). As even Descartes was to remark: "if an angel were in a human body he would not have sensations as we do, but would simply perceive the motions which are caused by external objects and in this way would differ from a real man."[5] So far from the soul's being any sort of ghost in a machine, it is matter that is close to being a figment, and given such being as it has by soul. Loosed from the body, we may be (as it were) an angel: loosed from the soul, the body is dissolved (see V.1.2).

Extended bodies are unified, and set in motion by soul; effects upon those bodies are experienced by the soul. By its involvement with corporeal, extended, being, the soul may lose touch with it own noncorporeality. It may be reminded by reckoning with the phenomena of memory, judgment, and self-awareness. A merely corporeal model of memory (impressions upon wax, perhaps) does not explain why later impressions do not obliterate the earlier (IV.7.6.38–50). Even if affections belong to the (ensouled) body, judgments (which class includes perceptions) are noncorporeal, not such as to affect the underlying substance of the soul (III.6.1.4–27). "The whole soul perceives the affection in the body without being affected by it" (IV.4.19.13). A fortiori, those forms of thought that deal with the incorporeal, the partless, must themselves be incorporeal. "How will something which is a size think what is not a size and think what is partless with something which has parts?" (IV.7.8.10–13). It is this last consideration which might create another duality, between human and subhuman soul.

II BEASTS AND INNER ANGELS

"Dualism," as this is commonly understood, postulates two sorts of substance, weirdly interwoven. If the defining character of "soul" is self-motion, or sentience, then plants and animals can be regarded as amphibia like ourselves (see IV.8.4.32–3): bodies and souls together. If the essence of soul is judgment, and the capacity to attend to noncorporeal substance, it will seem easier to place nonhuman creatures entirely in the corporeal camp (as Descartes's followers did with more enthusiasm than their master). Plotinus accepts neither of these hypotheses. The body of an animal or plant has a sort of shadow, or trace, of soul: when a body becomes a living body that is what it gains (VI.4.15.12–18). "And pain or bodily pleasure affect a body which is so qualified; but the pain of this body and pleasure of this kind result for us in a dispassionate knowledge" (IV.4.18.7–11). Animals (nonhuman animals, that is) do not realize that they are in pain, that pain is what they are in.[6] They are "angry because of their temperaments, but not because it appears to them that they have been ill-treated" (IV.4.28.33–4). Bodily affections may encourage us to make poor judgments, but their nature lies outside such judgments. "The beast is the body which has been given life. But the true man is different, clear of these affections" (I.1.10.7–8). And what of brute beasts (thêria), themselves? "If as it is said there are sinful human souls in them, the separable part of the soul does not come to belong to the beasts but is there without being there for them" (I.1.11.8–12).

Even in man "the better part does not always dominate" (III.4.2.6). Once "out of the body [the soul] becomes what there was most of in it. . . . Those, then, who guarded the man in them become men again. Those who lived by sense alone become animals; but if their sense-perceptions have been accompanied by passionate temper they become wild animals" (III.4.2.11–12, 16–18). "The man who practised community virtue becomes a man again; but one who has a lesser share of it a creature that lives in community, a bee or something of that sort" (III.4.2.28–31). The soul that was in man may turn aside to help make a lesser thing, though something just as necessary to the splendor of "the complete living being," which is the whole (VI.7.7.1–6, 31–2). "Hence Plato says that the soul enters into other living beings, in the sense that the soul becomes different and the rational principle is altered, in order that what was formerly the soul of a man may become the soul of an ox; so that the worse being is justly dealt with" (III.3.4.42–4). All those different shapes, and the cycle of predation, are no more than "transformations into each other of animals which could not stay as they are for ever" (III.2.15.18–19). "It is like on the stage, when the actor who has been murdered changes his costume and comes on again in another character" (III.2.15.22–3). The only difference, we may imagine, between men and brutes is that men are allowed to recognize that they are playing. Poor actors get worse parts (III.2.17.49).

Even within a human lifetime we have different parts to play, as Wordsworth, after many others, tells us.

> And with new joy and pride
> The little Actor cons another part;
> Filling from time to time his "humourous stage"
> With all the Persons, down to palsied Age,
> That Life brings with her in her equipage[7]

The Persons, or Parts, we play are not identical with the very self.[8] That self may, on the one hand, so far "bury itself" in corporeal concerns as to be detached, almost, from its own eternal being. It may, on the other hand, so far detach itself as to be reunified, or reidentified, with the abiding *daimon*, or angel, that is its real beginning. "If a man follows the spirit which is above him, he comes to be himself alone, living that spirit's life, and giving the pre-eminence to that better part of himself to which he is being led" (III.4.3.17–21).

There are in a way two men: the composite being "here below," and "the man Plato was defining [which] he indicated . . . rides upon the one which primarily uses a body" (VI.7.5.23–5). "Man, and especially the good man, is not the composite of soul and body" (I.4.14.1–4), but the soul directed upwards (or inwards) to the intellect. Such a man provides for what belongs to him: "that is, he seeks it for the body which is joined to him; and even granting that this is a living body, it lives its own life and not the life which is that of the good man" (I.4.4.27–31). "Even if the death of friends causes grief, it does not grieve him but only that in him which has no intelligence" (I.4.4.34–6):

For really here in the events of our life it is not the soul within but the outward shadow of man which cries and moans and carries on in every sort of way on a stage which is the whole earth. . . . For only the seriously good part of man is capable of taking serious things seriously; the rest of man is a toy. (III.2.15.47–51, 53–5)

That part of the soul which does not descend is at once the same and not the same as that which does: we may identify ourselves with either, but must look in different directions, so to speak, to do so. Our outer or lower selves may be distracted and confused by bodily perceptions, but do not wholly lose, as long as we are human, the chance to look toward that other. "Their heads are firmly set above in heaven. But they experienced a deeper descent because their middle part was compelled to care for that to which they had gone on, which needed their care" (IV.3.12.5–8).

There are four relevant possibilities. The first is the brute, incapable in its mortal life of looking back at its own eternal soul, as that is governed by intellect. The second is the ordinary, sensual human being, capable of remembering itself, but too deeply absorbed in sense to try. It is possible that the higher soul of someone like that is noble, even though the other soul is "a rather bad one, forcibly restrained by the higher soul" (IV.3.32.10–11). Once free of that particular incarnation the higher soul may recollect itself. The third possibility is the aspiring soul whose intellect, or whose intellect-inspired soul, is still distinguishable from his everyday living, but who is still trying to remember. Wordsworth again, addressing such a one:

> Thou, over whom thy Immortality
> Broods like the Day, a Master o'er a Slave,
> A Presence which is not to be put by,
> Thou little Child.[9]

The fourth is the good man, in whom intellect is active: "he is then himself a spirit or on the level of a spirit, and his guardian spirit is God [or a god]" (III.4.6.3–4). Porphyry suggests that this was the moral that Plotinus drew from his curious experience in the temple of Isis: when Plotinus's guardian spirit was evoked it turned out to be a god (*Life* 10.15–31).

Good men, in brief, are wholly identified, in thought, with what intellect requires, and treat their living bodies almost as animals in their charge – or even as a gardener cares about the maggots in the rotten part of a plant "for that is what the ensouled body is like in the all" (IV.3.4.29–33).

> Consume my heart away; sick with desire
> And fastened to a dying animal
> It knows not what it is; and gather me
> Into the artifice of eternity.[10]

The significant division does not lie between "humans" and "nonhumans," but between the eternal and the temporal selves. "There," in the eternal, we were (and are) indivisible, and even "here," spread thinly, the soul "is not divided in that it gives itself whole to the whole and is divided in that it is present in every part" (IV.2.1.20–2). How does it happen that we *are* "here"? Not, Plotinus thinks, because that is the sort of thing we are:

No, even before this coming to be came to be we were there, men who were different and some of us even gods, pure souls and intellect united with the whole of reality; we were parts of the intelligible, not marked off or cut off but belonging to the whole; and we are not cut off even now. But now, another man, wishing to exist, approached that man. . . . And we have come to be the pair of them, not the one we were before. (VI.4.14.17–23, 28–30)

That "other man" is presumably to be equated with the "restlessly active nature which wanted to control itself and be on its own [which] moved and time moved with it" (III.7.11.14–17). "It did not want the whole to be present to it altogether" (III.7.11.21–2). "There" there was (and is) no need of memory, since all is present (IV.4.1.12–16). "But if it comes out of the intelligible world, and cannot endure unity, but embraces its own individuality and wants to be different and so to speak puts its head outside, it thereupon acquires memory" (IV.4.3.11–13). What it remembers (earth or heaven) determines what it is (IV.4.3.7–8). "The shade of Heracles in Hades . . . remembers all that he did in his life," but Heracles himself, once he is freer from bodily contamination, "will go over again in its memory also what it did not have in this life" (IV.3.27.8–9, 19–20). During this life, if "one soul is in tune with the other, their image-making powers are not separate, and that of the better soul is dominant, the image becomes one" (IV.3.31.9–13). "And what will the soul remember when it has come to be in the intelligible world?" (IV.4.1.1–2). Not, we can be sure, the heroic deeds it has been involved with in this life, with an accompanying dictum "It was I did them (not those other, unheroic, acts)." In a way, it does not remember anything, since everything it might need is present to it, forever. Whether it will need to know any particular lifetime as "its own," who knows?

III INDIVIDUAL SOULS AND THE WORLD SOUL

That element of Plotinus's theory might well lead us to conclude that it is really wrong to think of oneself as one self among many. True wisdom should require us to reject the notion that "my" body and experience have any privileges: even if, in this world here, the soul experiences itself as multiple, having access only to individual occasions, we should remind ourselves that truth is the same for all. Coming to realize reality "I" find only what every "other" soul will find, and so recall my, our, unity. Remembering itself, "it will not even have the remembrance of itself, or that it is the man himself, Socrates for instance, who is contemplating" (IV.4.2.1–3). How could it, if what it contemplates is all and only what every other contemplative soul is (timelessly) contemplating? Even when, being embodied, there are different (partial) experiences in different parts, "it is what is judged that is different, not what judges" (VI.4.6.7–12).

Does it seem surprising that there is, "really," only one soul? How could there be, if there are many different living beings, each acquainted only with its own vicinity? But that difference, between the composites, proves nothing: "it is certainly not necessary that when I have a perception the other should also have exactly the same experience. For even in one body one hand does not perceive what happens to the other, but the soul in the whole body" (IV.9.2.7–10). The facts that "we suffer with others from seeing their pain and feel happy and relaxed [in their company]," that spells and magical acts draw men together, and that a quiet word affects far distant things also serve as evidence that the soul is one. (IV.9.3.1–9)

Is that one soul best understood as the world soul? According to Plotinus, no.

There could be no one world, no cosmos, if there were no unifying soul. Plotinus applies the same arguments to the world as a whole as to an individual organism: if all were corporeal "it would not be one soul which would direct this universe, but innumerable souls separate from each other. . . . For the talk about continuity, if this does not gather to a unity is futile" (IV.1.2.9–12). Without a unifying, noncorporeal principle, the All would be completely senseless, moving at random (IV.7.3.30–1). Any putative corporeal principle could only have one effect, "for it does not belong to fire to cool things, nor to the cold to make them hot" (IV.7.4.29–30), but whatever it is that keeps the All together does many different things (and so must be the noncorporeal principle, the soul). It is by its power that "the heaven is one, thought it is multiple in one part in one place and one in another" (V.1.2.39–40). "The universe extends as far as soul goes" (IV.3.9.46–7). The All is not like a soulless house: "it exists, all awake and alive differently in different parts and nothing can exist which does not belong to it" (IV.4.36.13–15). There never was a time when the cosmos was unsouled (IV.3.9.16–17), "For how could the parts have a soul when the All was soulless?" (IV.3.7.7–8). The distinction between the higher, detached soul and the lower, absorbed soul applies here too: "the administration of the universe is like that of a single living being, where there is one kind which works from outside . . . and another kind which works from inside (IV.4.11.1–3). On this account, it may seem clear that "we," these human animals, are no more than segments of the cosmos, of the well-ordered whole, and wisdom lies in realizing this. This body-here does only, and says only, what the whole decrees.

But Plotinus recognizes the many problems this creates.

On this assumption we are not ourselves, nor is there any act which is our own. We do not reason but our considered reasonings are the reasonings of another. Nor do we act, any more than our feet kick; it is we who kick through parts of ourselves. But really, each separate thing must be a separate thing; there must be actions and thoughts that are our own; each one's good and bad actions must come from himself, and we must not attribute the doing of bad actions at least to the All. (III.1.4.21–9)

"How if all things are well done, can the doers act unjustly or err?"
(III.2.16.3–4).

It is true that it is from the stars, the Spindle of Necessity, that
"we get our moral characters, our characteristic actions, and our
emotions: so what is left which is 'we'? Surely that which we really
are, we to whom nature gave power to master our passions"
(II.3.9.13–14). "As for the fact that we are begotten inside the universe, in the womb too we say that the soul which comes into the
child is another one, not that of the mother" (IV.3.7.29–31). The soul
descending into matter passes through the heavens, and has a celestial body before it reaches down as far as here. That is why our
earthly fortunes and lives "are indicated by the figures made by the
heavenly bodies" (IV.3.12.23–4). "All souls illuminate the heavens
and give it the greatest and first part of themselves, but illuminate
the rest of the world with their secondary parts" (IV.3.17.8–10). So
even if what we are and do is figured in the heavens it does not
follow that it is not *our* nature that is responsible. The soul of the
All does not simply extend to all that we are and do, although it is
open to "us" so far to forget ourselves as indeed to become no more
than parts (IV.3.15.11–15). "So we must fly from here and separate
ourselves from what has been added to us, and not be the composite
thing. . . . To the other soul . . . belongs the ascent to the higher
world." Whoever fails thus to withdraw "is bereft of this higher soul
and lives under destiny and then the stars do not only show him
signs but he also becomes a part and follows along with the whole of
which he is a part" (II.3.9.20–1, 24–31).

The Stoic wise man does what Nature requires of him, and knows
that he always did (even when he wasn't wise). The Plotinian wise
man is no such undivided part, but a real agent whose living body may
be swayed by the movements of that larger body, the cosmos, but who
is not identical with that body. His soul is a particular version of the
Soul (or else the Soul itself is present in all its temporal manifestations), but it is not therefore derived from the soul of the cosmos: that
latter soul is our sister, not our mother, and just as derivative. That
sister soul has made the cosmos ready for us, and looks toward the
Intellect itself, whereas our souls come to inhabit a world already
made, and look to our own partial intellects (IV.3.6.13–17). Our lives
really are *our* choices, and not just the working out of what our sister
chooses, because it is we who, "before time," choose what lot to enjoy

(III.4.5.2–5). Equivalently, "each soul comes down to a body made ready for it according to its resemblance to the soul's disposition" (IV.3.12.37–8). We have chosen, that is, the role already, but it is still entirely up to us how we shall play it.

The injustice one man does another is certainly an injustice from the point of view of the doer, and the man who perpetrates it is not free from guilt, but as contained in the universal order it is not unjust in that order, or in relation to the sufferer, but it was ordained that he should so suffer. (IV.3.16.18–22)

"No real being ever ceases to be" (IV.3.5.6): it does not follow that every single mortal individual abides as a really distinct being. Many such individuals, after all, are incarnations of one-and-the-same particular soul. But although the soul of the cosmos has greater power and purity it is not the only real soul. Socrates, at any rate, abides, rather as does a theorem belonging to a science: "each theorem contains the whole science potentially, but the science is none the less a whole" (IV.3.2.53–5; see IV.9.5.23–9).

IV TURNING FROM THE BODY

According to Porphyry (not necessarily the best witness) Plotinus "seemed ashamed of being in a body," and so "could never bear to talk about his race or his parents or his native country" (*Life* 1.2–5). Maybe this is how others thought Plotinus must feel (cf. IV.9.7.4–5: "the soul . . . should not be annoyed with itself because . . . it occupies a middle rank among realities"). Apollo's commemorative oracle claims that Plotinus, "freed from this tabernacle . . . and the tomb which held [his] heavenly soul" reaches the company of heaven, where dwell the spirits of the righteous (*Life* 22.95). According to the oracle (and Porphyry) he did "everything to be delivered and 'escape from the bitter wave of blood-drinking life here' " (*Life* 23.6–7). This is not to say that he sought to end his life.

Someone who manages to wipe away irrational desires and passions, may come to see the immortal god in himself, or else (equivalently) "self-control and justice . . . standing in itself like splendid statues all rusted with time which it has cleaned" (IV.7.10.10, 31–2, 44–7; see also I.1.12.12–17). The rust of time ensures that few souls, if any, are wholly in control while "in the body," since they then form part of an order with other things. "The better soul has power over more, the worse over less" (III.1.8.11–15), but any embodied soul will find the body something of a hindrance to thought and a source of pleasures, desires, and griefs (IV.8.2.43–5). All of us are "here" because we have been seduced, as it were, by our own images "in the mirror of Dionysus" (IV.3.12.1–3). That seduction cannot be reversed by suicide, nor even by self-hatred. "While we have bodies we must stay in our houses, which have been built for us by a good sister soul" (II.9.18.14–16). Suicide, in most cases, actually shows that we think too much about our bodies, not too little (I.9). "He once noticed," Porphyry says, "that I was thinking of removing myself from this life. He came to me unexpectedly . . . and told me that this lust for death did not come from a settled rational decision but from a bilious indisposition, and urged me to go away on holiday" (*Life* 11.12–16).

Our fall into matter (I.8.14.44) is at once the occasion and the cause of our mistaken belief or feeling that we are, each of us, a being at once all too dependent on material circumstance, and all too independent of all other beings. Our living bodies are like maggots in a plant, or like the rotten part of a plant which, qua gardener, we should care for. "The good man will reduce and gradually extinguish his bodily advantages by neglect, and will put away authority and office. He will take care of his bodily health, but will not wish to be altogether without experience of illness, nor indeed also of pain" (I.4.14.19–23). "One must understand that things do not look to the good man as they look to others; none of his experiences penetrate to the inner self" (I.4.8.10–13).

It is difficult to persuade good modernists that this is anything but pathological. It seems obvious to them that "decent" people welcome bodily pleasures, and must recognize all pain, their own and others', as the sort of evil that could never really be transformed into a good. To suggest, as Plotinus does, that one should not be inwardly affected by the suffering of others (I.4.8.13–24) merely confirms, for them, the essential "inhumanity" of dualism. But there is no reason to doubt that Plotinus was compassionate in a better sense: witness his care of orphans, and – in case they turned out *not* to be philosophers – their property (*Life* 9.13–16). He was not made miserable by the pain of others (nor by his own), but sought "to stand up to the blows of fortune like a great trained fighter" (I.4.8.24–6). The spurious "compassion" he and other philosophers have criticized is not the same as genuine compassion: that is not displayed by those who hide the sufferings of others away (lest they themselves be distressed by seeing them), nor those who think that suffering must make us worse. Those who take no more than they need, and find their own well-being in something that is inexhaustibly sufficient to share with everyone, have a better claim to virtue. No doubt – as Plotinus said – we should acknowledge what is beautiful, in the world, in beautiful bodies, in justice and the moral order (I.6.4.4–13). For that very reason, it is wise not to imagine that we can "possess" such beauty, except by becoming beautiful.

Our trouble is that, being bodily, we seek to possess things for ourselves: that is, indeed, the cause of being bodily. Being bodily, we are divided from each other, and easily assume that *our* good is something other than another's. Plotinus's conviction is that there is something spurious about a world spread out in space and time, where every apparent point is equally Now, Here, and I, but finds every other point opaque to it (so that they are at once entirely different and the same). Here we have to decode each other's meanings; "there" our whole body speaks, "and nothing is hidden or feigned" (IV.3.18.21–4). "The heavenly regions are better adapted to participate [in soul]. But the body of earth is the last and less naturally adapted to participate in soul and far from the bodiless nature" (IV.3.17.5–8). I am one, even though my body is extended over space and time, indefinitely divisible, and constantly losing touch with what it was. In becoming aware of my own unity my attention is already diverted from the world of sense (which only reveals disunities). Recognizing that "my body" is a part of a much greater whole, that even "my intellect" only realizes "a potentiality which the universal intellect includes" (IV.8.3.15–16), and that I may as easily be the same in many different bodies as on many different occasions, I can begin to recall myself. "Often I have woken up out of the body to my self," he says, "and have entered into myself, going out from all other things" (IV.8.1.1–3). "Man and especially the good man is not the composite of soul and body; separation from the body and despising of its so-called goods make this plain" (I.4.14.1–4). The true self neither thinks things through to an otherwise unknown conclusion (IV.3.18.2–5), nor remembers things that are not always present to it (IV.3.25.27–30).

Really, there is nothing that is truly ours that we can lose. Whatever seems to have been lost and divided from us, in this changing world, is There, where "all things are filled full of life, and, we may say, boiling with life" (VI.7.12.23–4). Aesop's fable of the dog who lost his *real* bone because he jealously required the bone he saw reflected in the water would have appealed to Plotinus. We are "here" because our souls mistook reflections for the Real, and our only way of escape is to recall what truly is, and whence we came.

> Hence in a season of calm weather
> Though inland far we be,
> Our Souls have sight of that immortal sea
> Which brought us hither.[11]

Plotinus's last words, allegedly, were " 'Try to bring back the god in you to the divine in the All,' and, as a snake crept under the bed on which he was lying and disappeared into a hole in the wall, he breathed his last" (*Life* 2.26–7). The symbolism is Porphyry's, not Plotinus's: the goal, to grow away from shadows, was Plotinus's.

NOTES

1 Which strictly, for Descartes, includes both matter and space.
2 All of which were written before Porphyry's arrival.
3 Porphyry left Rome after the forty-fifth treatise had been written (*Life* ch.5).
4 Wordsworth *Ode: Intimations of Immortality* section 5: 1950: 460.
5 Descartes 1981, 128 (January 1642).
6 It doesn't follow that they are not in pain.
7 Wordsworth *Ode* section 7: 1950: 461.
8 See Clark 1991.
9 Wordsworth *Ode* section 8: 1950: 461.
10 Yeats *Sailing to Byzantium:* 1950: 218.
11 Wordsworth *Ode* section 9: 1950: 462.

12 Human freedom in the thought of Plotinus

To the memory of Jean Trouillard

Freedom belongs to the category of issues that affect the whole of Plotinus's metaphysics. Insofar as they are not merely beings ranged in a hierarchy but also moments in an infinite process by which the One expresses itself and infinitely offers itself as the Good, all aspects of this metaphysics, whether subjective or objective, are brought into play by freedom. Metaphysics must give an account of this process; it must express its dynamic and offer an explanation of its principal stages in narrative form. Consequently, what is at issue is nothing other than the freedom of each being to evolve or act, depending on its nature, within the context of the whole conceived systematically as depending upon and manifesting the One. "Freedom" has the same meaning at every level: that of a being to be what it is. This meaning pertains to the identity of the Good and Being: "It is obvious that the Good is in being, and in being it would clearly be for each individual in himself" (VI.5.1.23–5). One can legitimately ask, therefore, in what sense can we say that freedom is not identical with necessity? Indeed, in what sense is there even a place for freedom in a universal emanationism?

It might seem paradoxical to turn to the concept of necessity in order to characterize a dynamic metaphysics of process. To interpret Plotinus in a way faithful to his intuitions, however, it is useful to distinguish two types of necessity. On the one hand, there is a preeminent form of necessity that is essentially set out in a polar relationship with the hazards of contingency but for all that no less opposed to the constraints of a vulgar determinism. According to Plotinus's interpretation of this concept in IV.8, that being is necessary which could be no other than it is and which owes its existence only to itself. In the case of the One, therefore, this necessity must be understood as self-engenderment and self-causation (VI.8.14.41–2), and it is in this sense that freedom and necessity are both equally opposed to chance and contingency. This pre-eminent necessity – of that which exists of itself – differs from another, lesser necessity, the conception of which is inherited from the fatalist tradition, in which necessity (*ananke*) is interpreted as inevitability or fate (*heimarmene*). The universe is represented as a causal chain and freedom is specifically excluded. Far from being the freedom of that which causes itself, this necessity appears as the consequence of an external determination and is the opposite of a power. Plotinus has always stressed the richness of an eminent concept of necessity, as opposed to the lower concept, which he nevertheless discusses in his treatises on Fate and Providence in the third *Ennead*.

The metaphysical process taken as a whole is distinguished by two symmetrical movements, for which Plotinus proposes a number of different images – the imagery of descent and ascent and that of radiation and concentration are only the best known of these. This might be the process by which the One makes possible the differentiation which then goes on to express itself as Life, or it might be the movement by which this Life, expressed in the diversity of souls, seeks infinitely to find its starting point and unite with it; in each case the problem of freedom is none other than the troubled and negative side of necessity. Only this necessity can constitute the true positivity within which Plotinus's monism can find its legitimacy. It contains freedom within itself, which in many ways links Plotinus's philosophy with the modern metaphysics of Spinoza or Bergson: for them as for Plotinus, freedom is accomplished through an unavoidable and irreducible necessity. Is this position paradoxical? This is the question to be addressed by this essay, with particular reference to human freedom.

We should begin by specifying that the concept itself, of freedom, only appears very indirectly in Plotinian metaphysics. An effort to reconstruct this concept can be based only on two sets of texts: *On Free Will and the Will of the One*, VI.8, and a scattered set of comments touching on the activity of the soul. The teaching of the former (VI.8) shows that human freedom constitutes only the weakest possible level of a superior, pre-eminent, and ineffable freedom characteristic of the One itself. Indeed, Plotinus allows himself to go so far as to ask about the freedom of the One itself. Even if a priori this might seem like a damning question, since it implies some form of subjectivizing, which is intolerable, he still formulates it in VI.8, if only to exclude the thesis of the contingency of the One. More than any other thesis, this exclusion of a contingent advent of the One, the refutation of any formulation that would imply some form of genesis, points to Plotinus's central intuition and the heart of his conception of freedom. Plotinus in effect adheres to necessity as the superior form of all existence and all essence, rather than to freedom conceived, for example, in Aristotle's moral philosophy, as the power to chose and to act, since this latter concept is immediately marked by hesitation and contingency and for this reason is irreconcilable with the Neoplatonic world-view. Within this necessity, the most important predicates standing against the hazards of weak, servile, and contingent action are those of power, sovereignty, and actuality. Thus, existence realizes itself only when it has attained the immutability conferred by virtue; within this virtue, it discovers at once its freedom and necessity.

Despite these strong metaphysical premises, a form of ethical liberty is predicated of the soul, though in an ambivalent and unsystematical way, as being conceivable in the context of human action. Here we must note, however, to what extent each text belonging to this set offers a different answer to the problem of freedom, inasmuch as this problem is neither central nor explicitly formulated. When one seeks to produce a reconstruction of these texts, the distinction between the conceptual concepts of descent (procession) and ascent (purification) allows one to separate two series of preoccupations: the first constitutes the metaphysics of the soul and of its movement and inclinations; the second concerns ethics properly speaking. In both cases – and this remark deserves a philological elaboration that cannot be offered here – it is necessary to insist on the inchoate and imprecise character of the philosophical lexicon of freedom. The distinctions between voluntary, deliberate, determined, free, and self-determined, which later on will become so important, are discussed neither in the description of moral action, which is principally inherited from Aristotle's ethics and the commentaries of Alexander of Aphrodisias, nor in the explanation of the metaphysical procession. In particular, it is clear that for Plotinus, as for Greek philosophy in general, voluntariness in no way implies deliberate choice. We shall briefly examine this point below.

I

The first series of ideas, then, involves the metaphysics of procession. At stake here is the voluntary nature of the descent of the soul (notably in *Enneads* II.9, IV.3, and IV.8). This issue belongs to the network of *quaestiones vexatae* of interpretation:[1] Does the soul descend voluntarily, that is, does it freely move toward the lower states of its realization, and in particular toward the body? Which soul or which type of soul is free to move in this way? Indeed, the World Soul and individual souls all represent the same type of being, to the extent that they all derive from the hypostatic soul:[2] they also differ substantially from it, due primarily to their different thoughts. As Plotinus teaches in several treatises (notably IV.3 and IV.9), the universe possesses a single soul; while we must conceive of individual liberty, this can only be if we separate this liberty from the global destiny of the living world. In regard to this, the eternal existence of the forms of individuals reinforces their specific destiny. It is very interesting to note that the scope of the Plotinian discussion of individuality is first of all ontological rather than ethical – that is, the discussion is animated by a desire to ensure, paradoxically by limiting it, the identity of the individual soul as a being which subsists, much more than it is motivated by the requirement of providing a foundation for ethics. At no point in this group of treatises does the problem of freedom take on a determining role, for the destiny of the individual appears to participate in a movement which differentiates it, that is, which draws a distinction between it and the very necessity which differentiates beings. Linked together as parts of the Intellect (IV.3.5.15–16), souls remain focused on it. But individual souls do not maintain this orientation, even though a part of each remains oriented toward the Intellect.

The very image of descent is itself inappropriate if intended to connote a spatial movement, since the standard meaning of this voluntary movement is self-abasement (VI.4.16). Inasmuch as it expresses an inclination of the individual soul, this is certainly voluntary (IV.7.13.4), though unintentional and nondeliberate (IV.3.13.17–

18).³ This movement results from a guilty will to be itself (V.1.1.5), but insofar as it participates in the general dynamic of that flow which constitutes the very heart of metaphysics, the self-abasement is determined.⁴ It at once expresses and fulfils the inferior necessity of the procession of Being (II.9.3.11–14), a necessity which represents the chain of begettings and which must not be confounded with the absolute and preeminent necessity of the self-causation characteristic of the One. Despite the differences in emphasis between IV.8, which is chronologically anterior, and II.9, which belongs to the anti-Gnostic polemic, the teaching of Plotinus on this matter is consistent and coherent.⁵

This matter of the freedom to descend echoes difficulties already found in Plato. Plotinus does not miss his chance to bring out what he thinks is in many ways a paradox (IV.8.1.26). His interpretation of the *Phaedrus* and the *Timaeus* is stimulated not only by what seems to him to be a contradiction concerning freedom but also by the role of myth in the expression of the negativity and the process of differentiation. Is it possible, following the *Phaedrus*, to seek to ground the freedom of myth in metaphysics? By interpreting the doctrines of Plato on this subject, Plotinus comes to the following conclusion:

There is then no contradiction between the sowing to birth and the descent for the perfection of the All, and the judgment and the cave, and necessity and free-will (since necessity contains the free-will) and the being in the body as an evil; nor [is there anything inconsistent about] Empedocles' flight from God and wandering nor the sin upon which judgment comes, nor Heraclitus' rest on the flight, nor in general the willingness and also the unwillingness of the descent. For everything which goes to the worse does so unwillingly, but, since it goes by its own motion, when it experiences the worse it is said to be punished for what it did. (IV.8.5.1–10)

This passage is important for two reasons: first because it reinforces the metaphysical compatibility of freedom and necessity, and secondly because it introduces a kind of responsibility which closely resembles fault and error. Within this fault, which comprises the movement specific to free will and submission to a sort of destiny, reside the primitive paradoxes of human freedom: first the basic liberty to proceed, which results from an original self-abasement, and then the empirical freedom of corporeal existence, which is the place and theatre of fault and failure, that is, of the victories of desire.

By using the Kantian empirical vocabulary to characterize lived freedom, that is freedom in existence, we accent the specific nature of
preempirical freedom, which is the freedom of the descending soul.
As long as it is freed from the contingencies of composite life, this
latter freedom is purer and more genuine.

Thus, Plotinus is very conscious of the tragedy of individuation.
He sees the contradiction between two inescapable demands: the
necessity of wishing for inferior existence and the impossibility of
remaining in the realm of the intelligible. He maintains, however,
that in general the descent belongs to the metaphysical order of
procession (II.9.8; IV.3.13.18) and thus takes on a necessary appearance. Thus, it is not exclusively a failing, as in the Gnostic drama-
turgy inherited from the Platonic myth, since the illumination it
brings with it in its inclination toward inferiority is an expression of
kindness (I.1.12.21–8) and a response to the needs of other beings
(IV.8.5.10–15). At this point, then, ontology makes up for the
obscurities – and in a sense for the absurdities – of the mythical
drama of the fall. Moreover, the body plays an essential role in the
process, which affects the soul: bodies are responsible for receiving
form and thus for receiving the soul, according to the principle that
each being receives form according to its capacity (VI.4.3.10). Soul,
body, and matter in interaction with one another are thus coexten-
sively responsible for that which is to become evil.[6] It is not exclusively matter or the material world that introduces evil into the
metaphysical structure, but, correlatively, the fact that the incorporation of the soul into the composite submits it to the wrenching pull
of desire and opens up the possibility of failure and defeat. This
issue, which is essential for understanding the destiny of liberty, is
dealt with in Chapter 7 of the present volume and forms a necessary
background to the problem of that specifically human freedom
which touches the human soul in the composite. Each soul gives
form to a different body; the body of the world soul is purer and more
durable than the bodies of individual living beings.

Insofar as the question of the voluntariness of incarnation first
arises in the context of the soul, and insofar as Plotinus does not
seem preoccupied with the question of whether the Intellect is free
to proceed, one might think that his treatment of these questions
excluded subjectivizing Intellect, even if this Intellect finds itself
involved in a complex relationship of return (epistrophê) and recon-

stitution of its identity in relation to the One, a relationship which lets us presuppose a sort of being of which freedom can be predicated. Intellect is not to be equated in Plotinus's metaphysics to Mind as subject. Not only does Intellect lack the lower desires (IV.7.13.3) but, we must stress, all desire is eternally satisfied in Intellect through the contemplation of the One. Although we must still keep freedom in mind in this context, it can only take the form of a quasi-subject, for when Plotinus spoke of the will of the Intellect to possess everything, he meant it metaphorically (III.8.8.34). This position is generalized in VI.8, where Plotinus insists upon the impossibility of predicating freedom of superior beings for which action is nonexistent (VI.8.4). The cardinal principle here is necessity, which is identified with nature and ultimately with the preeminent freedom characteristic of the One. Thus, the paradox of a freedom whose essence is fulfilled in necessity does not begin to unravel until it reaches the point where Plotinus agrees to ask about the freedom to descend; from here on he agrees to presuppose that this descent might be at once necessary and voluntary. By accepting this possibility, he makes possible a freedom which is later set within the soul and made its focus. The soul cannot stop itself from descending; it is here, in this natural momentum, that it achieves its existence. But this achievement is not complete without the reascension that liberates the soul from desire. The freedom exercised by the soul will then constitute a surpassing of this merely natural, voluntary momentum.

II

It is not easy to understand how the existence of the soul in the composite permits the conception of a sort of freedom which, for the first time in the metaphysical process, does not cancel itself out by becoming identified with necessity. This is nevertheless the position of Plotinus in a second series of texts dealing with his ethics of liberty. Human existence is the site of authentic freedom: a freedom the exercise of which leads back to the transcendental necessity of the Good. This active freedom is identified with the movement toward purification and implies a certain responsibility, for example, in disciplining the passions. So one cannot think in the same way about voluntary descent, which is the necessary form of this tendency, and the liberty of re-ascension. These are, in a manner of speaking, two different freedoms. While remaining voluntary, the descent is also necessary; its characteristic freedom is preempirical, thus conceptually absorbed by the reality of necessity. Ascension, on the other hand, expresses the freedom of risk taking, the sense of choosing or of making an effort, and is proportionately closer to a modern conception of freedom.[7] Indeed, this liberty escapes from the determinism of the system since the soul must struggle to redis-cover its purity, meaning that not all souls will liberate themselves. From here on it is a matter of understanding just how the freedom of liberation is an authentic form of freedom according to Plotinus.

Underlying this proposition is a complex philosophical anthropol-ogy. The theory of the individual soul, inherited from Plato, main-tains that only the superior part of the soul is immutable – this is the rational and divine part, the sovereign part of *Timaeus* 69d. This part of the soul is moreover impassive, as in Aristotle's philosophy (*De anima* 408b2). When the time comes to examine Plotinus's thinking about freedom, this thesis becomes fundamental. In several treatises it seems clear enough that Plotinus wishes to foster an impassive subject able to confront the contingent passions and be shown to be the bearer of freedom.[8] Freedom is in fact a predicate belonging to the human soul, insofar as it maintains its spiritual origin within itself and fulfills its destiny in the ascent and union with the One. Against Plato, Plotinus maintains the continuity of a nondescended part of the soul (IV.8.8). According to the premises of this anthropology, then, freedom is characteristic only of the higher soul.[9] The separation of soul and body fulfills this identification by making it possible to isolate the form of the soul. Through the asceti-cism of philosophy, this separation is then completed and led back to its original destiny, liberation.

One of the first chapters of *Ennead* I.1. unquestionably establishes this anthropology: only that which is composite experiences sensi-bles and passions; this composite alone has desires (I.1.6.4–7); and rational life – the practice of thought – is the prerogative of the soul alone, isolated in its noetic essence. The problem of freedom finds a fundamental resolution at this point, in two ways: first as a tendency toward the Good (I.1.5.27), and second as resistance to and control of the passions. The tendency toward the Good is not an ordinary affec-tion (*pathêma*), but rather an inclination proper to the unquestionably soul. It implies a driving force within the soul: its sovereignty or lordship which is created from reflection and intelligence:

> From these forms, from which the soul alone receives its lordship over the living being, come reasonings, and opinions and acts of intuitive intelligence; and this precisely is where "we" are. That which comes before this is "ours," but "we" in our presidency (hêgemonia) over the living being, are what extends from this point upwards.[10] (hêgemonia, I.1.7.14–19)

Now, this sovereignty is the power of reason. By opening up the soul's thought, understood as illumination (I.1.8.15), to the subjective thought of the self as such, Plotinus made it possible to reflect upon liberty: in its solitary sovereignty, the immobile and impassive soul is "free from all responsibility for the evils that man does and suffers; these concern the living being, the joint entity" (I.1.9.1–3). As for evil, it resides in the momentary power of the bad part of that manifold being which is Man – the victory of desire, of anger, and of the imagination. We can therefore ask how for Plotinus the free self, the sovereign soul, can bring to life this selfhood that can only exist in the composite world? It is a highly problematic relationship that is likely to exist between the sovereign soul, insofar as it is identified with the hegemonic principle of reason and insofar as it is an impassive self, and the empirical self which acts in the composite world. When he writes that "we are many" (polla gar hêmeis [I.1.9.7]), Plotinus might have wanted to insist upon the need to unify the plural nature of subjective experience. At the same time, he identifies the true self and points out its essential otherness. Nonetheless, his thought remains imprecise regarding the possibility of reconciling the two topical conceptions of self which appear to affect his moral psychology: impassive reason and empirical subjectivity which is expressed in the self.

In setting out his anthropology, Plotinus insists on the aspects of separation and struggle which result from the division of the various parts of the soul, aspects which are reinforced by life in the composite.[11] The sovereign soul is thus not only that being in which one accomplishes in a provisional or momentary way an identification with Intellect (V.3.3.34). It is also power over the inferior – power of perspective and of resistance. This links it to that which it resists. That which remains impassive, not having descended, nonetheless remains active insofar as reason plays a role in the life of the composite, that is, of the joint entity. The nature of subjectivity is thus complex (as can be seen in another essay in this volume) precisely due to the overdetermination of its context of moral liberation. The self is only what it is by freely turning toward that which it is not, that is, the Intellect. From this point of view, the thesis that the sovereign soul is faultless immediately confers upon the Plotinian conception of freedom the same intellectualistic character which determines the whole of Greek philosophy's moral psychology. Owing to its intellectual essence and impassivity, the soul is unable to exercise freedom contrary to the Good – it is a freedom which is devoted exclusively to this Good. Error and evil, in consequence, are not free in the strong sense of the word: they are not chosen by the sovereign soul and do not participate in the profound dynamic of metaphysics, of which they constitute the unfathomable material abyss. Rather, they represent the power of the inferior element and therefore result from irrational illusions. The bad soul is full of bad desires (I.6.5.26), but the soul in such a state is not free. It is merely weak and blind (I.8.14). In this Plotinus remains profoundly faithful to Platonic intellectualism (III.2.10; I.8.5.26). "No one does evil voluntarily" is the statement that characterizes this tradition.

Human life is composite life; it is the theatre of passion and desire. No doubt, the problem of the origin of desire is less crucial than that of its diversity and power; the Plotinian psychology is extraordinarily rich as concerns the analysis of desire and of inclination. The vocabulary in this area is complex (hormê, orexis, epithumia, ephêsis, e.g., IV.7.13.1–6) and directly intersects with what we might call the lexicon of freedom, mostly inherited from Aristotle and the Stoics (ekousion, eph'hêmin, boulêsis, autexousion): the boundary is often indistinct between simple inclination and a voluntary surge of fully willing spontaneity. But as we noticed above, this vocabulary does not clearly develop into a neat conceptual vocabulary of willingness and freedom as an autonomous power distinct from an inclination.[12] Desire is constitutive of the voluntary. Moreover, the inclination to act is adventitious for the soul (IV.7.13.4). Like desire, this tendency finds its origin in the living body (IV.4.20–1),[13] which is itself a product of nature. The cycles of development of desire are subject to the surveillance of nature and the soul can resist this desire as it can resist anything corporeal. In this fascinating analysis, the tensions are fundamental: in the separated state, the sovereign soul is an

unassailable power; in the composite, the rational part retains a
certain power, a certain strength. Only the superior part determines
whether the desire will be satisfied (II.2.28). The link between desire
and memory is itself problematic (IV.3.26.35), insofar as it affects the
work of reason. If one can control one's desires, can one become the
master of one's own memory? This question gives some idea of
the subtlety of the considerations in moral psychology within which
the problem of freedom is addressed. We must abandon the attempt
to find a doctrine of freedom in Plotinus's thought that is expressed
in the conventional lexicon of free will, yet, on the other hand, we
can find that doctrine in his rich and consistent reflection on the
power and sovereignty of the soul.

The essential nature of this control is problematized as an effect of
the will (IV.4.12.44): "But in work of which someone is master, and
sole master, what does he need except himself and his own will?" In
his critique of the Aristotelian notion of the soul as entelechy,
Plotinus wants primarily to maintain the possibility of an opposition between reason and desire (IV.7.9). The topical and dynamic
model of the soul elaborated by Plato, mainly in book four of the
Republic, seems essential to Plotinus.[14] The possibility of contrary
actions is evoked twice in this discussion in order to specify the
spirituality of the soul, and in the list of functions underlying this
possibility the will very clearly intervenes (IV.7.8.5–13). Insofar as
this opposition is the basis for a moral psychology where the sovereignty of reason might express itself in a victorious effort against the
inferior powers, one might then conceive of it as constituting the
foundation of Plotinus's thought regarding empirical freedom.

Plotinus recognizes that in this sense our identity is also vested in
our empirical corporeal existence – it would be incorrect to say that
we ourselves did not exist in the concrete composite, even though it
is true that we are preeminently only our impassive, sovereign soul
(I.1.10.5). We are dual beings, and this duality brings with it a double
liberty: the sovereign freedom of the perfect soul and the empirical
freedom of a self existing in action.

We should repeat that for Plotinus as for the whole Platonic tradition, reconciling these two identities is far from being the least of his
difficulties. For while it is true that freedom fulfills the transcendental essence of the soul, notably through the practice of philosophical
purification (and this follows the whole protreptic tradition deriving

from the *Alcibiades*), the question remains: How can freedom be exercised in empirical life? This question has two facets: first, how can we become liberated from the constraints of a life of multiplicity? This first facet has to do with the origin of philosophy and of the desire for union conceived as an expression of nostalgia for our origins. The world of the body can destroy this desire; if the risk is genuine then so must the freedom be. But in the question of individual liberation we cannot avoid more basic questions: How can one believe oneself to be free in this very life, and in moral decisions, when one is as distanced – not to say cut off – as we are from the very inspiration of this sovereign freedom? Must one already be free to free oneself? This second facet touches on the very possibility of ethics and politics. For if every freedom is purification and separation from existence, then what does it mean to live freely? Plotinus's reaction at this point is uneasy: he accepts double existence while maintaining the privilege of the other man – the one who is free because he has been liberated and purified (I.1.10.7). In our examination of Plotinus's theory of freedom, for which we have furnished the metaphysical context, we shall now discuss these two sides to his thought: freedom as the power of liberation, and the freedom in life. This distinction will become a useful instrument for going beyond what might seem to be a certain contempt on Plotinus's part for empirical freedom, and a preference for the spiritual ideal of liberation.

III

In this distinction we find profoundly articulated the second important moment of freedom, which is also the most evanescent in Plotinus's thought: the moment of ascension. Inasmuch as his interest in ethics and human action in general is entirely subjugated to an ideal of contemplation inherited from Plato, metaphysical liberation constitutes for Plotinus the highest requirement, whereas the freedom to act is merely its expression and consequence. The difficulties of interpretation encountered in this double framework and glimpsed by the first exegetes of these issues in Plotinus's work, notably Father Paul Henry,[15] should therefore not surprise us. Father Henry often settled for verbal solutions to these difficulties, perhaps because he was unduly concerned with finding a complete doctrine of freedom in Plotinus's work, a doctrine which might have provided a refutation of pantheism. It would be more useful, however, to adopt a perspective which takes account of the constraints of a deterministic and profoundly monistic metaphysics which is addressing questions of which the tradition had not yet made possible an independent treatment.

The principal problem is more or less as follows: freedom exists only on the higher plane of the soul, the plane where the soul can become identified with Intellect, participate in the superior hypostases, and tend toward the good. As in the thought of Kant, then, there is a priori only a transcendental freedom of the good which excludes any freedom to do evil. The consequence of this position would seem to be that no inferior freedom, immanent in human beings, bound to corporeal life, and affected by the passions, can exist: "Thus free-will is at all levels only to be found in the sense of identity with the appropriate level of intelligible being, and arises from the ultimate connection of all things with the One."[16] This formula is right: no empirical freedom can be any more than a reflection of transcendental freedom. Therefore, freedom is always liberation from manifold existence and a return to the One. This implies, as Jean Trouillard has pointed out, that an element of the divine freedom is present in each soul to the extent that all liberation presupposes the power to make oneself free. This power is divine; it is coextensive with the divine origin of the soul and with its immortal and beatific destiny. The appeal to a predicate of divinity is of course not only a metaphor: it fully expresses the essence of the soul and refers to the imposing analogy of freedom which structures VI.8. Human freedom can be imagined only through its original and essential participation in the freedom of the One through the mediation, at once ontological and spiritual, of Intellect. One can speak of an essential freedom, therefore, by which the soul is free as long as it refers back to its source, and of a spiritual freedom by which the soul is free in each spiritual act which liberates it in this life.[17]

We have seen the central importance of the unfallen part of the soul (IV.8.8) to Plotinus's metaphysical anthropology. Should the divine element we have just discussed be identified with this part? Free of fault and error (as I.1 insists),[18] this part of the soul represents our profound identity, our true self.[19] Examined from the perspective of freedom, this is a matter of consciousness and self-awareness. Plotinus occasionally risks using an expression which implies that the subject as will precedes thought (V.6.1.2), but the identity of the self and of the sovereign element remains the most constant element. Although it is true that the soul must want to forget what is inferior (IV.3.32.10), this willing never takes on a status which could modify the intellectualistic thesis by forming an empirical, autonomous subject. So what is the unfallen element? Only the preexisting form of Man can explain our identity and the burdens of our freedom: we have to discover this superior identity (VI.5.7.1–2) which will deliver us from the manifold nature of our positions in life. The limits of personal identity, which are discussed elsewhere in this volume, must always be called to mind when the time comes to ask, "Who is the subject of freedom?"

Furthermore, if Plotinus affirms that we are not the source of our own evils (I.8.5.26–34), this is not in order to dissolve all forms of identity – our identity is rather affirmed in the search for the Good. But, paradoxically, the further our identity goes along the road toward the Good, the more it is distanced from itself by becoming grounded in the intelligible universal. This idea is very nicely expressed in the commentary by Dean Inge, who is close on this matter to P. O. Kristeller. Inge holds that contrary to what goes on in modern thought, Plotinus's soul is not a fixed center of experience but rather consists in an entity which travels within and across experience – a wanderer.[20] Impassive, the soul remains completely spiritualized. Fallen, it accepts the risk of experience and the tensions of desire.

Therefore, when this soul finds itself in the state of corporeal existence, its freedom is that of its virtue – its merit (IV.7.7). Voluntary actions are only free to the extent that they suppose a choice of motives which do not belong to the body; they then constitute authentically free inclinations. The soul can in effect beget contrary actions (IV.7.4 and III.1.9) and make decisions: to will is a work that properly belongs to the soul; the act of a gaze that is fixed upon the pure and impassive Reason. Plotinus's thought on this question is entirely in the form of various sparse notations, but when we take the trouble to assemble them, we find that they are absolutely coherent.[21] The intellectual character of the will appears most especially in the analysis offered in the first chapters of VI.8, which can be considered as a synthesis of his thought on the subject. While taking up Aristotle's position concerning the voluntary and the involuntary, Plotinus suddenly turns from this discussion to show how the will is fulfilled only in the act of participation in the Intellect. Concrete deliberation (*prohairesis*), so important in the analysis of the *Nicomachean Ethics* (books III and VI), is for Plotinus only a stage, for this moment, itself inspired by the vision on the Intellect, is part of the process by which the soul orients itself toward the Good. The concepts of voluntariness, of self-determination, and of that which depends on us are not really differentiated when we take into account this unique teleology of Intellect.[22] When we reflect on its rich elaboration in the first chapters of VI.8, we see that it is fully inspired by Platonic ethics.[23]

To this moral psychology of freedom, III.4 adds an interesting mythological note since Plotinus introduces the influence of an active demon, a guardian spirit (III.4.3.14) whose role is taken from Plato's texts, most notably book ten of the *Republic*. Plotinus accords a great deal of importance to the choice of the demon, which he identifies with a choice of life, that is, with the will or the disposition of the soul in its entirety, such that empirical life, with its hazards and its retinue of difficulties – described in VI.8 – do not completely touch the will. This very subtle exegesis of Plato's demonology appears to be concerned mainly with one thing: maintaining a place in life for freedom and not wiping it out with a determinism that would transform our existence into nothing more than a series of consequences from prior lives. Our life is thus not directed by a demon: "Does the guardian spirit, then, always and in every way accomplish its task successfully? Not altogether since the soul is of such a disposition that it is of a particular kind in particular circumstances and so has a life and a purpose (*prohairesin*) according to its kind and circumstances" (III.4.6.8–10). This is also not a vain existence, since it is the site of true liberty: the risk of annihilation is constant and the threat of enslavement is real, even if, as this intellectualism paradoxically asserts, an orientation toward evil cannot be called "free." Plotinus is clear: as long as there are involuntary impulses, the soul is not truly the god it is in essence (I.2.6.3). There is thus no empirical will to self-abasement (IV.4.44.32).

What is at stake in concrete freedom in this life is therefore that it must try to maintain an internal orientation toward Intellect. This implies the practice of virtue, which constitutes the premier motif of an ethic centered upon our resemblance to God, to take Plato's expression. Plotinus devotes an entire treatise (I.2) to a commentary on this ideal. A number of treatises in the first *Ennead* reveal the straightforwardly Platonic visage of this ethic: the aspiration (*ephêsis*) toward the Good; the ideal of autonomy (*autarkeia*) in the context of wisdom (I.4.4). The entire treatise on happiness (I.4) defines the goal of the wise man's life and in so doing show how the will is essentially an orientation or a tension leading inward – in this passage the will is defined as the freedom to breakaway from exteriority (I.4.4.15–17). This distinction, between interiority and exteriority, even if it is never spelled out, remains constitutive of an idea of liberty made dynamic by the Good.[24] The intrinsic impulse of freedom is a turning (*epistrophê*) inward and an inner self-identification with intelligible life (V.1.12.13–14). In so doing, the soul merely reproduces in life the universal aspiration of all beings toward the Good (VI.7.20) – its desire is its freedom; its freedom is its desire. Plotinus continually restates this ideal of wisdom, insisting along the way on the full identity of a free will and a wisdom turned toward attaining the resemblance to God, mediated by Intellect.

The more or less explicit mentions of the free nature of this orientation are very numerous: they go all the way from expressing the mere tendency toward the Good to stating the soul's desire to exist in the intelligible realm (for example, IV.3.32.22) to expressing its desire to unite with God (for example, VI.9.9.34). The soul is in other respects attached to Intellect, provided that it does not want to leave it (V.1.5.2). This *apostasis* is not only the fall of the soul but the possibility of a more definitive rupture. This spiritual will manifests an authentic freedom, inasmuch as it is different from the circular motion of the universal soul. Plotinus evokes the persistence of God's desire in a cosmological context (II.2.2). This desire connects us to Him and also flows from Him (II.9.15.7).[25] The manifestations of this desire in Plotinus's work are so constant and so strong that one cannot help but be impressed by the depth of this desire (for example, in VI.7.31).[26]

Indeed, the reality of the spiritual life influences the development of moral psychology at this point – the experience of union, even in the simple exercise of thought, already annuls the will to diversify and liberates the soul (III.7.34.19). It is thus the progress of this union toward a superior liberation that fulfills the nature of free will. Plotinus expresses the principle of this will in an eternal seeking of the higher object, the thing that is elevated (I.4.7.6; V.3.16.24; VI.7.19). His treatise on Eros (III.5), by working out a commentary on the *Symposium*, seeks to give deep Platonic roots to this philosophy of desire.[27]

Moreover, another desire, linked to action and to exteriority, can come to contradict this spiritual will: this desire is an obstacle to self-knowledge and can block the movement toward conversion. This evil *orexis* (V.3.6.39) is the effect of the inferior part of the soul; it cannot be confused with the *thelêsis* directed by Intellect (V.3.11.3), and even less so with the spiritual *ephêsis* toward the One and the Good. Its power, coming from exteriority itself, is real inasmuch as it can constitute a weight, a constraint, a threat to liberty. But it is never itself free, since it is not turned toward the Good.

It is in VI.8, to which we must now return, that the dialectic of this freedom is taken to its most perfect expression. The part of this treatise which concerns human freedom cuts across the first seven chapters, as we have seen earlier; here Plotinus seeks to formulate a concept that will be able to include the sense in which the One is itself free and self-caused, as he will discuss in the section that will follow. After having briefly considered Aristotle's moral psychology, and especially his concepts of voluntary and unvoluntary, Plotinus hastens to substitute the Platonic ethic of the Good. His reading of the *Nicomachean Ethics* (book III) is tainted by Stoic elements, which doubtless come from the discussions put to work in the commentaries of Alexander of Aphrodisias: Plotinus is not merely interested in willingness as such, but in a concept of self-determination that will be able to guarantee that something will depend upon us (*eph'hêmin*, VI.8.2.33–7). Aristotle's definitions of willingness were based on the absence of constraint and the presence of knowledge (*NE* III.7.1135a23), but Plotinus cannot accept a purely formal definition of free will. For Plotinus, the voluntary (*hekousion*) does not depend on criteria which defined the free (*eph'hêmin*) according to Aristotle. It must be given a thoroughgoing Platonic definition, essentially founded on the conscience of the moral good. That action is voluntary which seeks the good. The beginning of Plotinus's discussion is sensitive to the fatalistic context of the period (VI.8.1.23–9), which creates a certain echo of the treatises on providence (III.2 and III.3).[28] But the fundamental preoccupation is the nature of the interior principle of self-determination, and Plotinus does not pause to discuss the Stoic conception.[29] Platonic reason is at the heart of his thought. How else can we define this self-determination, if not by means of a psychology of action which gives precedence to Intellect? The more an action conforms to the Good, the more it is self-dependent and the less it is enslaved by exteriority (4.33–5). Self-determination fulfills, in what seems to be a superior stage of freedom, the free determination of oneself (*autexousion*) which characterizes "one whose doings depend upon the activities of Intellect and who is free from bodily affections" (3.19–21). This liberation is concrete; it is fulfilled in action under specific circumstances (5.10–27), even though Plotinus holds that authentic freedom resides outside of action. In fact, it essentially belongs to reason and to virtue, both of which precede action. This fifth chapter of the treatise expresses more than any other the subordination of concrete freedom to a superior spiritual freedom, the one being, one might say, the pursuit of the other to the point where liberation, existence within Intellect, and union with the Good have all been achieved. Asceticism, disciplining the passions through action, is thus not the first moment of freedom, since the essence of virtue resides in an outflowing of action, that is in an immateriality which is identified with the life of the Intellect – in this sense one can say that virtue is a second intellect.

> If then virtue is a kind of other intellect, a state which in a way intellectualises the soul, again, being in our power does not belong to the realm of action but in intellect at rest from actions. . . . We shall assert that virtue and intellect have the mastery and that we should refer being in our power and freedom to them. . . . (VI.8.5.34–7 and 6.6–10)

The freedom to engage in *praxis*, the freedom to choose and to act, is thus destined to be displaced by a purely spiritual, free determination. This does not take away the authenticity of that freedom, since it accompanies the daily battle of empirical existence. But it cannot be conceived in and of itself. This part of VI.8, spiritually very profound, constitutes a complete reinterpretation of the moral psychology of antiquity. Here we find a remarkable achievement of classical intellectualism, inasmuch as Plotinus reinterprets the meaning of the mind as free will. Plotinus not only expresses a doctrine of the foundations of human freedom but actually shows how these foundations enlist an ascetic ethics which alone can guarantee liberation.

The affirmative conclusions of this set of texts concerning the fact of empirical liberty and its spiritual foundations are reinforced by a treatise from Plotinus's youth on destiny (III.1). This treatise offers a number of antifatalist arguments directed against the determinism of the atomists, the Stoics,[30] and the astrologers. Nourished mainly by a conception of the free subject, master of himself, the Plotinian arguments reject the concept of a vulgar necessity which would ruin the freedom of the activity of the soul. Already in this treatise then, Plotinus was linking freedom with the sovereignty of the soul:

> When in its impulse, the soul has as director its own and untroubled reason, then this impulse alone is to be said to be in our own power and free; this is our own act, which does not come from somewhere else but from within, from our soul when it is pure, from a primary principle which directs and is in control, not suffering error from ignorance or defeat from the violence of the passions. . . . (III.1.9.10–15)

Thus, rationality and sovereignty confer upon the soul the power to be the cause of its own action, which is the power in which liberty consists. This power is real: it is not annuled by the external determinations at work in the fatalistic theories. Certainly, liberty can vary according to the individual, as Plotinus will later say (IV.3.15), but it is destroyed neither by destiny nor by the laws regulating the cosmic order. The two later treatises of providence (III.2 and III.3) as well as the treatise on the influence of the heavenly bodies (II.3) take up this teaching again, modulating it to meet the needs of a providentialistic argument – the influence of providence is of course real, but not so real that it can cancel out freedom (III.2.9.1 and II.3.1.1).

This defense of freedom is enunciated in the context of an extremely complex theory of natural causation. Indeed, Plotinus distinguishes between near and distant causes which bring with them effects on the specific causality of the soul, which is truly an originating causality (III.1.8.8; III.2.10.12–19). Naturally, the motion of the heavens and the effects of universal sympathy count for much in the determination of the general framework of causation (see also IV.4.31). Nevertheless, the most constant thesis of these treatises, placed at the very heart of a majestic hymn to the beauty of nature and to the rationality that forms its necessity, is still the following: human beings possess an inalienable principle of freedom (III.3.4.6). Here more than anywhere else in his work resonates the force of the principle of that which depends on us (to eph'hêmin), the origin of the proper work of a human being. The accent placed on responsibility (III.2.7) is more significant for the interpretation of these treatises than whatever deterministic elements can be found there.[31] Plotinus, for his part, takes up the distinction, which is central to his anthropology, between a higher, impassive self and a fragile, vulnerable self assailed by the disorder of its desires.[32]

Plotinus also reiterates his intellectualism and he stresses the involuntariness of evil. But in his conception this does not exclude full responsibility for actions, whether good or bad: the wicked man remains responsible, he acts by himself, even though his action is not voluntary in the Platonic sense of this concept. This doctrine agrees with the whole of the moral psychology of the *Enneads*, and most notably with the first chapters of VI.8. Man is a free principle when he acts toward the Good: he then identifies with freedom, he is *arché autexousios*. He accomplishes the full nature of his liberty when he takes for guide pure and impassive reason (III.1.9.11).

In the Plotinian conception of human freedom, therefore, what strikes us most is the strength of the metaphysical premises. In a manner quite different from that of Aristotle, who appeared to be exclusively interested by the problems of choice and contingency, Plotinus conceives of liberty as the true property of virtuous life. By stressing this theme, he appropriates the great heritage of the Platonic tradition centered on the divine origin of the soul and the ideal of resemblance to God. His position regarding the freedom of the soul in the process of descent toward existence in the body is indeed the expression of his desire to preserve the metaphysical necessity of procession, but we must remember that he still is inclined to integrate in this framework a freedom to descend which resembles a form of consent. Compared to this passive liberty – the freedom to ascend – the freedom of return is the manifestation of a powerful conception of spiritual life. It is indeed in the act of ascent, an act which is identified with purification and will toward the Good, that freedom reaches its full dimension as essence of human nature. First and foremost, in its effort to triumph over the threats of bodily existence, virtue can here be conceived as free resistance. But this life would not be possible if it were not animated, from the inside, by an orientation toward impassive reason and contemplation. Human freedom in the thought of Plotinus is thus a true freedom; it is affirmed not only against all forms of vulgar determinism – and most notably against fatalism – but also against the sophisticated conceptions put forward by the Stoics. Human freedom accounts for the pure origin of the higher self, for the soul's vocation to return as bearer of this self in existence, for the moral sovereignty of the spiritual subject. The eminent model of human freedom is still the absolute freedom of the One: only the One can be seized in his act of extreme vigilance as absolutely free, as absolute cause of Himself. The greatness of Plotinus's vision is rooted in the spiritual experience of a philosopher who has always tried to fuse together the harmony of metaphysical hierarchy as expressed by necessity and the urgency of purification as the spiritual injunction to return.

NOTES

1 The best summary of this, accompanied by a very elaborate critical discussion, is to be found in O'Brien 1993, notably 5–18.

2 On this question, see the numerous works of Blumenthal, especially Blumenthal 1971b, 55–63 and Blumenthal 1987, 557. Blumenthal insists on a balanced interpretation which takes account of the unitary and differential aspects of the problem. Rist 1970 claims that Plotinus held to this thesis of the forms of individuals. A presentation of more recent scholarship, placing an accent on the difficulties of interpretation, may be found in Corrigan and O'Cleirigh 1987, 581–4.

3 Following the 1962 edition of Harder and Theiler, this text should be read with the correction at line 17; see the commentary by O'Brien 1993, 14.

4 This is the way Festugière (1953, 65–9) puts the matter. Dodds (1965, 24–6) has put forward the hypothesis that the aspects connected with freedom might have given way to a more deterministic position as a result of Plotinus's break with the Gnostics. Nevertheless, this account is somewhat confused, especially concerning the chronology of the Enneads, as O'Brien's analysis has shown (1993). See also Blumenthal's critique in Blumenthal 1971b, 5. For a synthetic discussion of the philosophical issues, see Himmerich 1959, 66.

5 I agree on this point with the analysis of O'Brien 1993, 12f.

6 See the numerous discussions in the work of O'Brien 1993, 42–9 and O'Brien 1971, 114–46. The parallel passages of I.2.4 and V.1.1 are less precise on the voluntary nature of the descent. But the expression to autoexousion (V.1.1.5–6 and IV.8.5.26) is rare and indicates a freedom that is specific to the human soul – a self-determination of its movement.

7 Trouillard (1949) thought that the freedom of descent was marked by a

great deal of confusion, whereas the spiritual freedom of ascension was the only true freedom in Plotinus's work. See his commentary on IV.8.5 (353–7).

8 Aside from I.1, see the discussion of the impassivity of incorporeal reality in III.6.5 and IV.6.9.

9 This is the conclusion reached by Rist 1967, 130–8 which is, albeit very brief, one of the best statements of this question.

10 This important passage has given rise to a rich body of commentaries on the idea of the self in Plotinus's work and to the problem of an internal humanism. See first of all O'Daly 1973 and Prini 1968, and the chapter by Himmerich 1959, "Ich," op. cit., ch. 8. This theme of the true self goes back to the thought of Plato in the *Alcibiades*, of which tradition a remarkable study has been produced by Jean Pépin (1971). See also the text in the *Republic* 589a7 and the parallel passage in Plotinus, at V.1.10.10. Against Porphyry (*Ad Marcellam*,8.15–17 and *De abstinentia* I.29.9), Plotinus does not want to identify this self with the Intellect. See his very subtle discussion at V.3.3.31, where his stance appears to be motivated by a concern for maintaining the life of the soul with its tensions and its own temporal nature.

11 The parts of the soul are powers, *dunameis*, which means that the soul is a composite whole. See VI.9.1.40.

12 These analyses were carried out by Zeeman 1946 who has corroborated the results attained by philosophical methods in the first commentators on these questions, for example, Gollwitzer 1900, 1902.

13 Following the commentary of Blumenthal 1971b, 38f.

14 In an important article, Igal 1979 has argued against Blumenthal in favor of the hypothesis of an evolution towards a more unitary, quasi-hylomorphic model of Plotinian anthropology. I think nonetheless that Platonic dualism remains fundamental and that this is explicitly shown in the remarks concerning liberation.

15 In a series of three articles, see Henry 1931.

16 Blumenthal 1987, 559, taking up the conclusions of Salmona 1967.

17 This distinction matches up with the distinction proposed by Kristeller 1929 in his brilliant study, between the objective point of view and the actual (subjective) point of view in Plotinus's philosophy. In his synthetic article, Blumenthal 1987, 548f. presents a similar distinction between metaphysics and ethics, while insisting on the importance of the work of Trouillard, who wanted to bring out (wrongly, thought Blumenthal) the prevalence of the ethical and spiritual perspective. According to Kristeller – and I should say that I believe that he has presented one of the most faithful interpretations of this double movement – these two perspectives were equally at work in the mind of Plotinus and are

equally constitutive of his genius. The Kantian aspects of this interpretation, which on the one hand allow metaphysics and ethics to spill over into each other, also open it to the risk of a certain formalism. As for me, I should say that there is no doubt that Plotinus's metaphysics is not a metaphorical objectification of the spiritual life.

18 See the comments of Trouillard 1953, 19–29. It is this part which represents the deep ego, the self.

19 See Himmerich's discussion, 1959, 92–100.

20 See Inge 1929, vol. I, 203. The same idea occurs in Emile Bréhier's introduction to his edition in the Budé series of treatise IV.3, 27.

21 Zeeman 1946 has produced very useful lexicographical research on the topics of will and freedom in Plotinus.

22 Rist 1975 shows how Plotinus distances himself from the Aristotelian and Stoic positions by marginalizing the experience of decision and choice. This attitude is particularly clear in the discussion of the fall of the soul.

23 I have tried to show this in detail in my commentary of treatise VI.8; see Leroux 1990.

24 See Salmona 1967, ch. 2, "Interiorità e liberazione," 30–70, which presents this thematic in a very inspired way. See also Trouillard 1957 and Fraisse 1989.

25 This theme has been studied in the important book by Arnou 1967.

26 See the commentary by Hadot 1988.

27 See the commentary by Hadot 1990.

28 The philosophical analysis of the arguments put up by Plotinus in these treatises has been well elaborated in Parma 1971 and Schubert 1968. I have not been able to read the study of Boot 1984.

29 For a comparison of these two conceptions see the essay by Graeser 1972, 112–25.

30 Graeser 1972, 48f. brings out several infidelities in Plotinus's presentation of the Stoic theses.

31 Here I agree with the excellent chapter by Rist, "Man's Free Will," in Rist 1967, 130–8, which proposes a more balanced interpretation, taking account of the whole of his work, than that of Clark 1943, 16–31, which seems to me to unduly exaggerate the determinism in the analysis of action.

32 This theme comes up at I.1.10; II.9.2; and IV.4.18.

13 An ethic for the late antique sage

"Our concern," remarks Plotinus, in the course of his treatise *On Virtues*, which is his chief discussion of the principles of ethics (I.2.6.2–3), "is not to be free of sin, but *to be god.*" This remark, while not by any means as hybristic as it might appear at first sight, nevertheless points to an important aspect of Plotinus's ethical thought, an aspect which must be addressed at the outset of any discussion of the subject.

To what extent, it must be asked, does Plotinus in fact have an ethical theory? This may seem a silly, even perverse question to ask, but I think we shall see that it has a point. Of course, Plotinus has an ethical *stance*. We can derive this from a perusal of Porphyry's *Life of Plotinus*, and from many remarks scattered throughout his writings. Like most late antique philosophers, especially those of a Platonist or Pythagorean persuasion, he tended to asceticism in his personal life, to celibacy, both heterosexual and homosexual, and even to vegetarianism.[1] He was also, as we learn (*Life* ch. 9), a kind and caring guardian of orphans, who took his financial and educational responsibilities very seriously and was therefore much in demand in this role. He was also a person of preternaturally powerful psychic powers (*ibid.* chs. 10–11), which he used for virtuous purposes.

But there is another significant aspect of Plotinus's character which also emerges clearly from the *Life*, which points us in the direction of an answer to the initial question. That is his overwhelming preoccupation with the life of the mind. As Porphyry tells us, à propos his methods of composition (ch.8):

> Even if he was talking to someone, engaged in continuous conversation, he kept to his train of thought. He could take his necessary part in the

315

conversation to the full, and at the same time keep his mind fixed without a break on what he was considering. When the person he had been talking to was gone he did not go over what he had written, because his sight, as I have said, did not suffice for revision. He went straight on with what came next, just as if there had been no interval of conversation between. In this way he was present at once to himself and to others, and he never relaxed his self-turned attention except in sleep: even sleep he reduced by taking very little food, often not even a piece of bread, and by his continuous turning in contemplation to his intellect. (trans. Armstrong)

What does ethics mean for such a man as this? Plotinus starts his enquiry into the nature of virtue in *Ennead* I.2 in the following significant way, drawing his inspiration from the much-quoted Platonic text *Theaetetus* 176a-b:

Since it is here that evils are, and "they must necessarily haunt this region," and the soul wants to escape from evils, we must escape from here. What, then, is this escape? "Being made like to God," Plato says. And we become godlike "if we become righteous and holy with the help of wisdom," and are in general in a state of virtue. (trans. Armstrong, slightly adapted)

But this identification of the route of "escape" with the mundane practice of the virtues is called into question directly by the raising of the *aporia* as to whether the deity to whom we wish to liken ourselves himself possesses all or any of the virtues (1.11ff.). Even if this deity is the world-soul (or more exactly, its "ruling element" [*hêgoumenon*]), it would not have any use for the virtues in their normal, "political" form – that is, the virtues as set out in the *Republic* – and so even if we were likening ourselves to it, the practice of those virtues would not advance our purpose. In fact, however, we, like the world soul itself, are intent on likening ourselves to a higher deity, the transcendent intellect, and it is characteristic of that to be above all virtue – even the "purificatory" virtues that Plotinus discerns in the *Phaedo*[2] – so that it would seem that for the attainment of divinity, which is asserted to be the aim of the sage, the practice of the virtues in any normal sense is not indicated.

That Plotinus took the ideal of self-divinization seriously can not, I think, be doubted. He plainly saw himself (like Empedocles, long before him) as a denizen of a higher realm, exiled for a space in the physical, sublunary sphere, whose proper business was not here, but there. His autobiographical remarks at the beginning of the early treatise IV.8 are most revealing in this connection:

Often I have woken up out of the body to myself and have entered into myself, going out from all other things; I have seen a beauty wonderfully great and felt assurance that then most of all I belonged to the better part; I have actually lived the best life and come to identity with the divine; and set firm in it I have come to that supreme actuality, setting myself above all else in the realm of Intellect. Then, after that rest in the divine, when I have come down from Intellect to discursive reasoning,[3] I am puzzled how I ever came down, and how my soul has come to be in the body, when it is what it has shown itself to be by itself, even when it is in the body.

When one has this sort of attitude to corporeal existence, any views that one might have on ethical questions might be expected to exhibit a very distinct perspective. And so indeed they do.

I propose to proceed by raising, first, the question as to what one might reasonably expect the topic of ethics to cover, in the later Platonist tradition, and then to examine how well Plotinus's concerns accord with this model.

If we take as a rough guide to what was considered "ethics" in later Platonism the second century A.D. *Didaskalikos,* or *Handbook of Platonism,* of Alcinous,[4] we will find the following topics covered (in chs. 27–34 of the work). We begin with the nature of the highest good, or well-being (*eudaimonia*). We then turn to the *telos,* or "end of goods," and the question of the overall purpose of human life. Next comes the subject of virtue, and the individual virtues. In Alcinous's case this is followed by a chapter (30) on the *euphuiai,* or "good natural dispositions," and a discussion of the (originally Stoic) theory of "moral progress" (*prokopê*), and this is followed by a chapter on the question of whether one can do wrong voluntarily. Alcinous then discusses the emotions (*pathê*), and lastly the topic of friendship and love. The more or less contemporary Middle Platonic treatise of Apuleius, *On Plato and his Doctrines,* covers very much the same ground, with much the same order of topics (II, chs. 1–23), so that we may take this as being a fairly standard treatment of the subject. As we shall see, Plotinus does have something to say on the first few topics, up to and including a discussion of the virtues, but little or nothing on the later, more specialized ones.

In his edition of Plotinus, Porphyry groups in the first *Ennead* those treatises which he discerns as dealing with "predominantly ethical" topics (ēthikōterai hupotheseis, Life ch. 29). We may note the cautious comparative, which indicates that Porphyry is well aware of what is obvious to any reader of the Enneads, that any aspect of Plotinus's philosophy may manifest itself in any one of his treatises, and that it is therefore something of a distortion to group them under the traditional divisions of philosophy.

Nevertheless, Porphyry knows what he is doing, and in fact a good conspectus of what passes for ethical speculation in Plotinus can be derived from a study of the treatises of the first Ennead. I propose to go through them in chronological order, picking out what seem to me salient features. What we shall end up with, I think, is very much of an ethic for the late antique sage, not one that offers much practical guidance to the common man.

First, however, let me raise a slightly anachronistic question derived from modern moral philosophy, since it helps, I think, to clarify Plotinus's position. In G. E. Moore's terms, is Plotinus a "naturalist" in his ethics – that is, does he commit what Moore would identify as the "naturalistic" fallacy of holding that his primary positive value word or words – for Moore, "good," for Plotinus kalos and agathos – can be defined in terms of something else?

It seems to me that there is no question but that Plotinus (like any Platonist, indeed) is a "naturalist" in this sense, and that the grasping of this fact is the key to understanding the nature of his ethical theory. For Plotinus, as we shall see, the "good" or the "fine" is simply that which conduces to our knowledge of, or communion with, true being, that is to say, the intelligible world of forms, the contents of the hypostasis of intellect (nous) – and more remotely, to union with the One. Any attempt by Moore to raise the troublesome question, "Is then such a statement as 'contemplation of the forms is good' a tautology or not?," would be met with the unequivocal rejoinder that it is: that is all that agathos means, "conducive to the contemplation of the forms," even as kalos means "manifesting the world of forms on the material plane," or something such. There is no "fallacy" involved here, it seems to me, so long as one is perfectly clear and straightforward about what one is doing, as Plotinus certainly is. Whether one might be accused of introducing a "persuasive definition," in C. L. Stevenson's terms, is another matter.

Be that as it may, this is a cornerstone of Plotinus's ethics, and it means that a certain dimension of modern ethical theory, influenced as it is by the Judaeo-Christian tradition as well as the Greek, is not to be found in it – that aspect concerned with love of, or care for, one's neighbor, *for his or her own sake*. Greek ethical thought in general, whether Platonist, Peripatetic, Stoic, or Epicurean, has been frequently and justly characterized as comparatively self-centered and intellectualistic, by comparison with modern theories,⁵ but that of Plotinus, I think it is fair to say, is more so than most. His care for others, as we can see from Porphyry's *Life*, was in fact exemplary, but his mind was firmly fixed on the noetic realm, and on his own attainment of union with it, and it is this concern that dominates his ethical theory.

That said, let us turn to the texts. The first one, the treatise *On Beauty* (I.6), is in fact that one which Porphyry identifies as Plotinus's earliest essay – though even that does not make it very early in his intellectual development, since he only began to write at about the age of fifty (*Life*, ch. 4) – and it thus occupies a significant position. It appears at first sight to be an essay on aesthetics, since it begins with a critique of existing theories of beauty, or *to kalon*, but in fact for Plotinus there is no independent sphere of aesthetics, and the subject matter is primarily ethical.

His opening move (ch.1) is to counter the traditional definition of beauty, or "the fine," as propounded originally by the Stoics,⁶ "a good proportion of parts to each other and to the whole, with the addition of good colour." The arguments he uses are of rather doubtful force (though he makes the good point that such a definition makes it difficult to explain the beauty of a simple substance like gold, or of a simple event, like a lightning flash at night),⁷ but that need not concern us in the present context.

What is important is the conclusion that Plotinus wishes to recommend, which is (2.13–14) that "things in this world are beautiful by participation in *form*." Using the imagery of the *Symposium* (206d), he speaks of the soul instinctively recognizing the presence of form in matter as *kalon*, but shrinking away from instances of its imperfect domination of matter as *aischron* (2.1–8). Indeed this whole essay is shot through with reminiscences of Diotima's speech in the *Symposium*, the central myth of the *Phaedrus* (particularly the regrowing of the wings of the soul, 250eff.), and the Cave Simile of *Republic* VII. For Plotinus, the role of beauty can only be to recall us to a knowledge of the forms. The ascent to the forms, that is, to true Beauty (chs. 4–6), is achieved through the practice of the virtues, seen as "purifications" (*katharseis*), as portrayed in the *Phaedo* (69b–e). This distinction of "cathartic" from "civic" virtues (as set out in *Republic* IV) will prove an important element in his later (but still "early") treatise *On Virtue* (I.2), to be discussed shortly.

The ethical stance emerging from I.6, then, is distinctly self-centered and other-worldly. To quote from the beginning of chapter 7:

So we must ascend again to the Good, which every soul desires. Anyone who has seen it knows what I mean when I say that it is beautiful. It is desired as good, and the desire for it is directed to the good, and the attainment of it is for those who go up to the higher world and are converted and strip off what we put on in our descent – just as for those who go up to celebrations of sacred rites there are purifications, and strippings off of the clothes they wore before, and going up naked; until, passing in the ascent all that is alien to the God, one sees with oneself alone That alone, simple, single and pure, from which all depends and to which all look and are and live and think; for it is the cause of life and mind and being. (7.1–12; trans. Armstrong)

The theme of "likeness to God" as the end of ethical activity, which becomes of central importance in the later treatise already mentioned, I.2, surfaces already here. It is clear that for Plotinus any action must be evaluated primarily from the perspective of its capacity to assimilate us to the divine realm. All earthly concerns, such as love for family or kin, not to mention care for the poor and oppressed, and all passions, such as pity or grief, must be shaken off (like clothes at an initiation ceremony) in the process of purification.

Plotinus's position here (which is after all only the Stoic one, with a transcendent aspect added) is well illustrated by a passage from the late treatise *On Well-Being* (I.4), to which I will come presently. The passage itself, however, may be quoted now (Plotinus is making the point that even if the sage ministers to the needs of his body, he will do it while still making a firm distinction between himself and it):

He knows its needs, and gives it what he gives it without taking away anything from his own life. His well-being will not be reduced even when fortune goes against him; the good life is still there even so. When his friends and relatives die he knows what death is – as those who die do also, if they are virtuous. Even if the death of friends and relations causes grief, it does not grieve him *but only that in him which has no intelligence, and he will not receive into himself the distresses proper to that element.* (4.29–36; trans. Armstrong, slightly modified)

That is what moral *katharsis* involves, then, cutting out the passions, and the material interests that go with them and stimulate them, and turning one's whole attention to assimilation to the intelligible world.[8]

The little note or fragment on suicide, *On Going out of the Body* (I.9), is imbued with the same spirit. Plotinus is in fact against suicide in most instances, despite his profound belief that it is far better for the soul to be free of the body, since it is generally not possible to effect this liberation deliberately without mental disturbance. Interestingly, he does not use the argument advanced by Socrates in the *Phaedo* (62b), that we are put here by the gods on guard duty, and should not desert our post (though he does refer to our possibly having an "allotted time," 1.16). He is simply concerned with the state of our soul when we depart this life. Once again, his position is not very far from that of the Stoics. While maintaining that there is no justification for suicide so long as there is any possibility of moral progress (*to prokoptein*), if this possibility no longer exists – and this is something that only the wise man will clearly understand – then he is not absolutely opposed to rational "withdrawal" (*exagôgê*),[9] if that can be managed.

We may next turn back to the treatise mentioned at the outset, that *On Virtues* (I.2), and its companion *On Dialectic* (I.3), which belong still to the "early" period of Plotinus's literary career, before Porphyry's arrival in 264. As I have said, we are here concerned with an analysis of what it can mean to say that we may attain likeness to God through the exercise of the virtues, when we agree that God cannot possess the virtues as normally conceived, since he would have no way of exercising them. Certainly, as Plotinus makes clear in chapter 1, the exercise of the "civic" virtues is inappropriate to the divinity (which in the present context may be taken to be primarily the hypostasis of Intellect), but, although even the "cathartic" virtues cannot properly be attributed to it, they can at least serve as means of ascent to it:

What then do we mean when we call these other virtues "purifications," and how are we made really like (sc. to God) by being purified? Since the soul is evil when it is contaminated with the body and shares its experiences and partakes in its whole outlook (panta sundoxazousa), it will be good and possess virtue when it no longer has the same outlook, but pursues its own activity by itself – this is intelligence and wisdom – and does not share the body's experiences – this is self-control – and is not afraid of departing from the body – this is courage – and is ruled by reason and intellect, without opposition – and this is justice. One would not be wrong in calling this state of the soul "likeness to God," in which its activity is intellectual, and it is free in this way from bodily affections. For the divine too is pure, and its activity is of such a kind that that which imitates it has wisdom. (3.11–23; trans. Armstrong, slightly modified)

These "cathartic" analogues of the four virtues of Republic IV are enumerated again in chapter 6 (20ff). They form the starting point for a remarkable doctrine of grades of virtue which was to be elaborated, first by Porphyry, and then by Iamblichus, until fully seven grades of virtue were discerned – a scholastic elaboration at odds with the spirit of Plotinus's philosophy, and which need not concern us here.[10]

However, behind this doctrine there lurks an important and most characteristic feature of Plotinian psychology, which comes to the fore more explicitly later in I.4,[11] but may profitably be brought out into the open now. Plotinus is strongly of the opinion that there is an element in us, which he identifies with the soul, and regards as our true self, which is in some way not subject to "passions" (pathê), both in the sense of not feeling emotions, and of not being affected by physical pleasures or pains.

This doctrine certainly takes its start from various Platonic utterances, most notably in the Phaedo, but in Plotinus's hands it becomes something far more radical than anything envisaged by Plato. As has been pointed out by Eyjólfur Emilsson,[12] "with Plotinus we can see a development towards a soul–body distinction closer to the one modern philosophers are familiar with ... Plotinus presents such a picture of the human soul that there is an ontological gap between it and bodies, even between it and the human body" (146).

This comes out vividly in the latter part of I.4, where Plotinus is concerned to hammer home the point that well-being (eudaimonia) should be quite independent of external circumstances. In chapter 13 (6ff.), he dismisses even the Stoic ideal of apatheia as based on an inadequate psychology:

But the "greatest study"[13] is always ready to hand and always with him, all the more if he is in the notorious "Bull of Phalaris" – which it is silly to call pleasant, even though people (sc. the Stoics) keep on saying that it is; for according to their philosophy that which says that its state is pleasant is the very same thing that is in pain.[14] According to ours that which suffers pain is one thing, and there is another which, even while it is compelled to accompany that which suffers pain, remains in its own company and will not fall short of the vision of the universal good.

It is this "other thing" which, as it turns out, is the true soul, while what is subject to passions is what Plotinus terms "the composite" (to sunamphôteron),[15] the combination of body and what might be termed an "animating force." This he is unwilling to grant the status of soul, but prefers to see as a sort of "illumination" (ellampsis) or "trace" (iknos) of soul in the body, which, though not corporeal, is yet not soul in the full sense. It is at this level of the human being that passions are experienced, Plotinus would maintain, and not at the level of soul proper. Back in chapter 8 of I.4 (1–6), he produces the following striking image of the soul proper:

> As far as his own pains go, when they are very great, he will bear them as long as he can; when they are too much for him, they will bear him off.[16] He is not to be pitied in his pain; *his light burns within, like the light in a lantern when it is blowing hard outside with a great fury of wind and storm.*

This image of the soul as a light shielded from the elements without by an impenetrable, though translucent, barrier expresses very well, I think, the view of the soul's relation to (animate) body which Plotinus sets before himself. It gives a new twist to the Stoic ideal of *apatheia*, which, as we have seen above, Plotinus declares to be incoherent on the Stoics' own materialist principles. This form of soul–body dualism is a difficult position to maintain (he makes a heroic effort in this regard in III.6.1–5), but it is central to Plotinus's ethical stance.

But let us return for a moment to I.2 and 3. I have suggested above that this single-minded pursuit of union with God which is Plotinus's only approved form of ethical activity does not really leave much room for that concerned interaction with our fellow man which constitutes the traditional arena of ethics. Plotinus actually raises this question himself at the end of the treatise (2.7.14ff.):

The question whether the possessor of the greater virtues has the lesser ones in actuality or in some other way must be considered in relation to each particular virtue. Take, for example, practical wisdom (*phronêsis*). If one is acting on other principles, how is it still there, even inactive? And how about if one type of virtue naturally permits so much, but the other a different amount, and one kind of self-control (*sôphrosunê*) measures and limits (sc. the passions), while the other totally abolishes them? And the same goes for the other virtues, once practical wisdom has been moved from its seat.

Plotinus answers his own question by asserting that, while the "civic" or vulgar virtues may remain present in the sage in some potential way, he will not act according to these:

But when he reaches higher principles and different measures he will act according to these. For instance, he will not make self-control consist in that former observance of measure and limit, but will altogether separate himself, as far as possible, from his lower nature and will live, not the life of the good man which civic virtue requires, but leaving that behind, he will choose another, the life of the gods: for it is to them, not to good men, that we are to liken ourselves.

This is a pretty uncompromising statement with which to end the treatise. Plotinus is not suggesting, of course, toleration of any form of antinomianism, or disregard for the norms of decent society, such as commended itself to certain contemporary Gnostic sects. Any such suggestion would have appalled him. He would, of course, observe the vulgar decencies; it is just that they would be subsumed into something higher.[17] One feels of Plotinus that he would have gladly helped an old lady across the road – but he might very well fail to notice her at all. And if she were squashed by a passing wagon, he would remain quite unmoved.

A further important clue to Plotinus's view of the nature of *eudaimonia*, as the end to be pursued by the practice of the virtues, is provided in the "middle-period" treatise I.5, *On Whether Well-Being Increases With Time.* Plotinus here takes his start from an interesting *aporia* as to whether, even as we can reckon in the past and future with the present when calculating such a thing as the duration of an illness or a belief,[18] so we can declare that yesterday's well-being can be added to today's, or rather the present moment's well-being, to make *more* well-being. It is certainly true that we would tend to feel that someone who had been *eudaimôn* for many years enjoyed a greater degree of *eudaimonia* than someone who had just attained it yesterday, but would we be right?

Plotinus's response to this problem, once again, reveals clearly the basic presuppositions of his ethics. The fact is, he asserts, that true *eudaimonia* is not a thing of time at all, but relates to the realm of eternity, and so cannot be measured by time. It is certainly reasonable to assert that extent of time can enable one to increase one's degree of insight into intelligible reality, but once one has attained a perfect vision of it (assuming such a thing to be possible), then extent of time ceases to be of any significance.[19] He addresses the relation of *eudaimonia* to time most particularly in chapter 7:

> But why, if we ought only to consider the present and not to count it along with the past, do we not do the same with time? Why do we count the past along with the present and say that it is more? Why, then, should we not say that well-being is equal in quantity to the time that it lasts? We should then be dividing well-being according to the divisions of time (whereas if we measure it by the present moment, on the other hand, we shall make it indivisible).
>
> Now it is not unreasonable to count time even when it does not exist any longer, since we can make a count of things which have been there in the past but no longer exist, such as the dead, for instance; but it is unreasonable to say that well-being which no longer exists is still there, and is *more* than that which is present. For well-being demands actual existence (*sumbebêkenai*), but time over and above the present allows of being more while not existing any longer.
>
> In general, then, extent of time means the dispersal of a single present. That is why it is reasonable to term it "the image of eternity" (*Tim.* 37d5), since it tends to bring about the disappearance of what is permanent in eternity by its own dispersion. . . .
>
> So if well-being is a matter of good life, obviously the life concerned must be that of real being; for this is the best. So it must not be counted by time but by eternity; and this is neither more nor less nor of any extension, but a "this-here," unextended and not time-bound. (7.1–25; trans. Armstrong, adapted)

That this is a somewhat counterintuitive conclusion would bother Plotinus not at all. In response to the argument (chs. 8–9) that a man who is presently in a state of well-being, but can also also enjoy the memory of past states of well-being, is plainly better off than a man who is presently *eudaimôn*, but has no such memories, his reply will be that the man who is truly *eudaimôn* does not *as such* make use of memory, any more than do the pure intellects in the intelligible world, and so his past *eudaimonia* can add nothing to his present state.

The concept of the essential impassibility of the soul proper (from which follows the timelessness of its proper state, *eudaimonia*) is very much the subject of another late treatise (I.1) which Porphyry has placed at the head of his whole edition, on the ground that it deals, broadly speaking, with the subject of the *First Alcibiades*, which was traditionally the starting point for any course in Platonism in later antiquity, that is to say, "Know thyself."[20]

In the process, however, of establishing the soul's impassibility, Plotinus is constrained to demonstrate that passions and affections properly belong, not to the soul, but to something else, the "composite" (*to sunamphôteron*) mentioned above, the combination of body and that life-principle which is a "trace" or "illumination" of soul. In this connection, he develops an interesting theory of the center of consciousness, the "we" (*hêmeis*), as he calls it (e.g., chs. 7–8), which is lower than our highest elements, the pure soul and "undescended" intellect, and higher than the subconscious processes going on all the time in the living body.[21] It is this entity that would be the proper subject of "vulgar" ethical behavior, the practice of the "civic" virtues, which are still concerned with the moderating or "fine tuning" of the passions and the direct processing of sense perceptions, while the true soul holds itself aloof from all this:

> Let us say that it is the composite which perceives, and that the soul by its presence does not give itself as such either to the composite or to either member of it, but makes, out of the given body and of a sort of light which it produces from itself,[22] the nature of the living being, another different thing, to which belong sense-perception and all other affections which are ascribed to the living body.
>
> But then, how is it *we* (*hêmeis*) who perceive?
>
> It is because we are not separated from this type of living body, even if other elements too, of more value than we are, enter into the composition of the whole essence of man, which is made up of many elements.
>
> And the power of sense-perception proper to the soul need not itself be of sense-objects, but rather it must be receptive of the impressions (*tupoi*) produced by sensation in the living being; these are already intelligible entities. (I.1.7.1–12 trans. Armstrong, slightly emended)

This distinction between primary sense perceptions and what the soul takes cognizance of, which are already intelligible entities (*noêta*), was made in III.6.1–5, and in an interesting chapter (23) of IV.4, but is reiterated here. Fear, for instance, and the perception which causes it (let us say, of a poisonous snake), are experiences of the *sunamphôteron*. We have also, however, within us an entity which does not experience fear, but simply "notes" the fear – and indeed only receives some kind of intelligible analogue of the visual image of the snake. The virtues of this entity are "cathartic" virtues, and its proper activity is contemplation and self-divinization. The "we" is not necessarily identical with this entity (indeed, in the vast majority of men it is not), but it can become so, and that is what we have to work toward.

One might, I suppose, raise the awkward question, since Plotinus wishes to make such a strong distinction between the soul proper and the "composite," whether one might not postulate a separate ethic for the composite – such as would involve, say, the practice of the *civic* virtues rather than the cathartic, and practice moderation of the passions, rather than their extirpation.

I think that Plotinus's response to this piece of troublemaking would be that the composite is not a sufficiently autonomous entity to merit a distinct ethical system. The only proper thing to be done about the composite is to purify it, or rather to separate our true selves from it. Indeed it is about this that all traditional Platonist talk of "purification" is concerned, not about the soul proper, as Plotinus makes clear in III.6.5.13–29:

"But what could the "purification" of the soul be, if it had not been stained at all, or what its "separation" from the body? (In the case of the intellective soul, it consists in "turning away" from the concerns of the body.) But the purification of the part subject to affections (*to pathêtikon*) is the "waking up" from inappropriate images and not seeing them, and its separation is effected by not inclining much downwards and not having a mental picture (*phantasia*) of the things below.

But separating it could also mean taking away the things from which it is separated when it is not standing over a vital breath (*pneuma*) turbid from gluttony and sated with impure meats, but that in which it resides is so fine that it can ride (*ocheisthai*) on it in peace. (trans. Armstrong)

This embodies one of Plotinus's rare references to the Middle Platonic doctrine of the "pneumatic vehicle of the soul,"[23] adopted once again by his successors, from Porphyry on, but it shows how he views this dubious level of the human being. All one can do with it is to fine-tune it and scarify it so that it provides the least possible disturbance to the soul proper. It should not have any concerns of its own.

The late treatise, *On What are Evils* (I.8), deserves some notice in this survey, since it serves to provide a metaphysical foundation for Plotinus's ethical position. For an essentially monistic philosophical system, such as is that of Plotinus, the origin and nature of evil is a difficult and sensitive question. It is not possible that there should be some other positive entity or force in the world independent of the first principle, but yet it is necessary to identify in some way that which makes all other things than the One, especially the contents of the physical world, less than perfect. At the level of Intellect or Soul, this element may be characterized as "otherness," or "intelligible matter" (as it is, for instance, in II.4), but this cannot yet be deemed "evil," *kakon*. That only arises in the physical world, and properly in the sublunary world.

In I.8.3.23–5, Plotinus makes the curious statement that "just as there is absolute good and good as a quality, so there must be absolute evil and the evil derived from it which inheres in something else." This has a dangerously dualistic ring to it, one would think, but it seems that all Plotinus wants to assert is that there is a source of evil in the physical world independent of the soul, and that there is no aspect of soul that is inherently evil. It is important to him to assert this, since the most influential of his predecessors, Numenius, who was also the most dualistic, had maintained the existence of an evil world soul (Fr. 52 Des Places), and this was too positive a force for Plotinus's liking.

For Plotinus, primal evil is the nonexistent (in the sense of what is *other than being*),[24] the absolutely deficient, the absolutely unmeasured (all this in ch. 3). It arises as the incidental, but unavoidable, consequence of the spontaneous overflowing of the One, or the Good. As he says in chapter 7:

Since not only the Good exists, there must be the last end to the process of going out (*ekbasis*) past it, or if one prefers to put it like this, a progressive going down (*hupobasis*) or departure (*apostasis*): and this last, after which nothing else can come into being, is Evil. Now it is necessary that there should be that which comes after the First, and therefore that there also should be a Last; and this is Matter, which possesses nothing at all of it any longer. And herein lies the necessity of Evil. (18ff.)

I do not feel called upon, in the present context, to enter into the vexed question of the origin of matter, on which Denis O'Brien has recently produced a trenchant monograph (contra Kevin Corrigan).[25] From the point of view of ethics, the important result of Plotinus's identification of the origin and nature of evil is that it has nothing essential to do with the soul, and that the soul can therefore purify itself by identifying and rejecting the measurelessness (ametria) and formlessness (to aneideon) in the physical world, and turning to pure Form.

In the two final chapters of the tractate (14–15), Plotinus presents an extraordinary picture of the confrontation between the soul and matter, neither of which can really affect the other, on the shadowy battlefield of the physical world, ending with the striking image of matter in the world as like a prisoner bound in chains of gold, by which he is completely hidden. Essentially, matter throws up a screen of attractive illusion, which the soul must see through, and evil is its not being able to do that. Thus does I.8 reinforce the basic thrust of Plotinus's ethical stance.

One final topic might be included under this heading, though for the ancients, strangely enough, it formed part of physics rather than of ethics, and that is the question of fate and free will. For us, the postulation of free will might seem to constitute the prerequisite for an ethical theory, but ancient thinkers, whether Platonist, Peripatetic, or Stoic, seem rather to have concentrated on the metaphysical implications of the concepts of fate or providence, and their consequences for the estimation of "what is in our power" (to eph'hêmin), though they certainly did not ignore the moral implications.

Plotinus addresses various aspects of the topic, first in an essay On Free Will and the Will of the One, which Porphyry placed in his sixth Ennead (VI.8), since it relates to Plotinus's doctrine of the One, and then in a long treatise On Providence, which Porphyry divided in two (III.2–3) and placed in the third Ennead, which is concerned primarily with "physical" issues.

Plotinus's position on the subject of free will and determinism is of considerable interest, and has an important bearing on his ethical doctrine as a whole, but it will only be possible to touch on it here. In VI.8 (the first section of which, chs. 1–6, concerns human free will) Plotinus makes clear that what would vulgarly be regarded as the essential characteristic of freedom, the ability to decide between alternative courses of action, is really not a lofty or admirable thing at all, but a function of our lowly and imperfect state as embodied intellects. Beings at the highest level of consciousness, that is to say, pure intellects, know already, without deliberating, the correct course of action, and their freedom is simply to do that. They do not require "freedom of choice." Our aim should be to attain their state as nearly as we can while still in the body, and to make as few choices as possible. What we think of as free choices and decisions are really just conditioned reactions to external impulses, or to desires generated by our own bodily needs, and they are thus, from a higher perspective, "unfree" (cf. esp. ch. 2).

From III.2–3 it becomes clear that Plotinus is in fact much affected by the Stoic arguments for determinism, and has not much use for the traditional Platonist or Peripatetic answers to them, as set out in the treatise *On Fate* of Pseudo-Plutarch, Alcinous's brief exposition in chapter 26 of the *Didaskalikos*, or Alexander of Aphrodisias's essay *On Fate*. If Plotinus is not a Stoic determinist, it is only, I think, because of a daring conception of his which sees the highest element in us, the "undescended" intellect, as in fact an autonomous component of the hypostasis of intellect, and thus in its own right (since every intellect in Intellect is in a way coextensive with the whole) a guiding principle of the universe. If one is oneself the author of the universal order, that is, of the providential dispositions of the *Logos*, then one cannot be properly regarded as constrained or determined by this order, since it is not something external to one. We can see something of this doctrine coming out in such a passage as III.3.4, but it must be connected with the doctrine of VI.8.1–6 before its full implications become clear. Plotinus's views on free will and determinism are austere, certainly, but not fatalistic in any vulgar sense, and they differ significantly in this way from those of the Stoics.[26] They also form an entirely appropriate background to his ethics, focused as it is on reassimilation to Intellect.

One might raise the question in closing, mindful of Porphyry's remark in chapter 14 of the *Life*, that Plotinus's writings are "shot through with both Stoic and Peripatetic doctrines in a hidden form," as to how far Plotinus's ethical concerns accord or conflict with those of his predecessors.

As for Plato, it was Plotinus's concern always to remain true to his teachings, and any deviations would be inadvertent. However, his strong distinction between intellect and soul, and his equally strong distinction between soul and animate body, do seem to give him a somewhat different perspective. In particular, the doctrine of two grades of virtues, the "civic" and the cathartic, though it builds on distinctions made by Plato, particularly in the *Phaedo*, is not to be found in Plato as such. Also, in his attitude to suicide, and to fate and free will, Plotinus seems closer to the Stoics, though, as we have seen from his criticisms of them in connection with his doctrine of *eudaimonia*, he likes to maintain his distance from them.

As regards Aristotle, the situation is more complex. Can we say that Plotinus's ethics is either Aristotelian, as for instance was that of Plutarch or Alcinous, or anti-Aristotelian, as was that of Atticus or Numenius? It seems to me that in fact Plotinus largely ignores the main doctrines of the *Nicomachean Ethics*. Where does he stand, for example, on the doctrine of virtue as a mean, or on the practical syllogism, or on friendship? He is not *opposed* to these doctrines, I think; he is just not much concerned with them.[27] On one important topic of dispute between Peripatetics and Stoics, the relative merits of *metriopatheia* and *apatheia*, the moderation or extirpation of the passions, as an ethical ideal, he was certainly on the side of the Stoics (though he recognized, as we have seen, that *metriopatheia* was an appropriate aim of the *civic* virtues). The one basic doctrine of Aristotle with which Plotinus was in thorough agreement was one in which Aristotle was not at odds with Plato, and that is the identification of the end of life as contemplation and divinization, as set out in *Nicomachean Ethics* X.7. But on the whole it is fair to say that the tone of Plotinus's ethical utterances is more Stoic than Aristotelian.

The Plotinian ethical system is, then, as I have said, an uncompromisingly self-centered and otherworldly one. If we feel that an ethical theory should include an element of concern for others *for their own sake*, then, I think, Plotinus cannot be said to have an ethical theory. But that would after all not be quite fair. It is by no means clear, after all, that an ethical system needs to involve more than a set of precepts regulating our behavior and attitudes toward our fellow men, or living creatures generally, and even toward the inanimate environment, without specifying the motives governing such behavior. We can observe Plotinus in practice behaving with admirable courtesy, considerateness, and public-spiritedness, but we must recognize that all that matters to him ultimately is, as he said in his last recorded utterance, on his deathbed, to his friend, the doctor Eustochius, that he "return the god in him to the divine in the universe" (*Life* 3.26–7).

NOTES

1 Cf. *Life of Plotinus* ch. 2, where we learn that Plotinus would not even make use of medicines derived from parts of wild animals, basing his refusal on his disapproval of eating the flesh of tame animals – a position with interesting modern resonances!

2 For a discussion of the distinction that Plotinus makes between the two grades of virtue, the "political" and the "purificatory," see Dillon 1983, 92–105.

3 *Logismos*, that is, in the present context, the level of consciousness proper to embodied soul.

4 See the excellent recent Budé edition of Whittaker 1990 and Dillon 1993.

5 Aristotle's theory of perfect friendship, as set out in book 8 of the *Nicomachean Ethics*, constitutes an exception, perhaps, involving as it does loving another person *for his own sake*. There is also an interesting passage of Plato's *Laws* (V.731d–e), of which Lloyd Gerson has reminded me, where Plato attacks what he identifies as the traditional attitude that "every man is by nature a lover of self," and condemns *excessive* self-love (*hê sphodra heautou philia*) as the root of all evil. But this, I think, is an attack on vulgar selfishness, not on the deeper self-centeredness that is at the core of Platonist ethics.

6 E.g. *SVF* III. (Arius *ap.* Stobaeus: "good proportion of the limbs with each other and with the whole." Cf. 279 (Cicero Tusculan Disputations 4.31) and 392 (Philo, *De Vita Mosis* 140), which add "good colouring" to the definition.

7 I do not, however, see the force of the following argument (1.29ff.): "If

the whole is beautiful, the parts must be beautiful too; a beautiful whole can certainly not be composed of ugly parts; all the parts must have beauty." Why should this be so? If beauty resides in the *symmetria* of parts, why need the parts as such themselves be beautiful? A given "part," let us say a hand, might well itself be beautiful, admittedly, and beautiful because adorned with, let us say, beautiful fingers, but sooner or later, surely, one comes to a "part" of which it makes little sense to declare that it is either beautiful or ugly, e.g., a segment of a finger.

8 There is a fuller exposition of Plotinus's doctrine of intellectual beauty and our mode of attaining it in the later treatise V.8, reading of which is warmly recommended, but we need not go into it now.

9 One of the interesting questions surrounding this piece is the fact that the later Aristotelian commentator Elias, in his *Prolegomena* (6.15.23–16.2), refers to a monograph (*monobiblon*) of Plotinus *On Rational Withdrawal* (*Peri eulogou exagôgês*), his account of which does not correspond very closely to what we have in I.9. Elias reports Plotinus as rejecting all of the traditional Stoic five reasons for suicide, and saying that suicide is wrong in all circumstances, whereas at 1.16f. he says "And if each man has a destined time allotted to him, it is not a good thing to go out before it, *unless, as we maintain, it is necessary.*" He makes it clear also in the late treatise I.4 that the sage will be able to decide in what circumstances to "withdraw" (8, 9–10; 16, 21–9).

10 For further discussion of this see my article quoted in note 1 above. It is interesting in this connection to note that Porphyry, in his interpretation of I.2 in his *Sententiae*, ch. 42, derives two further higher grades of virtue, the contemplative and the paradigmatic, out of Plotinus's discussion in chs. 6–7, where it does not in fact seem to be Plotinus's intention to postulate further grades of virtue.

11 And also, for instance, in the "middle period" treatise, III.6.1–5, *On the Impassibility of Things Without Body.*

12 In his most useful book, 1988, esp. ch. 8. See also Dillon 1990, 19–31. It might be more accurate to specify, as we shall see, that the distinction, in Plotinus's doctrine, is between soul and *animate body*. But basically Emilsson's observation is perfectly valid.

13 That is to say, the contemplation of the Good, the *megiston mathêma* of *Republic* VI. 505a.

14 Because the Stoic soul is unitary and material.

15 In ch. 14 of the present treatise, but also, most notably, in I.1, which we will turn to presently.

16 Borrowing here a well-known dictum of Epicurus, cf. Fr. 447 Usener.

17 Indeed, at the end of I.3, he makes just this point, that, although the lower virtues are imperfect without the accession of dialectic and theoretical wisdom (*sophia*), they will not be eliminated by its acquisition, but rather brought to completion: "So wisdom comes after the natural virtues, and then brings the character (*ta êthê*) to perfection; or rather, when the natural virtues exist, both increase and come to perfection together: as the latter progresses, it perfects the former" (6.19–23). As regards the final phrase, I take this to be the meaning, as I do not think that Plotinus can mean that progress in the lower virtues brings the higher to perfection; but all the Greek says is that, "as *the one* (*hê hetera*) progresses, it perfects *the other*" (*tên heteran*).

18 Even here, of course, one could make a distinction between saying that *A* had a worse bout of the flu than *B* because he had it for three days longer, and asserting that, at any given moment, *A* was sicker than *B*, *A* would not necessarily be sicker just because he had been suffering *longer*, unless his suffering at the given moment were also *more intense*.

19 Cf. ch. 3: "What, then, about the statement, 'he has been *eudaimôn* for longer, and has had the same thing (sc. the noetic world) before his eyes for longer'? If in the longer time he gained a more accurate knowledge of it, then the time would have done something more for him. But if he knows just the same all the time, the man who has seen it once has as much."

20 Although in fact Plotinus takes his start from certain remarks of Aristotle in the *De anima* 408b1ff.

21 On this entity, see the excellent monograph of O'Daly 1973.

22 I must say that I prefer to read here *par'autês*, with the corrector of the Laurentianus (A), and Ficino, to the *par'autên* of the mss., approved by H-S, though I grant that sense can be given to this – "of itself," as Armstrong translates it. The basic meaning is the same either way, though, I think.

23 Dodds gives a good account of the genesis of this doctrine in 1963, 313ff.

24 He actually describes it, in a bold phrase, as "a sort of form of non-existence" (*hoion eidos ti tou mê ontos*, ch. 3.5). He goes on to specify: "Non-being here does not mean absolute non-being, but only something other than being; not non-being, however, in the same way as the movement and rest which are co-ordinate with being, but like an image (*eikôn*) of being, of something still more non-existent."

25 1991 Cf. Corrigan 1986a, 167–81. And see his chapter in the present volume.

26 It seems fair to remark, however, that the Stoic sage was deemed to be "free" by the very act of assenting to the inexorable order of the *Logos*, as is evidenced by Zeno's image of the little dog tied to the cart (*SVF* II.975).

27 This does not, of course, mean that he will not frequently use Aristotelian formulations to buttress his own doctrine, but when he does, he will often use them for un-Aristotelian ends as, for example, in the case of *De anima* 408b1ff. in I.1, in connection with his doctrine of the self, or *Nicomachean Ethics* I.8 in connection with his doctrine of well-being in I.4.

14 Plotinus and language

I REPRESENTATION

Plotinus's highest metaphysical principle, the One or Good, is ineffable (V.3.13.1; cf. V.3.14.1–8; V.5.6.11–13; VI.9.5.31–2).[1] Indeed, Plotinus is hesitant to attribute "good," "is" (VI.7.38.1–2), or even "one" (VI.9.5.30–3) to it. If the heart of his philosophical enterprise is to make meaningful statements about this principle, and furthermore our understanding of all else is informed by it, we may well ask why, in the light of this apparent despair of language, he would continue in his quest (his work extends to nine hundred and seventy-four pages of Oxford text).[2]

Of course, in saying that the One is ineffable, Plotinus has already made a statement, albeit negative, about the One. So at least this negative statement is permissible. Further examination of the possibilities of negative language offers more fruitful ways out of the closure apparently imposed by the stricture of ineffability. Before we consider further the question of the One's ineffability, it will be useful to examine the uses that Plotinus makes of negation. Plotinus uses negation to avoid confusion of an incorporeal reality accessible only to the mind or spirit with a corporeal reality perceived by our senses.

We may begin our examination of negation by exploring complementary uses of positive and negative language. In a discussion of the omnipresence of the hypostasis of Soul (VI.4.7–8), Plotinus asks us to imagine a hand exerting its force upon a plank. The force of the hand is present to the entire plank without division, even if the hand itself is not thus present. Even so may the Soul be present to the many particulars of the corporeal world without division. Then

Plotinus qualifies this image. The hand is still bodily and thus not the best illustration of Soul, which is incorporeal. He asks us now to imagine a luminous mass in the center of a transparent sphere. We are now further invited to subtract the corporeal mass of the luminous body from the picture. For it was not qua body, but qua luminous that the luminous object exerted its presence upon the surface of the sphere. Light itself is incorporeal.

In both figures, the hand and the plank, and the luminous body and the sphere, the terms of the comparison, hand and source of light, are advanced to demonstrate presence without division. To accomplish this end, the corporeal character of the source must be removed. Thus the hand is interesting, not for its bodily nature, but for its force. The source of light is valuable, not for its corporeal character, but because it is a source of light that is itself incorporeal. In both cases Plotinus is practicing abstraction (*aphairesis*), a procedure by which he renders the comparison useful by negating those aspects that would disarm it (V.4.7.19).[3] Abstraction is a form of nonprivative negation, that is, it does not take away any attribute that is proper to its subject (cf. IV.7.10.30; V.3.9.3; V.5.7.20; V.8.9.11; VI.2.4.14; VI.8.8.14; VI.8.21.26, 28). By contrast, *sterêsis* or deprivation is a form of privative negation which Plotinus reserves for matter/evil (I.8.1.17–19 of matter–evil as deprivation of good; as deprivation of form: I.8.11; cf. II.4.13).[4]

Negative language may succeed in avoiding the confusion of intelligible with sensible reality. Nevertheless, it remains unsatisfactory. What has seemed to be a positive statement (e.g., Soul is light) unpacks as negative (Soul is like light because it is *not* corporeal). What Soul *is*, in a positive sense, is not here, though doubtless somewhere.[5]

How then can we make a positive statement about incorporeal and intelligible reality that will not confuse its subject with corporeal and sensible reality? Intelligible reality bears to sensible reality the relation of original to image. To understand the nature of that relationship, we must first distinguish between two models of the relationship between original and image. Using one corporeal and sensible artifact as a pattern, an artisan might make another that is like it in the sense that it effectively duplicates it. He makes one chair or table after the pattern of another. Each is like the other. The relation of likeness is one of similarity, a symmetrical relationship. On another model, the artist represents the pattern in the image through an accumulation of similar characteristics, a color here, a certain curvature there, so that the whole portrait looks like the original, without being another version of it. The image indeed is like the original, but the relationship is not one of duplication. An artist paints a portrait of his subject. Between that subject and the painting, there is, of course, a relationship of likeness, in the sense of the symmetrical relation of similarity we have just examined. On the other hand, there is also a relationship of imitation that transcends and yet embraces that symmetrical relationship. Plotinus then distinguishes two senses of likeness: (1) a symmetrical relation of likeness that exists between two things which bear to each other a mutual resemblance; and (2) an asymmetrical relationship of likeness that exists between a pattern and a copy (over and above the symmetrical relationship of likeness) (I.2.2.4–10; cf. 1.2.7.27–30). We may call the latter relationship "representation."

On the model of the subject and the portrait there is then a symmetrical relation of likeness. Thus, curvature of a certain kind is present both in the snub nose of the subject and in the portrait. The subject in fact has a snub nose, while the portrait has only the *appearance* of a snub nose that is represented in the portrait. The attribute "snub-nosed" is contained truly in the subject. The relation of imitation between the original and the image is a kind of likeness that, unlike the likeness of mere similarity that it embraces, is asymmetrical. Thus we predicate "snub-nosed" both of the subject and the portrait, but in a way that does not confuse the original with the image. The portrait image also analyzes and isolates characteristics that, in the original, are held in unity. Thus the artist who produces the portrait analyzes "snub-nosed" into a certain kind of curvature or, seeing that there is a certain color required for depiction of the eyes, employs it for that purpose. Yet in the original, the curvature is not in fact separated from the snub nose, nor is the color in fact separated from the eyes. These attributes are part of what the original is. Thus:

It is as if, the visible Socrates being a man, his painted picture, being colours and painter's stuff, was called Socrates; in the same way, therefore, since there is rational form according to which Socrates is, the perceptible Socrates should not rightly be said to be Socrates, but colours and shapes which are representations of those in the form; and this rational form in relation to the truest form of man is affected in the same way. (VI.3.15.31–8)[6]

The distinction that we make between substance and quality when we speak of objects in the sensible world does not pertain to the intelligible world, because it detracts from its organic wholeness:

Reality there, when it possesses an individual characteristic of substance, is not qualitative, but when the process of rational thinking separates the distinctive individuality in these realities, not taking it away from the intelligible world but rather grasping it and producing something else, it produces the qualitative as a kind of part of substance, grasping what appears on the surface of the reality. (II.6.3.10–20)

Notice that the process of rational thinking portrayed in this passage individuates and analyzes attributes in the intelligible world in the same manner as the artist in our example.

When we speak of the relationship between the Forms and the particulars as one of pattern and copy, our language suggests some kind of making. A craftsman makes a copy after a pattern and thus mediates between them. In Plato's *Timaeus* (28a5–b1) such a relationship is portrayed as the Demiurge fashions the world after the pattern of the Forms. This story is interpreted literally by Aristotle and his school and by Plutarch, who see the making of the world as taking place in time, but allegorically by Xenocrates, Crantor, and the Platonic Academy, who see it as a demonstration of the character of the relationship between the intelligible and sensible worlds that is fixed eternally.[7] Plotinus subscribes to the latter view. He nevertheless uses the imagery of the Demiurge to describe mediation among the hypostases and the sensible world. Thus Intellect, that mediates eternally between the One and the Soul, is a Demiurge (II.3.18.15) and the Soul, that mediates eternally between Intellect and the sensible world, is also a Demiurge (IV.4.9.9).[8]

II REFLECTION

Clearly Plotinus does not interpret the making of the world by the Platonic Demiurge literally. Yet a figurative interpretation of the Demiurge still has its uses for Plotinus. It introduces a separation between intelligible and sensible reality that allows us to compare them and to develop a careful method of predication which will avoid the confusion of intelligible with sensible reality.

On the other hand, Plotinus, who is in any case critical of the literal interpretation of the Demiurge, is not entirely happy with his own metaphorical uses of the story. He is particularly concerned with that very separation that is so convenient for the purposes of comparison where there is rather a relationship of ontic dependence between them established in the procession of sensible from intelligible reality. Plotinus states this relationship:

In each and every thing there is an activity (*energeia*) which belongs to substance and one which goes out from substance; and that which belongs to substance is the active actuality which is in each particular thing, and the other activity derives from that first one, and must in everything be a consequence of it, different from the thing itself: as in fire there is a heat which is the content of its substance, and another which comes into being from that primary heat when fire exercises the activity which is native to its substance in abiding unchanged as fire. So it is also in the higher world; and much more so there, while the Principle "abides (*menontos*) in its own proper way of life," the activity generated from the perfection in it and its coexistent activity acquires substantial existence, since it comes from a great power (*dunamis*), the greatest indeed of all, and arrives at being and substance. (V.4.2.27–37)

The words "abides in its own way of life" are taken from Plato's *Timaeus* 42e5–6 where the Demiurge, after the creation of soul and before leaving the creation of mortal bodies to his children, "abided in his own way of life." In the same chapter, Plotinus applies these words to the One in its production of Intellect (V.4.2.21). Plotinus is clearly taking liberties with the text of Plato to gain his result. The separation between the intelligible and sensible worlds that is suggested by the use of Demiurgic imagery is to be counterbalanced by the notions of abiding on the part of the source and procession on the part of the product.[9]

On this model, the product is not cut off from its source, but remains dependent upon it: "Just as it is not possible to have substance without power, so it is not possible to have power without substance" (VI.4.9.23–4). Thus the powers (*dunameis*) that proceed from the intelligible world, like light from light, are yet grounded in their respective substances (VI.4.9.25–8). Plotinus entertains the objection that a painter may produce a painting and withdraw from it, so that the product is not dependent upon its source (on the model of representation). He substitutes for the image in a painting the image in a mirror. It is true that, in a mirror image, the image only continues to exist so long as the reflected object continues to stand before the reflective surface. When the object is withdrawn, the image no longer exists. Now, in the case of intelligible reality, the object reflected in the mirror of the sensible world is eternal and remains where it is in its relationship to sensible reality. So the product remains in dependence upon its source.[10] We may refer to this latter relationship between the original and the image as one of "reflection."

Let us consider how the model of reflection corrects the model of representation. The artist represents the attributes of imitation in the original by means of attributes of similarity, curved lines for "snub-nosed," and so forth. Yet the attributes of the original are not truly present in the image, but only represented in it. On the model of reflection, the attributes of the original are truly present in the image, as they stand in dependence upon and continuity with it. Yet the product is not confused with the source, for it "abides" in what it is. Where the model of representation allows us to avoid the confusion of intelligible with sensible reality, the model of reflection introduces an optimism with respect to language. If the model is truly present in its image, then surely the image has promising veridical possibilities.[11]

III ILLUMINATION

Reflection is an instance of illumination and light is the master metaphor in Plotinus.[12] All figurative language other than illuminationist imagery is to be qualified in the direction of fulfilling the conditions for illumination. The light that we see with our eyes is, on Plotinus's view, incorporeal, even if its source is corporeal (IV.5.7.41–2). It is for this reason that the imagery of light and its source is preferable to the figure of the hand and the plank in VI.4.7–8. The source of the light is source of light, not qua corporeal, but qua luminous. So to remove body by abstraction is not to take out anything essential. Since the bodily character of the hand is essential to its exercise of force over the plank, to remove its corporeality is to render the hand and the force that it exerts an imperfect illustration of the presence of the incorporeal to the corporeal. Thus we need not qualify light to render it incorporeal. Now reflection is an obvious instance of illumination (IV.5.7). Therefore reflection and illumination do not presuppose the corporeal character of their source.

Light and the presence of light to the objects that it illumines are inseparable. Reflection is, of course, a species of illumination. For Alexander of Aphrodisias, reflection is to be accounted for by the juxtaposition of the subject of reflection and the reflective surface. Reflection is a joint effect produced by both (De anima 42.19–43 [Bruns]). Plotinus criticizes this idea by asserting that light is an activity (energeia) that proceeds from a luminous source, rather than an effect that arises both from the source of illumination and the illumined object. Thus the activity of projecting the image to be reflected is an effect of the source alone: if the reflective surface happens to be present, then it will reflect that image. Presence and withdrawal belong properly to the reflected object alone and do not describe an act of juxtaposition. Thus, for light to be is for it to be present. It is pure presence (IV.5.7.35–49).[13] Thus light, both sensible and intelligible, is not only accessible, but self-manifesting.

Light is both the means of vision that lends transparency to things seen and is in its own nature transparent. When we behold other objects, light is a marginal object of awareness. Yet it may become the focal object of awareness (V.5.7.1–10). This pattern of awareness is applied as well to the consciousness that Intellect has of the One. If intellect abstracts (aphêsei) the objects of its vision (the Forms), it sees the light by which it saw them, namely, the One (V.5.7.16–21). The One is light proprio sensu: it is the absolutely transparent that is seen when all else is abstracted.

We should notice here that Plotinus is reshaping the architecture of Plato's intelligible universe. In Plato, the philosopher turns around from the shadows of the cave toward the light of the sun. Thus he turns around from the sensible world to behold the intelligible world.[14] In the present passage in Plotinus, we see that no turning, no spatial metaphor is summoned to describe illumination. We have seen how the model of reflection overcomes the distance introduced by the model of representation. Here we may see how the language of illumination also stresses the continuity between awareness of sensible objects and illuminating Form.[15]

The imagery of "emanation" is used where Plotinus compares

the procession of all things from the One to the flowing forth of streams from a spring as from an undiminished source (III.8.10.5–10). Plotinus distinctly denies that light, which is incorporeal, emanates from its source (IV.5.7.46; cf. II.1.8.1–3). He describes the emanation of Intellect from the One by advancing, in addition to the imagery of light proceeding from its source, other imagery of emanation, of snow and cold and flower and scent (V.1.6.27–37). The imagery of emanation is successful to the degree that it expresses the relationship of dependence that exists between source and product, but unsuccessful to the degree that its figures are corporeal. A comparison with V.4.2.27–37 cited above will show that the principle of procession of an activity (*energeia*) from power (*dunamis*) is at work here. We have seen that that principle best corresponds to the procession of light from its source. Powers proceed from the intelligible to the sensible world as light from light (VI.4.9.25–7). The examples of spring and streams, snow and cold, and flower and scent work to the extent that they illustrate this principle. Yet its paradigmatic instantiation is the procession of light from its source. Thus the procession of sensible from intelligible reality is not merely *likened* to the procession of light from its source. It *is* such a procession.[16]

IV THE PROPOSITIONAL SENTENCE

Insofar as we speak, not in exclamations, but in propositional sentences, language is, in Beierwaltes's phrase, a phenomenon of difference.[17] The propositional sentence must consist of a subject, a copula, and a predicate. Yet this sentence cannot ostensibly represent an intelligible reality that transcends the difference required by the form of the statement. Thus a statement of the type, "The One is *x*," must necessarily misrepresent the simplicity and unity of the One, whatever the predicate that is used, by adding something (i.e., some thing) to it. Thus:

It [the One] is, therefore, truly ineffable: for whatever you say about it, you will always be speaking of a "something." But "beyond all things and beyond the supreme majesty of Intellect"[18] is the only one of all the ways of speaking of it which is true; it is not its name,[19] but says that it is not one of all things. (V.3.13.1–5)

Even a statement that would try to omit the copula will fail:

> Then when it [the One] says "I am this," if it means something other than
> itself by "this," it will be telling a lie; but if it is speaking of some incidental
> property of itself, it will be saying that it is many or saying "am am" or "I I."
> Well then, suppose it was only two things and said "I and this." It would
> already be necessary for it to be many: for, as the two things are diverse and
> in the manner of their diversity, number is present and many other things.
> (V.3.10.35–40)

The One is also ineffable as any propositional statement would presume a limitation on its essential indeterminacy (VI.9.3–4).[20]

  This vein of enquiry would again invite pessimism with respect to
the capacity of language. Language will never *disclose* the One:
"How then do we speak about it [the One]? Indeed we say something
about it (*ti peri autou*), but we do not say the One itself (*ou mên auto
legomen*)" (V.3.14.1–3). This passage offers two uses of the verb "to
say" (*legein*): (1) an intransitive use (*legein* with the preposition *peri*,
"about" and the genitive case, to "talk about," or "discuss" (the
One) and (2) a transitive use (*legein* and the accusative), "to say," or
to "disclose," the One. The first option is open to language, but not
the second (cf. VI.7.38.4–5).

  Yet we may use language to speak about, or discuss the One, so
long as we are aware of the limitations of speech. A blunt instrument may be better than none at all, although we should use it with
appropriate care. The project of negative theology that we have discussed so far has as its goal to make language do things that it
normally would not do while observing appropriate *caveats* at each
stage of its progress toward the One. Negative theology is not an
expression of mystical silence, but is always a function of speech
used in the service of philosophy.[21]

  If speech cannot disclose the One, can it disclose the nature of
Intellect? The statement "it is" (*estin*) is most true of the things we
say about Intellect (*tôn peri auto*)[22] and is itself (*auto*). By contrast,
"is" (*estin*) is not predicable of the One (VI.7.38.1–2). Thus it is not
the case that Plotinus entirely despairs of speech in its function of
disclosure.

  Apart from the simple statement "it is," which is most appropriate
to Intellect, there are predications made about the content of Intellect
that involve subject, copula, and predicate. Every Form in Intellect

contains every other Form by the interiority of its relations to the other Forms. We may say, for example "Beauty is good." However, we are not to think that some fragment of goodness is separated out from the Form of Goodness and attached to Beauty. Each Form is all the other Forms and each intellect is cognitively identical with each and every Form (V.5.1.19–43; V.8.3.30–4; V.9.8.3–7).[23]

We have already seen how for Plotinus, even as illumination is an activity of the source alone, so is reflection (itself an instance of illumination) the activity of the source of reflection and does not require the presence of a reflective surface for its completion. In our previous treatment of reflection, the context was the relationship between a superior model and an inferior image, for example, intelligible Form is reflected in the sensible world. However, in Intellect a Form is transparent to every other Form:

[The gods there] see all things, not those to which coming to be, but those to which real being belongs, and they see themselves in other things; or all things there are transparent, and there is nothing dark or opaque; everything and all things are clear to the inmost part to everything; for light is transparent to light. Each there has everything in itself and sees all things in every other, so that all are everywhere and each and every one is all and the glory is unbounded. A different kind of being stands out in each, but in each all are manifest (emphainei). (V.8.4.3–11)

The verb here translated as "are manifest" (emphainein) is used of reflection (Plato Republic 402b6; Plotinus I.4.10.14). Further (lines 23–4): "Here, however, one part would not come from another, and each would be only a part; but there each comes only from the whole and is part and whole at once: it has the appearance of a part, but the whole is seen in it (enhoratai) by a penetrating look." The verb enhorasthai (here translated by "seen in it") is also employed of reflection (IV.5.7.45; I.4.10.15). Plotinus proceeds (V.8.4.42–3): "All things of this kind there are like images seen (enhorômena) by their own light." Again, the verb enhorasthai ("seen," or, more accurately, "seen in"), associated with reflection, is used to demonstrate the reflection of each Form in all the others. What is truly remarkable in this passage is the notion that the Forms, in their mutual reflection, are like images (agalmata). We are so used to the idea that the relation of original and image (either representational or reflective) should describe the relationship between Form and particular that we are unprepared for the transposition of this relationship to the realm of Intellect and the Forms where it prevails among ontic equals.

In the sensible world, we see instances of reflection, either in the mirror as artifact or in other reflective surfaces, such as water. On Plotinus's view, we can be misled by our observations of reflection to believe that a reflective surface is required for the subject to project its reflective image. In fact, everything that is projects an image, but that image is not always received. The reflective image is always there, but under the opaque conditions of the world of sense, it does not always appear (IV.5.7.33–49). However, in Intellect, where there is no such opacity, the image of reflection is always received and is received by Intellect in all its parts. Every Form is at once a source and a receptacle of reflection under the conditions of total transparency where there is nothing to prevent such reflection.

I would like to make use of the phrase "speculative statement" here, without embroiling myself in the difficulties it brings with it in Hegel.[24] To this end, I would exploit the etymology of the English word "speculative," which is derived from the Latin *speculum*, or "mirror." In reference to the realm of Intellect, we may make the statement "Justice is beautiful." Now, at the level of Intellect, both terms of the statement, "justice" and "beautiful," have been purged by abstraction of their associations with the sensible world. Thus to say that Justice is beautiful is not to say that it is "a beautiful thing." Also, Beauty is utterly transparent to Justice as Justice is utterly transparent to Beauty. Each mirrors the other. Except for the form of the propositional sentence, it would be very difficult to say which is the subject and which is the predicate, even as it would be difficult to say which is the mirror and which the reflected object. We might well refer to each term of what I am calling a speculative statement as a subject–predicate. The copula is expressing, not an external, but an internal relationship. Each term of the speculative statement reflects the other in total transparency.[25]

Plotinus gives us a lively portrayal of what such discourse would be like in his account of Egyptian hieroglyphs:[26] "Inscribing in their temples one particular image of one particular thing, they manifested the non-discursiveness of the intelligible world, that is that every image is a kind of knowledge and wisdom and is subject of statements, all together in one and not discourse or deliberation"

(V.8.6.6–9). The descent into cursive script and the discursive thought that corresponds to it were a later development and a decline, both in writing and in thought (lines 9–12).

V PERSPECTIVE

In late antique and early medieval art, there is a habit of measuring perspective, not from the viewpoint of an ideal spectator, but from the central object in the piece. Plotinian optics corresponds to this practice of presenting perspective.[27] In a forthcoming paper, I argue that this principle informs Plotinus's understanding of the organization of internal space in architecture.[28] The progress of the soul toward the One is compared to a man entering a grand house, admiring its magnificent appointments, and then seeing the master of the house. As he fixes his gaze upon the master, "he mingles his seeing with what he contemplates, so that what was seen before (to horaton) has now become sight (opsis) in him and he forgets all the other objects of contemplation" (VI.7.35.7–16). I take opsis (vision) here to mean that angle of vision that belongs, no more to the spectator, but to the master of the house who has become the central piece from which perspective is measured. In another passage, again describing the progress of the soul to the One, Plotinus speaks of how a man enters a temple and passes through a series of rooms, each of which contains a statue of a god. At last he enters the immost shrine, and sees, not a statue, but the god himself, who is not an object of vision (horama), but another way of seeing (allos tropos tou idein) (VI.9.11.17–23). Although the objects seen are in a series rather than on the same plane, it remains true that the god, once seen, becomes the organizing principle of the whole piece. I take "another way of seeing" to represent the angle of vision belonging to the god.[29]

In an early medieval painting, the Virgin who is the central piece may organize the objects in the painting as seen from her perspective, so that, for instance, objects that would appear smaller from the angle of vision of the person looking at the painting will appear greater from the perspective of the Virgin. Now the One clearly cannot see, and definitely cannot see any object other than itself. Such vision would violate Eleatic principle by admitting duality. Yet everything below the One (if we must use the language of vertical space) may be organized as measured from the angle of vision that would belong to the One (if the One had vision). In both instances, this manner of organizing perspective belongs to a pious humility.

From our perspective the One, and indeed the whole of the intelligible world, is transcendent and hence other. Yet for Plotinus, difference belongs alone on our side and not on the side of the One (VI.9.8.33–5). Otherness belongs to a diminution of being. On the model of representation, we overcome our hybristic spectator-centered perspective through the refinements of negative theology. However, the model of reflection obviously runs in the other direction, for all things proceed from their source and center.

The painstaking exercises of negative theology that we undertake on the model of representation accustom us to speaking always of the intelligible world as pattern or model and the sensible world as copy or image. Now we have already seen how Plotinus can surprise us by locating the relationship of original and image within the mutual reflection of the Forms in Intellect (V.8.4.42–3). He can further astonish us by offering an image from the intelligible world to illustrate a phenomenon of the sensible world. Thus, he compares the procession of sensible light from its source to the procession of lower soul from higher soul (IV.5.7.33–51). Sensible fire "shines and glitters as if it was a Form" (I.6.3.25–6).[30] In the only passage in which he claims experience of the intelligible world in the first person, Plotinus speaks of the descent from this ecstasy to the sensible world as an interruption of his proper activity (IV.8.1.1–11).[31] Indeed there is an inversion of the relationship between sense and intellection, so that the soul "has seen" (eiden) the intelligible world, but has "understood" (katenoêsen) the sensible world (II.9.16.48–56).[32] Jerphagnon argues correctly that Porphyry offers in the Life of Plotinus a kind of docetic biography (my phrase) in which the sage Plotinus, his person, and the events of his life, are valuable mainly as a sort of stained glass window through which there shines intelligible light.[33]

The powerful imagery of "emanation," for example, the one spring source of the many streams or the one root source of the multiple life of the plant in III.8.10, should be interpreted perspectivally. In each case, Plotinus is maximizing the potential for unity.[34] It is not just the case that each example imperfectly represents the unity of the One. It is also that in each image the unity of the entity in question is measured from the perspective of the primal unity of the One that in its turn encodes the signifier.

VI LANGUAGE AND DECLARATION

We have seen that language may discuss the One, but never disclose it. There is a third way in which language may relate to the One that we may call "declaration." In declaration, our words may indeed not disclose the One, but our discussion is exalted as it points prophetically to the One and reflects and is charged with the One's presence.

Plotinus argues (V.3.14) that we do not have the One in the sense that we may disclose it, yet we may have it in the sense that it is the intentional object of our discussion. Another kind of having is to "have (or hold) toward" (echein pros, line 13) the One in a moment of mantic declaration of the One's presence. At this moment, we ourselves and our words are held or possessed (katochoi) by the One. The One, which is greater than what is said, holds forth or bestows (paraschôn) speech (together with intellect and perception, lines 17–19).[35] The One does not, of course, give us speech as parents give speech to children. Yet speech must proceed from the One as do the other things in our world.

We may notice here the colorful uses of echein, "to have, or hold." The One, which cannot be contained by our speech, may contain that speech both by its primary gift of language and by its possession of our words. Clearly, where discussion follows the model of representation, declaration follows the model of reflection. From the smooth transition between the modalities of having, from discussion which has the One as its intentional (though transcendent) object to declaration as a being held by the One which at first gave us speech, we may see that the mantic speech in question does not exclude, but rather embraces and exalts discussion.

We have seen that Plotinus measures perspective from the central piece in the scene rather than from the spectator. If we apply this principle to language, then we would see that the value and scale of our words are to be measured, not from the speaker, but from the object of his discourse. In one of the most beautiful and admired passages in Plotinus, Nature breaks her wonted silence to describe her creative contemplation (III.8.4.3–14). Employing the normal tools of literary criticism, we would see this passage as an exercise in personification. Perhaps we should be more subtle. If the perspective of discourse is measured from the object of speech, we should rather understand that Nature does speak, at least in the sense that Plotinus's words about her have their location, not in the speaker, but in the object of discourse. In the very speech of Plotinus Nature is not so much personified as hypostatized and is not possessed by, but rather possesses, his words. The same may be said of Plotinus's giving voice to the cosmos: "Looking upon it one might readily hear from it, 'A god made me.' " (III.2.3.19–21) and the statement: "Indeed this cosmos exists through him [the One] and each and every god and all that depends from him prophesies to men and proclaims what is dear to them" (II.9.9.39–42).[36]

VII THE LIMITS OF DISCOURSE

There is never an end to Plotinian discourse, for the reason that the limitations of discourse will always leave us demanding more. The soul, in union with its object of contemplation, still wishes to distance itself from what is has and to express it in words. There is a dialectical tension between silence and intuition, on the one hand, and words and discursive analysis, on the other (III.8.6.21–9).[37] The tension between saying and having that we observed earlier is also dialectical in nature. Having belongs to intuition, saying to discursive analysis, so that the same dialectical relationship that exists between intuition and discursive analysis belongs to saying and having. The restlessness of the soul, its wanting always to express what it has and thus distance itself from its having and its intuition, belongs to the very structure of the Plotinian universe. Intellect and the One are rich epistemic targets. Even in the moment of vision, we feel driven to (declarative) speech. Thus the Soul, even at the moment of its union (sunousia) with the One, proclaims (angellonta) that union (VI.9.7.22–3). In so doing, it becomes the reflective and declarative instrument of the One which, as we know from V.3.14.18–19, bestows speech.[38]

Declaration and prophecy are joined in V.3.14 as we declare the One "inspired and possessed" (enthousiôntes kai katochoi) (V.3.14.9).[39] Now discussion can never express the whole of Intellect or of the One. Nor can the act of interpretation, by its very nature, exhaust its text (unless we really believe with the positivists that there could be such a thing as a definitive interpretation). As Trouillard observes, discursive thought for Plotinus "oriented to the future, will never discover any true totality."⁴⁰ Of course, the future tense cannot really apply to the timelessness of the intelligible world, but its use can indicate that there is always more to come, that the subject is inexhaustible. Discussion is declarative in its pointing prophetically beyond its images to its intentional object. Thus, although the One is ineffable, "we speak and write impelling toward it" (VI.9.4.12–13).⁴¹ We can only point to, give a sign about, or indicate (sêmainein) the ineffable One (V.3.13.5). The Greek verb that is employed here may belong to prophecy. Thus, according to Heraclitus, "the god whose oracle is in Delphi neither says, nor conceals, but gives a sign (sêmainei).⁴²

Intellect is our king and sense perception is our messenger. Yet we too can be kings.⁴³ We can have Intellect in one of two ways: either as we have written laws, or as we have the mind of the lawgiver (V.3.3.4–V.3.4.4).⁴⁴ The lawgiver Minos produced his laws from ineffable contact (sunousia) with the mind of Zeus (VI.9.7.21–6).⁴⁵ Presumably those laws were not present in his mind as written texts, but in the mode of inspiration. Perhaps here we may think again of the passage in which Plotinus sees the Egyptian hieroglyphs as the perfect model of language without the syntax of discursive thought (V.8.6.6–9). The laws in the mind of the divine king are laid up in this heavenly script. All our attempts at discursive thought are partial restorations of this true language.

VIII CONCLUSIONS

The model of representation departs from the sensible world and attempts to account for intelligible reality in such a way that the two realms will not be confused with each other. The careful comparison which it undertakes suggests a separation between intelligible and sensible reality. The model of reflection, that counterbalances the model of representation, begins rather from the intelligible world and demonstrates both the real presence of intelligible to sensible reality and the ontic dependence of the latter upon the former. It stresses continuity, rather than separation.

The model of reflection opens up the avenue of measuring the perspective of language and its figures of speech from the intelligible center. Declaration, which participates in the model of reflection, participates in such a perspective, while discussion, which belongs to the model of representation, measures perspective from the sensible world.

The relationship between the two perspectives is not exclusive, but dialectical. Each requires the other. Speech can never exhaust its subject as interpretation is for Plotinus never definitive and belongs to a hermeneutical circle encompassing intelligible and sensible reality. A declarative statement will cry out for further discursive analysis. A statement belonging to discussion and discursive analysis will leave us feeling that there is something more not embraced by the narrow confines of the statement. Necessarily, because what is discussed is not some thing, Plotinian conversation will always resemble an attempt to recapture with frustrating partiality a seamless discourse that we have known but forgotten. Yet language, ever mantic, is transparent to reveal the One in and through the discursive operations of the mind.

NOTES

1 Cf. Plato *Parmenides* 142a; *Ep.* VII.341c5.
2 Reference throughout is made to the *editio minor* of Henry and Schwyzer, 1964–82.
3 The use of *huphairein*, V.4.7.33, is obviously equivalent to the use of *aphaireisthai* at V.4.7.19.
4 Cf. Mortley 1975, 374.
5 Cf. Alfino 1988, 279.
6 Trans. Armstrong 1966–88.
7 For the former position, cf. Plutarch *De animae procreatione* 1016cd and for the latter Proclus *In Timaeum* 89b (Diehl I 290/30 291/3); cf. Schroeder 1992, 36 and n37.
8 On the subject of representation, see further Schroeder 1978 and Schroeder 1992.
9 Cf. Schroeder 1992, 28–30; Dörrie 1985, 147 and n29, in addition to this text, adduces III.4.1; V.1.3.11; V.3.12.34. In this article, Dörrie argues that Platonism which, in contrast to the Peripatos, is convinced that we can think without language, systematically develops a use of language that deepens the ordinary senses of words so that the advanced student will see that the esoteric sense refers properly to an intelligible reality that transcends speech. He sees such a use of "abide" (*menein*) here.
10 Cf. Schroeder 1992, 31–2.

11 For the model of reflection generally, see Schroeder 1980; Schroeder 1984; Schroeder 1992, 24–65.

12 The metaphysics of light (*Lichtmetaphysik*) pervades Beierwaltes's work; the fundamental paper is Beierwaltes 1961; Ferwerda 1965, 6–7, 34, 46–7, 59–60, 194 argues against the Beierwaltian position. Essentially, he argues that Plotinus distinguishes between symmetrical and asymmetrical relations of likeness. It is only in the former that the two terms may share the same quality in common. From my argument above (under "Representation") it may be seen that this is not the case. His critique of Beierwaltes implies that before the absolute otherness and transcendence of the One, the value of all figurative language is relativized, i.e., that there is the sort of democracy of figurative language that I describe above. Beierwaltes 1971, successfully replies to Ferwerda's arguments. Cf. my defense of Beierwaltes in Schroeder 1992, 33n29 where I consider further scholarship that resists the Beierwaltian *Lichtmetaphysik*. Crome 1970 also sees a relativization of speech before the task of describing the transcendent; for my differences with Crome, see Schroeder 1985, 82–4; Mortley 1986, II, 238 correctly states Beierwaltes's position: "Beierwaltes has pointed to the way in which light symbolism becomes more than just an image of Neoplatonism: the image of light becomes a mode which actually casts and directs the terms of the analysis." Oosthout (1991, 120–1) objects that light merely illustrates the principle of procession of activity from power. For my opposing view that light is the larger category, see Schroeder 1994.

13 Schroeder 1992, 25–8.

14 Cf. *Republic* 514b2; 515c7; 516c6; 518d3; 521c5–6; 525c5; 526e3; and Beierwaltes 1991a, 180.

15 The language of conversion is also employed by Plotinus, but significantly it is used in the context, not of turning as from one thing to another, but of a turning inward to be aware of what already informs our awareness. Cf. V.3.1.3–4 and the further evidence presented in Beierwaltes 1991a, 175–82.

16 Cf. V.1.3.10–12; II.1.8.1–4; and Dörrie 1976, 34–5.

17 Beierwaltes 1985, 102–7; cf. Beierwaltes 1991a, 129–38.

18 Cf. Plato *Republic* 509b9.

19 Cf. Plato *Parmenides* 142a3.

20 Cf. O'Meara 1990, 148.

21 Cf. Mortley 1986, II, 251: " . . . in fact the negative way and the silence of the mystic are not closely related. The use of negatives is over and over regarded as a linguistic technique . . . the negative way is always a part of language: it is a linguistic manoeuvre."

22 Here Plotinus uses *peri* with the accusative, rather than with the geni-

tive (as in V.3.14 above), but the effect is the same: cf. Schroeder 1992, 68n6.

23 Cf. Schroeder 1992, 16; Trouillard 1961.

24 Beierwaltes 1972, 22, 45, 69 and 152 (on V.3.10.37: "I I" and "am am" as an attempt to avoid the copula) uses the Hegelian term *spekulativer Satz* to interpret Plotinus pushing the barriers of syntax.

25 On the question of whether there is propositional thought in Intellect see Lloyd 1970, who denies it, Sorabji 1982, who affirms it (*pace* Lloyd 1970; cf. further Lloyd's reply in Lloyd 1986 and 1990, 168), and Alfino 1988, who denies it. If by propositional thought, we mean that Intellect in thinking the Forms is also thinking their definitions and if further the defining term is introduced from without, then I would not see the presence of propositional thought in the Plotinian Intellect, even though I would admit a statement that is propositional in form.

26 Plotinus is doubtless thinking, not of the hieroglyphs normally accompanied by phonetic signs, but of the nonphonetic ideogram that represents an idea such as "life," or "happiness": cf. de Keyser 1955, 60–2.

27 Cf. II.8.1 and my discussion in Schroeder 1992, 21–3.

28 "Plotinus and Interior Space." Cf. Schroeder 1996.

29 Other interpretations, which I consider in "Plotinus and Interior Space," involve a metaphorical approach that would transfer "vision" and "another way of seeing" to ourselves. Obviously if these texts will admit of a strict construction, then that interpretation is to be preferred. Cf. Schroeder 1996.

30 Cf. Schroeder 1992, 3.

31 Cf. Schroeder 1992, 5–6 and O'Meara 1974 for a preference of MacKenna's translation (MacKenna 1962) over Armstrong's translation (Armstrong 1966–88) that presents the experience of intelligible reality as if it were an interruption of everyday experience.

32 Cf. Schroeder 1992, 20 and note 7 for further bibliography on this point.

33 Jerphagnon 1983.

34 Beierwaltes 1991a, 158: "*Steigerung* oder *Intensivierung* des ... Einheitspotentials."

35 For the view that these words must apply to the One as well as to pure intellect, the highest phase of the human soul that is in identity with the One, cf. Schroeder 1992, 69. This construction is supported by the following chapter whose subject is how the One can give what it does not have.

36 Cf. Schroeder 1992, 72–3; Plotinus's use of rhetoric (as, e.g., his use here of prosopopoeia) would be an excellent subject for further research.

37 Cf. Schroeder 1992, 76–7.

38 Cf. Schroeder 1992, 79–80.

39 Cf. Plato *Ion* 533e6–7; we may also think of poetry here: cf. Plato *Apology* 22c1; both the *Ion* 534b3–7 and the *Apology* 22c1–2 associate poetry and prophecy; cf. Schroeder 1992, 69–70.

40 Cf. Trouillard 1961, 132; cf. 130–1; cf. Mortley 1986, 1, 131.

41 Cf. Schroeder 1992, 78.

42 Diels and Kranz, vol. 1, 1964, B 93. Harder-Beutler-Theiler V b, 1960, properly refer V.3.13.6–9 to the Delphic self-knowledge knowledge of VI.7.41.22–5. Also, the mantic context is supplied in the following chapter, V.3.14.

43 The reference is to Plato *Philebus* 28c7.

44 Cf. V.3.4.20–7.

45 For the association of Minos with Zeus see Plato *Laws* 624a1; *Minos* 319e1; cf. Schroeder 1992, 72.

15 Plotinus and later Platonic philosophers on the causality of the First Principle

Within the history of philosophy, Plotinus is presented as the founder not only of a school, but of an entire current of thought, which we are accustomed to call "Neoplatonism." From Hegel onward, the relationship between later thinkers belonging to this current and its founder has been presented as an increasing systematization of a rich and somewhat chaotic thought into a deductive structure. This process is seen as having reached its summit with Proclus, who distinguishes himself from Plotinus precisely insofar as he gives to Neoplatonic philosophy a systematic order.[1] However, many relevant contemporary studies show that this model does not exhaust the complexity of the historical development of Neoplatonic thought.[2]

The first part of this study will deal with the most prominent features of Plotinus's interpretation of the Platonic doctrine of Ideas, and it is meant to elucidate the set of basic philosophic tenets issuing from this interpretation, which later Platonic thinkers endorsed as the common inheritance of their philosophy. In the second part I shall try to set out the reasons why, within the development of Neoplatonic thought, Plotinus's representation of suprasensible reality gave way to a more complex picture.

I

In two well-known passages (III.6.6.65–77 and V.5.11.16–22) Plotinus compares people who believe that bodies are the true beings (*onta*) with sleepers who consider as really subsistent the images of their dreams, unaware of their true nature. It is evident from the context that here he is not criticizing everyday assumptions, but the philosophical position which maintains that only bodies satisfy the re-

356

quirements for full reality: namely, the Stoic one.[3] By contrast, the characters of the true beings are conceived of as totally different from those of bodies. Bodily beings are subject to change, true beings are unchanging. Bodily beings need other principles for their subsistence, and moreover they necessarily possess magnitude and occupy space; true beings have their basis in themselves (idrumena eph'heautôn), and are independent of place and magnitude. Plotinus sums up all these features by saying that true beings possess an hupostasis noera, an intelligible reality (V.9.5.43–6).

This idea rests on the assumption that, in the search for an explanation of phenomena, an infinite regress can be avoided only if being is conceived of as having stability and intelligibility.[4] Does this mean that Plotinus thinks that the two kinds of being, the intelligible and the sensible, are totally opposed? Seemingly not, since in many passages he endorses the Platonic model of a relationship of imitation between sensible and intelligible reality. For instance, in VI.4.2.1–6 Plotinus follows the Platonic Timaeus, 48e6–49a1, in presenting the visible world as different from the true universe (to alêthinon pan), but at the same time as dependent on it (ex ekeinou êrtêmenon) insofar as it is a mimêma, an imitation, of it.

However, by saying that Plotinus shares with Plato the idea that the phenomena imitate intelligible patterns it is by no means implied that he takes for granted that such a doctrine is exempt from puzzling features. As a matter of fact, several treatises in the Enneads take into account difficulties regarding the participation of individuals in the Forms. In particular, VI.4 and 5, dealing with the presence of the suprasensible reality in the sensible, provide a wide discussion of the objections raised in the Platonic Parmenides against the relationship between sensible things and Forms.[5] At the end of this discussion intelligible realities are conceived of as having a set of characteristics which will be endorsed by all later Neoplatonic thinkers.

In the first part of the Parmenides the theory of the Forms is submitted to a series of criticisms. According to the first of them, an individual participating in a Form has to participate either in the whole of the given Form, or in a part of it (131a4–6). In the first case, the Form is credited with being in each individual with its entire nature; but since the hypothesis of the Forms requires that they exist apart from individuals, this would mean that the Form would be separate from itself. The answer provided by Socrates to this dilemma fails to demonstrate that there is a way in which the *eidos* can be present in its participants, while preserving its separateness. In fact, Socrates's attempt to compare the presence of a Form in many individuals to the way in which day can be present at the same time in different places prepares for his admission that the individual shares a part of the Form.[6] Parmenides's reply equates Socrates's analogy of the day with another analogy, according to which a Form can be present at the same time as a whole in many individuals (*en tauton ama pollachou*, 131b7) as a sail can cover several men. Accepting this equation, Socrates has no choice but to admit that the Form is present in its participant only in part, just as only a part of the sail covers one man among many.

When Porphyry entitled the treatise composed of VI.4 and 5[7] with the words of the Platonic "Parmenides" – *On the Presence of Being, One and the Same, Everywhere as a Whole (peri tou to on en kai tauton on ama pantachou einai olon)*[8] – he grasped that the Plotinian purpose was to state the way in which dilemmas about the relationship between intelligible and sensible realities could be solved. In turn, contemporary scholarship acknowledges that this treatise concerns Parmenides's aporias about Ideas.[9]

Plotinus's solution starts with the remark that our difficulties in understanding the omnipresence of intelligible realities result from believing that being (*to on*) has the same nature as the sensible world, and consequently from conceiving of its omnipresence as an everywhere distribution (VI.4.2.27–30). Plotinus introduces his well-known examples of the presence of the intelligible[10] with the observation that to subdivide intelligible being into its participants is tantamount to subdividing "what controls and holds together (*to kratoun kai sunechon*)" into the parts of what is controlled (VI.4.7.8–9).

Plotinus is here adopting the Aristotelian description of the relationship between soul and body provided in *De anima* 411b5–14, where Aristotle argues that soul is indivisible insofar as it is the principle giving to the body its unity. By so doing, Plotinus establishes two relevant points. First, he eliminates the criticisms against the doctrine of the Forms which are based on the interpretation of the presence of the Form in its participant as a local one. Secondly, he points to the fact that the causality of the Forms on their participants is by no means equivalent to an action or a production. It consists in "controlling and holding together" bodies, that is, in giving to them their inner *ratio* and the principle of their unity, as soul causes the life of the organized body.

The first point is directed at solving not only the aporia raised by "Parmenides" about the presence of Forms in their participants, but also Aristotle's objection regarding separation. In *Metaphysics* 1086b6–7, Aristotle argues that the main cause of the difficulties in the theory of Forms consists in their separation. The difficulty lies precisely in the fact that the doctrine of Forms postulates a set of principles which are meant to be, at one and the same time, subsisting apart from sensible things (*tines ousiai para tas aisthetas*, b8), and inherent in sensible things, giving them their characteristics. This position leads, in Aristotle's view, to the collapse of universals into particulars. Plotinus's remark that true being – that is, intelligible reality – does not share the localization of bodies is also directed against this criticism, insofar as he rejects the view that "to be in" has the same meaning in the case of bodies and in the case of intelligible characters. Such a reality escapes local extension, insofar as it is indivisible; consequently, it can be conceived of as present in an extended reality without subdivision (VI.4.8.34–8; see also VI.5.11.1–11).

Therefore, when Plotinus concludes that if this indivisible reality is participated in by some individual, it "will remain whole itself and whole in visible things" (VI.4.8.42–3), he is not making a choice between the two possibilities presented by "Parmenides," namely, participation in the Form as a whole or as a part. Both of these possibilities were in fact – in the Platonic *Parmenides* as well as by Aristotle – conceived of as features shared by the participated Form and the participant individual in one and the same manner. But according to Plotinus the participated Form cannot share with the participant individual the marks of corporeal reality, namely, spatiality and subdivision into parts (VI.4.11.6–9; see also VI.4.13.14–18 and VI.5.3.1–8). This analysis of the status of the intelligible model will give rise to the characteristic formula of Neoplatonic causality, according to which suprasensible causes are at the same time everywhere and nowhere.

Plotinus carefully distinguishes between the Idea as a property of an individual participant and the Idea as rational paradigm of all the particular instantiations (VI.5.6.11–12). The participated Idea obvi-

ously is particular, insofar as it is a property of an individual entity
But the rational paradigm considered in itself has to be "everywhere
(*pantachou*)" in the sense that in each instantiation there is present
the same "formula," as it were, even if no individual entity possesses it as its own property (VI.5.6.12–15). It follows that the rational paradigm is at the same time present in all the entities which
possess a particular instantiation of it, and separated from them as
well. Considered in itself, the Idea remains free from any relationship with particulars (VI.5.8.35); considered as the same "formula"
which is present in all the particular instantiations of it, it is present
everywhere.

This double status of transcendence and immanence can help
also in solving another set of objections about the Ideas, according
to which they are useless from the point of view of the explanation
of phenomenal reality, precisely because of their separateness. Plotinus's answer to this Aristotelian criticism consists in an analysis
of the causality of intelligible realities, which is intimately linked
with the idea of their presence "everywhere and nowhere."

A principle giving to a set of particular participants the character
which defines their nature has no need to "do" something in order to
be their cause. What is required, is the permanence of this principle
as the "formula" of all its different kinds of instantiation. Plotinus
uses the Platonic verb *menein* (which in *Timaeus* 42e5–6 describes
the status of the Demiurgic Intellect) to convey a double set of
meanings: first, immutability is not a supplementary feature of intelligible patterns, but the very nature of their causality; secondly, the
Forms cannot be charged with the failure to be efficient causes of
sensibles, since they are responsible not for their movement, but
only for their rational structure.

When Plotinus tries to explain how an indivisible reality can be a
cause, he argues that it does not pass through matter, but "remains"
in itself, *ou tês ideas dia pasês* [= *tês ulês*] *diexelthousês kai
epidramousês, all'en autêi menousês* (VI.5.8.20–2).

In the context of the discussion of the omnipresence of the intelligible in the sensible, Plotinus emphasizes the first meaning of
menein, namely, the immutability which is involved in the very
nature of eidetic causality (VI.4.7.22–9. See also I.7.1.13–19 and 23–
4; VI.5.10.8–11).

In the context of the discussion of the causality of the demiurgic *nous* in regard to the cosmos, Plotinus emphasizes the difference between eidetic and efficient causality. Intelligible paradigms need neither instruments nor deliberation in order to communicate their property to the participants. In III.2.1.38–45 Plotinus contrasts the production of effects by means of an activity with the causality of the principles which act only through the immutability of their nature. The intelligible – which is considered here in its double aspect of Intellect (*nous*) and intelligible paradigm (*kosmos alêthinos*) – does not "act" in the sense of producing. It is indeed by its not producing, *mê poiein*, that it gives rise to the great and magnificent reality of the visible cosmos. It does so precisely because of its being what it is, namely, by its *eph'heautou menein* (see also III.2.2.15–17 and V.8.7.24–31).

According to Plotinus, both these features of intelligible reality – the capacity to be present "within" physical reality in a nonlocalized manner and the capacity to be the cause of effects by being the immutable pattern of their inner rational structure – characterize the first principle itself, namely, the One.

Omnipresence characterizes the One insofar as it is conceived of as the condition *sine qua non* for the very reality of all things. In the famous beginning of VI.9 all beings (*panta ta onta*) owe their being to the One: *toi eni esti onta* (VI.9.1.1–2). Plotinus explains this relationship by means of a list of examples, starting from collective names and proceeding to continuous magnitudes, bodies, qualities, soul, and finally intellect. This list is meant to show that unity always is the basic condition for being. It is impossible to say what a reality is without considering it as an unity (VI.9.1.4–2.8; see also V.3.15.11–15 and V.5.4.31–8). Consequently, unity is the condition for predication, and since "to be" in the Platonic way of thinking means essentially "to be intelligible,"[11] to maintain that unity is the condition for predication is tantamount to affirming that it is the condition for being.

In a subsequent chapter of the same treatise, Plotinus expands on this idea by saying that when we are not "around" the One – that is, when any entity whatsoever, including ourselves, loses its unity – the dispersion is waiting for us, and we will be no longer (*ouketi esometha*: VI.9.8.41–2). The One is conceived of as continuously giving us participation in it, so long as it is what is: *aei chorêgountos eos an ê oper esti* (VI.9.9.7–11. See also V.6.3.2–4, and compare with

VI.6.18.46–7, where the same character is attributed to the intelligible reality). The first feature of eidetic causality, namely, omnipresence in the effects, is intimately linked in this passage with the second feature, namely, immutability as the *ratio* for the causality of intelligible models.

It is in fact by "being what it is" that an intelligible cause communicates itself to all the entities which share its character. But we have seen that according to Plotinus all beings share the character of unity. Hence, the One is conceived of as the cause of all beings. The model of this causality is analogous to that of the Ideas. Both of them, the One and the Ideas, are causes by immutably being what they are.

In V.4.2.19–22 Plotinus says that if something comes into being from the One which rests in itself, it is precisely because of the eternal permanence of its nature (see also V.3.10.16–17 and 12.33–8). Such a cause is conceived of as transcendent in respect to its participants, namely, subsistent apart from them and prior in respect to them. It is reached, in fact, as the only principle which is able to explain *all* the different instantiations of a given character. Consequently, it is conceived of as separate from, and prior to, the series which originates from it. Like the Platonic "Beauty in itself" in respect to the many beautiful things, the Plotinian eidetic cause transcends its participants, insofar as it is the principle which is required in order to explain the fact that many individuals share a common property. This feature is attributed also to the One.

When Plotinus is looking at the participation of all the realities in the unity as a common property, he deals with the One as with the *auto kath'auto* of this character. But beauty concerns only the set of beautiful things; on the contrary, unity concerns all that is. Consequently, the One transcends all realities.

In two well known passages, V.2.1.1–2 and III.8.9.44–54, Plotinus points out the fact that the transcendence of the One cannot be separated from its omnipresence. While the first passage is only a brief assertion that the One is all things and not one of them, in the second Plotinus uses a *reductio ad absurdum*, in order to demonstrate that the omnipresence of the One cannot be interpreted as immanence in things. The One, notwithstanding the universal presence that results from its causality, is totally transcendent (*ouden tôn pantôn, alla pro tôn pantôn*).

In several passages the double status of transcendence and immanence – *pantachou kai oudamou* – is formally presented as the
explanation for the derivation of things from the One. An excellent
example is III.9.4.3–9. Were the One only "everywhere," without
being at the same time "nowhere," it would have the same nature as
its effects. But since it is transcendent, "nowhere," it can satisfy the
basic requirement for the causality of the intelligible principles: to
precede all the particular instantiations of them. Accordingly, it is *pro
pantôn en*, and this is the reason why it is able to produce all things,
instead of coinciding with its products, which is absurd in Plotinus's
view.[12]

All the later Neoplatonic thinkers will endorse the main tenets
of the Plotinian vision of intelligible causality, as well as its extension to the One. Porphyry begins his *Sentences* by stating that
while bodies are always located in space, none of the suprasensible
realities are so located.[13] The second *Sentence* maintains that incorporeal and self-subsistent entities, namely, the intelligibles, are
everywhere, *pantachê*, in a simple and nonlocal way.[14] Porphyry
uses the metaphor of an "inclination" (*ropê, repein*) in order to
distinguish between the separateness of the substance of the intelligibles and the relationship (*schesis*) that they have with bodies.[15] In
Sentence 27 Porphyry attributes the double status of *pantachou kai
oudamou* to the incorporeals.[16]

Furthermore, Porphyry devotes a *Sentence* to stating that there is
a hierarchy among incorporeals, from the point of view of their
being *pantachou kai oudamou*. They all share this characteristic,
but only the First Principle, which is called here simply "God," is
"everywhere and nowhere" without qualifications. Intellect and
Soul are *pantachou kai oudamou* only in respect to their participants.[17] In describing the causality of the First Principle in terms of
its simultaneous omnipresence and separateness, Porphyry quotes
Plotinus literally.[18]

The Plotinian topic of the *menein* of intelligible causes appears in
Sentence 34 as the explanation of the omnipresence of true being in
the physical universe, which, in turn, clearly echoes the doctrine
and terminology of VI.4–5[19]

Marius Victorinus, the Latin Christian Neoplatonist of the fourth
century A.D. who translated into Latin the *Libri platonicorum*, later
quoted by St. Augustine and probably identical with the *Enneads*,[20]

adapts the Plotinian model of the causality of the One to the God of his own trinitary theology. Plotinus ruled out any "pantheistic" interpretation of the omnipresence of the One by repeatedly asserting that the One must fill all things and make them, rather than "being" itself all the things that it makes (see, for instance, the last sentence in the above-quoted passage of III.9.4.8–9: *plêroun oun dei auton kai poiein panta, ouk einai ta panta, a poiei*). In all likelihood Victorinus has in mind such an idea when he adds to the thesis that God is *causa . . . dator et pater* of beings the following clause: *et non est dicere haec* – for example, beings – *esse ipsum* – that is, God – *quibus ut essent, dedit.*[21] The famous passage of V.2.1.1–2 about the relationship between the One and *ta panta* is quoted literally by Victorinus,[22] so that a very typical feature of the Plotinian conception of the First Principle is transmitted in this way to the Latin readers of the age of St. Augustine.

Victorinus endorses both the conception of the simultaneous omnipresence and separateness of the One, and the doctrine of the immutability as the *ratio* of the causality of incorporeal principles. God is described as the *manens vel mansio . . . quies, quietus*[23] which, by its very rest, gives rise to all beings. In a passage of the *Adversus Arium* the two doctrines are linked together. God is *in semet ipso manens, solus in solo, ubique existens et nusquam.*[24] In turn, St. Augustine will repeat that God's creation does not involve any change (see, for instance, *De Trin.* V.1.2: *sine ulla sui mutatione mutabilia facientem, nihilque patientem*), and repeatedly will call God *ubique praesens, ubique totus.*[25] In the *Confessions* the double status of *pantachou kai oudamou* which characterizes the Plotinian One is referred to God: *ubique totus es . . . et nusquam locorum es.*[26]

In the Athenian School this model of causality is systematically exploited. Although in the surviving writings of Syrianus the formulas of the "everywhere and nowhere" and of *menein* of the principle in producing its effects are not present, Proclus's teacher substantially contributed to the systematization of the Plotinian causal doctrine. It was Syrianus who first used the well-known formula of causality "by being itself, *autôi tôi einai*," which sums up both the meanings involved in the Plotinian doctrine of the immutability of the cause and the absence of any "action," in the sense of the craftsmen's production.

In his commentary on the Aristotelian *Metaphysics* Syrianus maintains that the intelligible paradigm produces by being itself, *autôi tôi einai*. The context of this assertion is highly interesting, since Syrianus is here commenting on the passage of the *Metaphysics* where Aristotle argues that the argument which attempts to establish the Ideas as entities existing apart from sensibles (i.e., the one-over-many doctrine) rests on the assumption of the homonymy between the *ousia* of the sensible things and the (supposed) *ousia* of the suprasensible items (1079a31–b3). Syrianus's reply pivots on the notion of homonymy. He distinguishes between the mere casual homonymy and the one which exists between entities which actually have something in common. The model and the image worked out on its basis undeniably have a real link, in particular – Syrianus adds – when the *paradeigma*, having brought into existence the image by its being, *huphistan autôi tôi einai*, is able to "convert" the image into itself,[27] that is, to establish the effect as something which is more like to the cause, than different from it. Proclus will explain this idea by maintaining that in the relationship between an intelligible principle and its effects similarity prevails over difference: were it not so, the derived things would not be members of the "series" which originates in the principle.[28]

Not only the intelligible paradigms, but also the Intellect operates according to the Plotinian model of immutability. Syrianus describes the causality of the demiurgic Intellect as the capacity to produce all things by its being, according to its intellectual nature: *autô tôi einai kata tên heautou idiotêta*.[29] In his commentary on *Metaphysics* 1086b14–22, where Aristotle is once again criticizing the theory of the separated substances, Syrianus endorses the Plotinian distinction between production involving deliberation and change and the one which is owing only to the nature of the principle. The Intellect is cause of its effects *autôi tôi einai*, unlike the principles which act by deliberation and change.[30]

The pattern of the causality *autôi tôi einai* is largely adopted by Proclus,[31] who has recourse to it throughout his work to indicate the specific kind of action of the intelligible reality. It is worth noting that Proclus wants to distinguish between two levels of the causality of suprasensible principles. The kind of action *autôi tôi einai*, strictly understood, is appropriate only to intelligible realities (in Proclus's language, to the *noêton platos*) while Henads – the highest level of the Proclean universe, for example, the series of principles which culminate in the One – act by their "anteriority to being (tôi proeinai)."[32] This distinction is meant to avoid attributing "being" to the highest level of reality, which is conceived of as superior to being. In fact, this distinction obscures, at least partly, the original Plotinian idea that in the case of suprasensible principles "to produce" coincides with "to be itself."

As a matter of fact, the Proclean distinction will not survive in the two principal adaptations of the metaphysics of Proclus, namely, the De divinis nominibus by Pseudo-Dionysius Areopagite, and the Arabic Liber de causis, a short treatise about first principles extracted from Proclus's Elements of Theology. Neither Pseudo-Dionysius nor the author of the De causis will follow Proclus in distinguishing two meanings of the immutability of principles in their production, the one corresponding to the One above being, and the other to true being, that is, the intelligible causes. Indeed, both of them will attribute such a pattern of causality especially – not to say exclusively – to the First Principle itself.

Pseudo-Dionysius repeatedly maintains that God creates all reality by his being: he is cause of all beings by his being,[33] he gives being to every kind of beings by his being.[34] The adoption of the concept of causality autôi tôi einai is particularly consistent with Dionysian affirmative theology, according to which "being" is the best among the divine names,[35] though from the complementary viewpoint of negative theology God is above being, huperousios proon.[36] Being is the first and foremost among the divine bestowals. In the Platonic-Plotinian tradition "being" coincides with the status of intelligibility, which is in turn the condition for all the more specific perfections, like "life" or "intellectuality." Pseudo-Dionysius shares the Neoplatonic idea of the priority of "being" among all the intelligibles. The characteristic feature of his interpretation consists in thinking that if "being" is the first product of the First Principle, this implies that in our affirmative discourse about God "Being" is the first and more appropriate name.

Notwithstanding the obvious difference of the theological assumptions in the background with Plotinus and with Pseudo-Dionysius, the First Principle of the Dionysian universe in its creation acts in precisely the same way as the Plotinian One. It is described in several passages as undiminished and immutable in its production (*eph'eautou menon*)[37]; like the Platonic intelligible world, it is always the same (*aei kata ta auta kai ôsautôs echon*).[38] It is omnipresent (*pasin ôsautôs paron*).[39] In several passages the formulas of Pseudo-Dionysius seem to echo the Plotinian ones: see for instance the passage in which God – who is named here *ho proon*, "who is before being" – is present to all things and everywhere, in himself as unity and in the same way: *parôn tois pasi kai pantachou kai kata en kai to auto kai kata to auto*.[40] Pseudo-Dionysius endorses the basic Plotinian tenet about the transcendence of the principle as a correlative of its omnipresence. God is conceived of as overflowing in all creatures, and at the same time "remaining" in himself.[41] As with the Proclean Henads, the Dionysian God is everywhere by means of his providence, and his capacity to "comprehend" in himself all the lower entities is qualified by his transcendence.[42]

A similar picture appears clearly in the *Liber de causis*. In proposition 19 we are told that the First Cause governs (*tudbbiru, regit*) all created realities without any mixture with them (*ġayra anna takhlitu bihā, praeter quod commisceatur cum eis*).[43] The author attributes to the First Cause the feature of immobility in producing effects, which belongs to the divine Henads according to proposition 122 of Proclus's *Elements of Theology*, which directly inspires this proposition of the *De causis*.[44] As well as Pseudo-Dionysius, the author of the *Liber de causis* says that God acts by his being – *biannīhi faqaṭ, per esse suum tantum*[45] – meaning not only that he does not need deliberation, instruments, or motion in order to create, but also that he acts by giving being, insofar as he is the first and pure Being, *annīya faqaṭ, esse tantum*.[46]

Medieval theologians and philosophers who used the lemmas of the *Liber de causis* in order to explain the relationship between God and the world actually were reproducing an adaptation of the Neoplatonic doctrine of the causality of suprasensible entities. The innovation of equating God with pure Being does not prevent this adaptation from transmitting the decisive features of the original Plotinian thought.

However, even if the basic tenets of the Plotinian interpretation of Plato's doctrine of Ideas are unanimously shared by later Neoplatonic thinkers, this is by no means the case concerning the solutions that have been proposed in order to solve its intrinsic difficulties. In the following section I shall try to indicate the main difficulty, namely, the derivation of the multiplicity from an absolutely simple and unique first principle, and Plotinus's solution to it. Finally, I shall suggest some reasons for the abandonment of this solution by later Neoplatonic thinkers, in favor of a quite different approach to this crucial problem of Neoplatonic metaphysics.

II

According to the presentation I have given in the first section, Plotinus attributes to the One a kind of causality which has the same features as the causality of intelligible items. The only difference I have called attention to is that, while any intelligible principle whatsoever is "everywhere and nowhere" only in respect to a given set of derived entities, and produces by its immutability only a specific kind of effect, namely, its participants, the First Principle is "everywhere and nowhere" without qualifications, and what it is able to produce by its immutability coincides with reality itself.

It is evident that this point is far from being uncontroversial, and we must credit Plotinus with having grasped the puzzling character of such an assertion. Since my main concern here is the model of causality which is involved in the Plotinian conception of the First Principle, I will leave aside the problems about the "freedom" of the First Principle in producing the universe, as well as the ones about the "limit" of its production, that is, about the Plotinian conception of matter. The question I will deal with is the following: can the pattern of intelligible causality explain the fact that the One produces *ta panta*, all realities?

The difficulty lies in the fact that Plotinus maintains that the One is the universal principle of all that is, squarely refusing as irrational imagery the hypothesis of another principle, responsible for the production of matter and for the existence of the multiplicity.[47] This implies that the One is responsible not only for the unity of all the things which, insofar as they are, participate in unity, but also for their very multiplicity.

Consequently, the basic tenets of the pattern of causality described in the first part seem to be denied. Actually they all derive from conceiving of the relationship between cause and effect as similarity between the particular instances of a given form and the Form in itself. But if the One gives rise to the multiplicity qua multiplicity, that is, qua different from the principle instead of as similar to it, how in the world is it possible to preserve in this production the features of eidetic causality? For instance, the immutability of the cause in its production is nothing but an analysis of the identity in form between the effect and the cause. Therefore, if the One produces the multiplicity – that is, what is different from it – it cannot do so owing to the rules of eidetic causality: it cannot, for instance, produce the multiplicity qua multiplicity by its *menein*, as it does when it is considered as the separated cause of the unity within the things.

Plotinus seems to tackle such a perplexity when, in V.1.6.3–8, he tells us that the soul must acknowledge that the multiplicity exists, and

longs to answer the question repeatedly discussed also by the ancient philosophers, how from the One, if it is such as we say it is, anything else, whether a multiplicity or a dyad or a number, came into existence, and why it did not on the contrary remain by itself (*all'ouk emeinen ekeino eph'heautou*) but such a great multiplicity flowed from it as that which is seen to exist in beings, but which we think it right to refer back to the One (*anagein de auto pros ekeino axioumen*).

The core of the dilemma can be presented in the following alternative: either the One is not the principle of the multiplicity qua multiplicity, and consequently it is not the first and universal principle, or it actually produces the multiplicity qua multiplicity, and consequently it cannot "remain by itself," that is, it alters its nature in the production, in order to be able to produce what is different from it.

Plotinus's solution takes into account the second horn of the dilemma, in order to show that a way can be conceived in which the One gives rise to the multiplicity, without contradicting the basic tenets of the causality we must attribute to it, namely, the one in which the principle remains unaltered and undiminished. In V.2.1.3–5 he asks: "How then do all things come from the One, which is simple and has in it no variety, or any sort of doubleness?" It is evident from the very use of the term variety (*poikilia*) that he is not, or not primarily, thinking of the multiplicity of the sensible world, but of the multiplicity of the intelligible realm.

To ask how the One can be conceived of as the principle of what is different from it means primarily to ask how the One can produce intelligible items. They are in fact by definition a variety, insofar as they are rational formulas of qualities. Taking for granted that the First Principle actually is first and universal, Plotinus must explain the fact that it has to produce them (and through them all subsequent reality), in a double sense: insofar as they are *instances of unity*, and insofar as they are a true and original variety.

Roughly, Plotinus's explanation of the derivation of multiplicity qua multiplicity from the One pivots on the idea that, in this second case, the principle gives to its participants something that it does not possess. Far from concealing this crux of his metaphysics, Plotinus declares it. In the continuation of the passage quoted above he says that: "It is because there is nothing in it that all things come from it: in order that being may exist, the One is not being, but the generator of being" (V.2.1.5–7). Plotinus carefully analyzes this relationship between the One above being and being, that is, the intelligible reality or, what is the same for him, the Intellect. Contemporary scholarship has submitted this analysis to a detailed examination, because of its crucial importance as well as its controversial features, a debate our present purpose does not compel us to enter.[48] It is instead necessary to focus on the kind of causality by which the One produces what it does not possess. In the passage quoted above, as well as in all the relevant passages devoted to the generation of the Intellect from the One, Plotinus repeatedly tells us that what the First Principle sets out in its first product, namely, the Intellect, is not found, as such, in the principle itself. See for instance VI.9.3.40–1, where, dealing with the relationship between the Intellect and the One, Plotinus maintains that: "For since the nature of the One is generative of all things it is not any one of them,"[49] or, for instance, V.3.15.35–41:

How then does the One make what it does not have? . . . Now it has been said that, if anything comes from the One, it must be something different from it; and in being different, it is not one: for if it was, it would be that One. But if it is not one, but two, it must necessarily also be many: for it is already the same and different and qualified and all the rest.

See also VI.7.17.32–41, where Plotinus is more explicit in indicating what is the bestowal that the One gives to its final product, without having it in itself:

The life of Intellect, then, is all power, and the seeing which came from the Good is the power to become all things, and the Intellect which came to be is manifest as the very totality of things (*o de genomenos nous auta anephanê ta panta*). But the Good sits enthroned upon them, not that it may have a base but that it may base the "Form" of the first "Forms," being formless itself, *ina idrusêi eidos eidôn tôn prôtôn aneideon auto*. . . . Therefore Intellect too is a trace of that Good; but since Intellect is a Form and exists in extension and multiplicity, that Good is shapeless and formless; for this is how he makes forms.

The multiplicity the One gives without having it in itself is therefore the multiplicity of Forms, the variety of *eidê* which are in turn responsible for the rational structure of the various objects of our experience. The One is the principle of the Forms precisely by its not being a Form. In its producing the intelligible multiplicity of determinations the One "makes what it does not have," to recall the expression of the above-quoted passage from V.3.15. Plotinus expresses this idea by a wide range of formulas, among which prevails the theme of the One as the productive power of all things (*dunamis tôn pantôn*) giving rise to the Intellect, which possesses the intelligible patterns of all reality (*ta panta*).[50] He emphasizes that the One is the principle of being – Forms and Intellect – not in spite of the fact that it does not possess either being or Form, but precisely owing to this (V.5.6.1–11; see also V.3.14.18–19).

The problem we have to consider now lies in the fact that the pattern of causality according to which the One "makes what it does not have" seems hardly consistent *prima facie* with the one according to which the One gives to all realities the unity they possess. The right conclusion to draw, seemingly, is that the One is conceived of by Plotinus as having two different kinds of causality, the one reserved for the communication of unity and the other, truly different, that explains its production of multiplicity. However, the available evidence works against this interpretation. Plotinus does not seem disposed to distinguish two sets of rules in the causality of the One.

Perhaps the answer to this question can be approached by considering the following passage, where Plotinus compares the particular instance of a given Form with the Form itself – in this case, the Form of "Beauty":

But since it is the principle of beauty it makes that beautiful of which it is the principle, and makes it beautiful not in shape, but it makes the very beauty which comes to be from it to be shapeless, but in shape in another way; for what is called this very thing [shape] is shape in another, but by itself shapeless, *êph gar legomênê auto touto monon morphê en alloi, eph'heautês de ousa amorphon.* Therefore that which participates in beauty is shaped, not the beauty. (VI.7.32.34–9)

Plotinus is faced with the question: is the Form which is responsible for the beauty of all the beautiful things beautiful in itself, or not? He answers that it does not possess the beauty that it gives. There is no question here of distinguishing the intelligible kind of beauty from the complex of colors, lines, surfaces, in which consists the beauty of a given sensible thing. What Plotinus wants to single out is the difference between the Form of "Beauty" in itself and the various rational criteria of the beauty in any particular instance of beauty. The difference consists in the fact that the Form in itself is formless with respect to the criteria of the particular instances. The Form of Beauty does not possess in itself either the rational structure of a symphony as such, or one of a beautiful face as such. It is the principle of all the rational structures and serves as the ground of all the particular instances of beauty in our experience, but cannot coincide with any one among them. Consequently, it has to be formless in respect to them, and it becomes a specific form when it is "in another," namely, in its specific instances. What has a specific form, is the participant: the Form in itself gives it something that the Form does not possess as such. What the Form possesses, or, more precisely, what it is, is the capacity to generate both the rational pattern according to which a symphony is beautiful to listen to, and one according to which a face is beautiful to look at.

This Plotinian solution to the paradox of the self-reference of the Forms is meant not only to illuminate the common inheritance of the Platonic school, but also to provide a pattern for the understanding of the relationship between the various Forms and their principle. All the instances of beauty are what they are owing to the Beautiful in itself, which gives rise to them precisely by its not being any particular kind of beauty, but the "formula" for all them. In turn, the "formula" of the Beautiful differs from the "formula" of "Righteousness" or "Wisdom," to recall the Plotinian examples in the chapter immediately following the above-quoted passage. As a result, all the different Forms owe the very fact of their being Forms to a principle which generates them precisely by its not being one among them, namely, by its being formless in respect to them.

Nor, then, can it be a shape of any kind or an individual power, nor again all those which have come to be and exist here above, but it must be above all powers and above all shapes. The principle is the formless, not that which needs form, but that from which every intelligent form comes. (VI.7.32.6–10. See also V.1.7.19–20)

The production of the multiplicity of intelligible Forms by the One is not, therefore, an alternative kind of production in respect to the communication of unity, but a different analysis of the way in which suprasensible principles operate. When we consider the One as the principle of the unity of all the things which are, we are looking at the relationship of similitude which is involved in the pattern of eidetic causality. When we ask how the One can generate the multiplicity of Forms, and Plotinus answers that it occurs because of the One's being separated from all the Forms and formless in respect to them, we have before us the Plotinian answer to the paradox of self-predication, extended to the relationship between the set of the Forms and their principle.

A crucial consequence of this idea is that the principle is conceived of as being the power (*dunamis*) of all the specific instances of it. If the Form of Beauty is formless in respect to the rational models of a symphony and of a face which are beautiful, and if – by definition – it has to be the principle of both of them, this implies that it is not "a" beauty, but the power to give rise to all the possible kinds of beauty. If the One is formless in respect to all the Forms, this means that it has the power to generate them all, namely, that it is the *dunamis tôn pantôn*, without being one among them. To put it in Plotinus's words,

– What then are "all the things"? – All things of which that One is the principle. – But how is that One the principle of all things? Is it because as principle it keeps them in being, making each of them exist? – Yes, and because it brought them into existence. – But how did it so? – By possessing them beforehand. – But it has been said that in this way it will be a multiplicity. – But it had them in such a way as not to be distinct: they are distinguished on the second level, in the rational form. For this is already actuality; but the One is the potency of all the things. – But in what way is it the potency? – Not in the way in which matter is said to be in potency, because it receives: for matter is passive; but this [material] way of being a potency is at the opposite extreme to making. (V.3.15.26–35)[51]

To admit that the variety of the Forms in their actuality, *energeia*, comes from the *dunamis* of the One-formless is tantamount to admitting that the One possesses them beforehand, as all the possible rational criteria for beauty are implied in the Beautiful in itself.

Aware as he is of the strict necessity of safeguarding the first principle of his philosophy from any multiplicity, Plotinus does not hesitate to maintain that all the intelligible causes are "beforehand" in it. In VI.8.18.38–40, after having called the One "cause of the cause," that is, of the Intellect, he adds that: "He (i.e., the One) is then in a greater degree something like the most causative and the truest of causes, possessing all together the intellectual causes which are going to be from him, and generative of what is not as it chanced but as he himself willed."[52] The passages of the *Enneads* in which Plotinus refers to the Intellect as to the best or first image or trace of the One (*agalma* or *ichnos tou henos*,)[53] are meant to recall this same idea, as well as the remark, directed against the Gnostics, that *nous* immediately follows the First Principle, without any intermediary principle: *metaxu ouden*.[54]

Lack of space forbids here the treatment of this topic, and compels me to focus on the main problem about the causality of the One. Plotinus seems to have a sharp awareness of a double-sided meaning of his basic tenet, namely, that the hypothesis of the Forms rests on the ground of the causality of the One-Good. This idea is implied in the prominent feature of the Plotinian interpretation of Platonic philosophy, according to which the intelligible world is produced by the One above being and Intellect.

The first and most obvious meaning of this idea is that analogously as we discover the Form as the separate principle of a multiplicity which shares an intelligible character, so we discover the One-Good as the separate principle of the character shared by all the Forms. Following this way of thinking, the One acts like any intelligible item whatsoever, namely, insofar as it is in itself the character – unity – that participants possess in a derived manner. There is, however, a second meaning, according to which, while an intelligible Form is responsible only for the similarity to it which is in its participants, the One-Good is responsible also for the principles of the eidetic distinctions, which are the true beings and which are to be "referred back" to it, *anagein . . . pros ekeino,* as we have seen in the above-quoted passage from V.1.6. Following this way of thinking, the One acts like an intelligible item insofar as this latter is conceived of as a principle which gives what it does not possess as such, but which it has the power to produce (V.3.15.27–30).

It is clear that this is a subtle and difficult answer to give to the problem of the origin of the multiplicity from the One. The various and puzzling descriptions of the genesis of *nous* are to a large extent the result of this difficulty. But the Plotinian commitment to the idea that the intelligible world, with all its variety, comes straight away from the First Principle has the great merit of pointing out the difficulty. Later Neoplatonic thinkers did not follow Plotinus's footsteps on this issue.

Contemporary scholars call attention to the increasing complexity of the suprasensible realm in post-Plotinian Neoplatonism.[55] What Plotinus had forbidden – to insert supplementary hypostases between the One and the Intellect, and in turn between the Intellect and the Soul[56] – comes to be the rule in later developments of this current of thought, and in particular in Athenian Neoplatonism. As a result of this process, in the final picture of the Neoplatonic universe the First Principle does not give rise immediately to the intelligible multiplicity of the true beings, but to other principles which are responsible for their status as simple, but at the same time different, realities.

In Proclus this picture reaches its best formulation, in the sense that the process of removal of the First from the world of the Forms does not arrive at the paradox of refusing to attribute to it the character of "principle." This conclusion will be drawn by Damascius, according to whom to be a "principle" involves a relationship with the originated realities, and such a relative character is not consistent with the absolute transcendence of the First.[57] Proclus maintained that the One is indeed the principle of multiplicity, but at the same time he found unsatisfactory, at least to a certain extent, the Plotinian conception of this point. What this Proclean development implies will concern us later; for now, let me indicate some evidence about Proclus's critique of the Plotinian conception of the relationship between the One and the intelligible realm.

In the *Platonic Theology* Proclus criticizes the opinion of the "ancients, who follow the philosophy of Plotinus," insofar as they locate *nous* immediately after the One, failing to recognize that other degrees of divine realities exist between them. By contrast, the best interpreter of Plato's thought, Syrianus, distinguishes different degrees in the intelligible world which is below the One.[58]

A parallel passage in the commentary on the *Parmenides* shows that not only the followers of Plotinus, but the teacher himself is criticized by Proclus. Dealing with the order in which the characters of the multiplicity are removed from the One in the first hypothesis of this dialogue, Proclus endorses the exegetical pattern provided by Syrianus: all the characters removed from the One in the first hypothesis correspond in the subsequent hypotheses to the ones which individuate the subordinate degrees of the suprasensible realm.[59] Consequently, to single out what kind of multiplicity cannot be in the One is tantamount to finding out what kind of multiplicity exists immediately below the One. Having refused as absurd the possibility that this is the case with regard to the sensible multiplicity, Proclus quotes Plotinus literally in order to present the possibility that this is the case with regard to the multiplicity of the Ideas, the *noeron plêthos*.[60] This possibility is rejected, for the same reason as in the *Platonic Theology:* to set the Intellect with its intelligible contents immediately below the One is too simple a picture to represent the complexity of the suprasensible world.

But Proclus does not confine himself to maintaining that the Plotinian conception fails to grasp the complexity of the divine hierarchies. He gives us the key to understanding the reasons why he does not follow Plotinus when he maintains that the arising of the multiplicity from the One does not entitle us to hold that the intelligible causes of all subsequent reality existed beforehand in it, even if without their multiplicity. This thesis, which summarizes the Plotinian solution to the dilemma of the origin of multiplicity from the One, is criticized by Proclus in the context of his comment on the lemma of *Parmenides* 137c9–d3, where Plato says that if the one is one, it cannot be a whole or have parts:

There are other authorities, however, who have said that since the first principle is cause of all things, notwithstanding its superiority in respect to the Life, to the Intellect and to the Being itself, it possesses within itself in some way the causes of all these things unutterably and unimaginably (*anepinoêtôs*) and in the most unified way, and in a way unknowable to us but knowable to itself; and the hidden causes of all things in it are models prior to models, *paradeigmata pro paradeigmatôn*, and the primal entity itself is a whole prior to wholes, not having need of parts.[61]

The reason why the philosopher here criticized by Proclus, namely, Plotinus,[62] felt compelled to ascribe to the First Principle the *paradeigmata*, even if in the most unified way, lies in the fact that he wanted to avoid the conclusion that there is no way to distinguish the First Principle from nothing, if "everything absolutely is removed from" it.[63]

Taking for granted that Proclus has singled out the Plotinian answer to the crux of any Neoplatonic metaphysics, and has rejected it, we are in position to raise the following question: if the First Principle does not possess within it the *paradeigmata pro paradeigmatôn*, how do they arise? A full answer to this question is beyond the limits of this paper, but a synthetic outline of the Proclean way of thinking can be provided.

It is usually assumed that Athenian Neoplatonists, and Proclus in particular, added a "step" in the process of derivation of multiplicity from the One, by inserting between One and the intelligible reality the pair of principles "Limit–Unlimited," which are responsible respectively for the elements of sameness, stability, and determination, and otherness, "motion," and indetermination in the world of Forms. But the steps are at least two, since the multiplicity of intelligible Forms is conceived of by Proclus as present beforehand and in a "hidden" way within a principle which is a sort of sum of all the intelligibles, the "monad" of Being (*autoon, auto to on*).[64] This principle, in turn, derives from the couple "Limit–Unlimited," as the first "mixture" of them.

By this doctrine Proclus does not limit himself to endorsing the Plotinian reading of the interplay of identity, otherness, and being, in the *Sophist* as well as in the *Timaeus*,[65] even if within the relevant modification of interpreting the couple and its mixture as hypostases which transcend the Forms, instead of as constitutive principles of each Form. He proposes, moreover, his own explanation of the origin of intelligible multiplicity. The First Principle gives rise to the pair of determination–indetermination; the mixture of determination and indetermination provides the "model" of any Form. Such a model is meant to have the capacity of originating all the Forms, and this fact is expressed in Proclean language by saying that it is the "monad" of Being. In this way, the principle which possesses beforehand the intelligible variety of Forms ceases to be the One, which is credited with remaining totally transcendent and separate, and giving rise to the process of the production of multiplicity only through its first and decisive step, namely, the production of the pair "Limit–Unlimited."

One might raise the following objection: the difficulty of explaining how an absolutely simple principle can produce a variety of intelligible items is far from solved by such a multiplication of intermediate steps. As a matter of fact, the proliferation of intermediate entities in the Proclean metaphysics, reaching sometimes an uncontrolled kaleidoscope,[66] is exposed to the risk of merely obscuring this philosophical difficulty. The problem was raised by Plotinus in the following terms:

But how does he give them [i.e., being, intellect, thought, and awareness]? By having them, or by not having them? But how did he give what he does not have? But if he has them, he is not simple; if he does not have them, how does the multiplicity come from him? (V.3.15.1–3)

This problem can scarcely be answered by introducing intermediate principles which are simpler than the Forms but more complex than the One. In this case, in fact, the quoted alternative remains unresolved. We must credit Proclus with not having tried to solve it by this means.

Indeed, the origin of multiplicity is highly problematic for him too, as is witnessed by the fact that throughout his work it is possible to discover two distinct accounts of it.

To put it roughly, the first account is the one I have summarized: the First Principle gives rise to the pair of *archai* "Limit–Unlimited"; in turn, this couple generates, through its "mixture," namely, the "monad of Being" – the intelligible world (the *noêton platos*, in Proclus's language). Being "divine" in its nature, the intelligible world is actually a hierarchy of gods, that is, the supreme Ideas, which is organized according to "triads." The first and principal triad which governs intelligible gods consists of Being, Life, Intellect. This is meant to recall that in any Idea there is the mixture of Limit and Unlimited ("Being"); the capacity to communicate with other Ideas ("Life"); and, finally, the capacity to "return" to itself and to the One ("Intellect"). After the intelligible gods, there are other gods, namely, the "intelligible and intellectual" ones, and the "intellectual" ones. Below this, we encounter the class of Souls, with its inner hierarchies.

The second account differs from this one in that, after the One, there are principles which are called Henads, and are said to have been produced by the One in a special way, namely, without any "otherness" or, as Proclus says, according to the mode of unity, *kath'enôsin*.[67] These principles cooperate with the One in producing the supreme kind of Ideas. According to proposition 137 of the *Elements of Theology*, every Henad "is cooperative with the One in producing the real existent which participates in it."[68] Thus, the Henads are superior to the *noêton platos* and transcendent in respect to the *on*; they are often called *huperousioi*.[69] While in the first account all the divine orders appear as subordinated to the pair "Limit–Unlimited," in this second account the Henads, which are incontrovertibly gods, appear as independent from it.

One may ask if the two accounts are inconsistent or, rather, complementary, and this question might be answered only by means of an analysis which lies beyond the scope of this paper. What is important to emphasize here is the fact that Proclus feels compelled to provide two explanations for the origin of multiplicity, the one pivoting on the idea that if the intelligible realm has an intrinsic variety, this is owing to the presence of a hypostasis – the Unlimited – which intermingles with the Limit; and the other which tries to explain how it is possible that the variety of the Ideas comes from the One, without being beforehand "in" the One.

The main point I wish to make here is to call attention to the close relationship between the Proclean rejection of Plotinus's doctrine of the presence of intelligible causes "beforehand" in the One as *dunamis tôn pantôn*, and the attempt to explain the origin of intelligible multiplicity by means of intermediate hypostases, which accomplishes the task of avoiding a straight "contact" of the First Principle with the intelligible world. I suspect that the increasing importance of the so-called doctrine of principles in the last stage of pagan Neoplatonism plays an important role in explaining this Proclean way of thinking. It has been observed that the doctrine of principles is scarcely employed by Plotinus,[70] while in Iamblichus, Syrianus, and Proclus it takes on a decisive role in the structure of Neoplatonic metaphysics. This fact can help us in understanding the hidden assumptions in the Plotinian and Proclean pictures of the relationship between the One and the Forms.

Roughly speaking, the Plotinian solution seems to rest on the grounds of the pattern provided by Plato in the sixth book of the *Republic*, where the main realities of the suprasensible world are the Good – which lies beyond being in importance and power (*epekeina ousias presbeiai kai dunamei*) – and the Forms or true beings.[71] In the background of the Proclean solution we discover as a prominent feature the ancient Academic model, according to which the One and the Indefinite Dyad are responsible for the production of various levels of increasing complexity within reality.[72] In the Plotinian picture the First Principle has to explain the variety of true beings inside the divine Intellect; in the Proclean one, it is conceived of as directly responsible only for the first "step" of a linear process, in which each level of reality is deduced from the previous one. To put it into Proclus's words, this means that each level of reality is present in the previous one *kat'aitian*, for example, according to the mode of being of the cause. It does not come as surprising that, given this model, it is necessary to avoid contiguity between the One and the intelligible multiplicity. As Proclus says, in fact, "the cause of plurality is itself, in a way, causally plurality, *kat'aitian to plêthos*, just as the one, the cause of unity, is causally one.[73] Finally, it is interesting to observe that in the aftermath of Neoplatonic metaphysics this peculiar development will be abandoned. The direct production of intelligible perfections will again be conceived of as compatible with the absolute simplicity of the First Principle. For instance, according to Dionysius the Pseudo-Areopagite the First Cause is absolutely transcendent – it surpasses, in fact, the good itself, and it is called *autouperagathotês* – but, at one and the same time, possesses in itself beforehand being in itself, *auto to einai*, and the principles of being, *archai tôn ontôn*, without any multiplicity (*aschetôs kai suneilemmenôs kai eniaiôs*).[74] This is but one of the possible examples of the survival of the Plotinian account of the causality of the One in the history of late ancient and medieval thought.

NOTES

1 G. W. F. Hegel 1971, 469.

2 See note 57.

3 On the Plotinian critique to the Stoic assumption that true beings are bodies see the passages listed and commented by Graeser 1972, 24–6 and 36–7. On the philosophical meaning of the topic of awakening see the famous passage of IV.8.1.1–11.

4 On the Platonic relationship between stability and intelligibility see Vlastos 1965; Ketchum 1980; Kahn 1981; Frede 1988; Turnbull 1988. Plotinus squarely equates true being (for example, intelligible reality: see V.9.3.1–4) with unchangeable reality. See for instance III.7.6.12–14, where *to alêthôs einai* is explained as *to oudepote mê einai oud' allôs einai touto de ôsautôs einai touto de adiaphorôs einai*. See also VI.5.2.9–16 and III.6.6.8–23.

5 This fact was already recognized by Bréhier 1936, 161–7. Several contemporary studies deal with this topic: Fielder 1976, 1977, 1978, 1978a, 1980, 1982; Lee 1982; Regen 1988; D'Ancona 1992a.

6 See Allen 1983, 116–17.

7 As for the unity of the twin treatise VI.4 and 5 see Beutler-Theiler, 1962, II b 396.

8 See Porphyry, *Life of Plotinus* 5.8–9.

9 See note 5.

10 The true being is one and the same everywhere in the same way as a hand might control a whole body (VI.4.7.9–22), or as a light coming from a small luminous bulk into a transparent spherical body (22–39), or, finally, as the light of the sun, "if the sun was only a power which was without a body" (39–47). In VI.5.8.1–10 Plotinus states explicitly that the idea of the omnipresence of being rules out the main difficulties (*to dusphraston kai to aporotaton*) of the doctrine of participation in the Ideas.

11 The Platonic dichotomy between being and becoming (*Tim.* 27d5–28a4) involves the identity of true beings and intelligible items (see, for instance, *Phdr.* 247d5–e3) which is in turn a pivotal concept of Neoplatonic metaphysics. See, for instance, in Plotinus V.8.5.18–20; V.9.3.1–4; VI.6.18.31–5.

12 See also III.8.9.24–9; V.5.8.23–7; 9.11–26; V.9.4.24–8; VI.7.32.12–14; VI.8.16.1–12.

13 Porph. *Sententiae* 1, Lamberz 1.2–3.

14 Porph. *Sent.* 2, Lamberz 1.5–6. See also *Sent.* 33, 35.4–21.

15 Porph. *Sent.* 3, Lamberz 2.2, 3, 7, 8; *Sent.* 28, 17.5; *Sent.* 30, 21.1; 32, 35.3; 37, 45.1,2,5.

16 Porph. *Sent.* 27, Lamberz 16.5–16.
17 Porph. *Sent.* 31, Lamberz 21.9–16.
18 Porph. *Sent.* 31, Lamberz 21.16–22.5; see III.9.4.3–6.
19 Porph. *Sent.* 34, Lamberz 38.6–39.12.
20 Theiler 1993 rejected the identification of the *Libri platonicorum* mentioned by Augustine in *Confessions* VII.9.13 and VIII.2.3 with the *Enneads*; Henry 1934, 69–45, provided a wide range of proofs in order to show that these "books" were in fact primarily the *Enneads*. On the Augustinian *Libri platonicorum* see also Courcelle 1943, 159–76; 1950, 93–138, 1954; Pépin 1954; O'Meara 1958; O'Connell 1963. On the translation of the *Enneads* made by Victorinus, see Henry 1950; Hadot 1968; Hadot 1971.
21 Marius Victorinus Afer, *Ad Cand.* 12.1, Hadot 1968, II, 18.
22 Marius Victorinus Afer, *Adv. Ar.* IV. 22.6–10, Hadot II, 49.
23 Marius Victorinus Afer, *Adv. Ar.* IV. 24.32–6, Hadot 1968 II, 51. See also *Ad Cand.* 15.1, Hadot II, 20 (*secundum nullum progressum semper in semet manens*); *Adv. Ar.* I.52.21, Hadot 1968 II, 31 (*quiescente quod est esse patricum*); *Adv. Ar.* IV. 21.19–25, Hadot 1968 II, 48 (*Primum in rebus eternis, divinis maximeque primis manentia quieta et in eo quod sunt exsistentia nulla sui per motum mutatione generarunt*).
24 Marius Victorinus Afer, *Adv. Ar.* I. 50.9–10, Hadot 1968 II, 29.
25 The relevant passages are commented on by O'Connell 1963. See also Teske 1986.
26 Aug. *Conf.* VI.4. See also V.16: *ubique presens.*
27 Syr. *In Aristotelis Metaphysicam Commentarium*, Kroll 114.35–115.3.
28 Proclus, *Elements of Theology* 28, Dodds 32.10–34.2; 32, Dodds 36.3–10.
29 Syr. *In Arist. Metaph. Comm.*, Kroll 117.16–28.
30 Syr. *In Arist. Metaph. Comm.*, Kroll 163.27–34.
31 See for instance *Elements of Theology* 18, Dodds 20.3–22; 120, Dodds 106.7–8; *In Tim.* II, Diehl I, 268.6–13; 335.25–336.3; 390.9–21; 395.10–22. On the topic of the production *autôi tôi einai* see Trouillard 1977. The Plotinian law of the immutability of the principle in its production is squarely endorsed by Proclus: cf. *Elements of Theology* 26, Dodds 30.10–11. See also *In Tim.* II, Diehl I, 396.24–6, where the Demiurgic Intellect remains eternally in itself and because of its *menein* produces the universe.
32 Procl. *El. Th.* 122, Dodds 108.8–9. On this topic see Trouillard 1960.
33 Pseudo-Dionysius Areopagita, *De divinis nominibus* I.5, Suchla 117.11–12.
34 Pseudo-Dionysius Areopagita *De div. nom.* V.5, Suchla 184.5–6. See also IV.1, Suchla 144.1–5.
35 Pseudo-Dionysius Areopagita *De div. nom.* V. 5, Suchla 184.2–3: *archegikoteron ôs on o theos ek tês presbutêras tôn allôn doreôn umneitai;*

see also V.4, Suchla 182.17–18: *tagathon ôs ontôs on kai tôn ontôn apantôn ousiopoion anumnêsomen;* V.4, Suchla 183.4–5: *o theos ou pôs estin on, all'aplôs kai aperioristôs olon en eautôi to einai suneilefôs kai proeilephôs.*

36 Pseudo-Dionysius Areopagita *De div. nom.* IV.20, Suchla 166.14; V.4, Suchla 182.19; V.8, Suchla 188.9–10 *(uperousios)*; V.4, Suchla 183.7–8: *oute en oute estai oute egeneto oute ginetai oute genêsetai, mallon de oute estin;* ibid., 183.12–13 and 17; V.8, Suchla 186.9 and 15; *ibid.* Suchla 187.4–5; V.10, Suchla 189.7 *(o proon)*.

37 Pseudo-Dionysius Areopagita, *De div. nom.* IX.4, Suchla 209.9.

38 See IX.8, Suchla 212.16–17: *ti de allo [= ê theia stasis] ge para to menein auton en eautôi to theon;* X.2, Suchla 215.12: *en tôi aei kineisthai menonta eph'heautou;* XI.1, Suchla 218.12–13: *kai proeisin epi panta endon olê menousa [= e theia eirênê di'uperbolen tês panta uperechousês enôseos.*

39 Pseudo-Dionysius Areopagita, *De div. nom.* IX.4, Suchla 209.10.

40 Pseudo-Dionysius Areopagita, *De div. nom.* V.10, Suchla 189.10–11.

41 Pseudo-Dionysius Areopagita, *De div. nom.* V.10, Suchla 189.11–12.

42 Pseudo-Dionysius Areopagita, *De div. nom.* IX.9, Suchla 213.12–14. Compare Proclus, *El. Th.* 122, Dodds 108.1–4.

43 *Liber de causis*, section 19, Bardenhewer 95.2–3 (see the Latin text in Pattin, 1968, 177.97–8). This lemma depends *ad verbum* from *El. Th.*, prop. 122 (see note 42).

44 *Liber de causis*, section 19, Bardenhewer 95.5: *al-'illa al-ūlā thābit qā'im bi-waḥdanīyyatiha, causa prima est fixa stans cum unitate sua* (= Pattin 177.3). Compare Proclus, *El. Th.* 122, Dodds 108.5.

45 *Liber de causis* section 19, Bardenhewer 96.8 = Pattin 178.25.

46 *Liber de causis* section 8, Bardenhewer 79.1 = Pattin 158.2. On the doctrine of being in the *Liber de causis* see D'Ancona 1992a. On the doctrine of proposition 8 of the *Liber*, see D'Ancona 1990a.

47 II.9.4. On this chapter see Roloff 1970, 166–9; in general, on the Plotinian polemic against the Gnostic cosmology see Elsas 1975; O'Brien 1981, 1992b, Evangeliou 1992; Pépin 1992. On the generation of matter see O'Brien 1971, 1991c; Corrigan 1986; Narbonne 1993.

48 See Rist 1962; Igal 1971; Santa Cruz de Prunes 1979; Szlezák 1979, 52–108; Smith 1981; Gatti 1983; Corrigan 1986a; Schroeder 1986; Lloyd 1987; Bussanich 1988; D'Ancona 1990a.

49 On this passage see Hadot 1988, 133–4, and Bussanich 1988, 169. See also I.8.2.17; V.1.7.19–20; V.2.1.5–7; V.3.11.18; VI.7.17.3–6; VI.9.6.26–35.

50 III.8.10.1–2: *dunamis tôn pantôn;* V.1.7.10 *(to en dunamis pantôn)*; V.3.15.32–3 *(to de dunamis pantôn)*; VI.8.9.45 *(dunamin pasan autês ontôs kurian)*.

51 Hyphens not in the Armstrong's translation. I have inserted them to bring out the dialogic form implicit in Plotinus's writing.

52 See also V.5.9.7–11.

53 III.8.11.19 (ichnos tou agathou); see also V.5.10.2; V.1.6.14 (agalma to prôton).

54 II. 9.1.12–16; V.1.6.48–9.

55 According to Hadot 1968, 99–100, the main cause of this increasing complexity lies in the fact that the Plotinian nous has been split by Iamblichus into two distinct principles, the intelligible paradigm and the divine Intellect. On the Plotinian thesis of the coincidence of Intellect and intelligible paradigm see Armstrong 1960. On the later views on the structure of the intelligible world see Pépin 1956; Trouillard 1957; Dillon 1969; Wallis 1972; Beierwaltes 1973; Steel 1978; Blumenthal 1981; Sheppard 1981; Evangeliou 1988; D'Ancona 1991.

56 See note 55.

57 Dam. De Princ. I.7, Westerink–Combès I, 37.20–38.12. See Combès 1975 and Linguiti 1990, 15–21; 35–43.

58 Proculus Theol. Plat. I.10, Saffrey–Westerink I.42.4–10. On the relevance of Syrianus in the development of the Neoplatonic school see Dodds 1963, XXI–V; Merlan 1965; Wallis 1972, 144–5; Sheppard 1981; Madigan 1986; Saffrey 1987.

59 See Saffrey–Westerink, 1968, LXVIII–LXXXIX, and Saffrey 1984.

60 Compare Proclus, In Parm. VI, Cousin 1089.30–1090.5 (see trans. Morrow and Dillon 1987, 438), with Enneads V.1.8.23–6. On this Plotinian passage see Schwyzer 1935 and Atkinson 1983, 196–8.

61 In Parm. VI, Cousin 1107.9–17, trans. Morrow and Dillon 1987, 452, with the following modifications: I interpret as a concessive the clause pantôn aition on to prôton, and I indicate within asterisks the words "but knowable in itself," coming from the Latin translation by William of Moerbeke (see Steel 1985, 390.00–1).

62 For the evidence on this point see D'Ancona 1991, 285–7.

63 Proculus In Parm., VI, Cousin 1105. 32–1106.1; see Morrow and Dillon 1987, 451.

64 See for instance In Tim. II, Diehl I, 230.8–231.9; 420.3–11; IV, Diehl III, 15.11–21; 100.8–20; In Parm. I, Cousin 620.8–17; 699.18–28; 703.33–704.12; 707.28–708.26; 710.11–27; VII, Cousin 1219.33–9; Theol. Plat. II.4, Saffrey–Westerink II.34.9–35.9; III.3, Saffrey–Westerink III.13.12–16; III.6.23.11–24; III.9.34.21–35.7; 38.8–39.8; III.10.42.6–12.

65 On the interpretation of the genê of the Sophist as the principles of the intelligible world see Nebel 1929; Rist 1971; Wurm 1973; Strange 1981. On the transformation of them into hypostases between the One and the intelligible world see Merlan 1965; Sheppard 1981; D'Ancona 1992b.

66 See for instance the passage of *In Parm.* IV, Cousin 969.16–32, where the intelligible world is conceived of as a hierarchy of eight principal levels of Ideas (cf. trans. Morrow and Dillon 1987, 316–17).

67 *Theol. Plat.* III.3, Saffrey–Westerink III, 11.23–13.5.

68 *El. Th.* 137. 120.31.

69 See D'Ancona 1992c, 281–90.

70 See Szlezák 1979, 34–6.

71 See for instance VI.7.16.22–31.

72 See O'Meara 1989.

73 *In Parm.* I, Cousin 712.2–5, trans. Morrow and Dillon 1987, 85.

74 Pseudo-Dionysius Areopagita *De Div. Nom.* V.6, Suchla 184.17–185.3.

16 Plotinus and Christian philosophy

A study of the relationship between Plotinus and Christian philosophy is far less than an investigation of the overall influence of Platonism on Christianity. It treats of the effect on Christianity of a particular Platonist philosopher of the third century A.D.: A task at once more manageable in scope and more difficult to identify precisely. For Platonism had influenced Christian philosophers before Plotinus (particularly Justin Martyr, Clement of Alexandria, and Origen) and it was to be influential over hundreds of years on later Christians, many of whom knew Plotinus as just a prominent name in the tradition. However, to discuss the influence of Plotinus on Christianity is not only to discuss those who knew Plotinus at first hand, and liked (or reacted against) what he taught; it is also to consider the thought of those whose understanding of Platonism was affected *indirectly* by the particular brand of Platonism established as dominant by Plotinus and which in modern times we have learned to call Neoplatonism.[1]

We are not immediately concerned with the influence of Neoplatonism as a whole on Christianity: that again is too wide a topic, for Plotinus was merely the founder of Neoplatonism, not perhaps even the most typical Neoplatonist, and many of his successors developed his basic insights plus additions of their own, in ways which he did not know, and which he would often not have approved. In treating of Plotinus's *indirect* influence we can at this stage do little more than observe that the later Neoplatonists of antiquity reinforced many of his original claims, and therefore his reputation, both among those who read him personally and among those who knew him through second-hand sources, and second-hand sources might be Christian as well as pagan. We shall return to this subject, but notice at once that

386

from the sixth century until the fifteenth the text of the *Enneads* was unknown in Western Europe, though still available in the Greek- (and later Arabic-) speaking East where it was sometimes put to philosophical purposes.[2] On the other hand the indirect influence of Plotinus can be found not only in later writers who were "obviously" Neoplatonists, but also in the vast majority of the Greek commentators on Aristotle – after Alexander of Aphrodisias and with the striking exception of Themistius – whose Neoplatonism has only been generally recognized by modern scholarship in very recent times.[3]

· For our present purposes Neoplatonism is the modern name for a particular sort of Platonism which, from Plotinus's time and in its own different versions, came to dominate the Platonic schools of late antiquity and thence to influence Christianity. Its appearance did not immediately cause earlier kinds of Platonism to be forgotten or even, for a while, to become obsolete. For by the time of Plotinus some form of Platonism was the intellectual air of most ancient society, to be breathed by Christians and pagans alike, and by pagans moving toward Christianity as well as those who rejected the newfangled religion and persevered to the end in what they thought of as traditional "Hellenism." Among Christian writers, however, we should also notice that the "Platonism" may at times be little more than a linguistic veneer, Platonic words and phrases being radically redirected to quite novel purposes. Gregory of Nyssa, as we shall see, at times provides good examples of this. Finally, though it is often said that Christian Platonists after Plotinus are Christian Neoplatonists, one needs to determine which of them would be better described as Platonists of a largely pre-Plotinian sort, which as Plotinian Neoplatonists, and which as Neoplatonists influenced by some post-Plotinian version of Neoplatonism and thus only indirectly by Plotinus himself. In many, indeed most, cases the effect of the philosophizing of Plotinus was to direct Christians to a broadly Platonic way of thinking and only to a limited extent to render them Plotinians.

Neither Plotinus nor any of his successors labeled themselves Neoplatonists: they are simply Platonists. Converting someone to a Platonic way of thinking would never have been called converting him to Neoplatonism. Both in antiquity and indeed down to the nineteenth (and even often the twentieth) century, the problem of who is a Platonist, who a Neoplatonist, and who a Plotinian is complicated by the fact that the Platonic tradition was thought to be and was preached to be more or less a unity. In the fifteenth century it would have been hard to persuade Marsilio Ficino or Pico della Mirandola of the significance of differences between Plotinus and Proclus or even between Plato and Proclus); the same would be true of the Cambridge Platonists of the seventeenth century and of many later Christian Platonist thinkers. If that situation has now changed, it is because modern scholarship has been effective in distinguishing between often radically different modes of Platonism, and because it has been willing to believe that many "Platonists" more than marginally distort some of the basic notions of Plato himself, while still remaining well within the broader Platonic tradition. Since antiquity it is only comparatively recently that it might be said of a philosopher that he is a Plotinian who despises Proclus, or that he thinks that Proclus is significantly more of a genuine Platonist – that is a teacher of the spiritual inheritance of Plato – than Porphyry. Of course, ancient Neoplatonists and Renaissance Platonists differed among themselves, but the notion that while they are all broadly within the Platonic tradition they are also at times *radically* diverse is a modern thesis. Above all, it is modern to say that Plotinus is a real philosopher while Proclus is not.

If Plotinus introduced a new brand of Platonism, what are its most important features? What did Plotinus emphasize, or de-emphasize, in the Platonic tradition, in ways which marked him out from others? That leads to a more basic question: what did the ancients, both Christian and pagan, see as the most important claims of Platonist philosophy, both before Plotinus and in its Plotinian version? And what did Plotinus add – whether he realized it was novel or not? To answer such questions properly would involve nothing less than a full-scale exposition of the thought of Plotinus as a whole and a detailed comparison of that thought with the ideas of many of his Middle Platonist predecessors. Such an enterprise – once again – is beyond the scope of the present introductory essay, and it would perhaps suffice if among Plotinus's personal contributions we could separate those areas in which he developed (and in particular those in which he tidied up) some rather unassimilated Middle Platonic themes from those other areas where, for his own philosophical reasons, he broke more radically new ground. Even this distinction cannot but appear arbitrary at times, but it will at least serve as a broad basis for broaching the following questions: How far did

Plotinus have a particular effect on the notions about Platonism which Christian thinkers, especially those of the early centuries, imbibed?; how far did Christian thinkers derive ideas from Plotinus which they could not have derived from earlier philosophers in the Platonic tradition?; and (most difficult of all) how far did the thought of Plotinus enable Christian thinkers to think more philosophically, and generally more intelligently, within the Platonic tradition than they would have been able to do had they had no direct or indirect access to his ideas?

Plotinus has been famously described as a *Plato dimidiatus*, as "half a Plato,"[4] and that description indicates that for a variety of reasons many features of the Platonic dialogues have been omitted or downplayed in Plotinus's presentation of Platonism: the tentative, more "Socratic," perhaps even more skeptical side of the early writings; above all the social and political themes and the concern with public life which permeate the whole of Plato's work, even when he is treating of apparently personal morality and more abstruse questions of philosophical logic and metaphysics. Furthermore, Plotinus quotes very selectively even from dialogues such as the *Sophist* and *Theaetetus* from which he quotes regularly.

Such reflections are scarcely helpful in identifying what is distinctively Plotinian: the title *Plato dimidiatus* (or even "Plato further fragmented") could be affixed to virtually all (if not all) pre-Plotinian writers in the Platonic tradition, perhaps even back to the first generation after the master's death, the era of Speusippus, Eudoxus, and Xenocrates, though perhaps with increasing aptness as we pass from the classical to the Hellenistic to the Roman periods of ancient thought. The end of the *polis* as the essential focus of human life carried with it a certain removal of philosophy from those concerns with society as a whole which intensely mattered to Plato.

Our search for the distinctively Plotinian will center on specifically metaphysical claims, and in particular on Plotinus's blending of the varying forms of the Platonic and Pythagorean traditions which existed before his time. Plotinus is said by Porphyry to have combined the Pythagorean and Platonic first principles better than his predecessors (*Life of Plotinus* 20), and this can be taken to mean, *inter alia*, that he combined traditions which identified as the first principle (which he normally called the One) not only the Neopythagorean One (supposedly also discussed in the first hypothesis of the second part of the *Parmenides*⁵), but also the Good of the sixth book of the *Republic* which is said to be "beyond the finite existence and nature [of other Forms]." Furthermore, developing the anti-Aristotelian strain of Middle Platonists like Atticus, Plotinus argues (and not merely asserts) that this first principle is no Aristotelian mind, but transcends the Aristotelian dualism of mental subject and object.⁶

It is not only the Aristotelian account of God as a thought thinking itself which Plotinus has subordinated to his "Neoplatonic" first principle. As Porphyry has also told us (*Life* 14), he has assimilated a great deal of Stoicism. Much of this is to be found in his ethics, but Plotinus also built the Stoic notion of the "sympathy" of the physical cosmos into his third "hypostasis," which he called Soul. He was helped in this reconstruction by his imaginative transposition into a metaphysical law of the Platonic principle of psychology, whether human or divine, that goodness is necessarily productive. Recall that for human beings the notion that to love beauty is to wish to create in beauty (*Symposium* 206b) and the related theme, applied to the gods in general in the *Phaedrus* (247a) and to the Demiurge in particular in the *Timaeus* (29e), that grudgingness is no divine characteristic; indeed that it is absent from the highest living beings, whether human or divine. The result of this blending of a Platonic psychological-cum-metaphysical principle, seen as indicating something of the nature of love (Eros) itself, with the Stoic notion of a pantheistic universe, enabled Plotinus to formulate as a cosmic as well as a metaphysical law that famous triad (rest in God or the One, procession, and return to God) which attracted mystical Christians from Gregory of Nyssa to Thomas Aquinas and beyond.⁷ And as we shall see, the effects of this principle in Christianity were not limited to what has been called cosmic theology: it had a particularly important role to play in ethics and the theory and practice of asceticism.

Plotinus constructed his Neoplatonic synthesis from the disparate strands which had been handed down to him by weaving them into a vision of the universe in which a single first principle, the One, is the first of three "hypostases" or types of enduring reality which are strictly subordinated to one another: from the One comes the Divine Mind and from the Divine Mind comes Soul. This set of subordinated divinities, a final form of the various attempts made by Plotinus's predecessors to organize the untidy bundle of "contents" of the universe which Plato and his immediate successors had bequeathed to their philosophical posterity, was to provide as much a stumbling block (and a potential source of heresy) to those Christians who came to know it as pre-Plotinian subordinationisms had been to (some of) their earlier co-religionists.

Plotinus's most important tidying-up of all, perhaps, was his not entirely successful attempt to argue (in fact against Plato himself, though that was not admitted) that everything in the world, including matter, ultimately derived from the One. This was to lead to a certain amount of confusion among Christians since Plotinus's account of divine production was (again, it seems, contrary to the intention of Plato's *Timaeus*) an unhistorical one. All depends on the One in that it could not exist without the One's productive power, but there is no beginning of the physical universe: hence matter has always existed, though it has always been dependent for its existence on the One itself.[8] But Christians normally asserted that all physical objects (if not also all non-physical objects) are ultimately *ex nihilo* productions with a temporal origin. Hence Plotinus's tidier version of previous Platonism, insofar as its metaphysics is anti-historical, was no more satisfactory to the majority of them than its less tidy Middle Platonist predecessors.

If the Plotinian One is to be dramatically transcendent, and Plotinus's Platonism is to be a unified system in which the One is responsible for the existence of all else, that is, in Neoplatonic terms, the single and indivisible cause of all that in any way partakes of multiplicity, then Plotinus has given a further boost to the tradition of negative theology – that is, to the view that we say of the first principle only what it is not, not what it is – already well developed in many of the Middle Platonists,[9] visible in Philo and from both sources attractive to Platonizing Christians.[10] It is probably safe to say that the influence of Plotinus, whether direct or indirect, played a major role not in founding but in securing the philosophical tradition of negative theology, via such writers as Gregory of Nyssa (c. 335–94) and Pseudo-Dionysius (early sixth century), as a permanent feature of Christianity.

One of the effects of Plotinus's attempt to integrate matter into a single universe caused in its totality by the One is a comparative upgrading of the world of physical nature, against the Gnostics (as particularly in *Ennead* II.9), and a softening of the soul–body dualism of the *Phaedo*, under the influence of other Platonic dialogues such as the *Timaeus*. In place of a cruder metaphysical form of immaterial–material (or soul–matter) dualism, Plotinus maintained only a moral "dualism" whereby material objects and the body, far from evil in themselves insofar as they exist, are a source of temptation, perhaps of almost inevitable temptation, to the soul.

Plotinus's views never hardened into the Porphyrian tag "*omne corpus est fugiendum*" deprecated by Augustine in the *Retractationes* (1.4.3) and which may be seen as a partial reversion to a cruder dualism than the *Enneads* themselves are prepared to tolerate. Nevertheless, there is a certain conflict between the Platonic notion that the soul is naturally immortal, which Plotinus endorsed wholeheartedly (and which was unacceptable to Christians who had always held that it is only made immortal by God or his grace),[11] and the Christian belief, always fundamental, in the resurrection of the body: first that of Christ, then of each member of the human race. It is true that Christians, while maintaining the resurrection of the body, were still often inclined, at least before Augustine,[12] to define the human being (or person) in ways which seemed to suggest, in Plotinian fashion, that "real" man is in some sense just a soul, but more normally they avoided the problem by talking perhaps too Platonically about the perfection of the human soul, while keeping that doctrine in a separate compartment of their minds, refusing to juxtapose it (and see its possible disharmony) with the theology of bodily resurrection.

Yet despite all this, there is no doubt that Plotinus's account of the return of the soul by the power of Eros from the world below to the heavenly world above – note that Augustine was to reproach himself in the *Retractationes* (1.3.2) for assimilating the Kingdom of God to the Platonic intelligible world in his early writings – was an added incentive for Christians (directly or indirectly) to follow him as he led the soul, following Plato's *Symposium*, as Porphyry put it (*Life* 23), up the ladder of divine ascent to God. As we shall see, fairly soon after Plotinus's death a side effect of the Council of Nicaea (A.D. 325) may have been to make this part of the Platonic inheritance especially attractive to Christians.

Yet Plotinus's doctrine of the soul which remains above and cannot sin – a doctrine which he seems rightly to have regarded as essential if his ethics are to be consistent – could not be acceptable to orthodox Christians: rather than being a support for orthodox Christianity, it remained a persistent invitation to heterodoxy, indeed to that very heterodoxy which early Christian hostility to the "Platonic" notion of the natural immortality of the soul hoped to rule out. For although the Iamblichean revision of Plotinian ethics, whereby the whole soul falls (and needs somehow to be retrieved, theurgically, by action of the gods),[13] was more suitable to Christianity, its ready redescription by Christians as mere magic, as opposed to Christian sacramentalism, told against it, perhaps paradoxically making the Plotinian "heresy" of the unfallen soul that much the more attractive.

Although it is far beyond the scope of this essay to tackle it thoroughly, the question of ancient notions of self-perfection, and of how far they are alien to and superseded by Christianity with its doctrine of the acts of a Redeemer, indeed of God himself, if human perfectability is to be achieved, cannot be entirely evaded. For where two doctrines have apparently much common ground, as is the case with Christian and Platonic notions of the ultimate perfectability of man (or of the human soul), there is also likely to be confusion between them. Within the history of Christianity one can trace the tension and antagonism between those Christians who welcomed the Platonic theory of self-perfection as some kind of adumbration of Christianity and those who thought it a curiously misleading, if not blasphemous, parody of Christian Truth. (Sometimes the two types of reaction can be seen within the same author, as in the case of Augustine, and sometimes they are even to be found, confusingly, at the same time of an author's life.) Into such a protracted history of the general interaction of Platonism and Christianity the influence of the peculiarly *Plotinian* version of human perfectability would have to be fitted.

Dialogue between Platonism and Christianity began early, and a complete history of our present topic would have taken account in detail of how they were both compatible and incompatible, how Platonism both aided the development of Christian theology and perverted that growth; and that would present us with further theological problems of what kind of thought would be such as to develop Christianity as "true" Christianity and what kind of thought would pervert it – which in its turn would demand some kind of account, regrettably implicit if not honestly explicit, of what kind of thing "Christian orthodoxy" must be. But for us much of that daunting project can be avoided, for Plotinus was not the first Platonist to influence Christianity, nor was he the last, and, as already stated, our primary concern is to identify the specific areas in which the thought of Plotinus himself, directly or indirectly, has been decisive. A question which cannot be deferred, however, concerns the specific aspects of Christianity which Plotinus was able to influence – given the time at which he lived and the exact development of Christian thought up to and shortly after that time.

Plotinus makes no mention of Christianity, and with the possible exception of VI.8 there seem to be no passages in the *Enneads* indicating any concern with what may be crudely called the mainline Christianity of his day. In chapter 16 of his *Life of Plotinus*, however, Porphyry notes that he and other pupils were encouraged to refute the views of certain sectaries with Christian connections whom he also identifies as Gnostics, the targets of Plotinus himself in several of the *Enneads*. After Plotinus's death, if not before, Porphyry himself was to become an implacable foe of all forms of Christianity, so it is particularly striking that he does not associate Plotinus with this more generalized hostility.

Thus, Plotinus's activity as a philosopher occurs at a time when most Platonists (there were exceptions like Celsus, to whose work Origen had devoted a lengthy reply) were not yet as aware of the Christian "threat" as Porphyry was to become. But the *Enneads* were published, as distinct from composed, during the greatest of the anti-Christian persecutions, launched by the emperors Maximian and Diocletian; and some twenty years after their publication the general Constantine, who had emerged from the struggles of the early fourth century as the unchallenged master of the Roman world and a Christian – with the bishop of Cordova as his theological advisor – was able to arrange for the assembling of the most important of all Christian "Councils" (excluding that described in *Acts* at Jerusalem), the Council of Nicaea.

Although the Council of Nicaea was far from having Platonism, or any directly philosophical matters, high on its agenda, its effects on the future relations between Christianity and Platonism, and therefore on Christian attitudes to Plotinus himself, were of the greatest importance. For the primary concern of the Council was the "heresy" of Arius, a priest of Alexandria who had run into trouble with his bishop Alexander for claiming that Christ, the Logos, the Second

Person of the Christian Trinity, was inferior to, not of the same substance as, God the Father, indeed that he was a created intermediary between God the Father and the created universe.

Dispute has raged as to whether Arius himself was in any way, directly or indirectly, influenced by Platonizing notions of a hierarchy of divine beings such as (but only by way of example) the One, *Nous*, and Soul of Plotinus,[14] or whether his theories derive from a mixture of earlier, but as yet uncondemned, Christian theology and a sprinkling of biblical exegesis perhaps dependent on the mysterious but obviously influential figure of Lucian of Antioch.[15] But the precise origin of Arianism (or origins if, as at least came to be the case, Arianism was a theological syndrome rather than a single necessarily fixed set of doctrines), is not our present concern.

.What mattered for the reception of Platonism, and especially the Platonism of Plotinus, into Christianity, was that after Nicaea, forms of Platonism which might look like (or be claimed to look like) the subordinationism of Arius were increasingly impossible for orthodox Christians. One traditional part of Platonism was thus excluded, and Christians who read Plotinus after Nicaea, if they wished to remain orthodox, as most of them did, or thought they did, now found it necessary to telescope the Plotinian hypostases of the One and *Nous*, making the Forms God's thoughts (though not concepts) in a more Middle Platonic manner, and for the most part concealing their Neoplatonic sources, if any, by referring to the first principle as the Good rather than the One.[16] The alternative was to run the risk of being damned as Arians if they indulged even in the rather more sophisticated speculations about Christ as a subordinate Logos which were not wholly out of place in Plotinus's own lifetime, as the career of Origen, his slightly older contemporary, shows, and which can be found earlier in the writings of the Jewish "Platonist" Philo – read by Christians at least as a helpful Old Testament exegete.

If Athanasius, the successor of Alexander, and the pro-Nicenes (eventually) gained a more or less complete victory in driving subordinationism (including therefore its Plotinian form) from mainstream Christianity, there were other areas in which the Council of Nicaea, and especially the prestige of Athanasius himself, gave Platonic and Plotinian notions free rein, for though Athanasius tends to despise philosophers as of vanishing importance in the new Christian world,[17] and could scent Arianism like a police dog sniffing out drugs, his love of the ascetic way to holiness could only (unwittingly) encourage the Platonic and Plotinian asceticism (of which he himself appears to be ignorant or at least disdainful), to enter the Christian fold and receive a warm welcome.

Plotinus did not enter the Christian world during his own lifetime, nor even as soon as his writings began to circulate. Indeed the process of assimilation was such that the antisubordinationist effects of the Council of Nicaea and its dependent theology were already visible before he became at all significant in Christian writings. There is, however, one interesting exception to this: Eusebius of Caesarea. Eusebius knows a small amount of Plotinus, though he seems to make little use of his knowledge. Nevertheless, as a supporter of Arius and certainly a subordinationist, he gives us an opportunity to imagine what effects Plotinian metaphysics might have been able to produce within Christianity had not the Council of Nicaea intervened.[18]

One result of that Council, then, was to ensure that negative theology, doctrines of asceticism and of the mystic way, combined with the general structure of cosmic rest, procession and return, not the schema of hypostases itself, were to be the Plotinian themes most apparent in subsequent Christianity.

We have seen something of the specifically Plotinian version of Platonism. We must now turn to particular Christian writers in whose texts Plotinian features may appear, thus observing the actual mode of Plotinus's reception into the Christian community. We shall recall that his writings may be received either directly, that is by those who read the *Enneads* (or other Plotinian texts, if any) firsthand, or indirectly by those who learn of Plotinus first of all through Porphyry, then later, and less specifically, through other more or less well informed intermediaries.

There is little or no evidence of Christian knowledge of Plotinus during the third century, which may seem hardly surprising since Porphyry's edition of the *Enneads* only appeared in about A.D. 301. But other sources of knowledge might have been available. Plotinus's pupil Amelius set up a school in Apamea in Syria (*Life* 2–3), and Porphyry tells us (19–20) that his own former master Longinus, who died in about 272, received from Amelius copies of the greater part of Plotinus's work. Longinus himself wrote a reply to material

on Forms now to be found in *Ennead* V.5, and he urged Porphyry to
bring him any further texts of Plotinus which might be available.
But there is no way of knowing whether Christians had access to
such texts.[19]

More problematic is what seems to have been an edition of at least
some (but by no means necessarily all) of Plotinus's work by his doctor Eustochius. The only secure piece of evidence for such an edition
is a scholion which appears in several manuscripts of the *Enneads* (A
E R J C) at the end of chapter 19 of *Ennead* IV.4. It says that in
Eustochius's edition book 2 of the *On Difficulties About the Soul*
ended here, and that book 3 began with what is chapter 20 of book 2
in Porphyry's text. But this edition of Eustochius, whatever size it
may have been, has left no trace at least until Eusebius's *Praeparatio
Evangelica*, composed some time after A.D. 313 at Caesarea.[20]

Eusebius's knowledge of Plotinus seems to be limited to material
to be found in *Ennead* IV.7 (*On the Immortality of the Soul*) and V.1
(*On the Three Primary Hypostases*),[21] and it may be noted that the
"Oration of Constantine to the Assembly of the Saints," a document
of not long after A.D. 320, seems to reflect the Middle Platonism of
Numenius rather than the Neoplatonism of Plotinus. Similar Christian ignorance of the text of Plotinus persists in most of the Christian East until about A.D. 380: there is nothing particularly Plotinian
in Athanasius, whose interest in philosophy is minimal, as we have
observed;[22] nor, as we have also argued, in Arius.[23]

If then there is little evidence of the specific influence of Plotinus
among Eastern Christian writers of the earlier part of the fourth century, when does the situation change? With the Cappadocians, it is
often suggested, but care is needed here too. Certainly it would be
ultra-skeptical to deny that, when Basil was a student in Athens for
four or five years from about 351 the intellectual air was Platonic, and
some effect of the theories of the great Plotinus and his pupils could
be recognized in the very thickness of that air. But to say that is far
from saying that the special features of Plotinian Neoplatonism
would have been obvious even to the fairly attentive observer. At any
rate they do not seem to have much penetrated the mind of Basil, who
gives no indication of taking more than minimal interest in Plotinus
until very near the end of his life, perhaps under the influence of his
more mystically-minded brother Gregory (of Nyssa). There may be
more to this neglect than Basil's obtuseness or absence of texts of the

Enneads. That more has to do with the difference between modern accounts of the history of ancient Platonism and the way in which ancient Platonists looked at the matter themselves.

By the time Basil came to Athens as a student Plotinus had been dead for about eighty years, and in the East his work and that of his proselytizing pupil and editor Porphyry had already begun to fade into the general tradition of Platonism. A new Platonic star, Iamblichus, whose ideas were beloved of the neo-pagan Emperor Julian and hated as magic and idolatry by many Christians, was in the ascendent. Although the modern reader of Neoplatonic texts wants to emphasize the philosophical superiority of Plotinus to his fellows, the ancients were not normally of that opinion. Indeed insofar as Plotinus was idiosyncratic in his wealth of detailed argument and more individualized theses, he may be said even at times to have been neglected. Hence a Christian looking at the Platonic tradition in the mid-fourth century "University" of Athens would have no particular reason to seek him out as the master *par excellence.* That said, it is possible only to summarize what seem to be the established facts about Basil's use of Plotinus.[24]

There is a text *On the Spirit* which is traditionally attributed to Basil, though I am inclined to think that Gregory of Nyssa or some other unknown party is the author.[25] This text, as is universally admitted, makes very extensive and respectful use of *Ennead* V.1 (one of the two treatises certainly known also to Eusebius, as we have seen),[26] but apparently of no other parts of the *Enneads.* A second work, certainly by Basil, *On the Holy Spirit,* seems to contain at least indirect echoes of *Ennead* VI.9 and V.2 (and just possibly of I.7 and II.9) in its ninth chapter, and there is a little more Plotinus in other parts of the same text.[27] The conclusion must be that before 375 Basil had come across parts of *Enneads* V.1 and IV.7, if only in Eusebius, but took little interest in them: by 375, when he wrote *On the Holy Spirit,* he probably knew V.1 directly and VI.9 indirectly. (It may be significant that these are numbers 10 and 9 on Porphyry's chronological list.)

Though it is commonly held that the influence of Plotinus entered Christianity extensively through the Cappadocians, it thus appears that even in his old age Basil took a rather limited interest in the *Enneads.* What about Gregory of Nazianzus? Again the pickings are slim. Gregory knows something of Greek philosophy, especially of

Plato, but he is critical and often hostile. He regards Aristotle, the Stoics, the Cynics, and the Epicureans as only worthy of refutation and he comments little on contemporary thinkers: of Plotinus in particular his knowledge is very limited, perhaps only to *Ennead* V.2.[28] He makes use of the schema of rest, procession and return, and thus can broadly be called a Christian Platonist, perhaps owing his emphasis on this schema at least indirectly to Neoplatonic rather than earlier Platonist texts, and he calls the Platonists "those who have thought best about God and are nearest to us" (*Oration* 31.5), but he contrasts faith with reason and merely breathes a general Platonic air when he muses on the nature of an immaterial God.[29]

The last of the Cappadocians is Basil's younger brother, Gregory, bishop of Nyssa. He is usually and rightly supposed to be much more affected than his namesake or than Basil by Greek philosophical ideas. "In the pages of the *On Virginity*, in particular, formulations from Plato and Plotinus dropped easily from his pen."[30] But it is also true that those formulations are often set in a very different, specifically Christian framework, and that the end-product is far removed from the thought of Plotinus. Gregory is certainly a Platonist if a Platonist is one who emphasizes an ontological distinction between the sensible and the intelligible, and holds that the power of *erôs* leads a man back to God. And Gregory believes in the infinity of God in his essence, a view which Plotinus almost certainly held, and held to be the theory of the *Republic* – and Plotinus's formulation of this may (though need not) have influenced Gregory.[31] Yet for Gregory the doctrine of infinity is central, clear, and unambiguous, while for Plotinus the debates and uncertainties of modern scholars result from the fact that infinity is not a central and constant topic. There can be little doubt that Gregory's different, and remarkable, attitude is in part the result of the fact that the dichotomy Creator–creature has subsumed the more generally Platonic and Plotinian contrast between the One and the many.

It cannot be denied that the major source of Gregory's Platonism (as of the Platonism of the other Cappadocians) is the Christian Origen – that is, his Platonism is largely derived from pre-Plotinian sources; it is reinforced by, rather than based on, Neoplatonic texts. It is also true for Gregory of Nyssa, almost as much as for the other Cappadocians, that much of his Platonism in general, let alone his Plotinianism, is unspecific enough as to be easily fitted into a Christian framework. It would probably be most correct to say that Gregory's Christian Platonism grows from the "Middle Platonism" of Origen largely in parallel to the specifically Neoplatonic developments of Plotinus, though not entirely uninfluenced by them.

It is often, and probably rightly, said that the influence of Plotinus on Gregory of Nyssa is particularly apparent in his account of the soul[32] and on related questions of the return of the purified soul to God – a theme we have already noticed. But Gregory is no different from other Christian Fathers in rejecting the soul's natural divinity, and for all the power of the Platonic ladder of ascent in its Christian guise, it should also be emphasized that in Gregory such ideas are closely associated with theories of virginity and bride-mysticism which came primarily from Origen (in his *Commentary on the Songs of Songs*), Athanasius,[33] and Methodius's *Symposium*.[34] It is worth noting that in their index of direct citations of Plotinus Henry and Schwyzer manage (though stingily) to cite only one instance from Gregory.

That brings us back to the question of direct and indirect influence. Perhaps, like Augustine, as we shall argue, Gregory derived much more from Plotinus and Neoplatonism than the direct quotations would indicate. Perhaps the air he breathed was Neoplatonic as well as Origenist, and perhaps he too was inclined to think consciously of Platonism, even of Neoplatonism, as a propaedeutic, even a necessary halfway house, to Christianity.

There is little, however, to support any such interpretation of Gregory's conscious views, and we may identify a few further features of his thought which are obviously un-Plotinian: such, in addition to the matter of virginity and his unwillingness to depart from Nicene orthodoxy in the matter of the nonsubordination of the Divine Persons of the Trinity, would be his notion of the *epektasis*, or continuing expansion of the understanding of God to be obtained in the beatific vision: his emphasis on a radical difference between God and man as indicated by the historical creation of man and the rest of the cosmos from nothing; his emphasis in the mystical ascent on the Dark Night of the Soul (a theme derived in part from Philo); his belief that man has reached his present state in three stages: first his soul is created in the intelligible world, then again in the sensible world, then it is muddied by the fall.

In all, this Gregory's specific background, as distinct from his more

general two-world background, is Christian, and what Platonism
there is comes, directly or indirectly, from Plato himself – influential
texts and traditions being often identical with those which influenced Plotinus: the central books of the *Republic*, for example, and
the Myth of the Charioteer of the *Phaedrus*.[35] It is not unimportant
that the cult of the untarnished body of the virgin, which Gregory and
others attached to the Platonic doctrine of *erôs*, was significantly
alien to the Platonic tradition in that it is related to the doctrine of the
resurrection of the body, implying the necessity of keeping the body
as well as the Platonic soul ready for immortality.[36]

So it seems that the specific influence of Plotinus on Greek Christian thought down to the late fourth century was rather limited, that
even Gregory of Nyssa should be seen as a man who expressed a
number of Christian themes in a Platonic way rather than one whose
basic beliefs were dependent on Platonic philosophizing or who
thought of Neoplatonism as a way of justifying or grounding his Christianity philosophically. Gregory's Platonism is thus unselfconscious,
and although further investigation of the indirect effects of Porphyry
might alter this picture in some details, the differences would be
marginal.

Perhaps the greater emphasis in Porphyry than in Plotinus on
escape from the body helped to encourage those in the Christian
tradition who played down the theological importance of the doctrines of the Incarnation and the Resurrection. That at least, as we
shall see, is what Augustine came to believe had happened in his
case in Milan. In any case, not only is there little emphasis on
specifically Plotinian features of the Platonic tradition among the
Greek-speaking Christians so far examined, but it is also true that
the *argumentative* side of Plotinus's work, that is, his campaign to
update Platonism against its various critics, particularly Aristotelians, has left almost no trace on these writers at all. We must now
consider whether the situation was any different in the fourth century West.

Plotinus wrote in Greek, and although no-one else copied his idiosyncratic style, the writers we have considered, as Greek-speakers,
would have been familiar with the standard philosophical sense of
Greek technical terms. When we shift our attention to the West,
however, the situation changes. Over a long period of time, and with
obvious exceptions to the general pattern, we can see that Roman

intellectuals were once bilingual in Greek and Latin, then become Latin-speakers with limited competence in Greek, and later lost the use of Greek altogether. Marius Victorinus and Augustine are examples of the first two types. Furthermore, it had always been a problem that Greek philosophical terms could not be rendered exactly in Latin, and that their approximate Latin equivalents introduce new overtones of meaning unknown to the Greek. Both Cicero and Seneca complain of such difficulties, and a good example of them can be seen in the use by Seneca of the word *voluntas* (will, moral personality) where the equivalent Greek (in Epictetus) seems to be *prohairesis.*

Marius Victorinus, a distinguished and bilingual African *rhêtor* resident in Rome in the mid-fourth century, is the first Latin author to know Plotinus and Porphyry well.[37] His anti-Arian treatises, though hardly affected by contemporary Greek theology, are dominated by the metaphysics of Porphyry which he attempts to adapt to Christian Trinitarian speculation, specifically to a defense of Nicene "orthodoxy." He uses the Porphyrian language of "being alone" (*to einai monon* or *huparxis*) to represent the Plotinian sense of "beyond being" when applied to the First Principle – Victorinus is often easier to understand if his literal-minded Latin is turned back word for word into the Porphyrian Greek from which it derives – and his One is consubstantial with the Logos–Son in an anti-Plotinian "telescoping" of the first two Neoplatonic hypostases – which some have again seen as indebted to, though developed from, Porphyry,[38] but which enables him to avoid the Neoplatonic "subordinationism" which he knows Nicaea has disallowed.[39]

Victorinus's Neoplatonizing theology has been called the first systematic exposition of the doctrine of the Trinity,[40] but Jerome found him difficult (*De viris illustribus* 101) and he was little read. His most significant contribution to Christianity was his translation of a number of Neoplatonic texts, chiefly, though not necessarily only by Plotinus himself.[41] The effect of these translations was first particularly felt in Milan, at that time the most important center of Christian thought in the West, where a number of priests and laity interested in Platonism, and indeed in Neoplatonism, can be identified well before the arrival of Augustine in 384.

Milan in the last decades of the fourth century seems to have been the site of the first substantial Christian "circle" devoted to Plotinus's work. The learned priest Simplicianus who not only knew and influenced Victorinus but who also baptized both Ambrose and Augustine and later succeeded Ambrose as bishop, was the intellectual center of the group.[42] The position and theology of Ambrose himself is more difficult to determine. His main impact on Augustine was threefold: to persuade him that allegorization in the manner of the Alexandrians, and of Origen in particular, was an effective answer to Manichaean attacks on the "grossness" of the Old Testament; to encourage him to think of God and the soul as immaterial substances, a view – surprisingly to us – unusual among Western Christians of the age, though long familiar in the East;[43] to convince him that for fallen man belief is the essential prerequisite for understanding (Confessions VI.5.7–8).[44]

Ambrose was fairly well read in Greek theology, especially that of Origen, Methodius, Athanasius, and Didymus the Blind, as well as of Philo and his own nearer contemporaries. He knew something too of Plotinus and Porphyry in the original Greek, as well as in Victorinus's Latin versions, but it is not entirely clear when he read the Neoplatonic texts, and how much they added to his basically Alexandrian (sometimes Cappadocian) and Middle Platonic outlook.[45] In the manner of Gregory of Nazianzus, Ambrose was willing to call the Platonists the "aristocrats of thought" (Ep. 34.1),[46] but despite his willingness to cite Plotinus (though perhaps sometimes indirectly via one of the Greek Fathers) in the De Isaac, the De bono mortis, and the De Iacob,[47] there is no reason to think of any special respect or devotion of the sort which Augustine, in the Happy Life, attributes to his fellow Milanese Manlius Theodorus.

Ambrose's Platonism, besides deriving from Origen's Commentary on the Song of Songs and other Christian texts, is, however, also particularly indebted to a tradition deriving especially from the pseudo-Platonic dialogue Alcibiades Maior[48] (which like Plotinus Ambrose assumed to be genuine),[49] whereby we are simply to be identified with our souls, and this fitted well with the belief of Porphyry to which we have already referred that we should strive to separate the soul from all else, including, of course, the body, which is a tattered garment, a mere instrument of the soul to be cast off in the return to God.

There is no doubt that Ambrose uses Plotinian ideas, though not the major themes of Plotinus, in the three "Plotinian" sermons mentioned above, just as he used themes from Cicero's De officiis in his

De officiis ministrorum, but merely to say that is to remain far from knowing whether Ambrose should in any sense be called a Plotinian. Those who wish so to describe him are too ready to blend the Platonism of various thinkers in Milan into a homogeneous pattern, thus assuming for all what might have been true for Simplicianus – whose strictures on Platonism as well as his knowledge of the *Enneads* are well known – or Manlius Theodorus; on the other hand they greatly underestimate the tradition which came down to Ambrose from the vast majority of his Christian sources: the sheer originality of Christianity, and the normal subordination (even sometimes the alleged historical dependence) of Platonism to it or to its Old Testament precursor. If the Cappadocians were among Ambrose's sources, as seems certain especially for his *Hexameron*, recall that the specifically Plotinian impact on these thinkers is often overrated, and that Ambrose is at least as suspicious of philosophy, even of Platonism, as they are.

If Simplicianus was a genuine, though critical, admirer of Plotinus, there seems to be no evidence that Ambrose can be so described;[50] indeed he tends to equate philosophy with paganism.[51] Like the Cappadocians, he sees Platonism in general as sharing important beliefs about the priority of the non-sensible world, the separation of the soul from the body, and other themes, with Christianity, but he is far less influenced by the details of Platonism than Origen, or even than Clement of Alexandria. Certainly the thought of Plotinus neither brought him to Christianity nor affected the essentials of his presentation of Christianity in more than marginal fashion.

All of which means that there remains but one further candidate for the source of the belief that by A.D. 400 ancient Christianity had not only been marked by Platonism, as indeed it had often been since the time of Justin Martyr, Clement, and Origen, but by specifically Neoplatonic ideas (as in Victorinus). If Christianity is thought to be *Neoplatonic*, or to find Neoplatonism an essential explanatory tool, it must be Augustine who first saw it to be so, or made it so.[52] An attempt to see that that is so, how far it is so, and why it is so, is almost the last theme that can be introduced in the present discussion.

We have already noticed that the Council of Nicaea forms a watershed in the relations between Christianity and Platonism. Before that, as in Origen, Platonic metaphysics could be used without radical reformulation in what was later to be called Trinitarian debate;

after Nicaea that is no longer kosher. But Platonism, often exotically blended with a doctrine of virginity (symbolizing the Christian thesis of the resurrection of the body), could still be important: contrary to the other philosophical systems of antiquity, it could offer belief in a non-material world (including Platonic Forms as God's thoughts) governed by Providence, as well as a doctrine of love and desire for the Good which could lead man back to that immaterial world at least dimly grasped by Platonic and Neoplatonic metaphysicians. Hence when Augustine, still not a Christian, was convinced by Ambrose and others of the existence of a spiritual universe, where could he turn but to the Platonists, and what more natural but that in such a mood he should be overwhelmed, as on his own admission he was, by reading "very few" of the books of Plotinus,[53] the philosopher in whom he found that Plato lived again? And as we shall see, what more natural than that a perceived flaw in the account of that very *erôs* which is so essential to Platonism was also to provide a key to his understanding that, if Platonism had one flaw, it could have many?

Yet Augustine remained sufficiently impressed by what he saw of the Platonism that seemed to form part of Christianity – and can be glimpsed by non-Christians – to retain a lifelong respect for the Platonist, or rather Neoplatonist, who had played such an important role in the intellectual part of his own journey to Christianity. For it is above all Augustine's belief that Christianity can subsume Platonism, but that the Platonism it subsumes is part of the essence of Christianity, which more than any other single factor has led us to think of an almost essential relationship between Platonism and an *intellectual explanation* of Christianity itself. Plotinus was the Platonist who led Augustine to that view. Augustine was the most able Christian of antiquity whose conversion to Christianity had been intellectually supported by Neoplatonic theory. It is therefore not surprising that he saw the Christian possibilities of Neoplatonism more clearly than the rest of his coreligionists.

Augustine's reading of the *Enneads* was not that of a scholar, but that of a determined seeker for the way to a good life based on truth. Hence a hunt for verbal parallels between his text and that of Plotinus cannot do justice to the impact the *Enneads* had upon him.[54] Certainly such parallels can be found, but modern scholars have become bogged down in the details of which exactly were the very few of the treatises of Plotinus Augustine had actually read at the time of his conversion. The debate is endless, and no objective means is available to settle it. It is much more important to notice that had Augustine read only two or three of the *Enneads* (say I.6, V.1, and VI.9), he could have creatively combined them to reconstruct much more of the work and mindset of their author than could have been achieved by a more literal-minded reader, for he was mentally in tune with much of Plotinus's thought and found it inspiring and compelling. Reading Plotinus taught him to be no slavish disciple but to create a Platonism of his own, while retaining important Plotinian themes (such as the account of *tolma* in V.10) when he found they could be harmonized with Scripture and Catholic tradition.[55]

When Augustine first heard Ambrose preach – it is by no means certain that he heard any of the "Plotinian sermons" we discussed earlier – it was Ambrose's resolution of Manichaean difficulties with the Old Testament, as we have seen, which impressed him, along with the insistence that God and the soul are immaterial substances. But Augustine never claims that he was introduced to Neoplatonism by the bishop of Milan, and from what we have noted of Ambrose's attitude to philosophy that is understandable. When Ambrose did make recommendations to Augustine, it was to read Isaiah – which Augustine found too difficult. But when, through the intermediary of a "man of outstanding vanity," Augustine began to read some of the *Enneads*[56] in Victorinus's translation, he found Ambrose's preaching supported by philosophical theorizing and Plotinian argument. He may, for example, have met the Plotinian views which influenced his own argument for the existence of God in the second book of the *De libero arbitrio* at this time.

There is no reason to suppose that Augustine read all the Plotinus he ever knew in the crucial months before his conversion to Christianity: if he enjoyed the *Enneads*, or those parts of them with which he first became acquainted, he would have continued his study later. In fact his acquaintance with Neoplatonism is probably to be divided into three stages: before his conversion; in the 390s; after about 400, when he seems to have become concerned in particular with the anti-Christian arguments of Porphyry and those whom he influenced. What he found on his first encounter with the "Platonic books" was evidence about God and his eternal Word: that is, he explains (*Confessions* 7.9.14), about the Trinity but not about the Incarnation. Secondly he discovered that a man must return to himself (7.10.16); he must look within for God, toward his own soul rather than to the world "outside." Thirdly he learned that all things exist insofar as they derive their being from God: this is certainly a Neoplatonic thesis, not merely a Platonic one, and of course Augustine relates it to the more general Platonic thesis that the truth is something incorporeal (7.20.26).

Why then did Augustine become a Christian, not a Neoplatonist? The answer to that shows both how Augustine related Neoplatonism to Christianity, and how he found, almost at the outset of his reflections on Neoplatonism, a weakness – which perhaps enabled him to see more clearly, as time passed, that there are other weaknesses too: that Platonism failed to account for creation *ex nihilo* (and its possible corollary the coming end of the present temporal dispensation), that we are not simply our naturally divine souls, but a marriage of our souls with our bodies, which unplatonically are, as Paul had taught, the temple of the Holy Spirit. Neoplatonism did not, however, enable him to recognize that Christian theology demands a direct confrontation with the concept of omnipotence in a way that Platonism did not. Had he seen that, some of his problems about grace, divine love, and predestination might have proved rather easier to solve.[57]

What then was the weakness in Platonism which Augustine seems to have noted at the outset? Roughly it was that while the Neoplatonists seemed to have some idea of where the soul must go (though Augustine blames himself in the *Retractationes* for having too easily assimilated the Kingdom of Heaven with the Platonic Intelligible World [1.3.2]), they had little idea of how to travel from here to there. Indeed because of their inability to live the life which could lead to happiness, they had recourse to "theurgy," which for Augustine was little more than a magical attempt to take heaven by storm.

Well before the time of Augustine a crisis had arisen in Neoplatonic ethics and theory of asceticism. Both Plato himself (most of the time at least) and Plotinus had supposed that the natural divinity of the human soul (part of which could remain sinless) provides us with sufficient means to climb to "heaven," to the perfect life. Within us is a pearl in the oyster, a pure, uncontaminated part of the self, which we can with effort free of its contaminations derived from empirical life, so that once again we become perfect. But even Porphyry, and more markedly Iamblichus, had lost this confidence in our innate goodness, and Iamblichus teaches directly that the whole soul is fallen. That means that we have inadequate resources within ourselves to return through *erôs* to the One. We need the help of the gods: hence theurgy.

Hence, for Augustine, we need the help of God himself – what he was soon to call God's grace. The Platonists are wrong to suppose, in the words of a famous phrase of Symmachus, one-time patron of Augustine, that there are many ways to so great a mystery. On the contrary there is only one Way, the way revealed to us by God (How else could we know it?). God himself has descended in Christ to bring us where on our own, *pace* Plotinus, we could not ascend.[58] Thus, as Augustine saw it, Neoplatonism could describe, metaphysically, something of the "end" for man, but it failed to provide the means, being in fact mistaken about the depth of our present fallen condition and, in effect, confusing the would-be wise man with Adam before the fall.

There is a widespread belief that Patristic Christianity was deeply imbued with Platonism. If that means that the Fathers thought at least in part in the categories of Platonism more than in those of other schools, that they often accepted something like Plato's theory of Forms, talked about participation (though often of the created in the uncreated as much as of particulars in Forms)[59] or of the Platonic Form of the Good, the belief is largely correct. If it means that they had a conscious theory that Platonism forms a halfway house to Christianity, and that it can be fitted in, modified, reformed, and above all completed so as to become Christianity, that view (though adumbrated in the attitudes of Clement of Alexandria and Origen) is really due to Augustine, who saw that Platonic thinking is not peripherally but essentially helpful not so much in being a Christian but in becoming a Christian and in giving an intellectual account of much (though by no means all) Christianity. It reflects his own experience and his own reflection on the conversion of the thinking man to Christianity. If Augustine is right (and I believe he is), then barring extraordinary acts of grace, it will be through Platonism, especially in its Neoplatonic form, that philosophical intellectuals may most readily be led to Christianity. A corollary of that will be that insofar as Christianity tries to purge itself entirely of Platonic modes of self-explanation, it will falter into little more than a fundamentalism.

What then is the role of Plotinus himself in all this? Historically it was the Plotinian version of Platonism which led Augustine toward Christianity, though it did not make him a Christian. Of course, Augustine did not see this as *Neo*platonism. He thought it was Platonism, in that following in the footsteps of Plotinus himself. The greatest effect, therefore, which Plotinus produced in the development of Christianity, was that it was his inspired presentation of Platonism which brought an enormously influential figure, Augustine, toward the Christian fold. For it is from Augustine that, at least in the mediaeval West, most Western Christians of a Platonic turn of mind (Anselm, Bonaventure, even later François de Sales) have drawn their more immediate inspiration. Almost all the other effects Plotinus has had, at least until modern scholarship separated out the peculiar nature of Plotinianism within the wider stream of the Platonic tradition as a whole, have been within that wider stream: that is, less specifically "Plotinian."

We may close by noticing this latter phenomenon in a particularly influential case, that of Pseudo-Dionysius, for what can be said of Pseudo-Dionysius in the sixth century might equally well be said of Marsilio Ficino and Pico della Mirandola in the fifteenth, and of the Cambridge Platonists in the seventeenth. When "Dionysius" produced his curious blend of Neoplatonism and Byzantine Christianity, he began a process of assimilating not only Plato and Plotinus, but now Iamblichus (even – in a way – the theurgy) and Proclus as well. Plotinus has taken his place within that general tradition to which he had always wished to belong, and from which, at least in part, modern scholars have recently excavated him. But the necessity for some part of Plotinian (and not simply Platonic) underpinning for Christian *theology* is as strong now as when Augustine first came to grasp the facts of the case.

NOTES

1 For the purposes of the present discussion we may leave aside the much controverted question of the role of Plotinus's teacher, Ammonius "Saccas," in the development of the sort of Platonism which is Neoplatonism.

2 Note, however, the comment of Walzer 1967, 644 that "philosophy never succeeded in reaching in the Islamic world the position which it had maintained in the ancient world for more than a thousand years." One might add, in considering the effect of philosophy in general upon various societies, let alone the influence of Plotinus in particular, that philosophy never obtained the status in the Islamic world, despite the efforts of Farabi, Avicenna, Averroes, and others, which it obtained in Catholic Western Europe.

3 The best introduction to the Neoplatonism of the commentators is to be found in parts of Sorabji 1990.

4 By Theiler 1960, 67.

5 See especially Dodds 1928. The topic has now been reopened in a new and challenging fashion by Tarrant 1993. Chapter 6 of Tarrant's book (148–77) is entitled "The Neopythagorean *Parmenides*."

6 See especially Whittaker 1969.

7 For a powerful statement of the importance of this principle and the originality of Plotinus in formulating it see especially Trouillard 1955b. For a perhaps over-exotic account of something of its effects on (some) Christians see von Balthasar 1961. For an unhistorical and unfortunately influential account of its workings in Christianity in general (it is described as the "Alexandrian world-scheme") see Nygren 1953.

8 For an introduction to some of the problems of Plotinus's account of the production of what is not the One see Gerson 1993.

9 See Dillon 1977.

10 For example, for Origen see Crouzel 1962.

11 Cf. Tatian, *Oratio and Graecos* 13.1 and Nygren 1953, especially 280–7.

12 Cf. *Ep.* 137 and Hölscher 1986, 213–20.

13 See Rist 1992.

14 See for example Rist 1981, 170–3; Hanson 1988, 84–94.

15 For Lucian see Rist 1981, 170–3; Hanson 1988, 79–83.

16 For Gregory of Nyssa as an example of this see Balás 1966, 54–75.

17 See Rist 1981, 173–8.

18 See the interesting papers of Ricken 1967, 1969, 1978.

19 More detailed discussion of the spread of direct knowledge of Plotinus is to be found in Rist 1981.

20 Cf. Barnes 1976, 240.

21 See Rist 1981, 159–65. Eusebius knows something about the views of Plotinus's pupil Amelius (see *Praeparatio Evagelica* 11.18.26), or at least about his comments on St. John's Gospel.

22 Note the comments of Hanson 1988, 861–2 on the fact that the mere use of Platonic tags by Athanasius does not make him a Platonist.

23 For a balanced state of the debate about possible *Middle* Platonic influence on Arius see Hanson 1988, 84–94.

24 For a detailed account of Basil's "Neoplatonism" see Rist, 1981 190–220, which includes comment on the most recent full-length account of the matter, that of Dehnhard 1964. Hanson 1988, 687, 865–6, dislikes Rist's "minimizing" version of the influence of Plotinus on Basil, but his own account also minimizes the substantive effects of Neoplatonism (rather than the merely verbal ones), and he offers no direct objections to the view, discussed again below, that the partly Plotinian *De spiritu* is not by Basil.

25 See especially Rist 1981, 218.

26 V.1 is also known to Cyril of Alexandria and Theodoret.

27 See Rist 1981, 195–9.

28 For details see Rist 1981, 215–6. Hanson 1988, 867, offers a few more vague parallels as evidence for the claim that Gregory was influenced "not least by Neoplatonism." But they are too vague to be helpful (except as confirming Gregory's limited interest in Platonism in general), and Hanson has to admit that "we cannot attribute a decisive influence upon his Trinitarian theology to this (viz., Neoplatonic) source" (p. 868).

29 Needless to say the comment of I. P. Sheldon-Williams in Armstrong 1967 ("Gregory's assimilation of Christianism to Platonism is thus much more profound and has wider implications than Basil's" [p. 446]) is misleading. Certainly he uses Platonic themes, such as the purification and ascent of the soul, but this is "higher" commonplace. The difference from Basil is rather to be seen in terms of Basil's more down-to-earth character.

30 Brown 1988, 300. For more general accounts of Gregory, and in particular of his Platonism, see Daniélou 1953, Balás 1966, and more broadly Mühlenberg 1966. In the Armstrong 1967 (p. 456), I. P. Sheldon-Williams claims that "He [Gregory of Nyssa] constructed a philosophy which was as faithful to the Platonic tradition as that of Plotinus, which it closely resembles." The misleading nature of such claims – they are not at all uncommon – will become evident.

31 For Plotinus's development of Plato's idea see Rist 1967, 27–37, with references to further discussion. For Gregory on infinity see Balás 1966, 131–2.

32 Cf. Daniélou 1953, 42–3; Meredith 1982.

33 See Aubineau 1955.

34 For Middle Platonism in Methodius's *On Free Will* see Pépin 1975.

35 *Vita Moysis* (PG 44, 353CD = p. 62.9ff. Musurillo. Cf. Methodius, *Symp.* 8.12.

36 See Brown 1988, 294, 299–300 (for Gregory) and more generally p. 222 on the Desert Fathers: "The ascetics thought of themselves as men and women who had gained a precious freedom to mourn for their sins and to suffer in this life so that they might regain a future glory *for their bodies*" (my italics).

37 For defense of this claim see Rist, 1981 "Basil," 144–7. For a modicum of Middle Platonism, not Neoplatonism, in Lactantius see (e.g.) Perrin 1978. For the very limited knowledge of Plotinus and Porphyry in Firmicus Maternus (nothing of great philosophical significance) see Rist 147, note 36. Calcidius is a special problem, since his date is uncertain (see Rist 151–5). If, as Waszink 1962, xvi supposes, he is an Imperial official in Milan of about 395, he does not affect our argument. If, however, he is associated with bishop Ossius of Cordova and his work to be dated c. 324 or earlier, then it matters what kind of Platonism he knows. One should note, however, that he cites no Neoplatonic writers by name. It is usually held (I think wrongly) that his knowledge of the Middle Platonist and Neopythagorean Numenius, as well as of other Platonic lore, derives from Porphyry's *Commentary on the Timaeus*. If this is true, it is remarkable that his commentary could have been produced with so little evident use of specifically Neoplatonic themes. Hence, whatever his own relationship to Christianity, he is no direct source of the Christian use of Plotinus, though his influence on the spread of Platonism in general was immense.

38 For "telescoping" the hypostases see A. C. Lloyd, in Armstrong (ed.) 1967, 291, commenting on an anonymous commentary on the *Parmenides* which Hadot (followed by many) has ascribed to Porphyry. For Porphyry and Victorinus in general see especially Hadot 1968.

39 For recent accounts see Clark 1981, Hanson 1988, 531–56.

40 Henry 1950.

41 For Victorinus's translations see Augustine, *Confessions* 8.2.3. There has been much scholarly debate as to how much Plotinus (and how much Porphyry) was actually translated. For an introduction to the tedious and largely unprofitable debate see O'Connell 1984, 11–13: a refreshing treatment.

42 For Ambrose's opinion of him see *Ep.* 65.1: "You grasp the intelligibles with an especially keen mind, seeing that you are accustomed to show how far even the books of the philosophers have diverged from the truth. . . ."

43 See Masai 1961; Teske 1985, 45, n37.

44 Cf. Du Roy 1966, 113, n5.

45 It would be irrelevant here to comment on the strong Stoic influences, from Cicero and elsewhere, apparent in Ambrose's thought: see further Colish 1985 V.2, 51–70.

46 Cf. Holte 1962, 111–64. It is uncertain whether Ambrose had any first-hand familiarity with Plato. Many of his quotations are via a later intermediary such as Plotinus (who seems for example in I.6 and V.9 to be the source of Ambrose's knowledge of the *Symposium*).

47 The fullest treatment of Ambrose's debt to philosophers, including Plotinus (whom he never mentions but whom Madec thinks he knew directly, p. 167), is to be found in Madec 1974, especially 61–71; also (e.g.) Courcelle 1950a, Hadot 1956, Solignac 1956.

48 It seems quite likely, as Madec argues (1974, 320–3), that Ambrose's knowledge of the *Alcibiades* is firsthand.

49 For the inauthenticity of this dialogue see De Strycker 1942; and De Vogel 1986, 185, 229, 243.

50 On differences between the Alexandrian exegesis of Ambrose and that of Simplicianus see Holte 1962, 147.

51 See Madec 1974, 94–5.

52 For an introduction to Augustine's Platonism see Hadot 1979; Regen 1983.

53 I.4, *On Well-Being* accepting Henry's reading *Plotini*; cf. *Contra academicos* 3.18.41.

54 On this point notice the useful methodological attitudes of Mandouze 1968.

55 For illuminating evidence of Augustine's ability to "recontruct" a Platonic text from "fragments" see Burnyeat 1987. From readings in Cicero's *Tusculans* Augustine can construct much of the epistemology of Plato's *Meno*.

56 See Rist 1991 for discussion of the man's identity.

57 See Rist 1994, 262–6.

58 For more detailed discussion of this crisis in Neoplatonic ethics see Rist 1992, 140–5.

59 For the illuminating case of Gregory of Nyssa see Balás 1966, 31.

BIBLIOGRAPHY

Alexander of Aphrodisias. 1989. *On Aristotle's Metaphysics I.* Translated by W. Dooley. Ithaca, New York: Cornell University Press.

Alfino, M. R. 1988. "Plotinus and the Possibility of Non-Propositional Thought," *Ancient Philosophy* 8, 273–84.

Allen, R. E. 1983. *Plato's Parmenides.* Minneapolis: University of Minnesota Press.

Anatolius 1900. *De decade.* Edited by J. L. Heiberg, *Congrès international d'histoire compareé. Ve section* Paris, 27–41.

Armstrong, A. H. 1960. "The Background of the Doctrine 'That the Intelligibles are not Outside the Intellect,' " in *Les sources de Plotin*, 393–413, reprinted in Armstrong 1979, Study IV.

1967. (Ed.) *The Cambridge History of Later Greek and Early Mediaeval Philosophy.* Cambridge University Press.

1966–88. *Plotinus.* 7 volumes. Cambridge, Mass.: Heinemann.

1971. "Eternity, Life and Movement in Plotinus' Accounts of *Nous*," in *Le Néoplatonisme.* Edited by P. Hadot. Colloques internationaux du Centre National de la Recherche Scientifique (Royaumont: 9–13.6.1969). Paris: Éditions du Centre National de la Recherche Scientifique, 67–74; reprinted in Armstrong 1979, Study XV.

1972. "St. Augustine and Christian Platonism," in *Augustine: A Collection of Critical Essays.* Edited by R. A. Markus, New York: Doubleday, 3–37.

1973. "Elements in the Thought of Plotinus at Variance with Classical Intellectualism," *Journal of Hellenic Studies* 93, 13–22.

1974. "Tradition, Reason and Experience in the Thought of Plotinus," in *Plotino e il Neoplatonismo in Oriente e in Occidente.* Atti del Convegno internazionale dell' Accademia Nazionale dei Lincei (Roma: 5–9.10.1970). Rome: Accademia Nazionale dei Lincei, 171–94.

1975. "The Escape of the One. An Investigation of Some Possibilities of

Apophatic Theology Imperfectly Realised in the West," *Studia Patristica* 13, 77–89. Berlin: Akademie-Verlag.

1977a. "Form, Individual and Person in Plotinus," *Dionysius* 1, 49–68, reprinted in Armstrong 1979, Study XX.

1977b. "Negative Theology," *Downside Review* 95, 176–89.

1979. *Plotinian and Christian Studies*. London: Variorum.

1986. (Ed.) *Classical Mediterranean Spirituality*. New York: Crossroad.

Arnou, R. 1935. "Platonisme des Pères," *Dictionnaire de théologie catholique* XII. 2, coll. 2258–92. Paris: Librairie Letouzey et Ané.

1967, 2nd edition. *Le désir de Dieu dans la philosophie de Plotin*. Roma: Presses de l'Université Grégorienne (1st edition, 1921, Paris: Alcan).

Atkinson, M. 1983. *Plotinus: Ennead V.1. On the Three Principal Hypostases*. Oxford: Oxford University Press.

Aubineau, M. 1955. "Les écrits de saint Athanase sur la virginité," *RAM* 31, 140–73 = *Recherches patristiques*, 163–96. Amsterdam: A. M. Hakkert, 1974.

Balás, D. L. 1966. *Metousia Theou: Man's Participation in God's Perfections According to Saint Gregory of Nyssa*. Rome: Herder.

Balthasar, H. U. von 1961. *Kosmische Liturgie*. Einsiedeln: Johannes-Verlag.

Barnes, T. D. 1976. "Sosianus Hierocles and the Antecedents of the Great Persecution," *Harvard Studies in Classical Philology* 80, 239–52.

Beierwaltes, W. 1961. "Die Metaphysik des Lichtes in der Philosophie Plotins," *Zeitschrift für Philosophische Forschung* 15, 334–62.

1967. *Plotin über Ewigkeit und Zeit*. Frankfurt am Main: Vittorio Klostermann.

1971. "Nachwort to 'Plotins Metaphysik des Lichtes,'" in the reprint of that article in *Die Philosophie des Neuplatonismus*. Edited by C. Zintzen, *Wege der Forschung* 186, 116–17. Darmstadt: Wissenschaftliche Buchgesellschaft.

1972. *Platonismus und Idealismus*. Frankfurt am Main: Vittorio Klostermann.

1973. "Die Entfaltung der Einheit. Zur Differenz plotinischen und proklischen Denkens," *Theta-Pi* 2, 126–61.

1985. *Denken des Einen: Studien zur neuplatonischen Philosophie und ihrer Wirkungsgerchichte*. Frankfurt am Main: Vittorio Klostermann.

1986. "The Love of Beauty and the Love of God," in *Classical Mediterranean Spirituality*. Edited by A. H. Armstrong, New York: Crossroad, 293–313.

1991a. *Selbsterkenntnis und Erfahrung der Einheit. Plotins Enneade V 3. Text, Übersetzung, Interpretation, Erlauterungen*. Frankfurt am Main: Vittorio Klostermann.

1991b. *Il paradigma neoplatonico nell'interpretazione di Platone.* Napoli: Istituto Suor Orsola Benincasa.

1991c. *Pensare l'Uno. Studi sulla filosofia neoplatonica e sulla storia dei suoi influssi.* Traduzione di M. L. Gatti. Introduzione di G. Reale. Milano: Vita e Pensiero.

Beutler, R., and W. Theiler. 1962. *Plotins Schriften.* Übersetzt von R. Harder, Neubearbeitung mit griechische Lesetext und Anmerkungen fortgeführt. 1960–7. Hamburg: Felix Meiner Verlag.

Blum, P. R. 1989. "Platonismus," *Historisches Wörterbuch der Philosophie* 7, coll. 977–85. Basel–Stuttgart: Schwabe Verlag.

Blumenthal, H. J. 1966. "Did Plotinus Believe in Ideas of Individuals," *Phronesis* 11, 61–80, reprinted in Blumenthal 1993, Study IV.

1968. "Plotinus *Ennead* IV.3.20–1 and its Sources: Alexander, Aristotle and Others," *Archiv für Geschichte der Philosophie* 50, 254–61.

1971a. "Soul, World-Soul and Individual Soul in Plotinus," in *Le Néoplatonisme*, 55–63, reprinted in Blumenthal 1993, Study III.

1971b. *Plotinus' Psychology. His Doctrine of the Embodied Soul.* The Hague: Martinus Nijhoff.

1974. "Nous and Soul in Plotinus: Some Problems of Demarcation," in *Plotino e il Neoplatonismo in Oriente e in Occidente.* Atti del Convegno internazionale dell' Accademia Nazionale dei Lincei (Roma: 5–9.10.1970). Rome: Accademia Nazionale dei Lincei, 203–19, reprinted in Blumenthal 1993, Study II.

1976. "Plotinus' Adaptation of Aristotle's Psychology," in *The Significance of Neoplatonism.* Edited by R. B. Harris, Albany: State University of New York Press.

1981. "Plotinus in Later Neoplatonism," in *Neoplatonism and Early Christian Thought.* Edited by H. J. Blumenthal and R. A. Markus, London: Variorum, 212–22.

1987. "Plotinus in the Light of Twenty Years' Scholarship," in *Aufsteig und Niedergang der römischen Welt.* Edited by W. Haase and H. Temporini, Teil ii, Band 36.1. Berlin/New York: Walter De Gruyter, 528–70.

1988. "Simplicius and Others on Aristotle's Discussions of Reason," in *Gonimos. Neoplatonic and Byzantine Studies presented to Leendert G. Westerink. Arethusa.* Supplementary volume. Edited by J. M. Duffy and J. Peradotto, Buffalo: SUNY, 103–19.

1989. "Plotinus and Proclus on the Criterion of Truth," in *The Criterion of Truth. Essays Written in Honour of George Kerferd Together with a Text and Translation of Ptolemy's On the Kriterion and Hegemonikon.* Edited by P. Huby and G. Neal, Liverpool: Liverpool University Press, 257–80, reprinted in Blumenthal 1993, Study IX.

1993. *Soul and Intellect. Studies in Plotinus and Later Neoplatonism.* Aldershot and Brookfield, VT: Variorum.

Boot, P. 1984. *Plotinus. Over voorzienigheid (Enneade III 2–3).* Amsterdam: VU Boekhandel.

Bréhier, E. 1936. "Notice" in *Plotin. Ennéades* VI (1). Paris: Les Belles Lettres.

Brisson, L., M. O. Goulet-Cazé, R. Goulet, and D. O'Brien. 1982. *Porphyre. La vie de Plotin. I.* Paris: J. Vrin.

1992. *Porphyre. La vie de Plotin. II.* Paris: J. Vrin.

Brown, P. 1988. *The Body and Society.* New York: Columbia University Press.

Burge, T. 1986. "Cartesian Error and the Objectivity of Perception," in *Subject, Thought, and Context.* Edited by P. Pettit and J. McDowell, Oxford: Oxford University Press, 117–36.

Burnyeat, M. 1982. "Idealism in Greek Philosophy: What Descartes Saw and Berkeley Missed," *Philosophical Review* 3, 3–40.

1987. "Wittgenstein and Augustine's *De Magistro,*" *Proceedings of the Aristotelian Society* 61, 1–24.

Burrell, D., and B. McGinn. 1990. (Eds.) *God and Creation: An Ecumenical Symposium.* Notre Dame: Notre Dame University Press.

Bury, R. G. 1933–49, reprinted 1961–83. (Ed.) *Sextus Empiricus.* 4 volumes. Cambridge, Mass.: Harvard University Press.

Bussanich, J. 1987. "Plotinus on the Inner Life of the One," *Ancient Philosophy* 7, 163–90.

1988. *The One and its Relation to Intellect in Plotinus.* Leiden: E. J. Brill.

1990. "The Invulnerability of Goodness in the Ethics and Psychology of Plotinus," *Proceedings of the Boston Area Colloquium in Ancient Philosophy* 6. Edited by J. Cleary, Lanham/New York/London: University Press of America, 151–84.

1994. "Mystical Elements in the Thought of Plotinus," in *Aufstieg und Niedergang der römischenWelt.* Edited by W. Haase and H. Temporini, 36.7 Berlin/New York: Walter De Gruyter, 5300–500.

Callahan, J. F. 1958. "A New Source for St. Augustine's Theory of Time," *Harvard Studies in Classical Philology* 63, 437–59.

1979. *Four Views of Time in Ancient Philosophy.* Westport: Greenwood Press.

Charrue, J. M. 1978. *Plotin lecteur de Platon.* Paris: Les Belles Lettres.

Cilento, V. 1963. "La radice metafisica della libertà nell' antignosi plotiniana," *Parola del Passato* 18, 94–123.

1971. *Plotino. Paideia antignostica.* Firenza: Felice le Monnier.

Clark, G. H. 1943. "Plotinus' Theory of Empirical Responsibility," *New Scholasticism* 17, 16–31.

Clark, M. T. 1981. "The Neoplatonism of Marius Victorinus the Christian," in *Neoplatonism and Early Christian Thought.* Edited by H. J. Blumenthal and R. A. Markus, London: Variorum.

Clark, S. R. L. 1991. "How Many Selves Make Me?" in *Human Beings.* Edited by D. Cockburn, Cambridge University Press, 213–33.

Cleary, J. 1988. *Aristotle on the Many Senses of Priority.* Carbondale: Southern Illinois University Press.

Colish, M. 1985. *The Stoic Tradition from Antiquity to the Early Middle Ages.* Leiden: E. J. Brill.

Combès, J. 1975. "Damascius lecteur du Parménide," *Archives de philosophie* 38, 33–60.

Corrigan, K. 1984. "A Philosophical Precursor to the Theory of Essence and Existence in St. Thomas Aquinas," *The Thomist* 48, 219–40.

1986a. "Is There More Than One Generation of Matter in the Enneads?" *Phronesis* 21, 167–81.

1986b. "Plotinus, Enneades 5,4(7),2 and Related Passages: A New Interpretation of the Status of the Intelligible Object," *Hermes* 114, 195–203.

1990. "A New Source for the Distinction between *id quod est* and *esse* in Boethius' *De Hebdomadibus*," in *Studia Patristica* 18, 4. Edited by E. A. Livingstone. Papers of the 1983 Oxford Patristic Conference, Kalamazoo, Mich.: Cistercian Publications, 133–8.

1993. "Light and Metaphor in Plotinus and St. Thomas Aquinas," *The Thomist* 57, 187–99.

Corrigan, K., and P. O'Cleirigh. 1987. "The Course of Plotinian Scholarship from 1971 to 1986," in *Aufstieg und Niedergang der römischen Welt.* Edited by W. Haase and H. Temporini, 36.1, Berlin/New York: Walter De Gruyter, 571–623.

Courcelle, P. 1943. *Les lettres grecques en Occident de Macrobe à Cassiodore.* Paris: Bibliothèque des Écoles Françaises d'Athènes et de Rome.

1950a (2nd edition, 1968). *Recherches sur les Confessions de saint Augustin.* Paris: de Boccard.

1950b. "Plotin et saint Ambroise," *Revue de philologie* 76, 29–56.

Crome, P. 1970. *Symbol und Unzulänglichkeit der Sprache.* München: Wilhelm Fink Verlag.

Crouzel, H. 1962. *Origene et la philosophie.* Paris: Aubier.

D'Ancona Costa, C. 1990a. "Cause prime non est yliathim. Liber de Causis, prop. 8[9]: Le fonti e la dottrina," *Documenti e studi sulla tradizione filosofica medievale* 1, 327–51.

1990b. "Determinazione e indeterminazione nel sovrasensibile secondo Plotino," *Rivista di storia della filisofia* 45, 437–74.

420   Bibliography

1991. "Primo principio e mondo intelligible nella metafisica di Proclo: Problemi e soluzioni," *Elenchos* 12, 271–302.

1992a. "ΑΜΟΡΦΟΝ ΚΑΙ ΑΝΕΙΔΕΟΝ. Causalité des formes et causalité de l'Un chez Plotin," *Revue de philosophie ancienne* 9, 69–113.

1992b. "La doctrine néoplatonicienne de l'être entre l'antiquité tardive et le Moyen Age. Le Liber de Causis par rapport à ses sources," *Recherches de théologie ancienne et médiévale* 59, 41–85.

1992c. "Proclo. Enadi e archai nell'ordine sovrasensibile," *Rivista di storia della filosofia* 47, 267–95.

Daniélou, J. 1944, reprinted 1953. *Platonisme et théologie mystique*. Paris: Aubier.

Dehnhard, H. 1964. *Das Problem des Abhängigkeit des Basilius von Plotin*. Berlin: Walter De Gruyter.

Delbrück, M. 1971. "Aristotle-totle-totle," in *Of Microbes and Life*. Edited by J. Monod and E. Borek, New York: Columbia University Press.

Descartes, R. 1981. *Philosophical Letters*. Edited by A. Kenny, Oxford: Blackwell.

1990. *Meditations on First Philosophy*. Edited by G. Hefferan, Notre Dame: Notre Dame University Press.

Diels, H., and W. Kranz. 9th edition, 1960. (Eds.) *Die Fragmente der Vorsokratiker*. 3 volumes. Berlin: Weidmann.

Dillon, J. 1969. "Plotinus Ennead 3.9.1. and Later Views on the Intelligible World, "*Transactions and Proceedings of the American Philosophical Association* 100, 63–70.

1977. *The Middle Platonists*. Ithaca, New York: Cornell University Press.

1983. "Plotinus, Philo and Origen on the Grades of Virtue," in *Platonismus und Christentum*. Edited by H.-D. Blume and F. Mann, Münster: Aschendorffsche Verlagsbuchhandlung, 92–105, reprinted in J. Dillon (1990). *The Golden Chain*. London: Variorum.

1990. "Plotinus the First Cartesian?" *Hermathena* 149, 19–31.

1993. *Alcinous. The Handbook of Platonism*. Translation, Introduction, and Commentary. Oxford: Clarendon Press.

Dodds, E. R. 1928. "The *Parmenides* of Plato and the Origin of the Neoplatonic One," *Classical Quarterly* 22, 129–42.

1951. *The Greeks and the Irrational*. Berkeley/Los Angeles: University of California Press.

1960. "Numenius and Ammonius," in *Les sources de Plotin. Entretiens Hardt V*, Vandoeuvres-Genève: Fondation Hardt, 3–61.

1963. *Proclus. The Elements of Theology*. A Revised Text with Translation, Introduction and Commentary. Oxford: Clarendon Press.

1965. *Pagan and Christian in an Age of Anxiety*. Cambridge University Press.

1973. *The Ancient Concept of Progress and Other Essays on Greek Literature and Belief.* Oxford: Oxford University Press.

Dörrie, H. 1965. "Emanation: Ein unphilosophisches Wort im spätantiken Denken," in *Parusia: Studien zür Philosophie Platons und zur Problemgeschichte des Platonismus: Festgabe für Johannes Hirschberger.* Edited by K. Flasch, Frankfurt am Main: Minerva, 119–41, reprinted in (1976) *Platonica Minora. Studia et testimonia antiqua,* 70–88.

1974. "Plotino. Tradizionalista o innovatore?" in *Plotino e il Neoplatonismo in Oriente e in Occidente.* Atti del Convegno internazionale dell' Accademia Nazionale dei Lincei (Roma: 5–9.10.1970). Rome: Accademia Nazionale dei Lincei, 195–201.

1976. *Platonica Minora.* München: Wilhelm Fink Verlag.

1985. "Denken über das Sprechen hinaus. Untersuchungen zu den Denk- und Sprachgewohnheiten der platonischen Philosophen des 2.–4. Jahrhunderts nach Christus," in *Collectanea Philologica, Festschrift für Helmut Gibber.* Edited by G. Heintz and P. Schmitter, Baden-Baden: V. Körner, 139–67.

Du Roy, O. 1966. *L'intelligence de la foi en la Trinité selon saint Augustin.* Paris: Études Augustiniennes.

Ebert, T. 1983. "Aristotle on What is Done in Perceiving," *Zeitschrift für Philosophische Forschung* 37, 181–98.

Elsas, C. 1975. *Neuplatonische und gnostische Weltablehnung in der Schule Plotins.* Berlin/New York: Walter De Gruyter.

Emilsson, E. K. 1988. *Plotinus on Sense-Perception: A Philosophical Study.* Cambridge University Press.

1991. "Plotinus and Soul–Body Dualism," in *Psychology.* Companions to Ancient Thought 2. Edited by S. Everson, Cambridge University Press, 148–65.

1993. "L'ontologie de Plotin dans l'Ennéade VI.4.5," in *Contre Platon.* V.1. Edited M. Dixsaut, Paris: Vrin, 157–73.

1995. "Plotinus on the Object of Thought," *Archiv für Geschichte der Philosophie,* 21–41.

Evangeliou, C. 1988. *Aristotle's Categories and Porphyry.* Leiden: E. J. Brill.

1992. "Plotinus's Anti-Gnostic Polemic and Porphyry's against the Christians," in *Neoplatonism and Gnosticism.* Edited by R. T. Wallis and J. Bregman, Albany: State University of New York Press, 111–28.

Everson, S. 1991a. *Psychology.* Companions to Ancient Thought 2. Cambridge University Press.

1991b. "The Objective Appearance of Pyrrhonism," in *Psychology.* Companions to Ancient Thought 2. Edited by S. Everson, Cambridge University Press, 121–47.

Faggin, G. 1992. Plotino. *Enneadi. Porfirio. Vita di Plotino.* Traduzione, introduzione, note e bibliografia. Milano: Rusconi.

Ferwerda, R. 1965. *La signification des images et des métaphores dans la penseé de Plotin.* Groningen: J. B. Wolters.

Festugière, A. J. 1953. *La Révélation d'Hermès Trismégiste* 3: *Les doctrines de l'âme.* Paris: Gabalda.

1954. *La Révélation d'Hermès Trismégiste* 4: *Le Dieu inconnu et la gnose.* Paris: Gabalda.

Fielder, G. 1976. "Chorismos and Emanation in the Philosophy of Plotinus," in *The Significance of Neoplatonism.* Edited by R. B. Harris, Albany: State of New York University Press, 101–20.

1977. "Plotinus' Copy Theory," *Apeiron* 11, 1–11.

1978a. "Plotinus' Reply to the Argument of Parmenides 130a–131d," *Apeiron* 12, 1–5.

1978b. "Plotinus' Responses to Two Problems of Immateriality," *Proceedings of the American Catholic Philosophical Association* 52, 96–102.

1980. "A Plotinian View of Self-Predication and TMA," *The Modern Schoolman* 57, 339–48.

1982. "Plotinus and Self-Predication," in *The Structure of Being. A Neoplatonic Approach.* Edited by R. B. Harris, Albany: State University of New York Press, 83–9.

Fraisse, J. C. 1989. *L'intériorité sans retrait.* Paris: J. Vrin.

Frede, M. 1987. "Stoics and Sceptics on Clear and Distinct Impressions," in *Essays in Ancient Philosophy.* Minneapolis: University of Minnesota Press, 151–76.

1988. "Being and Becoming in Plato," *Oxford Studies in Ancient Philosophy* 6. Supplementary volume. Edited by J. Annas and R. H. Grimm, Oxford: Oxford University Press, 37–52.

Früchtel, E. 1970. *Weltentwurf und Logos. Zur Metaphysik Plotins.* Frankfurt am Main: Vittorio Klostermann.

Gatti, M. L. 1982. *Plotino e la metafisica della contemplazione.* Milano: Cooperativa universitaria studio e lavoro.

1983. "Sulla teoria plotiniana del numero e sui suoi rapporti con alcuni aspetti della problematica delle 'dottrine non scritte,' " *Rivista di filosofia neoscolastica* 75, 361–84.

Gerson, L. P. 1990. *God and Greek Philosophy. Studies in the Early History of Natural Theology.* London/New York: Routledge.

1991. "Causality, Univocity and First Philosophy in *Metaphysics* II," *Ancient Philosophy* 11, 331–49.

1992. "The Discovery of the Self in Antiquity," *The Personalist* 8, 249–57.

1993. "Plotinus' Metaphysics: Creation or Emanation?" *Review of Metaphysics* 46, 559–74.

1994. *Plotinus*. London/New York: Routledge.

Gill, C. 1990. (Ed.) *The Person and the Human Mind*. Oxford: Clarendon Press.

1991. "Is There a Concept of Person in Greek Philosophy?" in *Psychology. Companion to Ancient Thought* 2. Edited by S. Everson, Cambridge University Press, 166–93.

Gilson, E. 1952. *Being and Some Philosophers*. Toronto: Pontifical Institute of Mediaeval Studies.

Gollwitzer, T. 1900, 1902. *Plotins Lehre von der Willensfreiheit*. 2 volumes. I Kaiserlaufern: P. Rohr. Kempten. II. Kaiserlaufern: P. Rohr Kempten.

Graeser, A. 1972. *Plotinus and the Stoics*. Leiden: E. J. Brill.

Gurtler, G. M. 1984. "Sympathy in Plotinus," *International Philosophical Quarterly* 24, 395–406.

1988. *Plotinus. The Experience of Unity*. New York: Peter Lang.

Hadot, P. 1956. "Platon et Plotin dans trois sermons de saint Ambroise," *REL* 34, 202–20.

1960. "Etre, vie, pensée chez Plotin et avant Plotin," in *Les sources de Plotin. Entretiens Hardt V*. Vandoeuvres-Genève: Fondation Hardt, 105–41.

1963. "La distinction de l'être et de l'étant dans le *De Hebdomadibus* de Boèce," in *Miscellanea Mediaevalia*. Edited by P. Wilpert, Berlin: Walter De Gruyter.

1968. *Porphyre et Victorinus*. 2 volumes. Paris: Études Augustiniennes.

1970. "*Forma essendi*: Interprétation philologique et interprétation philosophique d'une formule de Boèce," *Les Études Classiques* 38, 143–56.

1971. *Marius Victorinus*. Paris: Études Augustiniennes.

1973. "L'être et l'étant dans le Néoplatonisme," *Revue de théologie et philosophie* 23, 101–13.

1979. "La présentation du platonisme par Augustin," in *Kerygma und Logos. Festschrift C. Andresen*. Edited by A. M. Ritter, Gottingen: Vandenhoeck and Ruprecht, 272–9.

1986. "Neoplatonist Spirituality: Plotinus and Porphyry," in *Classical Mediterranean Spirituality*. Edited by A. H. Armstrong, New York: Crossroad, 230–49.

1987a. "L'Union de l'Ame avec l'Intellect divin dans l'Expérience mystique plotinienne," in *Proclus et son Influence. Actes du Colloque de Neuchâtel*. Edited by G. Boss and G. Seel, Zürich: GMB Editions du Grand Midi, 3–27.

1987b. *Plotinus or the Simplicity of Vision*. Chicago: University of Chicago Press. Translation by M. Chase of *Plotin ou la simplicité du regard* (1963, 2nd edition, 1973) Paris: Plon.

1988. *Plotin. Traité 38 (VI,7)*. Introduction, traduction, commentaire et notes. Paris: Les Éditions du Cerf.

1990. *Plotin. Traite 50. III, 5. L'amour est-il un Dieu, ou un démon ou un état de l'âme?* Paris: Les Éditions du Cerf.

Hager, F. P. 1964. "Die Aristotelesinterpretation des Alexander von Aphrodisias und die Aristoteleskritik Plotins bezüglich der Lehre von Geist," *Archiv für Geschichte der Philosophie* 46, 174–87.

Hahm, D. E. 1977. *The Origins of Stoic Cosmology*. Columbus: The Ohio State University Press.

Hanson, R. P. C. 1988. *The Search for the Christian Doctrine of God*. Edinburgh: T. & T. Clark.

Harder, R., continued by R. Beutler and W. Theiler. 1956–60. *Plotins Schriften*. 5 volumes. Hamburg: Felix Meiner.

Hatfield, G. 1986. " 'The Senses and the Fleshless Eye.' The Meditations as Cognitive Exercises." in *Essays on Descartes' Meditations*. Edited by A. Rorty, Berkeley/Los Angeles: University of California Press, 45–79.

Hegel, G. W. F. *Vorlesungen über die Geschichte der Philosophie* (1971). Edited by E. Moldenhauer and K. M. Michel, Frankfurt am Main: Suhrkamp Verlag.

Helleman-Elgersma, W. 1980. *Soul-Sisters. A Commentary on Enneads IV 3(27), I–8 of Plotinus*. Amsterdam: Rodopi.

Henry, P. 1931. "Le problème de la liberté chez Plotin," *Revue néoscholastique* 33, 50–79; 180–215; 318–39.

1934. *Plotin et l'Occident*. Louvain: Spicilegium Sacrum Lovaniense.

1950. "The 'Adversus Arium' of Marius Victorinus, the First Systematic Exposition of the Doctrine of the Trinity," *Journal of Theological Studies* 1, 42–55.

Henry, P., and H. R. Schwyzer. 1951, 1959, 1973. *Plotini Opera* 3 volumes (*editio maior*) (v.1, Bruxelles: Edition Universelle, *Enneads* I–III); (v.2, Bruxelles: Éditions Universelle and Paris: Desclée de Brouwer, *Enneads* IV–V); (v.3, Paris: Desclée de Brouwer and Leiden: E. J. Brill, *Ennead* VI)

1964, 1976, 1982. *Plotini Opera*. 3 volumes (*editio minor*). Oxford: Clarendon Press (v.1, *Enneads* I–III); (v.2, *Enneads* IV–V); (v.3, *Ennead* VI).

Himmerich, W. 1959. *Eudaimonia. Die Lehre des Plotin von der Selbstverwicklung des Menschen*. Würzburg: Tritsch.

Hölscher, L. 1986. *The Reality of the Mind. Augustine's Philosophical Arguments for the Human Soul as a Spiritual Substance*. London/New York: Routledge and Kegan Paul.

Holte, R. 1962. *Beatitude et Sagesse. Saint Augustin et la problème de l'homme dans la philosophie ancienne.* Paris: Études Augustiniennes.

Hyman, A., and J. J. Walsh. 1973. (Eds.) *Philosophy in the Middle Ages. The Christian, Islamic and Jewish Traditions.* Indianapolis: Hackett.

Igal, J. 1979. "Aristoteles y la evolución de la antropologia de Plotino," *Pensamiento* 35, 315–46.

Inge, W. R. 1929, 3rd edition 1968. *The Philosophy of Plotinus.* 2 volumes. London: Longmans.

Irwin, T. H. 1988. *Aristotle's First Principles.* Oxford: Clarendon Press.

Jerphagnon, L. 1983. "Epiphanie de Nous," *Diotima* 11, 111–18.

Jones, R. M. 1926. "The Ideas as the Thoughts of God," *Classical Philology* 21, 317–26.

Judovitz, D. 1988. *Subjectivity and Representation in Descartes.* Cambridge University Press.

Kahn, C. H. 1981. "Some Philosophical Uses of 'To Be' in Plato," *Phronesis* 26, 105–34.

Kenny, A. 1992. *The Metaphysics of Mind.* Oxford: Oxford University Press.

Ketchum, R. J. 1980. "Plato on Real Being," *American Philosophical Quarterly* 17, 213–20.

Keyser, E. de 1955. *La signification de l'art dans les Ennéades de Plotin.* Louvain: Bibliothèque de l'Université.

Klibansky, M. A. 1939. *The Continuity of the Platonic Tradition during the Middle Ages.* London: The Warburg Institute.

Krämer, H. J. 1964. *Der Ursprung der Geistmetaphysik. Untersuchungen zur Geschichte des Platonismus zwischen Platon und Plotin.* Amsterdam: Verlag P. Schippers.

    1982. *Platone e fondamenti della metafisica.* Milano: Vita e Pensiero.

Kraut, R. 1992. "Introduction to the Study of Plato," in *The Cambridge Companion to Plato.* Edited by R. Kraut, Cambridge University Press, 1–50.

Kripke, S. A. 1982. *Wittgenstein on Rules and Private Language.* Cambridge, Mass.: Harvard University Press.

Kristeller, P. 1929. *Der Begriff der Seele in der Ethik des Plotins.* Tübingen: Mohr.

Lee, J. S. 1982. "Omnipresence and Eidetic Causation in Plotinus," in *The Structure of Being. A Neoplatonic Approach.* Edited R. B. Harris, Albany: State University of New York Press, 90–103.

Leroux, G. 1990. *Plotin. Traité sur la liberté et la volonté de l'Un* [Ennéade VI, 8 (39)]. Paris: J. Vrin.

Linguiti, A. 1990. *L'ultimo platonismo greco. Principi e conoscenza.* Firenze: Olschki.

Lloyd, A. C. 1962. "Genus, Species and Ordered Series in Aristotle," *Phronesis* 7, 67–90.

1964. "*Nosce Teipsum and Conscientia,*" *Archiv für Geschichte der Philosophie* 46, 188–200.

1969. "Non-Discursive Thought – An Enigma of Greek Philosophy," *Proceedings of the Aristotelian Society* 70, 261–74.

1981. *Form and Universal in Aristotle.* ARCA: Classical and Medieval Texts, Papers and Monographs 4. Liverpool: Francis Cairns.

1986. "Non-Propositional Thought in Plotinus," *Phronesis* 31, 258–65.

1987. "Plotinus on the Genesis of Thought and Existence," in *Oxford Studies in Ancient Philosophy* 5. Edited by J. Annas, Oxford: Oxford University Press, 155–86.

1990. *The Anatomy of Neoplatonism.* Oxford: Oxford University Press.

Long, A. A., and D. N. Sedley. 1987. (Eds.) *The Hellenistic Philosophers.* 2 volumes. Cambridge University Press.

MacIntyre, A. 1967. "Essence and Existence," in *Encyclopedia of Philosophy* 2. Edited by P. Edwards, New York: Macmillan, 58–62.

MacKenna, S. 1962. *Plotinus. The Enneads,* 3rd edition revised by B. S. Page. London: Faber and Faber.

Madec, G. 1974. *Saint Ambroise et la philosophie.* Paris: Études Augustiennes.

Madigan, A. 1986. "Syrianus and Asclepius on Forms and Intermediates in Plato and Aristotle," *Journal of the History of Philosophy* 24, 149–71.

Manchester, P. 1978. "Time and the Soul in Plotinus, III 7 [45]," *Dionysius* 11, 101–36.

Mandouze, A. 1968. *L'aventure de la raison et de la grace.* Paris: Études Augustiniennes.

Marion, Jean-Luc. 1993. "Generosity and Phenomenology. Remarks on Michel Henry's Interpretation of the Cartesian *Cogito,*" in *Essays on the Philosophy and Science of Rene Descartes.* Edited by S. Voss, Oxford: Oxford University Press, 52–74.

Masai, F. 1961. "Les conversions de saint Augustin et les débuts du spiritualisme en Occidente," *Le Moyen Age* 67, 1–40.

Mayr, E. 1988. *Toward a New Philosophy of Biology.* Cambridge, Mass./London: Belknap Press.

McDowell, J. 1986. "Singular Thought and the Extent of Inner Space," in *Subject, Thought, and Context.* Edited by P. Pettit and J. McDowell, Oxford: Oxford University Press, 137–68.

McGinn, B. 1990. "Do Christian Platonists Really Believe in Creation?," in *God and Creation: An Ecumenical Symposium.* Edited by D. Burrell and B. McGinn, Notre Dame: Notre Dame University Press.

Meinhardt, H. 1984. "Neuplatonismus," *Historisches Wörterbuch der Philosophie* 6, coll. 754–6. Basel/Stuttgart: Schwabe Verlag.

Meredith, A. 1982. "Gregory of Nyssa and Plotinus," *Studia Patristica* 3, 1120–6.

Merlan, P. 1965. "Monismus und Dualismus bei einigen Platoniker," in *Parusia. Studien zur Philosophie und zur Problemgeschichte des Platonismus Festgabe für Johannes Hirschberger.* Edited by K. Flasch, Frankfurt am Main: Minerva, 143–54.

——— 1975. *From Platonism to Neoplatonism.* The Hague: Martinus Nijhoff.

——— 1990. *Dal platonismo al neoplatonismo.* Milano: vita e Pensiero. Italian translation of 1975.

Mihlenberg, E. 1966. *Die Unendlichkeit Gottes bei Gregor von Nyssa.* Göttingen: Vandenhoeck and Ruprecht.

Moravcsik, J. 1992. *Plato and Platonism.* Oxford: Blackwell.

Morrison, D. 1987. "The Evidence for Degrees of Being in Aristotle," *Classical Quarterly* 37, 382–401.

Morrow, G. R., and J. Dillon. 1987. *Proclus Commentary on Plato's Parmenides.* Translated with introduction and notes. Princeton: Princeton University Press.

Mortley, R. 1975. "Negative Theology and Abstraction in Plotinus," *American Journal of Philology* 96, 363–77.

——— 1986. *From Word to Silence. I. The Rise and Fall of Logos; II. The Way of Negation: Christian and Greek.* Bonn: Hanstein.

Müller, H. F. 1914. "Plotinos über Notwendigkeit und Freiheit," *Neue Jahrbücher für die Klassische Altertum* 17, 462–88.

——— 1917. "Die Lehre vom Logos bei Plotin," *Archiv für Geschichte der Philosophie* 30, 20–60.

Nagel, T. 1974. "What is it Like to be a Bat?" *Philosophical Review* 83, 435–50.

——— 1986. *The View from Nowhere.* Oxford: Oxford University Press.

Narbonne, J. M. 1993. *Plotin. Les deux matières [Ennéade II 4 (12)].* Introduction, texte grec, traduction et commentaire. Paris: J. Vrin.

Nebel G. (1929). *Plotins Kategorien der intelligibilen Welt.* Tübingen: J. C. B. Mohr.

Nicomachus, *Introductio arithmetica* (1866). Edited by R. Hoche, Leipzig: Teubner.

Nussbaum, M., and A. Rorty. 1991. (Eds.) *Essays on Aristotle's De Anima.* Oxford: Oxford University Press.

Nygren, A. 1953. *Eros and Agape.* Translated by P. S. Watson. London: S.P.C.K.

O'Brien, D. 1967–8. "The Last Argument of Plato's *Phaedo*," *Classical Quarterly* 17, 198–231; 18, 95–106.

1971. "Plotinus on Evil: A Study of Matter and the Soul in Plotinus' Conception of Human Evil," in *Le Neoplatonisme*. Edited by P. Hadot, Colloques internationaux du Centre National de la Recherche Scientifique (Royaumont: 9–13:61969) Paris: Éditions du Centre National de la Recherche Scientifique, 113–46.

1977a. "A Metaphor in Plato: 'Running Away' and 'Staying Behind' in the *Phaedo* and the *Timaeus*," *Classical Quarterly* 27, 297–9.

1977b. "Le volontaire et la nécessité. Réflexions sur la descente de l'âme dans la philosophie de Plotin," *Revue philosophique* 167, 401–22.

1981. "Plotinus and Gnostics on the Generation of Matter," in *Neoplatonism and Early Christian Thought. Essays in Honour of A. H. Armstrong*. Edited by H. J. Blumenthal and R. A. Markus, London: Variorum, 108–23.

1990. "The Origin of Matter and the Origin of Evil in Plotinus' Criticism of the Gnostics," in *Herméneutique et histoire de l'être. Mélanges en hommage à Pierre Aubenque*. Edited by R. Brague and J.-F. Courtine, Paris: Presses Universitaires de France, 181–202.

1991a. "Platon et Plotin sur le doctrine des parties de l'autre," *Revue philosophique de la France et de l'etranger* 181, 501–12.

1991b. "Le non-être dans la philosophie grecque," in *Études sur le 'Sophiste' de Platon* in *Elenchos. Collana di testi e studi sul pensiero antico*, diretta da Gabriele Giannantoni, n.21. Napoli: Bibliopolis, 317–64.

1991c. *Plotinus on the Origin of Matter. An Exercise in the Interpretation of the Enneades* in *Elenchos. Collana di testi e studi sul pensiero antico*, diretta da Gabriele Giannantoni, n.22. Napoli: Bibliopolis.

1992a. "Il non essere e la diversità nel Sofista di Platone," *Atti dell' Accademia di Scienze Morali e Politische di Napoli*, 102, 271–328.

1992b. "Origène et Plotin sur le roi de l'univers," in ΣΟΦΙΗΣ ΜΑΙΗΤΟΡΕΣ, *Chercheurs de sagesse, hommage à Jean Pépin* in the series *Collection des études augustiniennes, série Antiquité*, n.1331. Paris: Institut des études augustiniennes, 317–42.

1993. *Théodicée plotinienne, théodicée gnostique* in the series *Philosophia Antiqua* 57, Leiden/New York/Köln: E. J. Brill.

1995. *Le non-être, deux études sur le 'Sophiste' de Plata*, in the series *International Plato Studies*. Volume 6. Sankt Augustin: Akademia Verlag.

O'Connell, R. J. 1963. "Enneades VI, 4 and 5 in the Works of Saint Augustine," *Revue des Études Augustiniennes* 9, 1–39.

1984. *Saint Augustine's Platonism*. Villanova: Villanova University Press.

O'Daly, G. J. P. 1973. *Plotinus' Philosophy of the Self*. Shannon: Irish University Press.

O'Meara, D. J. 1974. "A propos d'un témoignage sur l'expérience mystique chez Plotin," *Mnemosyne* 27, 238–44.

1975. *Structures hiérarchiques dans la penseé de Plotin*. Leiden: E. J. Brill.

1985. "Plotinus on How Soul Acts on Body," in *Platonic Investigations*. Studies in Philosophy and the History of Philosophy 13. Edited by D. J. O'Meara, Washington, D.C.: Catholic University of America Press, 247–62.

1987. "The Chain of Being in the Light of Recent Work on Platonic Hierarchies," in *Jacob's Ladder and the Tree of Life*. Edited by M. L. and P. G. Kuntz, Bern New York: Peter Lang, 15–30.

1989. *Pythagoras Revived. Mathematics and Philosophy in Late Antiquity*. Oxford: Clarendon Press.

1990. "Le problème du discours sur l'indicible chez Plotin," *Revue de théologie et de philosophie* 122, 145–56.

1993. *Plotinus. An Introduction to the Enneads*. Oxford: Oxford University Press.

O'Meara, J. J. 1958. "Augustine and Neoplatonism," *Recherches Augustiniennes* 1, 91–111.

Oosthout, H. 1991. *Modes of Knowledge and the Transcendental. An Introduction to Plotinus Ennead* 5.3[49]. Amsterdam/Philadelphia: B. R. Grüner.

Owen, G. E. L. 1953. "The Place of the *Timaeus* in Plato's Dialogues," *Classical Quarterly* 3, 79–95, reprinted in Allen, R. E., ed., *Studies in Plato's Metaphysics*. London: Routledge and Kegan Paul, 1965, 313–38, with a reply by H. Cherniss, 339–78, "The Relation of the *Timaeus* to Plato's Later Dialogues," originally in *American Journal of Philology* 78 (1957), 225–66; and in *Logic, Science and Dialectic. Collected Papers in Greek Philosophy*. Edited by M. Nussbaum, London: Duckworth and Ithaca, N.Y.: Cornell University Press, 1986, 65–84.

Owens, J. 1958. "The Accidental and Essential Character of Being in the Doctrine of St. Thomas Aquinas," *Mediaeval Studies* 20, 1–40.

1965. "Quiddity and Real Distinction in St. Thomas Aquinas," *Mediaeval Studies* 27, 1–22.

Parma, C. 1971. *Pronoia und Providentia. Der Vorsehungsbegriff Plotins und Augustins*. Leiden: E. J. Brill.

Pépin, J. 1954. "Une curieuse déclaration idéaliste du *De Genesi ad litteram* (XII, 10.21) de saint Augustin et ses origines plotiniennes (Enn. 5, 3, 1–9 et 5, 3, 1–2)," *Revue d'histoire et de philosophie religieuses* 34, and now in, *Ex platonicorum persona. Études sur les lectures philosophiques de saint Augustin*, 1967. Amsterdam: Hakkert, 183–211.

1956. "Eléments pour une histoire de la relation entre l'intelligence et l'intelligible," *Revue philosophique* 81, 39–64.

430   Bibliography

　　1964. *Théologie cosmique et théologie chrétienne*. Paris: Presses Universitaires de France.

　　1971. *Idées grecques sur l'homme et sur Dieu*. Paris: Les Belles Lettres.

　　1975. "Platonisme et Stoicisme dans le *de Autexousio* de Méthode d'Olympe," in *Forma futuri. Studi in onore del cardinale Michele Pellegrino*. Torino: Bottega d'Erasmo, 126–44.

　　1986. "Cosmic Piety," in *World Spirituality: An Encyclopedic History of the Religious Quest* 15. Edited by A. H. Armstrong, New York: Crossroad, 355–408.

　　1992. "Theories of Procession in Plotinus and the Gnostics," in *Neoplatonism and Gnosticism*. Edited by R. T. Wallis and J. Bregman, Albany: State University of New York Press, 297–335.

Perrin, M. 1978. "Le Platon de Lactance," in *Lactance et son temps*. Edited by J. Fontaine and M. Perrin, Paris: Éditions Beauchesne, 203–34.

Pistorius, P. V. 1952. *Plotinus and Neoplatonism. An Introductory Study*. Cambridge: Bowes and Bowes.

Prini, P. 1968. *Plotino e la genesi dell'umanesimo interiore*. Roma: Edizioni Abete. 4th edition titled *Plotino e la fondazione dell'umanesimo interiore*, 1993, Milano: Vita e Pensiero.

Radice, R., and D. T. Runia. 1992. *Philo of Alexandria. An Annotated Bibliography 1937–1986*. Leiden/New York/Köln: E. J. Brill.

Reale, G. 1983. "I fondamenti della metafisica di Plotino e la struttura della processione," in *Graceful Reason: Essays in Ancient and Medieval Philosophy Presented to Joseph Owens*. Edited by L. P. Gerson, Toronto: Pontifical Institute of Mediaeval Studies, 153–75.

　　1991. *Storia della filosofia antica*. Volume 5. Milano: Vita e Pensiero. English translation of volumes 1–4 by J. R. Catan as *A History of Ancient Philosophy* (1985–1990). Albany: State University of New York Press.

Regen, F. 1983. "Zu Augustins Darstellung des Platonismus am Anfang des 8 Buches der *Civitas Dei*," in *Platonismus und Christentum. Festschrift H. Dörrie*. Edited by H. Blume and F. Mann, Münster: Aschendorffsche Verlagsbuchhandlung, 208–27.

　　1988. *Formlose Formen. Plotins Philosophie als Versuch die Regressprobleme des platonischen Parmenides zu lösen*. Gottingen: Vandenhoeck and Ruprecht.

Rich, A. N. M. 1954. "The Platonic Ideas as the Thoughts of God," *Mnemosyne* 4, 123–33.

　　1960. "Plotinus and the Theory of Artistic Imitation." *Mnemosyne* 13, 233–9.

Ricken, F. 1967. "Die Logoslehre des Eusebios von Caesarea und der Mittelplatonismus," *Theologie und Philosophie* 42, 341–58.

1969. "Nikaia als Krisis des altchristlichen Platonismus," *Theologie und Philosophie* 44, 321–41.

1978. "Zur Rezeption der platonischen Ontologie bei Eusebios von Kaesareia, Areios und Athanasios," *Theologie und Philosophie* 53, 321–52.

Rist, J. M. 1961. "Plotinus on Matter and Evil," *Phronesis* 6, 154–66.

1962. "The Indefinite Dyad and Intelligible Matter in Plotinus," *Classical Quarterly* 12, 99–107.

1963. "Forms of Individuals in Plotinus," *Classical Quarterly* 13, 223–31.

1964. *Eros and Psyche. Studies in Plato, Plotinus and Origen.* Toronto: University of Toronto Press.

1967. *Plotinus. The Road to Reality.* Cambridge University Press.

1970. "Ideas of Individuals in Plotinus. A Reply to Dr. Blumenthal," in *Revue internationale de philosophie* 24, 298–303.

1971. "The Problem of Otherness in the Enneads," in *Le Néoplatonisme.* Edited by P. Hadot. Colloques internationaux du Centre National de la Recherche Scientifique (Royaumont: 9–13.6.1969). Paris: Éditions du Centre National de la Recherche Scientifique, 77–87.

1975. "Prohairesis: Proclus, Plotinus et alii," in *De Jamblique à Proclus.* Edited by H. Dörrie, Vandoeuvres-Genève: Fondation Hardt, 103–22.

1981. "Basil's 'Neoplatonism.' Its Background and Nature," in *Basil of Caesarea: Christian, Humanist, Ascetic. A Sixteen Hundredth Anniversary Symposium.* Edited by P. J. Fedwick, Toronto: Pontifical Institute of Medieval Studies Press, 137–220.

1985. *Platonism and its Christian Heritage.* London: Variorum.

1989. "Back to the Mysticism of Plotinus: Some More Specifics," *Journal of the History of Philosophy* 27, 183–97.

1991. "A Man of Monstrous Vanity," *Journal of Theological Studies* 42, 138–43.

1992. "Pseudo-Dionysius, Neoplatonism and the Problem of Spiritual Weakness," in *From Athens to Chartres: Essays in Honour of Édouard Jeauneau.* Edited by H. Westra, Leiden: E. J. Brill, 135–61.

1994. *Augustine. Ancient Thought Baptized.* Cambridge University Press.

Robinson, H. M. 1993. (Ed.) *Objections to Physicalism.* Oxford: Oxford University Press.

Roloff, D. 1970. *Plotin. Die Grossschrift III,8–V.8–V.5–II.9.* Berlin: Walter De Gruyter.

Rorty, A. 1976. (Ed.) *The Identities of Persons.* Berkeley/Los Angeles/London: University of California Press.

Rorty, R. 1979. *Philosophy and the Mirror of Nature.* Princeton: Princeton University Press.

Ross, W. D. 1936. *Aristotle's Physics. A Revised Text with Introduction and Commentary.* Oxford: Clarendon Press.

Saffrey, H. D. 1969. "Saint Hilaire et la philosophie," in *Hilaire et son temps.* Edited by E. R. Labande, Paris: Études Augustiennes, 247–65.

1984. "La théologie platonicienne de Proclus, fruit de l'exégèse du Parménide," *Revue de théologie et de philosophie* 16, 1–12.

1987. "Comment Syrianus, le mâitre de l'école néoplatonicienne d'Athènes, considérait-il Aristote?" in *Aristoteles Werk und Wirkung.* Volume 2. Edited by J. Wiesner, Berlin/New York: Walter De Gruyter, 205–14.

Saffrey, H. D. and L. G. Westerink 1968–87. *Théologie platonicienne.* 5 volumes. Paris: Budé.

Salmona, B. 1967. *La libertà in Plotino.* Milano: Marzorati.

Santa Cruz de Purnes, M. I. 1979. "Sobre la generación de la Inteligencia en las Eneàdas de Plotino," *Helmantica* 30, 287–315.

Schibli, H. S. 1989. "Apprehending Our Happiness: *Antilepsis* and the Middle Soul, in Plotinus, Ennead I 4.10," *Phronesis* 34, 205–19.

Schroeder, F. M. 1978. "The Platonic *Parmenides* and Imitation in Plotinus," *Dionysius* 2, 51–73.

1980. "Representation and Reflection in Plotinus," *Dionysius* 4, 37–59.

1984. "Light and the Active Intellect in Alexander and Plotinus," *Hermes* 112, 239–48.

1985. "Saying and Having in Plotinus," *Dionysius* 9, 75–84.

1986. "Conversion and Consciousness in Plotinus, Enneads 5,1(10)9, 7," *Hermes* 114, 186–95.

1987a. "Synusia, Synais, Synesis. Presence and Dependence in the Plotinian Philosophy of Consciousness," in *Aufstieg und Niedergang der römischen Welt.* 36.1. Edited by W. Haase and H. Temporini, Berlin/New York: Walter De Gruyter, 677–99.

1987b. "Ammonius Saccas," in *Aufstieg und Niedergang der römischen Welt.* 36.1. Edited by W. Haase and H. Temporini, Berlin/New York: Walter De Gruyter, 493–526.

1992. *Form and Transformation. A Study in the Philosophy of Plotinus.* Montreal/Kingston, Ontario: McGill-Queen's University Press.

1994. Review of Werner Beierwaltes, *Denken des Einen. Studien zur Neuplatonischen Philosophie und Ihrer Wirkungsgeschichte, Ancient Philosophy* 14, 469–75.

1996. "Plotinus and Interior Design," in *Plotinus and Indian Thought.* Edited by P. Gregorios, Albany: State University of New York Press.

Schubert, V. 1968. *Pronoia und Logos. Die Rechtfertigung der Weltordung bei Plotin.* München: Verlag Anton Pustet.

Schwyzer, H. R. 1935. "Zu Plotins Interpretation von Platon 'Timaeus' 35a," *Rheinisches Museum* 84, 360–8.

1960. "Bewusst und Unbewusst bei Plotin," in *Les sources de Plotin.* *Entretiens Hardt V.* Vandoeuvres-Genève: Fondation Hardt, 343–90.

1970. "Plotin und Platons *Philebos*," *Revue internationale de philosophie* 92, 181–93.

1973. "Zu Plotins Deutung der sogenannten platonischen Materie," in *Zetesis. Festschrift E. de Strijcker.* Antwerp: De Nederlandsche Boeklandel, 266–80.

1974. "Plotinisches und Unplotinisches in den 'Αφορμαι des Porphyrios," in *Plotino e il Neoplatonismo in Oriente e in Occidente.* Atti del Convegno internazionale dell' Accademia Nazionale dei Lincei (Roma: 5–9.10.1970). Rome: Accademia Nazionale dei Lincei, 221–52.

Searle, J. 1983. *Intentionality.* Cambridge University Press.

Sellars, W. 1963. *Science, Perception and Reality.* London: Routledge and Kegan Paul.

Sells, M. 1985. "Apophasis in Plotinus: A Critical Approach." *Harvard Theological Review* 78, 47–65.

1994. *Mystical Languages of Unsaying.* Chicago: University of Chicago Press.

Sharples, R. W. 1987. "Alexander of Aphrodisias: Scholasticism and Innovation," in *Aufstieg und Niedergang der römische Welt.* 36.2. Edited by W. Haase and H. Temporini, Berlin/New York: Walter De Gruyter, 1176–1243.

Sheppard, A. D. 1981. "Monad and Dyad as Cosmic Principles in Syrianus," in *Soul and the Structure of Being in Late Neoplatonism. Syrianus, Proclus and Simplicius.* Edited by H. J. Blumenthal and A. C. Lloyd, Liverpool: Liverpool University Press, 1–14.

Simons, J. 1985. "Matter and Time in Plotinus," *Dionysius* 9, 53–74.

Sleeman, J., and Pollet, G. 1980. *Lexicon Plotinianum.* Leiden: E. J. Brill.

Smith, A. 1974. *Porphyry's Place in the Neoplatonic Tradition.* The Hague: Nijhoff.

1981. "Potentiality and the Problem of Plurality in the Intelligible World," in *Neoplatonism and Early Christian Thought.* Edited by H. J. Blumenthal and R. A. Markus, London: Variorum, 99–107.

1992. "Reason and Experience in Plotinus," in *At the Heart of the Real.* Edited by F. O'Rourke, Dublin: Irish Academic Press, 21–30.

Solignac, A. 1956. "Nouveaux parallèles entre saint Ambroise et Plotin. Le *De Iacob et Vita beata* et le *Peri eudaimonias* (Ennéade I.4)," *Archives de philosophie* 19, 148–55.

Sorabji, R. 1980. *Necessity, Cause and Blame. Perspectives on Aristotle's Theory.* London: Duckworth.

1982. "Myths About Non-Propositinal Thought," in *Language and Logos. Studies in Ancient Greek Philosophy Presented to G. E. L. Owen.* Edited by M. Nussbaum and M. Schofield, Cambridge University Press, 295–314.

1983. *Time, Creation and the Continuum: Theories in Antiquity and the Early Middle Ages*. London: Duckworth.

1990. *Aristotle Transformed: The Ancient Commentators and Their Influence*. Ithaca, N.Y.: Cornell University Press.

Steel, C. G. 1978. *The Changing Self. A Study on the Soul in Later Neoplatonism: Iamblichus, Damascius and Priscianus*. Brussel: Verhandelingen van de Koninklijke Academie voor Wetenschappen.

1985. (Ed.) *Proclus. Commentaire sur le Parménide de Platon. Traduction de Guillaume de Moerbeke*. Leuven University Press.

Strange, S. K. 1981. *Plotinus' Treatise "On the Genera of Being." An Historical and Philosophical Study*. Ph.D. diss., The University of Texas at Austin, 1981. Ann Arbor: University Microfilms International.

1992. "Plotinus' Account of Participation in Ennead VI.4–5," *Journal of the History of Philosophy* 30, 479–96.

1994. "Plotinus on the Nature of Eternity and Time," in *Aristotle in Later Antiquity. Studies in Philosophy and the History of Philosophy* 27. Edited by L. P. Schrenk, Washington, D.C.: The Catholic University of America Press, 22–53.

Strycker, E. de 1942. "L'authenticité du *Premier Alcibiade*," *Études classiques* 11, 135–51.

Sweeney, L. 1992. *Divine Infinity in Greek and Medieval Thought*. New York/Berlin: Peter Lang.

Szlezák, T. A. 1979. *Platon und Aristoteles in der Nuslehre Plotins*. Basle and Stuttgart: Schwabe.

Tardieu, M. 1992. "Les gnostiques dans la *Vie de Plotin*, analyse du chapitre 16," in *Porphyre, La vie de Plotin*. Études d'introduction, texte grec et traduction française, commentaire, notes complémentaires, bibliographie. Edited by L. Brisson, et al., Paris: J. Vrin, 503–63.

Tarrant, H. 1993. *Thrasyllan Platonism*. Ithaca, N.Y.: Cornell University Press.

Teske, R. 1985. "Vocans Temporales. Faciens Aeternos: St. Augustine on Liberation from Time," *Traditio* 41, 24–47.

1986. "Divine Immutability in St. Augustine," *The Modern Schoolman* 63, 233–49.

Theiler, W. 1960. "Plotin zwischen Platon und Stoa," in *Les sources de Plotin. Entretiens Hardt V.* Vandoeuvres-Genève: Fondation Hardt, 63–103.

1966. "Porphyrios und Augustin," in *Forschungen zum Neuplatonismus*. Berlin: Walter De Gruyter, 160–251.

Trouillard, J. 1949. "La liberté chez Plotin," in *La liberté*. Actes du IVème Congrès de philosophie de langue française. Neuchâtel: La Baconnière, 353–7.

    1953. "L'impeccabilité de l'esprit selon Plotin," *Revue de l'histoire des religions* 143, 19–29.

    1955a. *La purification plotinienne*. Paris: Presses Universitaires de France.

    1955b. *La procession plotinienne*. Paris: Presses Universitaires de France.

    1957a. "Le sens des médiations proclusiennes," *Revue philosophique de Louvain* 55, 331–42.

    1960. "Notes sur *proousios* et *pronoia* chez Proclus," *Revue des études grecques* 73, 80–7.

    1961. "The Logic of Attribution in Plotinus," *International Philosophical Quarterly* 1, 125–38.

    1977. "Les degrés du *poiein* chez Proclos," *Dionysius* 1, 69–84.

Turnbull, R. G. 1988. "Becoming and Intelligibility," *Oxford Studies in Ancient Philosophy* 6. Supplementary volume, 1–14.

Viellard-Baron, J.-L. 1979. *Platon et l'idéalisme allemand (1770–1830)*. Paris: Beauchesne.

Vlastos, G. 1965. "Degrees of Reality in Plato," in *New Essays on Plato and Aristotle*. Edited by R. Bambrough, 1–19, and now in *Platonic Studies* (1973, 2nd edition, 1981), Princeton: Princeton University Press, 58–75.

    1973. *Platonic Studies*. Princeton: Princeton University Press.

Vogel, C. J. de 1953. "On the Neoplatonic Character of Platonism and the Platonic Character of Neoplatonism," *Mind* 62, 43–64.

    1986. *Rethinking Plato and Platonism*. Leiden: E. J. Brill.

Wagner, M. F. 1982a. "Vertical Causation in Plotinus," in *The Structure of Being*. Edited by R. B. Harris, Albany: State University of New York Press, 51–72.

    1982b. "Plotinus' World," *Dionysius* 6, 13–42.

    1985. "Realism and the Foundation of Science in Plotinus," *Ancient Philosophy* 5, 269–92.

    1986. "Plotinus' Idealism and the Problem of Matter in *Enneads* VI.4 and 5," *Dionysius* 10, 57–83.

    1993. "Sense Experience and the Active Soul: Some Plotinian and Augustinian Themes," *Journal of Neoplatonic Studies* 1, 37–62.

Wallis, R. T. 1972. *Neoplatonism*. London: Duckworth.

    1976. "*Nous* as Experience," in *The Significance of Neoplatonism*. Edited by R. B. Harris, Albany: State University of New York Press, 121–54.

    1989. "Scepticism and Neoplatonism," in *Aufstieg und Niedergang der Römische Welt*. 36.1. Edited by W. Haase and H. Temporini, Berlin/New York: Walter De Gruyter, 911–54.

Walzer, R. 1967. "Early Islamic Philosophy," in *The Cambridge History of Later Greek and Early Mediaeval Philosophy.* Edited by A. H. Armstrong, Cambridge University Press, 643–69.

Warren, E. 1964. "Consciousness in Plotinus," *Phronesis* 9, 83–97.

Waszink, J. H. 1962. *Timaeus a Calcidio translatus commentarioque instructus. Plato Latinus* 4. Leiden: E. J. Brill.

Watson, G. 1988. *Phantasia in Classical Thought.* Galway: Galway University Press.

Whittaker, J. 1969. "Epekeina nou kai ousias," *Vigiliae Christianae* 23, 91–104.

　1990. *Alcinous, Enseignement des doctrines de Platon,* Paris: Les Belles Lettres.

Wilkes, K. 1988. *Real People.* Oxford: Oxford University Press.

　1991. "Psuche Versus the Mind," in *Essays on Aristotle's De Anima.* Edited by M. Nussbaum and A. Rorty, Oxford: Oxford University Press, 109–27.

Witt, R. E. 1931. "The Plotinian Logos and its Stoic Basis," *Classical Quarterly* 25, 103–11.

Wolfson, H. 1952. "Albinus and Plotinus on Divine Attributes," *Harvard Theological Review* 45, 115–30.

Wordsworth, W. 1950. *Poetical Works.* Edited by T. Hutchinson and E. de Selincourt, Oxford: Oxford University Press.

Wurm, K. 1973. *Substanz und Qualität. Ein Beitrag zur Interpretation der plotinischen Traktate VI 1, 2 und 3.* Berlin/New York: Walter De Gruyter.

Yeats, W. B. 1950. *Collected Poems.* London: Macmillan.

Zeeman, C. W. 1946. *De Plaats van de Wil in de Philosophie van Plotinus.* Arnhem: Van Loghum Slaterus 'Uitg. Mij N.V.

Zintzten, C. 1977. (Ed.) *Die Philosophie des Neuplatonismus.* Darmstadt: Wissenschaftliche Buchgesellschaft.

　1981. (Ed.) *Der Mittelplatonismus.* Darmstadt: Wissenschaftliche Buchgesellschaft.

INDEX OF PASSAGES

INDEX OF NAMES AND SUBJECTS